W9-AJO-197

Taking SIDES

Clashing Views on Controversial Issues in Childhood and Society

Taking SIDES

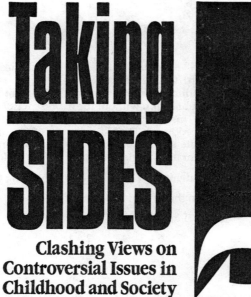

Clashing Views on Controversial Issues in Childhood and Society

Edited, Selected, and with Introductions by

Robert L. DelCampo
New Mexico State University
and
Diana S. DelCampo
New Mexico State University

The Dushkin Publishing Group, Inc.

Photo Acknowledgments

Part 1 DPG/Pamela Carley
Part 2 DPG
Part 3 United Nations/Photo by Marcia Weistein
Part 4 DPG

Cover Art Acknowledgment

Charles Vitelli

Copyright © 1995 by The Dushkin Publishing Group, Inc.,
Guilford, Connecticut 06437

Copyright law prohibits the reproduction, storage, or transmission in any form by any means of any portion of this publication without the express written permission of The Dushkin Publishing Group, Inc., and of the copyright holder (if different) of the part of the publication to be reproduced. The Guidelines for Classroom Copying endorsed by Congress explicitly state that unauthorized copying may not be used to create, to replace, or to substitute for anthologies, compilations, or collective works.

Taking Sides ® is a registered trademark of The Dushkin Publishing Group, Inc.

Manufactured in the United States of America

First Edition

10 9 8 7 6 5 4 3 2 1

Library of Congress Cataloging-in-Publication Data

Main entry under title:
  Taking sides: clashing views on controversial issues in childhood and society/edited, selected, and with introductions by Robert L. DelCampo and Diana S. DelCampo.—1st ed.
  Includes bibliographical references and index.
  1. Children—Social conditions. I. DelCampo, Robert L., *comp.* II. DelCampo, Diana S., *comp.*
    HQ767.9.T34   305.23—dc20
    1-56134-333-1   95-121

 Printed on Recycled Paper

The Dushkin Publishing Group, Inc.

PREFACE

Children are society's most valuable resource, and however clichéd that idea may be, there can be no doubt about the urgency of the issues confronting children today and the people who care for them and care about them. Each day we are bombarded with media reports on issues affecting children—complex issues related to child care, schooling, violence, sexuality, gangs, divorce; the list goes on. In this book we look at 17 of those controversial issues and ask you to think about them, perhaps for the first time, or perhaps in ways you may not have previously considered.

For the student who likes to memorize facts and learn *the* right answer, the controversies in this book could be most unsettling! However, a good education should include the nurturing of your ability to think critically and to be an active learner. This book endeavors to put you on the path toward further developing these skills. As you read each side of an issue and grapple with the points made by the authors, you will be moved to consider the merits of each position. In the process, you may adopt the point of view of one side, or the other, or formulate an opinion completely your own on the issue. And when you attend class, you will be exposed to your classmates' and instructor's ideas on the issue as well. This may further challenge you to reconsider and defend your position, which is the essence of critical thinking and a primary purpose of this book.

Plan of the book   *Taking Sides: Clashing Views on Controversial Issues in Childhood and Society* is designed to be used for courses in child development, or human development, or parenting. The issues can be studied consecutively or in any order, as each is designed to be independent of the other. We have included 17 issues encompassing 34 selections from a wide variety of sources and authors. Each part of the book deals with one of four developmental phases of childhood: infancy, early childhood, middle childhood, and adolescence. Within each part are issues related to aspects of child development at that stage. Each issue has an *introduction*, which provides some background about the controversy, briefly describes the authors, and gives a brief summary of the positions reflected in the issue. Each issue concludes with a *postscript*, which contains some final thoughts on the issue and offers a bibliography of related readings should you want to explore the topic further.

A listing of all the *contributors* to this volume is included at the back of the book to give you additional information on the scholars, practitioners, educators, policymakers, and social critics whose views are debated here.

A word to the instructor   An *Instructor's Manual With Test Questions* (multiple-choice and essay) is available through the publisher for the instructor using this volume of *Taking Sides*. A general guidebook, *Using Taking Sides in the Classroom*, which discusses methods and techniques for integrating the pro-con approach into any classroom setting, is also available.

Acknowledgments   We are most grateful to our son, Robert G. DelCampo, and graduate students A. Elaine Crnkovic and Joellyn M. Johnson for their enthusiasm and perseverance in helping us to undertake the research for this volume. The process of searching for and identifying appropriate selections, and preparing background information for the issues, was difficult and trying at times. Sharing this challenge with these three competent individuals was instrumental in our realizing success in completing this project.

We also want to extend a warm thanks to Mimi Egan, publisher for the Taking Sides series, for her guidance, editorial expertise, and support, as well as to David Dean, administrative editor, and David Brackley, copy editor, at The Dushkin Publishing Group.

We will look forward to receiving feedback and comments on this first edition of *Taking Sides: Clashing Views on Controversial Issues in Childhood and Society* from both faculty and students who experience the book. We can be reached via the Internet (ddelcamp@nmsu.edu or rdelcamp@nmsu.edu), or you can write us in care of the Taking Sides series at The Dushkin Publishing Group.

Robert L. DelCampo
New Mexico State University

Diana S. DelCampo
New Mexico State University

CONTENTS IN BRIEF

CONTENTS

Researchers Nazli Baydar and Jeanne Brooks-Gunn argue that maternal employment during a child's infancy has detrimental effects on the development of the child. Child development researchers Deborah Vandell and Janaki Ramanan assert that a mother's employment during a child's infancy leads to higher achievement test scores in elementary school.

Developmental psychologist Marguerite Barratt, assistant scientist Mary Roach, and lecturer Karen Colbert conclude that maternal age correlates with positive parenting skills. Andrew Yarrow, a researcher and journalist, contends that the children of older parents often feel that they are forced to grow up too fast.

Professor Charlotte Goodluck argues that putting a child into a family with a different racial and ethnic background can lead to problems in identity development, a loss of cultural values, and problems in dating and mate selection. Christopher Bagley, a professor of social work, maintains that transracial adoptions can adequately meet the psychosocial and developmental needs of the children involved.

Doreen Kimura, a neuropsychologist, believes that biological differences in the male and female brain explain behavioral differences between the genders. Carol Tavris, a social psychologist, concludes that there is no scientific evidence that the brains of males and females are different.

Murray Straus, a social science researcher, argues that the physical punishment children experience when they are young correlates with the violent acts they themselves commit later in life. Joan McCord, a professor of criminal justice, concludes that later violence is caused by faulty reward-and-punishment systems of behavior control, not by physical punishment.

Professors Barbara Byrd, Arnold DeRosa, and Stephen Craig assert that only children are less autonomous than firstborn children. Steven Mellor, a psychology professor, reports that only children are similar to firstborns in terms of their developmental path.

Barbara Whitehead, a researcher and journalist, argues that children of divorce are more likely than children from intact families to live in poverty, drop out of school, and commit criminal acts. David Gately and Andrew Schwebel, both university educators, contend that children of divorce show enhanced levels of maturity and self-esteem.

Brandon S. Centerwall, an epidemiologist, argues that children act out the violence they see on television shows and carry the violent behaviors into adulthood. Brian Siano, a writer and researcher, argues that variables other than TV violence are to blame for aggression in children.

Lawrence Schweinhart and David Weikart, from the High/Scope Educational Research Foundation, conclude that a quality preschool education leads to success later in life. Professor Michael Meyers maintains that preschool-age children should not be separated from their parents to attend a formal preschool program.

Carol Mills, Karen Ablard, and Heinrich Stumpf, all associates of the Center for Talented Youth Research at Johns Hopkins University, report that boys perform better than girls on tests for math reasoning ability. A report developed by the Center for Research on Women at Wellesley College for the American Association of University Women concludes that the differences in math achievement between boys and girls are not significant.

Child advocate Sherryll Kraizer and her colleagues found that children in self-care did not respond to dangerous situations safely. Professors John Woodard and Mark Fine conclude that self-care can be a positive learning experience for children.

David Guterson, an English teacher in the public schools, argues that home schooling is more effective than public schooling. Professors Jennie F. Rakestraw and Donald A. Rakestraw argue that interaction with a school peer group, which is usually missing in home schools, is imperative for the healthy social development of children.

Professor Diane Ravitch, who has written widely on educational issues, suggests that bilingual education programs are ineffective and that they have become simply a means to attain certain political ends. Linguistics professor Donaldo Macedo maintains that bilingual education programs are effective for educating children who cannot speak or read English and that they improve the academic performance of non-English-speaking children.

William J. O'Malley, a professor of theology and English, posits that children lack the ability to understand the implications of adulthood and its responsibilities because parents shield them from any real decision making and encounters with adversity. Kathleen Kennedy Townsend, who was a key administrator for the Maryland Department of Education at the time she wrote this selection, contends that expecting parents to instill values is not realistic and that teaching values in the schools instead can yield excellent results for children and for society.

Scott A. Hunt, a writer with a special interest in transpersonal psychology, suggests that current research has failed to adequately examine the issue of suicide among homosexual youths and offers reasons as to why it is important to undertake more research in this area. Douglas Foster, a former editor of *Mother Jones* magazine, contends that sexual orientation is but one variable in the risk factor equation that leads to youth suicide.

Thomas Lickona, a developmental psychologist, states that Americans need to promote a higher standard of sexual morality through sex education that promotes abstinence before marriage. Jessica Gress-Wright, a researcher and writer, argues that the problems of teen childbearing and abortion cannot be solved by sex education programs alone.

Jim Burke, a high school English teacher, contends that if children feel no security at home, they will seek it through the group affiliation that gangs provide. John M. Hagedorn, a researcher at the Urban Research Center, University of Wisconsin–Milwaukee, claims that economic problems, such as low wages and lack of jobs, are the reasons why young people join gangs.

INTRODUCTION

Children in Society

Robert L. DelCampo
Diana S. DelCampo

Childhood can be a wondrous time when days are filled with play and new discoveries, nights provide rest and security, and dedicated, loving parents nurture their children and meet their needs. This is a romantic notion of childhood and is the type of childhood all of us would wish for children. Some children do indeed experience the full joy of childhood; however, and regretfully so, there are other, more sobering scenarios of childhood. There are children who do not have nurturing adults to guide them and provide a sense of what it means to experience the magic of childhood. There are children who go to bed hungry, with at best one parent who struggles just to endure daily life. Some children are even without homes. Most typically, childhood experiences fall between these two extremes. So there is a wide variety of experiences that can impact the developing child; you should keep this in mind as you become involved with the issues debated in this book. Beyond the immediate circumstances of a child's family, there are larger social forces at work as well. Ask yourself as you debate these issues the extent to which society must collectively address and resolve these issues in order to encourage the protection and positive development of all children. This is a vital function of society because society's children are society's future.

PAST VIEWS OF CHILDHOOD

In order to further understand and appreciate children in contemporary society, it may be useful to briefly review how society's views of children have changed over time. In their book *Looking at Children: An Introduction to Child Development* (Brooks-Cole, 1992), David and Barbara Bjorklund discuss the history of adult perceptions of children in western European society. Would it surprise you to know that in ancient times children were sometimes killed as religious sacrifices and buried in the walls of buildings? People believed that this practice would strengthen a building's structure. Up until the fourth century, parents were legally allowed to kill their newborns if the children were not in good health at birth. They were also permitted to do away with a child if they already had too many children, if the child was female, or if the child was illegitimate. In 374 A.D., the Romans outlawed infanticide, hoping that this would end the killing. Since parents could no longer legally kill their children, unwanted infants began to be abandoned. This practice endured for over 1,000 years. It was not until the 1600s that child abandonment was outlawed throughout most of Europe.

During the seventeenth century, foundling homes were established to provide for the needs of unwanted children. In their text *Middle Childhood: Behavior and Development*, 2d ed. (Macmillan, 1980), Joyce W. Williams and Marjorie Smith describe how during this period children were considered to be miniature adults. They were dressed like adults and were expected to act as adults would act. By our contemporary standards, parents took a rather casual attitude toward their children. This was probably due to the high child mortality rate at the time. Since parents thought it likely that their children would die in infancy or childhood, they did not get as emotionally close to their young children as parents typically do today. It was not until the end of the century that society began to look upon children as different from adults.

Early in the 1700s, European societal attitudes about children underwent further change. Children were no longer considered to be miniature adults, and literature written specifically for children began to emerge. By the end of the century, children who went to school were grouped by age, reflecting an awareness of stages of growth. The eighteenth century also marked the rise of the systematic study of children, which centered around the moral development of children and child-rearing problems.

According to Williams and Smith, it was not until the beginning of the twentieth century that three distinct age groupings emerged in the study of human development: infancy through age four or five; childhood to late puberty or early adulthood; and adulthood. This time period also marked the beginnings of the distinct field of child study. Early child study emphasized descriptive accounts of individual children and was mainly concerned with aspects of physical growth. As the century progressed, the term *child study* was changed to *research in child development*. Mothering became an important concept in the study of early child development, and the psychological aspects of development began to be examined more rigorously. Today, in the latter part of the twentieth century, research in child development focuses on issues related to family systems and the larger social issues that affect child development.

NATURE-NURTURE CONTROVERSY

There are many things that impact individuals as they progress through the human life cycle. People, places, events, illnesses, education, success, failure —have you ever thought about the number of experiences each of us encounters in our lives? If one were to place all of the variables that influence human development into two general categories, those categories would be heredity and environment. As you may know, your genetic blueprint was determined at the moment of conception with chromosomes contributed by your father and mother. In a sense, for many of us, environment is also determined at the moment of conception. A good portion of the major elements of what makes up one's environment is often determined before a person is born. The society in which one will live, one's cultural and ethnic heritage, and one's family and subsequent socioeconomic status, for example, are usually predetermined for a child.

In *Taking Sides: Clashing Views on Controversial Issues in Childhood and Society*, rather than giving you, the reader, clinical case examples of issues related to a certain child or children, we have selected articles that look at children in general and how they affect or are affected by the issues raised. For the purposes of this book, we make three assumptions: (1) When we discuss a child's environment, we are usually describing elements of the society in which a child is growing, developing, and otherwise being socialized. (2) All child development occurs within this social context. (3) Children cannot help but affect and be affected by the societal forces that are around them. In most university classes, students derive a certain sense of security in receiving definitions of terms that are used frequently in a given class. We offer the following one for *society*, which we have adapted from Gelles's 1995 textbook *Contemporary Families*:

> Society is a collection of people who interact within socially structured relationships. The only way that societies can survive their original members is by replacing them. These "replacements" are the children about whom the issues in this book are concerned.

Determining an appropriate group of societal issues and fitting them into the confines of only one work on children and society is a challenging task. Consider, for example, the diversity of our contemporary society. We live in a sea of divergent and unique subcultures and ethnicities. Categorizing and describing the myriad values, customs, and belief systems of these groups could fill many volumes. In America and Canada, for example, there are many ethnic subgroups of citizens, such as English, Irish, Italians, Polish, Germans, Greeks, Russians, Scots, etc., all of whom are considered to be Anglos. There are people of native descent, sometimes referred to as Indians, who are affiliated with scores of different tribes and subtribes. Some Canadian and American citizens trace their heritages to a variety of Asian countries, including China, Japan, Vietnam, Cambodia, Thailand, and the Philippines. Even among Blacks, there are those that trace their roots to the Caribbean region and those that identify with different regions of Africa.

In light of the above, it may be reasoned that there are really no "typical" children in society! Although there are strong arguments supporting similarities within each of these general groups, there is a wide array of subgroupings and differences in customs and beliefs. As a consequence, when reading a book such as this one, it is important to be mindful of the extent to which differences might exist for those who may be of another race, ethnicity, religion, or socioeconomic status than the target group of children about which a selection focuses. It would also be prudent to consider geographic locale: rural, urban, northeastern, southwestern, etc., in considering the relevancy of a given argument to a specific subgroup of children.

CHILDREN IN CONTEMPORARY SOCIETY

It is worthy to understand children's points of view as they are impacted by society. It can be astonishing to take a step back and observe children as they undergo the socialization process in contemporary society. They come into the world totally helpless, unable to feed, care for, or protect themselves. As they grow and develop, children undertake the process of acquiring a sense of identity and learning the rules of the society in which they live. This process of socialization is fostered by many of the subsystems of society that provide prescriptions for behavior in particular areas of life. These subsystems include the family, the peer group, the school system, religion, and the media.

One important consideration is that up to about age five, children are oblivious to most racial, ethnic, religious, or socioeconomic differences. Typically, children can only realize differences in external appearance. One implication of this fact is that children can be much more amenable to learning and embracing a variety of cultural behaviors, attitudes, and even languages when they are young. Only as children move into middle childhood do they begin to recognize and understand other, more subtle differences. It is important to note that although young children may be oblivious to these differences, they are nonetheless impacted by them in the way they are socialized by their parents, families, and the significant others in their lives. This is done through family rituals, traditions, and outings, religious ceremonies, types of food prepared in the home, location where children live, and things that are found in the home, like books, magazines, music, and such.

Societal influences on children do not stop within the family system. As children grow, other institutions in society, such as schools, the economy, politics, and religion, expand their life experiences. Controversy arises as to how children react to these experiences. Consider, for example, what happens to children when both parents are employed outside the home. There are factions in our society who adamantly ascribe many of the problems associated with children growing up in contemporary society to the fact that many parents are overly involved with work at the expense of time with their children. They contend that one parent (usually the mother) should stay home with the children, especially when they are young. Children who care for themselves after school and the quality of after-school child care are also hotly contested, related issues.

Few readers of this book will be unfamiliar with the attacks on the mass media for its portrayal of violence in action movies, television programming, and video games targeted at children. Again, researchers, clinicians, teachers, policymakers, and others fall on both sides of what should be done to address this problem.

As children move toward adolescence and become more independent, concerns regarding identity, values, morals, and sexual behavior become issues of controversy. Homosexuality, for example, which often is first evidenced by a person in adolescence, is considered by many to be a learned and abhorrent form of sexual expression. Others believe that there are people who are predisposed to homosexuality for reasons that are as yet unclear.

Events in contemporary society always impact children directly or indirectly, despite attempts to protect them. Violence, inflation, war, poverty, AIDS, racism, and new technology are just a few of the phenomena that shape the society in which our children are socialized.

RESEARCHING CHILDREN

In finding answers to controversial topics, policymakers and the public alike oftentimes look to research literature for clues. The typical beginning college student might think of researching a topic as going to the library and looking up information on a subject, reading that information, formulating a conclusion or opinion about the topic, and writing a paper that conveys the student's findings. This is not the type of research about which we are referring! The type of research that we refer to here is called empirical research. This means that there is some question or group of interrelated questions to be answered about a topic. Data are then collected relative to the topic, which typically sheds light on how one goes about answering the question.

Data collection in research on children is undertaken from a variety of approaches. It could entail things like observing children at play in preschool or interacting with their parents at home. This is called observing children in a natural setting. With this method, observers must code behavior in the same way each and every time it is seen. Most of the information we have today on physical growth and developmental stages was acquired through observation by child development pioneers such as Arnold Gessell and Louise Bates Ames. You can imagine how time-consuming this form of study must be.

Another type of data collection is called an experiment. Experimental researchers systematically control how certain things happen in a situation and then observe the results. In this type of research, an experimental group and a control group are chosen. Both groups are examined to determine that they are the same before the experiment begins. The experimental group then receives some kind of treatment, while the control group receives no treatment. Then tests are conducted to see what kind of change, if any, has occurred between the two groups.

Interviewing children with a structured set of questions or giving children a structured questionnaire on a given research topic are other ways of collecting data. Projective techniques, where children might reveal their first thoughts about a picture or word that is presented to them, is also a form of the interview method.

The study of children can be organized in a variety of ways. One is by stages. The parts of this book (i.e., infancy, early childhood, middle childhood, and adolescence) are one type of stage organization. Another way to organize research endeavors is by topics. Topics are usually organized within the context of social, emotional, intellectual, physical, creative, and even spiritual aspects of development.

The time frames used to gather data on children also varies. In longitudinal data collection, information is collected from the same subjects over a long period of time. For example, one could examine the effects of preschool education on performance in elementary school by following and testing the same children during the preschool years and all the way through the elementary years. Because this type of research can take years to complete, a shorter method, cross-sectional research, could be used. In the previous example, one group of preschoolers would be compared to a similar group of elementary school children in order to answer the research question.

There are ethical considerations in studying children that some other disciplines may not face. Children should never be manipulated or put in danger in designing an experiment to answer research questions. Similarly, experiments that would not be in a child's best interests should not be conducted. For example, studies of abuse and neglect rely on retrospective techniques in which children who have already been abused report what has previously happened to them. No ethical researcher would ever put children at risk in order to observe the effects of abuse on children. Because of these ethical constraints, it can be frustrating for a researcher to fully answer questions raised in a research project. Additionally, it may take years to demonstrate the effectiveness of intervention for a particular social problem. Consequently, research on children and resultant intervention initiatives rarely offer "quick fixes" to the problems of children and society.

PROFESSIONAL ORGANIZATIONS

There are several major national and international professional organizations that promote research and policy making on issues related to children. It would behoove the beginning student of child development to become familiar with one or more of these organizations. Ask the instructor of this and similar classes for the names of the professional organizations to which they belong and for additional ones that they believe are important. Also ask them why they believe these particular organizations are important. Most of these organizations publish professional journals and host annual conferences where the latest information about issues related to children is presented. They can also provide students with contacts in the professional communities that share similar interests. Members of these organizations possess the expertise for undertaking research, education, and clinical practice related to issues of interest. There are numerous intangible benefits in affiliating with professional organizations as well. Typically, student members enjoy significant reductions in fees for membership dues and subscriptions to professional journals published by the organizations. Some of the major organizations that examine issues and promote policies related to children include:

- The Association for Childhood Education International
  11141 Georgia Avenue, Suite 200
  Wheaton, MD 20902
  (800) 423-3563

- The American Counseling Association
  5999 Stevenson Avenue
  Alexandria, VA 22304
  (703) 823-9800

- The American Association for Marriage and Family Therapy
  1100 17th Street, NW, 10th Floor
  Washington, DC 20036
  (202) 452-0109

- The American Association of Family and Consumer Sciences
  1555 King Street
  Alexandria, VA 22314
  (703) 706-4600

- The American Association of Sex Educators, Counselors and Therapists
  435 N. Michigan Avenue, Suite 1717
  Chicago, IL 60611
  (312) 644-0828

- The American Psychological Association
  750 First Street, NE
  Washington, DC 20002-4242
  (202) 336-5500

- The American Sociological Association
  1722 N Street, NW
  Washington, DC 20036
  (202) 833-3410

- The Canadian Home Economics Association
  151 Slater Street, Suite 901
  Ottawa, Ontario K1P 5H3
  Canada
  (613) 238-8817

- The Children's Defense Fund
  122 C Street, NW, Suite 400
  Washington, DC 20001
  (202) 628-8787

- Le Conseil de la Famille
  1245, chemin Sainte-Foy
  Bureau 342
  Quebec, Quebec G1S 4P2
  Canada
  (418) 646-7678

- The Family Service of Canada
  600 220 Laurier Avenue W
  Ottawa, Ontario K1Y 4G1
  Canada
  (613) 230-9960

- The National Association for the Education of Young Children
  1509 16th Street, NW
  Washington, DC 20036-1426
  (800) 424-2460

- The National Association of Social Workers
  750 First Street, NE, Suite 700
  Washington, DC 20002-4242
  (202) 408-8600

- The National Council on Family Relations
  3989 Central Avenue, NE, Suite 550
  Minneapolis, MN 55421
  (612) 781-9331

- The Sex Information and Education Council of the United States
  130 W. 42nd Street, Suite 2500
  New York, NY 10036
  (212) 819-9770

- The Society for Research in Child Development
  5720 S. Woodlawn Avenue
  Chicago, IL 60637
  (312) 702-7470

FUTURE DIRECTIONS

The study of children in society can begin to offer solutions to many of the more pressing societal problems. Quality child care, parenting skills education, stress reduction, affordable housing, job training, and humane political policies are a few ideas for solutions to some of the controversies that will be raised in this book.

The imbalance between work and family in the United States has created problems in the economy as well as in the family system. Workers are expected to produce quality goods and services but they receive little social support in raising their families. When it comes to caring for children, each family is on its own, piecing together supervised child care with self-care and hoping for the best until the children graduate from high school, only to enter the same workforce with the same problems. Employers must acknowledge the strain that workers feel as they are pulled between work and family responsibilities. Health insurance, family-friendly work policies, flexible work schedules, parental and dependent care leave, exercise facilities, quality child care and sick child care, on-site or nearby one-stop service centers with post offices, grocery stores, and dry cleaners would be ways of providing support for families in the workplace.

Schools contribute to the problems of child care arrangements by keeping to an antiquated schedule that was first developed to meet the needs of the farm family. Years ago, schools were let out in the early afternoon and all summer so that children could help with the crops, livestock, and other farm-related chores before sunset. However, ours has been a predominantly industrial society for a large part of the twentieth century. As a result, a different type of schedule is required. Many concerned families advocate activities for children after school and schools that are open all year long to match the schedules of society's workers. The economy has changed and families have changed; why have educational institutions remained static?

The majority of children somehow manage to grow and develop successfully in a variety of family forms. However, the stressors on all families are constantly increasing, which may, in turn, decrease the likelihood of continued success. Parents worry that the cost of a college education will be more than they can afford; parents worry about their children and AIDS, violence, and drugs. Parents are concerned that in adulthood their children will not be able to live as well as they have lived. Families need emotional support, and parents need opportunities to learn stress management and parenting skills.

Society can promote the optimal growth and development of its children by taking responsibility for them. There is an old saying, "It takes a village to raise a child." Our society can raise its children by establishing policies in schools, workplaces, and other institutions that reflect the importance of nurturing children.

PART 1

Infancy

Infancy and toddlerhood encompass the time period from birth to age two or three. During this time, the most dramatic growth of a child's life takes place. Traditionally, much of the literature on infancy has dealt with the physical aspects of development; more recently, however, researchers, practitioners, and policymakers have begun to be concerned with the social and emotional aspects of development during infancy. Some of these issues are examined in this section.

■ Does a Mother's Job Have a Negative
   Effect on Children?

■ Do Older Parents Provide a More
   Nurturing Environment for Children?

■ Is Transracial Adoption Harmful to a
   Child's Development?

■ Are Gender Differences Rooted in
   the Brain?

ISSUE 1

Does a Mother's Job Have a Negative Effect on Children?

YES: Nazli Baydar and Jeanne Brooks-Gunn, from "Effects of Maternal Employment and Child-Care Arrangements on Preschoolers' Cognitive and Behavioral Outcomes: Evidence from the Children of the National Longitudinal Survey of Youth," *Developmental Psychology* (vol. 27, no. 6, 1991)

NO: Deborah Lowe Vandell and Janaki Ramanan, from "Effects of Early and Recent Maternal Employment on Children from Low-Income Families," *Child Development* (vol. 63, 1992)

ISSUE SUMMARY

YES: On the basis of their analysis of available data, Nazli Baydar, a researcher with the Battelle Human Affairs Research Center, and Jeanne Brooks-Gunn, a researcher at Columbia University, conclude that maternal employment during a child's infancy has detrimental effects on the cognitive and behavioral development of the child.

NO: Child development researchers Deborah Vandell and Janaki Ramanan found that a mother's employment during a child's infancy was a predictor of higher achievement test scores in elementary school.

As more women have moved into the workforce over the course of the last 20 years, maternal employment and its effects on children has become a popular topic for researchers to study. Although maternal employment was once studied as a single, isolated factor affecting child development, most people who study children have come to view the study of maternal employment as a much more complex issue. Whereas researchers once thought that maternal employment had a direct influence on development, they now agree that the issue must be studied within the context of the family system and that research must simultaneously address many interrelated questions, such as: What quality of care does the child receive? How does the mother feel about her work? What societal and family support do the mother and child receive?

Researchers are divided over what variables to study, as well as what methods to use to study the effects of maternal employment. Should researchers combine several social classes to study the interactive effects of working mothers and types of child care arrangements? Would a study of one social class and its interaction with a mother's personality traits and type of family environment yield useful information?

Maternal employment effects are dependent on many variables, such as a mother's work satisfaction and morale; the amount of work; and a mother's perception of quality of time verses quantity of time spent with children. Depending on which study one reads, how the data were collected, and which combination of variables were studied, different conclusions are reported. For example, some research states that employed moms spend more quality time with their children, while other studies show that nonemployed moms spend more quality time with their children.

Research on maternal employment has become more sophisticated in recent years, yet the question still remains: Should mothers stay home with their babies? Often women will drop out of the workforce at least for the first few years to stay home and care for their children. The belief that an attachment to the mother in the first few years is critical to a child's later development may indeed have validity, according to some researchers. Conversely, some research suggests that quality child-care providers may be able to meet the same needs that mothers meet.

In the following debate, the authors of both the yes and no selections use the database produced from the National Longitudinal Survey of Youth to examine the effects of maternal employment. Although the authors of the following selections studied the same database, they came up with opposing conclusions. This is characteristic of the debate concerning whether or not mothers should work during their children's infancies.

YES

Nazli Baydar and
Jeanne Brooks-Gunn

EFFECTS OF MATERNAL EMPLOYMENT AND CHILD-CARE ARRANGEMENTS ON PRESCHOOLERS' COGNITIVE AND BEHAVIORAL OUTCOMES: EVIDENCE FROM THE CHILDREN OF THE NATIONAL LONGITUDINAL SURVEY OF YOUTH

Research on the effects of maternal employment on children grew in part out of a concern for the effects of maternal separation on young children, particularly regarding social and emotional development in the first year (Bowlby, 1969; Bretherton & Waters, 1985; Bronfenbrenner, 1979; Rutter, 1981a; Sroufe, 1979). Few studies address the effects of maternal employment in the first year on children's cognitive functioning (see for exceptions, Hock, 1980; Pedersen, Cain, Zaslow, & Anderson, 1982). The bulk of the research on the effects of maternal separation during infancy is focused on the mother and infant in a laboratory-based setting, using the Strange Situation to assess infants' responses to separation from and reunion with the mother (see Campos, Barrett, Lamb, Goldsmith, & Sternberg, 1983). The studies looking at employment effects tend to have small samples composed of primarily White middle-class families. Many report that 1-year-old White, middle-class boys whose mothers work are more likely to be insecurely attached (as evidenced by avoidant and anxious behavior) than same-age boys whose mothers do not work (Barglow, Vaughn, & Molitor, 1987; Belsky & Rovine, 1988; Chase-Lansdale & Owen, 1987; Doyle & Somers, 1978; Hock & Clinger, 1980; Schwartz, 1983). However, it is not known whether such behavior among boys with employed mothers is associated with later maladjustment. Links between insecure attachment and later social and emotional problems are reported in studies that do not focus on maternal employment (Farber & Egelan, 1982; Sroufe, 1983; Vaughn, Deane, & Waters, 1985). Research to date has been unable to elucidate possible mechanisms underlying the phenomenon: Insecure attachment may be indicative of problems associated with separation or may be

From Nazli Baydar and Jeanne Brooks-Gunn, "Effects of Maternal Employment and Child-Care Arrangements on Preschoolers' Cognitive and Behavioral Outcomes: Evidence from the Children of the National Longitudinal Survey of Youth," *Developmental Psychology*, vol. 27, no. 6 (1991). Copyright © 1991 by The American Psychological Association. Reprinted by permission. Notes omitted.

a reflection of earlier independence and autonomy (Clarke-Stewart, 1989). Maternal characteristics associated with entry into the labor force may also play a role in increasing insecure attachment (Clarke-Stewart, 1989; Rutter, 1981b; see study results of Hock, 1980).

Most studies on maternal employment do not consider either the type or the quality of care that infants are receiving, even though the latter is known to be associated with child functioning (Phillips, 1987). The effects of timing of maternal entry into the labor force during the first 3 years have also not been examined, although the significance of the development during the first year suggests that this period might be a particularly vulnerable developmental period.

A separate body of research focuses on the child care received, rather than on maternal employment. Almost no research compares the effects of different types of nonmaternal care. Instead, most of the research to date focuses on center-based care and, more recently, on family-based care (Hayes et al., 1990). One line of research concentrates on children in poverty who receive early educationally oriented intervention services through home visiting, center-based care services, or both (Beller, 1979; Bronfenbrenner, 1975; Bryant & Ramey, 1987; Clarke-Stewart & Fein, 1983; Haskins, 1989; Zigler & Valentine, 1979). For children who participate in center-based intervention, negative effects on social or emotional functioning are not found (Haskins, 1989). On the contrary, more positive mother-infant interaction and infant social development are shown in over one half of the studies evaluating social and emotional outcomes (Benasich, Brooks-Gunn, & Clewell, in press; Hask-

ins, 1989). Almost all program evaluations report enhanced cognitive functioning through the preschool years (Lazar, Darlington, Murray, Royce, & Snipper, 1982). Although the provision of daily center-based care services might facilitate entry into the work force, most of the early intervention programs did not have this as an explicit goal. The studies that investigate maternal employment find it to be higher in the families who participated in these programs than in the families in the control groups (Benasich et al., in press; Clewell, Brooks-Gunn, & Benasich, 1989). These studies have neither looked at differential effects of intervention for children whose mothers were employed versus children whose mothers were not employed nor looked at the effects of child-care arrangements in the comparison groups (many of whom were probably receiving some nonmaternal care).

Two other avenues of research on child care exist. One focuses on the variations in the quality of child care, and the other considers the links between the quality of family and child-care environment (Hayes et al., 1990). To date, these research lines have had center-based child care as their primary focus.

The intersection of maternal employment and child-care type was considered in this article, vis-à-vis its effects on subsequent cognitive and behavioral outcomes in children at preschool ages. Such an analysis requires a large and heterogeneous sample, and the Children of the National Longitudinal Survey of Youth (NLSY) data set is well suited to addressing the outcomes of intersecting life circumstances of children and their families. In keeping with the preceding two articles (Brooks-Gunn, Phelps, & Elder, 1991; Chase-Lansdale, Mott, Brooks-Gunn, & Phillips, 1991), we also considered various methodological issues that arose when using the Children of the NLSY data: How to operationalize child care and employment; whether retrospective and prospective child care data are similar; whether to analyze results for ethnic groups separately; and ways to construct multivariate models to examine differential effects of independent variables on the dependent variable as a function of background characteristics such as sex and poverty status. Although these methodological issues do not constitute an exhaustive list of problems that might be encountered when analyzing the data from the Children of the NLSY, they are illustrative of the issues pertaining to the use of this or other national data sets to address developmental issues.

Three sets of questions were addressed. The first set inquired about the effects of maternal employment in the first 3 years of life on cognitive and behavioral functioning of 3- and 4-year-old children and the factors that possibly mediate these effects. The effects of timing of maternal entry into the labor force were examined by estimating the effects of entry in each of the first 3 years on subsequent child outcomes, controlling for maternal characteristics that are associated with entry into labor force. In keeping with previous studies, we expected maternal entry into the labor force during the first year of life to have a negative effect on cognitive and behavioral functioning of preschoolers (cf. reviews by Chase-Landsdale, Michael, & Desai, 1991; Hayes et al., 1990). We expected the negative effects of maternal entry into the labor force to decline over the first 3 years with minimal effects of entry in the third year. On the basis of previous studies, effects of maternal employment in the first year were expected to vary by gender, with

stronger effects for boys. Another analysis of the NLSY data set (Desai, Chase-Lansdale, & Michael, 1989) found gender variation in maternal employment effects only for high-income families. Hence, we investigated the differential effects of maternal employment by poverty status as well as by gender.

Previous studies have not identified the particular aspects of maternal employment in the first year that might be most detrimental. The second set of questions related to the continuity, intensity, and timing of maternal employment in the first year of life. Among the children whose mothers were employed in the first year, those whose mothers were employed continuously throughout the first 3 years were expected to experience more detrimental effects than those whose mothers remained home during some of those years. Maternal employment was expected to have stronger negative effects with increasing weekly number of hours worked by the mother. A few studies suggested that negative effects appeared when the number of hours worked per week was over 20, although few direct tests of the amount of hours worked per week were made (Barglow et al., 1987; Belsky, 1988; Belsky & Rovine, 1988; Heynes & Catsambis, 1986; Milne, Myers, Rosenthal, & Ginsburg, 1986). In addition, the timing of maternal entry in the labor force during the first year was expected to have substantial impact on children. Children of mothers who enter the work force later in the child's first year could be expected to fare better than children whose mothers enter the work force earlier in the first year, possibly because of the amount of time spent with the mother. We expected more negative effects from maternal entry into the work force during the second and third quarters of the first year than from entry during the first or fourth quarter. This prediction is based on the admittedly speculative premise that infants in the last quarter of their first year have more sophisticated cognitive conceptions of object and person permanence (Harris, 1983; Lewis & Brooks-Gunn, 1979), rendering the older infant less vulnerable to the coming and going of a mother who has been available earlier than infants in the second or third quarters of their first year (Chase-Lansdale & Owen, 1987; Hoffman, 1984). During the first quarter of the first year, person permanence is not yet formed, as such, and maternal entry into the labor force at this time may be less detrimental than later (Hock, 1980), during its formation.

The third set of questions investigated whether the types of child-care arrangements influence child outcomes over and above the expected maternal employment effect. Quality of child care could not be explored with the Children of the NLSY data set because the characteristics of child-care arrangements used in the first, second, and third years of life were not asked. Note that information on child-care type was not used to test hypotheses regarding the effects of quality of child care. Care by relatives was expected to be beneficial for infants of employed mothers when compared with care by nonrelatives in the first year. On the basis of scanty evidence, grandparents and fathers were posited to enhance functioning as compared with other relatives because of their stability (i.e., presence in the child's life even when not performing primary child care) and long-lasting relationship and presumed commitment to the child (Furstenberg, Brooks-Gunn, & Morgan, 1987; Lamb, 1976; Parke, 1979; Tinsley & Parke, 1984).

Whether care by other relatives operates in a similar beneficial fashion is not known. Nonrelative care in the first year was expected to have particularly negative effects for poor children, because the quality of paid care that is affordable for families in poverty is likely to be low. Hence, the comparative advantage of relative child care as compared with paid child care was expected to be larger for children in poverty than for children not in poverty....

RESULTS

Intersection of Maternal Employment and Child-Care Arrangements

Of the children whose mothers were employed, 48.6% were employed for the child's first year, 56.6% for the child's second year, and 59.7% for the child's third year. These percentages are similar to those from other nationally representative samples (Bureau of Labor Statistics, 1988; see Figures 2 and 3 in Hayes et al., 1990)....

During the first year, grandmother care was the most prevalent type of nonmaternal care for all employment status groups, and the most common child-care arrangement for the children of employed mothers. During the second year, nonrelative care was the most prevalent nonmaternal care type for the children of employed mothers irrespective of the intensity of employment. For the children of mothers who were not employed, grandmother care remained the most prevalent nonmaternal care type during the second year. During the third year, center-based care gained prevalence for all children and became the type of nonmaternal care most frequently used for the children of mothers who were not employed. For the children of part-time employed mothers, grandmother care was the most common nonmaternal care type in the third year of life. For the children of mothers who were employed more than an average of 20 hr per week, nonrelative care was the most common care type. Employment status and the intensity of employment of the mothers were clearly associated with the type of child-care arrangements that the children experienced....

Effects of Child-Care Arrangements in Infancy

Before presenting results pertaining to the effects of infancy-care arrangements on cognitive and behavioral outcomes in preschool children, it is important to reiterate that very few children whose mothers were not employed during the first year of their life received nonmaternal care. Hence, during infancy, non-maternal care was closely linked with maternal employment, and it was not possible to compare the effects of most forms of nonmaternal care between children whose mothers were employed and children whose mothers were not employed. Two regression models were estimated to quantify the effects of various child-care arrangements on preschoolers whose mothers were employed during infancy. The first model includes the main effects of having experienced various child-care arrangements during infancy. The second model includes a set of interaction effects allowing the effects of child-care arrangements to vary by sex and poverty status. These models are presented in Table 1.

... The main effects of child-care arrangements on the BPI scores were significant. Model 1 for the BPI (Table 1, column 3) indicates that for the children

of employed mothers, baby-sitter care, grandmother care, and mother care in infancy resulted in significantly lower BPI scores than father (or father figure) care. Similar to the results of the effects of child care on the PPVT–R, the effects of various forms of child care on the BPI depended on the sex of the child. The beneficial effects of baby-sitter care or grandmother care were stronger for girls than for boys. The size of the interaction effect of sex and maternal care was relatively small. The interaction effect of mother care with poverty status on the BPI scores was not significant, indicating no poverty status differentials in the beneficial effects of maternal care in infancy.

Table 2 shows the predicted mean PPVT–R and BPI scores of children in each care type during infancy, classified by sex and poverty status. These predicted means pertain to the children whose mothers were employed during infancy. When the PPVT–R was considered, it was seen that mother and grandmother care were the most beneficial types of care for children in poverty. For children who were not in poverty, relative care for boys and baby-sitter care for girls appeared to be the most beneficial. When the BPI was considered, mother care emerged as the most beneficial type of care for boys, and baby-sitter care emerged as the most beneficial type of care for girls.

Mother and grandmother care were the only two care types for which effects can be compared between the children whose mothers had different employment statuses. Grandmother care was received by 5.4% of children whose mothers were not employed as well as 22.9% of children whose mothers were employed during the first year of

Table 1

The Effects of Child-Care Arrangements on the Cognitive and Behavioral Outcomes of 3–4-Year-Old White Children Whose Mothers Were Employed in Infancy: Unstandardized Regression Coefficients

Variable	PPVT–R[a]		BPI[b]	
	Model 1	Model 2	Model 1	Model 2
Controls				
Male	−2.382	−11.134	−0.863	−5.491
In poverty	−2.982	−13.117	2.375*	3.022
Mother employed 10–19 hr	−4.807*	−3.599	–	–
Mother employed 20+ hr	−4.043†	−4.400	–	–
Mother's AFQT score	0.030*	0.030	–	–
Child-care arrangements[c]				
Mother care	1.219	−4.545	−3.076*	−4.106
Father care	−3.663	−3.176	CC	CC
Grandmother care	4.901	−4.076	−3.483*	−6.431
Baby-sitter care	5.462	3.404	−4.383*	−8.494
Relative care	3.495	−5.366	EX	EX
Center-based care	CC	CC	EX	EX
Interaction of child care and poverty status[d]				
Mother care × In poverty[e]	–	13.692^F	–	−0.372
Grandmother care × In poverty	–	14.698	–	–
Interaction of child-care and sex				
Mother care × male	–	6.988^F	–	1.975^F
Grandmother care × male	–	14.758	–	6.248
Baby-sitter care × male	–	3.667	–	9.207
Relative care × male	–	20.859	–	–
r^2	0.159	0.218	0.081	0.175

Note: PPVT–R = Peabody Picture Vocabulary Test—Revised; BPI = Behavioral Problems Index; AFQT = Armed Forces Qualification Test; CC = comparison category; EX = excluded from the analysis. [a]Models are based on 252 3–4-year-old White children of mothers who were employed during their 1st year of life. [b]Models are based on 116 4-year-old White children of mothers who were employed during their 1st year of life, excluding those children who were in center-based or relative care. [c]The comparison categories are center-based care for the models of PPVT–R and father (figure) care for the models of BPI. [d]The significance of the interaction effects are shown by a superscript F when the sum of squares accounted by that group of interaction effects are significant at $p < .05$. The significance of each coefficient cannot be tested due to the multicollinearity of dummy variables representing the main effects and interaction effects. [e]The interaction effects are estimated only if the category of interest is represented by at least 10 observations. Consequently, for children in poverty, only the differential effects of mother and grandmother care could be estimated.
†$p < .10$ *$p < .05$.

life. For all children who were cared for either by their grandmothers or by their mothers, we estimated models that quantified the effects of these care types and the interactions of these effects with the maternal employment status (results not shown). These models did not support the hypothesis that the effects of maternal and grandmother care differed by maternal employment status.

Hence, grandmother care was not more beneficial to the children of employed mothers than to the children of mothers who were not working in this sample.

DISCUSSION

As the Children of the NLSY data set demonstrates, maternal employment and child-care choices are closely linked during the first 3 years of life, especially during infancy. Very few infants whose mothers are not employed receive non-maternal care. Very large proportions of infants whose mothers work more than half time receive care from relatives and nonrelatives, though the proportion of children who receive center-based care during the first year of life is negligibly small. Because maternal employment leads to profound changes in an infant's experiences and interactions, it is important to know if maternal employment has any negative effects on children. Our analyses indicate that maternal employment in infancy had significant negative effects on cognitive and behavioral outcomes in White children of age 3 to 4 years. Once maternal employment was postponed to the second or third years, it had negligible effects. At the same time, continuous employment throughout the first 3 years was not more detrimental than intermittent employment following the first year. Because the trends in maternal employment are socially and economically driven, factors that might counteract its possible negative effects need to be identified. . . .

The association of the timing of maternal entry into the labor force during the first year with cognitive and behavioral development is a question that has not been studied before. Postponement of labor-force entry to the last quar-

Table 2

Predicted Scores of the PPVT–R and BPI by Infancy-Care Arrangements for the Children of Mothers Who Were Employed During the First Year of Life

Child-care arrangement	Not in poverty		In poverty	
	Boys	Girls	Boys	Girls
	PPVT–R			
Mother	69.4	73.6	70.0	74.2
Father	63.8	75.0	50.7	61.8
Grandmother	77.7	74.1	79.3	75.6
Relative	82.5	72.8	69.4	59.7
Baby-sitter	74.1	81.5	61.0	68.4
Center	67.0	78.1	53.9	65.0
	BPI			
Mother	8.1	11.6	10.7	14.2
Father	10.2	15.7	13.2	18.7
Grandmother	10.0	9.3	13.0	12.3
Baby-sitter	10.9	7.2	13.9	10.2

Note: PPVT–R = Peabody Picture Vocabulary Test —Revised; BPI = Behavioral Problems Index. The predicted PPVT–R scores were computed on the basis of the regression equations given in Table 1 (Model 2). It was assumed that the mother's Armed Forces Qualifications Test score was 39.2 (the mean value for the sample concerned), that the child in question was a first-born and that the mother worked more than 20 hr per week. Expected scores are given by sex and poverty status, because characteristics were shown to interact with the type of child care to affect cognitive development. Only sex of the child interacted with the type of child care to determine behavioral development; however, poverty status had a significant independent effect. Hence, a two-way breakdown is given for the expected behavioral problem scores as well.

ter of infancy compared with the first 3 quarters had beneficial effects for White preschoolers' cognitive and behavioral development. A variety of factors may have accounted for this beneficial effect, such as the amount of time spent with the mother, the cognitive and emotional developmental level of the child at the time of separation, or some unmeasured differences in the characteristics of mothers who entered the work force late in the child's life (although our findings controlled for the usual socioeconomic factors, other differences might exist; Hock, Christman, & Hock, 1980; Rutter, 1981b). These analyses suggest that the former (i.e., the amount of time) is not the only factor; returning to the labor force in the second quarter was associated with lower preschool cognitive scores than was returning in the first quarter. What factors might render the second quarter (and possibly the third quarter) of the first year the most vulnerable to the effects of maternal employment and render the fourth quarter the least vulnerable? It is possible that in the second (and third) quarter, children are forming representations of their parents vis-à-vis dimensions such as constancy, consistency, and differentiation (Bell, 1970; Decarie, 1965; Mahler, Pine, & Bergman, 1975; Stern, 1977). Separation from the mother during this period may be more detrimental than earlier or later separation. If the mother returns to the labor force before the second quarter, a child might develop a notion of maternal constancy that includes regular absence. If the mother returns to the labor force during the fourth quarter, maternal representations may be better established and changes in maternal routine may be more easily incorporated into maternal representations.

This study shows that the intensity of maternal employment during infancy is associated with later cognitive and behavioral outcomes. However, the effects of intensity of maternal employment on cognitive and behavioral outcomes are not linear. Under 10 hr of employment is the least detrimental, whereas 10–20 hr and more than 20 hr of employment a week exhibit negative effects on cogni-

tive and behavioral outcomes. We found slightly larger detrimental effects for 10–20 hr of employment than for more than half-time employment. Children whose mothers were employed less than 10 hr per week could still receive maternal care for substantial proportions of time. Our data do not allow for a detailed look at the processes that account for differential effects of 10- to 20-hr versus more than 20-hr maternal employment. We speculate that children whose mothers are more than half-time employed may be more likely to be placed into more stable and possibly higher quality child-care arrangements because the mother knows that the child will spend a substantial number of hours every day in that care type and because the mother might be able to afford higher quality care. Furthermore, children of mothers who are employed more than half-time might develop an attachment to their caregiver (Hayes et al., 1990; Howes, Rodning, Galluzzo, & Myers, 1988). Children whose mothers are employed 10–20 hr a week might be placed in more ad hoc care, less stable arrangements, or lower quality care arrangements than children of more intensively employed mothers.

Type of child-care arrangements may alter the effects of maternal employment on children in the first year of life. Our results suggest that types of child-care arrangements have different effects on cognitive development as compared with behavioral development. The cognitive development of boys and children in poverty was vulnerable to child-care effects. The behavioral problems of all children were influenced by child-care arrangements regardless of the poverty status of the family and sex of the child. Mother care and grandmother care were more beneficial for the cognitive development of children in poverty than for children of nonpoverty families. Grandmother care was found to be associated with preschoolers' cognitive functioning in two studies of Black, mostly poor children (Furstenberg et al., 1987; Kellam, Adams, Brown, & Ensnubger, 1982). However, these studies did not focus on care in the first year or on working mothers. Our findings on the beneficial effects of grandmother care were not solely due to residence with the grandmother, because 75% of the children in grandmother care were not residing with her. The care that poor families could afford (or that is available in their communities) might not be of high quality, or poor children may be especially vulnerable to the low-quality care provided in many paid (nonrelative) care arrangements. Each of these hypotheses needs to be tested because the mechanisms through which child care influences cognitive development will determine the policy formulations. For example, if children in poverty receive low-quality care because their families cannot afford better care, child-care subsidies might alleviate the problem. On the other hand, if children in poverty are especially vulnerable to the care provided by nonrelatives (i.e., baby-sitter and center-based care), then programs such as those developed by the early intervention field might be necessary compensation for the negative effects of poverty.

Among the children of employed mothers, boys were found to be more sensitive to the type of care provided than were girls. Boys were likely to have higher PPVT–R scores if they were cared for by their grandmother or a relative other than their father. Perhaps as others have speculated, boys are more vulnerable to a variety of factors, such as low-quality care, less attentive or less attached caregivers (presuming relatives are more attentive or attached), and lack of stability. Negative effects of maternal employment found by the earlier studies might be because of the heightened vulnerability of boys to unstable care arrangements or less attentive caregivers in infancy.

We found that types of infancy-care arrangements are predictive of behavioral outcomes in preschoolers and that these associations are mediated by child gender. For the children of mothers who were employed in infancy, baby-sitter care for girls and mother care for boys are the most beneficial in terms of behavioral outcomes. These results point to the particular significance of child-care arrangements, especially for boys.

Father care appears to be associated with low cognitive scores and high behavioral problem scores in all children. This is contrary to our hypothesis that father care would be similar to grandmother and other relative care in its effects on early development. One could speculate that the fathers who were the main care providers were probably unemployed, with associated problems in emotional well-being and self-esteem....

The Children of the NLSY data set allowed us to examine maternal employment and child-care effects on children simultaneously, which, to our knowledge, has not been done previously. The size of the NLSY sample facilitated the examination of possible differential effects by gender and poverty status. Children in poverty are known to be at risk of delays in cognitive development irrespective of child-care arrangements (McLoyd, 1990). On the other hand, families in poverty are targeted by numerous policies for increased female labor-force participation. Hence, it is crucial to accumulate evidence regarding the effects of child-care arrangements on children in poverty. However, this data set does not allow for process-oriented studies of effects of the quality of child-care arrangements and the relationship between the care-giver and the child. Both types of studies are necessary to understand the mechanisms underlying maternal employment and child-care effects and to inform policy on child care.

REFERENCES

Barglow, P., Vaughn, B., & Molitor, N. (1987). Effects of maternal absence due to employment on the quality of infant-mother attachment in a low-risk sample. *Child Development, 58,* 945–954.

Bell, S. M. (1970). The development of the concept of object as related to infant-mother attachment. *Child Development, 41,* 291–311.

Beller, E. K. (1979). Early intervention programs. In J. D. Osofsky (Ed.), *Handbook of infant development* (pp. 852–894). New York: Wiley.

Belsky, J., & Rovine, M. J. (1988). Nonmaternal care in the first year of life and the security of infant-parent attachment. *Child Development, 59,* 157–167.

Benasich, A. A., Brooks-Gunn, J., & Clewell, B. C. (in press). Who benefits from intervention programs begun in infancy? A review of maternal and child outcomes. *Journal of Applied Developmental Psychology.*

Bowlby, J. (1969). *Attachment and loss: Attachment.* New York: Basic Books.

Bretherton, I., & Waters, E. (1985). Growing points of attachment theory and research. *Monographs of the Society for Research in Child Development, 50*(1–2, Serial No. 209).

Bronfenbrenner, U. (1975). Is early intervention effective? In M. Guttentag & E. L. Struening (Eds.), *Handbook of evaluation research* (Vol. 2, pp. 519–603). Beverly Hills, CA: Sage.

Bronfenbrenner, U. (1979). Contexts of child rearing: Problems and prospects. *American Psychologist, 34,* 844–850.

Brooks-Gunn, J., Phelps, E., & Elder, G. E., Jr., (1991). Studying lives through time. Secondary data analyses in developmental psychology. *Developmental Psychology, 27,* 899–910.

Bryant, D. M., & Ramey, C. T. (1987). An analysis of the effectiveness of early intervention programs for high-risk children. In M. Guralnick & C. Bennett (Eds.), *The effectiveness of early intervention for at-risk and handicapped children* (pp. 33–78). San Diego, CA: Academic Press.

Bureau of Labor Statistics. (1988). [Marital and family characteristics of the labor force]. Unpublished raw data, U.S. department of Labor, Washington, DC.

Campos, J. J., Barrett, K. C., Lamb, M. E., Goldsmith, H. H., & Sternberg, C. (1983). Socioemotional development. In P. H. Mussen (Ed.), *Handbook of child psychology: Vol. 3* (pp. 783–916). New York: Wiley.

Chase-Lansdale, P. L., Michael, R. T., & Desai, S. (1991). Maternal employment during infancy: An analysis of "Children of the National Longitudinal Survey of Youth (NLSY)." In J. V. Lerner & N. L. Galambos (Eds.), *The employment of mothers during the childrearing years* (pp. 37–61). New York: Garland Press.

Chase-Lansdale, P. L., Mott, F. L., Brooks-Gunn, J., & Phillips, D. H. (1991). Children of the National Longitudinal Survey of Youth: A unique research opportunity. *Developmental Psychology, 27,* 918–931.

Chase-Lansdale, P. L., & Owen, M. T. (1987). Maternal employment in a family context: Effects on infant-mother and infant-father attachments. *Child Development, 58,* 1505–1512.

Clarke-Stewart, K. A. (1989). Infant day care: Maligned or malignant? *American Psychologist, 44,* 266–273.

Clarke-Stewart, K. A., & Fein, G. G. (1983). Early childhood programs. In P. H. Mussen (Ed.), *Handbook of child psychology: Vol 4. Socialization, personality, and social development* (4th ed., pp. 917–1000). New York: Wiley.

Clewell, B. C., Brooks-Gunn, J., & Benasich, A. A. (1989). Evaluating child-related outcomes of teenage parenting programs. *Family Relations,* 201–209.

Decarie, T. G. (1965). *Intelligence and affectivity in early childhood.* Madison, CT: International Universities Press.

Desai, S., Chase-Lansdale, P. L., & Michael, R. T. (1989). Mother or market? Effects of maternal employment on the intellectual ability of 4-year-old children. *Demography, 26,* 545–561.

Doyle, A., & Somers, K. (1978). The effect of group and family day care on infant attachment behaviors. *Canadian Journal of Behavioral Science, 10,* 38–45.

Farber, E. A., & Egelan, B. (1982). Developmental consequences of out-of-home care for infants in a low income population. In E. Zigler & E. Gordon (Eds.), *Day care* (pp. 102–125). Boston: Auburn.

Furstenberg, F. F., Jr., Brooks-Gunn, J., & Morgan, S. P. (1987). *Adolescent mothers in later life.* Cambridge, England: Cambridge University Press.

Harris, P. L. (1983). Infant cognition. In P. H. Mussen (Ed.), *Handbook of child psychology: Vol. 4. Socialization, personality and social development* (4th ed., pp. 689–782). New York: Wiley.

Haskins, R. (1989). Beyond metaphor: Efficacy of early childhood education. *American Psychologist, 44,* 274–282.

Hayes, C. D., Palmer, J. L., & Zaslow, M. E. (1990). *Who cares for America's children? Child care policy for the 1990s.* Washington, DC: National Academy Press.

Heynes, B., & Catsambis, S. (1986). Mothers' employment and children's achievement: A critique. *Sociology of Education, 59,* 140–151.

Hock, E. (1980). Working and non-working mothers and their infants: A comparative study of maternal care-giving characteristics and infant social behavior. *Merrill-Palmer Quarterly, 46,* 79–101.

Hock, E., Christman, K., & Hock, M. (1980). Factors associated with decisions about return to work in mothers of infants. *Developmental Psychology, 16,* 535–536.

Hock, E., & Clinger, J. (1980). Behavior toward mother and stranger of infants who have experienced group day care, individual care, or exclusive maternal care. *Journal of Genetic Psychology, 134,* 49–61.

Hoffman, L. W. (1984). Maternal employment and the young child. In M. Perlmutter (Ed.), *Parent-child interaction and parent-child relations in child development. The Minnesota Symposia on Child Psychology.* (Vol. 17, pp. 101–127). Hillsdale, NJ: Erlbaum.

Howes, C., Rodning, C., Galluzzo, D. C., & Myers, L. (1988). Attachment and child care: Relationships with mother and caregiver. *Early Childhood Research Quarterly, 3,* 403–416.

Kellam, S. G., Adams, R., Brown, C. H., & Ensnubger, M. (1982). The long-term evolution of the family structure of teenage and older mothers. *Journal of Marriage and the Family, 44,* 539–554.

Lamb, M. E. (1976). *The role of the father in child development* (Vol. 1). New York: Wiley.

Lazar, I., Darlington, R. B., Murray, H., Royce, J., & Snipper, A. (1982). Lasting effects of early education: A report of the Consortium for Longitudinal Studies. *Monographs of the Society for Research in Child Development, 47*(2–3, Serial No. 195).

Lewis, M., & Brooks-Gunn, J. (1979). *Social cognition and the acquisition of self.* New York: Plenum Press.

Mahler, M. S., Pine, F., & Bergman, A. (1975). *The psychological birth of the infant.* New York: Basic Books.

McLoyd, V. C. (1990). The impact of economic hardship on Black families and children: Psychological distress, parenting, and socioemotional development. *Child Development, 61,* 311–346.

Milne, A. M., Myers, D. E., Rosenthal, A. S., & Ginsburg, A. (1986). Single parents, working mothers, and the educational achievement of school children. *Sociology of Education, 59,* 125–139.

Parke, R. D. (1979). Perspectives on father-infant interaction. In J. D. Osofsky (Ed.), *Handbook of infant development* (pp. 549–590). New York: Wiley.

Pedersen, F. A., Cain, R., Zaslow, M., & Anderson, B. (1982). Variation in infant experience associated with alternative family role organization. In L. Laosa & I. Sigel (Eds.), *Families as learning environments for children* (pp. 87–95). New York: Plenum Press.

Phillips, D. A. (1987). Socialization of perceived academic competence among highly competent children. *Child Development, 58,* 1308–1320.

Rutter, M. (1981a). *Maternal deprivation reassessed.* Harmonsworth, Middlesex, England: Penguin Books.

Rutter, M. (1981b). Social-emotional consequences of daycare for preschool children. *American Journal of Orthopsychiatry, 5,* 4–28.

Schwartz, P. (1983). Length of day-care attendance and attachment behavior in eighteen-month-old infants. *Child Development, 54,* 1073–1078.

Sroufe, L. A. (1979). The coherence of individual development. *American Psychologist, 34,* 834–841.

Sroufe, L. A. (1983). Infant-caregiver attachment and patterns of adaptation in the preschool: The roots of maladaptation and competence. In M. Perlmutter (Ed.), *Minnesota Symposium in Child Psychology,* (pp. 41–83). Hillsdale, NJ: Erlbaum.

Stern, D. (1977). *The first relationship: Mother and infant.* Cambridge, MA: Harvard University Press.

Tinsley, B. J., & Parke, R. D. (1984). Grandparents as support and socialization agents. In M. Lewis & L. Rosenblum (Eds.), *Social connection: Beyond the dyad* (pp. 161–194). New York: Plenum Press.

Vaughn, B. E., Deane, K. E., & Waters, E. (1985). The impact of out-of-home care on child-mother attachment quality: Another look at some enduring questions. *Monographs of the Society for Research in Child Development, 50*(1–2, Serial No. 209).

Zigler, E., & Valentine, J. (1979). *Project Head Start: A legacy of the war on poverty.* New York: Macmillan.

NO

Deborah Lowe Vandell
and Janaki Ramanan

EFFECTS OF EARLY AND RECENT MATERNAL EMPLOYMENT ON CHILDREN FROM LOW-INCOME FAMILIES

The norm in the United States is for mothers to be employed outside the home. Recent U.S. Bureau of Labor Statistics figures (1988) indicate that 73% of the married mothers of school-age children and 57% of the married mothers of infants and preschoolers are employed. Employment figures for single mothers are even higher: 84% of the single mothers of school-age children and 70% of the single mothers of children under 6 years are employed. In part because of this high level of labor force participation by mothers of young children, researchers, policymakers, and families are asking whether and in what ways maternal employment affects children's development.

There are considerable difficulties in trying to ascertain the effects of maternal employment on children. One difficulty is that mothers who are employed may differ a priori from mothers who are not employed. There is accumulating evidence that employed mothers have less traditional views about child rearing (McCartney, 1984), are less anxious about separating from their children (Hock, DeMeis, & McBride, 1988), and are more committed to their careers (Greenberger & Goldberg, 1989) than are women who are not employed or who resume employment later. In addition to these psychological differences, there are demographic differences associated with the likelihood that women are employed. Women who return to the workforce more quickly following the birth of their children are more likely to be black (as opposed to Hispanic or white) and to have higher family incomes (Garrett, Lubeck, & Wenk, 1991) than do women who resume employment more slowly. If these demographic and psychological characteristics contribute to differences in children's development, it is necessary to control for them when studying maternal employment. Unfortunately, many studies examining the effects of maternal employment on children do not have longitudinal designs that adequately permit the consideration of selection factors.

From Deborah Lowe Vandell and Janaki Ramanan, "Effects of Early and Recent Maternal Employment on Children from Low-Income Families," *Child Development*, vol. 63 (1992). Copyright © 1992 by The Society for Research in Child Development, Inc. Reprinted by permission.

The study of maternal employment is further complicated by the possibility that its effects may depend on the child's age when the mother is employed. Belsky (1988) and others (Bogenschneider, 1990; Heyns & Catsambis, 1986; Vandell & Corasaniti, 1990) have argued that maternal employment during infancy and early childhood is a more powerful influence on children's later development than is subsequent maternal employment. Historically, however, researchers (see the review by Hoffman, 1989) have focused on the concurrent effects of maternal employment on older preschool and elementary school children. Typically, researchers have not simultaneously examined early and subsequent maternal employment in order to determine which is the better predictor of children's development.

Yet another difficulty in studying maternal employment is a growing awareness that the effects of maternal employment may be moderated by child and family characteristics (Belsky & Eggebeen, 1991; Desai, Chase-Lansdale, & Michael, 1989). Because of the possibility that maternal employment affects families differentially, it is risky to assume a priori that results from studies involving maternal employment within middle-class white families are generalizable to low-income, single-parent, and racial minority households.

The current study seeks to examine further this complicated question of the effects of maternal employment by focusing on children from economically disadvantaged families. Analyses were conducted on a national data set, the National Longitudinal Survey of Youth (NLSY). The current study focuses on the second-grade children within the 1986 NLSY data set. These were the oldest children for whom detailed maternal employment histories from birth were available in sufficient numbers for analysis.

This study differs in significant ways from other recent papers that have used the NLSY to examine questions relating to maternal employment. Both Desai et al. (1989) and Belsky and Eggenbeen (1991) used the NLSY to examine the effects of early maternal employment on preschoolers. These preschool-age children had mothers who were older at their birth, were better educated, and were more affluent than the mothers of the second-grade children examined in the current study. Recent work by Brooks-Gunn (personal communication) using the NLSY also examines younger children than those in the current study and does not include the array of child outcomes examined within the current study.

Two conflicting hypotheses concerning the effects of maternal employment on children from economically disadvantaged families can be proposed. One is that maternal employment, poverty, and single-parent status act as cumulative stresses on families, thereby resulting in poorer social and academic outcomes in low-income children when their mothers are employed. An alternative hypothesis is that the financial and emotional benefits associated with maternal employment are so substantial that children whose mothers are employed demonstrate better developmental progress than low-income children whose mothers are not employed. Recent efforts at welfare reform in the United States, as exemplified by the JOBS and New Chance programs, are based on the assumption that maternal employment has positive effects in low-income families and children, but this assumption is largely untested.

Several studies conducted 20 years ago are consistent with the assumption of advantageous effects of maternal employment on low-income children. Within a group of low-income, black fifth graders, IQ scores were highest when mothers were employed full time (Woods, 1972). Similarly, within a sample of single-parent families living in poverty, Rieber and Womack (1968) reported children having higher achievement test scores when mothers were employed rather than not employed. More recently, others (Cherry & Eaton, 1977; Milne, Myers, Rosenthal, & Ginsburg, 1986) have found that black children whose mothers were single parents scored higher on standardized cognitive assessments when their mothers were employed rather than not employed.

The current study is a notable improvement over these earlier investigations. First, it utilizes a longitudinal data set to examine possible self-selection differences associated with maternal employment. These selection factors include mother's mental aptitude, self-esteem, and attitudes about employment and child rearing. The earlier studies of low-income families have not typically included the consideration of selection effects. A second improvement is that the current study utilizes a national data set rather than the small convenience samples that were typically used in the past. A third improvement is that the effects of both early and subsequent maternal employment were tested, whereas the previous work has focused only on the effects of concurrent maternal employment.

Another difference between this study and previous studies examining economically disadvantaged children is that sev-

eral potential moderators of maternal employment are examined. Given evidence that middle-class boys and girls react differently to maternal employment (Bogenschneider, 1990; Desai et al., 1989; Gold & Andres, 1978; Montemayor, 1984), interactions between maternal employment and child gender are tested. Also, family marital composition and child race/ethnicity are examined as possible moderators of the effects of maternal employment in accordance with suggestions (Brooks-Gunn, personal communication; Scarr, Lande, & McCartney, 1989) that these factors can result in maternal employment differentially affecting children.

A final difference between the current study and other studies involving economically disadvantaged families is that we examine possible processes and experiences by which maternal employment affects children. Maternal employment can provide families with greater financial resources, thereby reducing the likelihood that the family is living in poverty. It can change the emotional climate in the family by either reducing (or increasing) family stress and emotional support. Consequently, we examined ways in which family functioning might vary as a result of maternal employment in order to ascertain possible mechanisms by which maternal employment exerts effects on children.

METHOD

Subjects

One hundred eighty-nine second-grade children whose mothers were part of the National Longitudinal Survey of Youth served as subjects. The children ranged in age from 80 to 100 months

(M = 7 years 9 months). The sample consisted of 104 girls. Forty-six percent of the children were African-American; the remainder were white. Hispanic children were not included in the analyses because all 1986 assessments were conducted in English, and the data set does not specify how many of the Hispanic children had sufficient English skills to complete the tasks. Forty-one percent of the children lived in households whose incomes fell below the poverty line. Forty-eight percent lived in single-parent households. Most of the children (80%) were born to adolescent mothers (M mother age at the child's birth was 18 years). Seventy-five percent of the children resided in urban areas. Maternal education, on average, was 11.3 years.

Procedures...

Family Characteristics.
The 1986 NLSY data set includes information collected from the children's mothers beginning in 1979. These measures include yearly updates on demographic variables such as mothers' age, education, marital status, family income, and child race. During 1980, measures of maternal attitudes, values, and aptitudes were collected when the focal children in the current study were infants and toddlers. The 1980 assessment included the Armed Forces Qualification Test [AFQT], Rosenberg's (1965) Self-Esteem Scale, and the women's attitudes about women's roles.

The Armed Forces Qualification Test is a general measure of the mothers' intellectual aptitude and trainability (Baker & Mott, 1989). It consists of the sum of raw scores from the following sections of the Armed Services Vocational Battery (ABVAB): Section 2—Arithmetic Reason-ing; Section 3—Word Knowledge; Section 4—Paragraph Comprehension; and one-half of the score from Section 5—Numerical Operations.

Women's self-esteem was assessed using 4-point ratings for the 10 items that make up Rosenberg's (1965) Self-Esteem Scale. Cronbach's alpha for this scale within the current data set was .82.

The traditionality of attitudes about women's roles was measured using 5-point scales in response to four statements previously used in NLS studies: (*a*) "A woman's place is in the home, not in the office or shop," (*b*) "A wife who carries out her full family responsibilities doesn't have time for outside employment," (*c*) "It is much better for everyone concerned if the man is the achiever outside the home and the woman takes care of the family," and (*d*) "Women are much happier if they stay at home and take care of their children." Cronbach alpha within the current sample for these four items was .75.

During 1986, observers completed the standard NLSY. In addition, observers completed a shortened form of Caldwell and Bradley's HOME [Home Observation for Measurement of the Environment] scale. Ratings of the quality of the home environment were determined by mothers' responses to questions and by direct observations. The HOME scale assessed the extent to which children's home environment provided cognitive stimulation (14 items) and emotional support (12 items). Cronbach's alpha was .70 for the total scale.

Child Assessments.
During the 1986 interview, mothers also completed a questionnaire describing their children's behavior using a revised form of the Behavior Problems Index

(Pedersen & Zill, 1986). These 28 questions assessed six domains (peer conflicts, hyperactivity, anxiety, dependence, antisociability, and headstrong). A total behavior problems score standardized with a mean of 100 has been established using data from the National Health Survey. A higher score on this measure designates more behavior problems. For the NLSY children, Cronbach's alpha for the total behavior problems score was .87.

A battery of cognitive assessments was completed by the children during 1986. Subscales from the Peabody Individual Achievement Test (PIAT) were administered to measure children's mathematics and reading achievement. The Peabody Picture Vocabulary Test (PPVT) was used as an indicator of the children's verbal functioning, while the Digit Span Subscale of the WISC-R was used to assess children's short term memory and attentiveness. Standardized scores for each child were provided for the PIAT, PPVT, and digit span attention. The Digit Span was normed against a distribution with a mean of 10 and a standard deviation of 3. The PIAT and PPVT were standardized on a mean of 100.

RESULTS...

Associations Between Early and Recent Maternal Employment and Child Outcomes

... Duncan post hoc analyses revealed that both math and reading achievement scores were higher for those low-income children whose mothers were employed both early and recently in comparison to those low-income children whose mothers were not employed during either period ($p < .05$) or those children whose mothers were only recently employed

($p < .05$). PPVT scores were higher for children whose mothers were employed both early and recently in contrast to those children whose mothers were not employed during either period ($p < .05$). There were no associations between maternal employment and child behavior problems or child attention.

Maternal Selection Factors Associated With Early and Recent Maternal Employment

... Extent of maternal employment during the children's first 3 years was positively correlated with mothers' mental aptitude scores on the 1980 AFQT, $r(182) = .25, p < .001$. Selection factors were also indicated for mothers' employment during the previous 3 years (i.e., recent employment).... [R]ecent maternal employment hours were positively correlated with the mothers' 1980 AFQT scores, $r(180) = .23, p < .001$, and mothers' level of education, $r(183) = .21, p < .01$. These analyses suggest that economically disadvantaged women who were more intellectually competent and more highly educated were more likely to be employed than were economically disadvantaged women who were less intellectually competent.

Associations Between Maternal Employment and Family Functioning

A third set of analyses examined associations between maternal employment and the children's current home environment.... [M]aternal employment hours during the children's first 3 years was related to current family conditions in the second graders' homes. Early maternal employment hours were correlated with the quality of the second graders' home environment as assessed using the HOME, $r(156) = .17, p < .03$, and with the family being a two-parent household, $r(185) = -.16$, $p < .03$. Early maternal employment was negatively correlated with the second graders' families living in poverty, $r(170) = -.24$, $p < .001$. Significant correlations were also apparent between mothers' recent employment hours (i.e., employment during the previous 3 years) and current family conditions. Recent employment hours was negatively correlated with family poverty, $r(170) = -.38$, $p < .0001$, and positively correlated with quality of the HOME environment, $r(155) = .19$, $p < .01$, and with family income, $r(155) = .18$, $p < .05$.

Mothers' Employment During the First Three Years and Recently as Predictors of Child Development

The next question was whether maternal employment predicted children's development after controlling for selection factors. To test this question, a series of hierarchical multiple regressions were conducted. Within the first equation, maternal factors assessed in 1980 (AFQT, self-esteem, and traditional values) and implicated significantly or marginally significantly in differential rates of maternal employment were used in conjunction with child demographic variables (age and race) to predict the children's behaviors. In the second, third, and fourth regression equations (respectively), the increments of variance explained by the additions of (a) hours of early maternal employment, (b) hours of recent employment, and (c) both early and recent employment to the family selection variables were tested.

The first regression equation composed of the selection variables was a significant predictor of the children's math achievement, adjusted $R^2 = .32$, $p < .0001$, reading achievement adjusted $R^2 = .33$, $p < .0001$, attention, adjusted $R^2 = .10$, $p < .005$, and PPVT, adjusted $R^2 = .27$, $p < .0001$. Within these regressions, inspection of the individual betas indicated that mother's AFQT score was a significant positive predictor of children's reading achievement ($b = .51$, $p < .01$), math achievement ($b = .56$, $p < .01$), and PPVT ($b = .26$, $p < .05$) scores. Child age was a significant negative predictor of the PPVT ($b = -.17$, $p < .05$), reading ($b = -.36$, $p < .01$), and math achievement ($b = -.18$, $p < .05$) scores.

The second, third, and fourth equations tested the increments to the R^2 for the first equation provided by (a) early maternal employment hours, (b) recent employment hours, and (c) both early and recent employment. Early maternal employment contributed a significant increment to the R^2 for children's math achievement scores over and above the selection factors. The adjusted R^2 for selection factors alone was .32; the adjusted R^2 after adding early maternal employment was .35. This increment was a significant increase in R^2, $p < .05$. The addition of recent maternal employment did not improve the prediction of math achievement.

Recent maternal employment did contribute a significant increment to the R^2 for children's reading achievement ($p < .02$). The adjusted R^2 for selection factors alone was .33. The adjusted R^2 after adding recent maternal employment was .36. Recent maternal employment also contributed a significant increment ($p < .05$) to the prediction of the children's PPVT. The adjusted R^2 for the selection factors was .27. The addition of recent maternal employment increased the adjusted R^2 to .29. Early maternal employment did not contribute significant increments to the R^2's for these variables.

Neither early nor recent maternal employment contributed significantly to the variance explained for the children's behavior problems or attention span.

The next set of hierarchical regressions used as its first equation both selection factors and measures of current family conditions (poverty, marital status, HOME score) as predictors of child outcomes. The increments to R^2 provided by (a) early maternal employment, (b) recent maternal employment, and (c) both early and recent maternal employment were then tested. Thus, this set of hierarchical regressions enabled us not only to control for selection factors when examining the effects of maternal employment but also to determine if current family conditions might serve as mediators of maternal employment effects.

... [T]he addition of early maternal employment to the initial selection factors and the current family measures significantly improved the prediction of the children's math achievement ($p < .05$). The R^2 for the first equation consisting of family selection factors and current family functioning was .31. The addition of early maternal employment improved the prediction to .34. Recent maternal employment significantly improved the prediction of reading achievement ($p < .01$) and the PPVT ($p < .05$) over and above that predicted by the selection factors and current family conditions.

Tests for Moderating Factors

Because of suggestions that maternal employment effects are moderated by child gender, child race, and family marital composition, regression equations in which these interactions were added to the models... were tested. In no case did these interactions add a significant increment to R^2.

Tests for First Year and Current Year Effects

A final issue was whether single year employment records would be better predictors of child behaviors than the 3-year cumulative employment records. For these analyses, hierarchical regressions were conducted in which first year maternal employment and current year maternal employment were substituted for the 3-year cumulative scores. Results using a single year of data paralleled the 3-year cumulative data, but the adjusted R^2 and betas for the cumulative employment hours were higher in every case.

DISCUSSION

This study underscores the importance of several factors that make the study of the effects of maternal employment on children complicated: (1) self-selection results in maternal employment not being randomly distributed across families, (2) maternal employment contributes to differences in family environments that should be considered as possible mediators of maternal employment effects, (3) the timing of maternal employment must be considered because early employment and recent maternal employment predict different aspects of low-income children's development, and (4) the effects of maternal employment on children and families must be placed within a broader ecological context. Each of these points is discussed in turn.

Controlling for Self-Selection Effects

The longitudinal design of the NLSY allowed for a better test of selection effects than has typically been the case for research concerning maternal employment. In the current study, early maternal employment was associated with a number of maternal characteristics. In comparison to low-income women who were not employed during their children's first 3 years, low-income employed women (a) scored higher on a measure of mental aptitude (the Armed Forces Qualification Test) and (b) were more highly educated. These associations suggest that maternal employment is not randomly distributed across economically disadvantaged families but occurs selectively, resulting in more competent women being employed.

The nature of these associations underscores the importance of controlling for selection factors when studying the effects of maternal employment. Before taking at face value the better performance of low-income children with employed mothers on the math, reading, and language tests, it was necessary to control for selection effects. To this end, hierarchical regressions were conducted that controlled for selection factors. From these hierarchical regressions, it appeared that children from low-income families benefited from maternal employment. Children's math achievement scores were positively predicted by early maternal employment, even after controlling for the maternal and demographic selection factors such as AFQT, maternal self-esteem and attitudes, and child race. Reading achievement and PPVT scores were positively predicted by recent maternal employment, after controlling for selection factors. Within these analyses, it did not appear that the positive effects of maternal employment on the children were solely an artifact of self selection. Although one might argue that we failed to include the "right" selection factors as controls, the number of potential selection factors that were considered was large and diverse. Conse-

quently, we turn to aspects of the children's current family environment for possible processes that contribute to differences in child behavior.

Associations Between Maternal Employment and Current Family Conditions

The longitudinal design of the NLSY permitted an examination of the associations between early maternal employment and family functioning over time. In comparison to families in which mothers were employed, unemployed mothers were more likely to have families that were living in poverty when the children were in second grade. Maternal employment, on the other hand, was associated with the second graders having higher quality home environments as assessed by the HOME scale. These associations are counter to one cultural ideal in the United States, namely, that young children should be cared for in their own homes by their own mothers. This ideal could be a costly one for economically disadvantaged families. Staying home with mother can deprive families of the financial wherewithal to escape from poverty. Staying home can result in low-income families being less able, because of their economic or emotional circumstances, to provide their children with an environment that fosters development.

Although the associations between family conditions and maternal employment are important in their own right, the primary reason for including them in the current study was to use them to aid in the interpretation of the associations between maternal employment and child development. Consequently, a second set of hierarchical regressions were conducted in which both selection factors and measures of current family conditions were used as "controls." While current family conditions such as poverty were negatively associated with maternal employment and other family conditions such as quality of the HOME environment and a two-parent household were positively associated with maternal employment, it does not appear that these factors alone explain why maternal employment positively predicted children's behaviors. Early maternal employment continued to be a positive predictor of math achievement, and recent maternal employment continued to be a positive predictor of reading achievement, even after controlling for these measures of current family functioning.

It appears, then, that the study of maternal employment must turn to other child experiences in order to understand the processes by which maternal employment influences children's development. One critical aspect of children's experience not directly measured in the NLSY are children's experiences in alternate forms of child care. Interestingly, Field (1991) has reported higher math grades for children who attended high-quality infant day-care programs in contrast to children who began high-quality day-care programs later; and Andersson (1989) reported similar beneficial effects of early day-care experiences on Swedish children's math performance. The results of the current study are consistent with the contention that alternative forms of child care can be a positive force in the lives of young, low-income children. Unfortunately, the retrospective early child care questions and the limited questions about current after-school care administered as part of the NLSY do not include adequate measures of the nature of quality of the alternate child care experiences

in order for us to ascertain if the children's child care experiences were the mechanism by which maternal employment was associated with positive effects on low-income children.

Importance of Both Early and Recent Maternal Employment

Although the current study was unable to test for the potential contribution of alternate child care experiences, the results of the current study are quite clear on another issue. Whereas some (Belsky, 1988) have emphasized the importance of early experiences for child development, others have highlighted the role of recent experiences for children (Hoffman, 1989). The results of the current study point to the independent contributions of both early and recent experiences within the context of maternal employment for children's development. These differential contributions highlight the importance of including measures of both early and recent maternal employment in any study of school-age and adolescent children.

Ecological Context of Maternal Employment

Finally, the results of this study should be placed within a broader ecological context. The children observed in the current study were from economically disadvantaged families. Most had adolescent mothers who had limited education. Many of the children lived in single parent households. Within this ecological context, maternal employment was a significant positive predictor of children's math, reading, and language scores. Interestingly, these positive effects were not moderated by child gender, child race, or family marital composition.

It is premature, however, to assume that maternal employment inevitably affects low-income families in positive ways. Effects of maternal employment may be quite different for families in which mothers choose to be employed as opposed to those families in which mothers are forced by either personal circumstances or governmental regulations to be employed during their children's early years. Observations of middle-class mothers (Gold & Andres, 1978; Hock et al., 1988) suggest that the congruence between actual employment situation and preferred employment situation is a significant predictor of mothers' and children's reactions to maternal employment. Congruence may be an important moderator of the effects of maternal employment in low-income households as well.

Caution must also be taken in generalizing these results to children from middle-class or affluent families. The balance of trade-offs between financial needs, employment preferences, job stresses, and availability of child care may shift in families with different economic resources. Maternal employment may have a different meaning and different consequences for middle-class families and children.

REFERENCES

Andersson, B. E. (1989). Effects of public day-care: A longitudinal study. *Child Development*, 60, 857–866.

Baker, P. C., & Mott, F. L. (1989). *NLSY child handbook: 1989*. Columbus: Center for Human Resource Research, Ohio State University.

Belsky, J. (1988). The "effects" of infant day care reconsidered. *Early Childhood Research Quarterly*, 3, 235–272.

Belsky, J., & Eggebeen, D. (1991). Early and extensive maternal employment and young children's socioemotional development: Children of the National Longitudinal Survey of Youth. *Journal of Marriage and the Family*, 53, 1083–1110.

Bogenschneider, K. (1990). *Maternal employment and adolescent academic achievement: Mediating, moderating and developmental influences*. Unpublished doctoral dissertation, Department of Child and Family Studies, University of Wisconsin—Madison.

Cherry, F. F., & Eaton, E. L. (1977). Physical and cognitive development in children of low-income mothers working in the child's early years. *Child Development*, 48, 158–166.

Desai, S., Chase-Lansdale, P. L., & Michael, R. T. (1989). Mother or market? Effects of maternal employment on the intellectual ability of 4-year-old children. *Demography*, 26, 545–561.

Field, T. (1991). Quality infant day-care and grade school behavior and performance. *Child Development*, 62, 863–870.

Garrett, P., Lubeck, S., & Wenk, D. (1991). Childbirth and maternal employment: Data from a national longitudinal survey. In J. S. Hyde & M. J. Essex (Eds.), *Parental leave and child care*. Philadelphia: Temple University Press.

Gold, D., & Andres, D. (1978). Developmental comparisons between 10-year-old children with employed and nonemployed mothers. *Child Development*, 49, 75–84.

Greenberger, E., & Goldberg, W. A. (1989). Work, parenting, and the socialization of children. *Developmental Psychology*, 25, 22–35.

Heyns, B., & Catsambis, S. (1986). Mother's employment and children's achievement: A critique. *Sociology of Education*, 59, 140–151.

Hock, E., DeMeis, D., & McBride, S. (1988). Maternal separation anxiety: Its role in the balance of employment and motherhood in mothers of infants. In A. E. Gottfried & A. W. Gottfried (Eds.), *Maternal employment and children's development: Longitudinal research* (pp. 191–230). New York: Plenum.

Hoffman, L. W. (1989). Effects of maternal employment in the two-parent family. *American Psychologist*, 44, 283–292.

McCartney, K. (1984). Effects of quality of day care environment on children's language development. *Developmental Psychology*, 20, 244–260.

Milne, A. M., Myers, D. E., Rosenthal, A. S., & Ginsburg, A. (1986). Single parents, working mothers, and the educational achievement of school children. *Sociology of Education*, 59, 125–139.

Montemayor, R. (1984). Maternal employment and adolescent's relations with parents, siblings, and peers. *Journal of Youth and Adolescence*, 13, 543–557.

Pedersen, J. L., & Zill, N. (1986). Marital disruption, parent-child relationship, and behavioral problems in children. *Journal of Marriage and the Family*, 48, 295–307.

Rieber, M., & Womack, M. (1968). The intelligence of preschool children as related to ethnic and demographic variables. *Exceptional Children, 34,* 609–614.

Rosenberg, M. (1965). *Society and the adolescent self-image.* Princeton, NJ: Princeton University Press.

Scarr, S., Lande, J., & McCartney, K. (1989). Child care and the family: Cooperation and interaction. In J. Lande, S. Scarr, & N. Gunzenhauser (Eds.), *Caring for children: The future of child care in the United States* (pp. 1–21). Hillsdale, NJ: Erlbaum.

U.S. Bureau of Labor Statistics (1988). *Special labor force reports.* Nos. 13, 130, and 134. Washington, DC: Government Printing Office.

Vandell, D. L., & Corasaniti, M. A. (1990). Child care and the family: Complex contributors to child development. In K. McCartney (Ed.), *New directions in child development research* (pp. 23–37). San Francisco: Jossey-Bass.

Woods, M. B. (1972). The unsupervised child of the working mother. *Developmental Psychology, 6,* 14–25.

POSTSCRIPT

Does a Mother's Job Have a Negative Effect on Children?

Baydar and Brooks-Gunn found that preschoolers whose mothers worked during their children's first year of life scored lower on cognitive and behavioral scales than did those children whose mothers were not employed. These findings held regardless of the child's gender or the family's poverty status.

On the other hand, Vandell and Ramanan discovered that math and reading scores for second graders whose mothers worked during their children's infancy were higher than for children whose mothers were not employed. Their research was conducted on low-income families only.

Both sets of researchers used the same database, children and mothers from the National Longitudinal Survey of Youth, yet they came up with opposing conclusions on the effects of maternal employment. This illustrates the confusion surrounding maternal employment effects. In addition, the researchers disagreed on the relationship of their findings to social class. One study found negative maternal employment effects for children regardless of economic status, while the other study found positive maternal employment effects in only low-income families.

Although researchers agree that maternal employment studies need to examine the interaction of several variables, they do not agree on which sets of variables combine to give an accurate picture of how a mother's employment affects children. An up-to-date and balanced perspective on maternal employment effects can be found in *Working Women and their Families* by Jacqueline Lerner (Sage Publications, 1994).

As you review the cumulative research on this topic, you will find that it is apparent that maternal employment effects have been altered by new technology, in the form of time-saving appliances (e.g., dishwashers, automatic washers and dryers, self-cleaning ovens, microwaves), and by societal changes: the women's liberation movement, the widespread debate over the Equal Rights Amendment, and the election of more women to political office.

With the current political talk about welfare reform, it is more important than ever to examine maternal employment effects in a critical and realistic light. If single welfare mothers are required to work, how will their children fare? Does the research tell us anything about the need or lack thereof for mothers to be with their children during their first years of life? Should mothers stay home with their young children and delay entrance into the workforce? Can other caregivers provide for young children's needs?

SUGGESTED READINGS

Bogenschneider, K., & Steinberg L. (1994, January). Maternal employment and adolescents' academic achievement: A developmental analysis. *Sociology of Education, 67,* 60–77.

Greenberger, E., & O'Neil, R. (1992). Maternal employment and perceptions of young children: Bronfenbrenner et al. revisited. *Child Development, 63,* 431–448.

MacEwen, K., & Barling, J. (1991, August). Effects of maternal employment experiences on children's behavior via mood, cognitive difficulties, and parenting behaviors. *Journal of Marriage and the Family, 53,* 635–644.

Richards, M., & Duckett, E. (1994). The relationship of maternal employment to early adolescent daily experience with and without parents. *Child Development, 65,* 225–236.

Goldman, K. W. (1993). *My mother worked and I turned out OK.* New York: Garnet Press.

ISSUE 2

Do Older Parents Provide a More Nurturing Environment for Children?

YES: Marguerite Stevenson Barratt, Mary A. Roach, and Karen K. Colbert, from "Single Mothers and Their Infants: Factors Associated With Optimal Parenting," *Family Relations* (October 1991)

NO: Andrew L. Yarrow, from *Latecomers: Children of Parents Over 35* (Macmillan, 1991)

ISSUE SUMMARY

YES: Developmental psychologist Marguerite Barratt, assistant scientist Mary Roach, and Karen Colbert, a lecturer at Iowa State University, conclude that maternal age correlates with positive parenting skills.

NO: Andrew Yarrow, a researcher and journalist, contends that the children of older parents he studied were forced to grow up too fast and were expected to be more mature than their chronological age required.

If you could pick your parents, what qualities would they have and how old would they be? The age of one's parents carries with it many implications. Physical, social, and emotional development usually vary depending upon one's parents' ages. Younger parents may have more energy, while older parents may have more experience and wisdom. A child who wants to run and play but has an older, sedentary parent could feel cheated, while another child with a younger parent who does not know how to listen to the child's problems could feel likewise. It's a trade-off.

Pamela Daniels and Kathy Weingarten, in their 1982 book *Sooner or Later: The Timing of Parenthood in Adult Lives* (W. W. Norton), found that the age at which the people whom they studied became parents had little to do with the *number* of problems those parents experienced. However, the *nature* of the parents' problems with their children did vary according to parental age. Younger parents (20 years old) were faced with raising children while they were still trying to establish themselves in a career and in the social world. Older parents (30 years old), although financially stable and ready to nurture their children, felt a disruption in their routines and the lifestyles they had established.

The concept of older parents has changed since Daniels and Weingarten wrote their book and identified as "older" those parents who were 30 years of age or older. Current books and articles now describe as older those parents who are in their late 30s or 40s, as in Andrew Yarrow's 1991 book *Latecomers: Children of Parents Over 35.* And news stories have reported on women over 50 who have given birth with the aid of in vitro fertilization and other biomedical advances.

Because women can choose to bear children later in life than ever before, it is important to examine the ways in which children's lives are affected by the age of their parents. As compared to young parents, who are relatively closer in age to their children, older parents may be more formal and less understanding of the values and attitudes that shape their children's generation. On the other hand, older parents may possess more patience and a better understanding of their children's emotions than young parents.

For just about every positive point connected with having older parents there is a negative counterpoint. Older parents who are financially and emotionally stable are ready to spend time with and give attention to their children. While some children may see this as a positive, other children may feel burdened by the responsibility of being the center of their parents' lives. These children may feel overprotected or faced with excessively high expectations. Many adult children of older parents report feeling comfortable around older people but not with children. Also, while children of older parents may feel more secure and stable, they may also have a greater fear that their parents could die and leave them alone.

Each of the following articles takes a different view of the effects of parental age on a child. Marguerite Barratt, Mary Roach, and Karen Colbert, in a study of single mothers, conclude that older mothers are more responsive to their children than their younger counterparts. In a selection from his book, Andrew Yarrow presents the negative consequences of having older parents, based on interviews with adults who grew up with older parents.

YES Marguerite Stevenson Barratt, Mary A. Roach, and Karen K. Colbert

SINGLE MOTHERS AND THEIR INFANTS: FACTORS ASSOCIATED WITH OPTIMAL PARENTING

Within the past decade, there has been increasing recognition that multiple factors contribute to optimal parenting. Models suggest various maternal, infant, and contextual factors that may impact independently and in concert on parenting practices. Lamb and Easterbrooks (1981) outline sources of individual differences in parental sensitivity; Belsky, Robins, and Gamble (1984) identify multiple determinants of parental competence. If progress is to be made in understanding associated influences on parenting, well-designed empirical research within a theoretical framework must be conducted.

The present study provides a model designed to examine factors associated with optimal parenting by single mothers. Approximately 24% of infants are born to single mothers (National Center for Health Statistics, 1987), and Parke and Tinsley (1987) have urged research on single-parent families, particularly those with infants. In addition, research within special populations suggests that caregiving environments differ with marital status (Allen, Affleck, McGrade, & McQueeney, 1984; Bradley, Elardo, Rosenthal, & Friend, 1984; Kimball, Stewart, Conger, & Burgess, 1980). Thus, models developed to explain variations in parenting among married families may not be directly applicable to single-parent families.

Given the scarce resources available for parent intervention, counselors and educators could benefit from a suitable knowledge base detailing whom to target and how to design intervention curriculum. Heath (1987) has argued that parent education courses must take into account changing family configurations. Identification of factors potentially contributing to optimal parenting might also be useful for policymakers concerned with the issue of parenting by single mothers. The factors selected for this study were chosen specifically for their particular relevance for single mothers. Single mothers are more likely than married mothers to be young (Moore, Wenk, Hofferth, & Hayes, 1987), to have been reared in single or stepparent families (Eiduson,

From Marguerite Stevenson Barratt, Mary A. Roach, and Karen K. Colbert, "Single Mothers and Their Infants: Factors Associated With Optimal Parenting," *Family Relations*, vol. 40, no. 4 (October 1991). Copyright © 1991 by The National Council on Family Relations, 3989 Central Avenue, NE, Suite 550, Minneapolis, MN 55421. Reprinted by permission.

Kornfein, Zimmerman, & Weisner, 1982), and to have experienced depression (Pearlin & Johnson, 1977).

Accordingly, the first factor in the proposed model necessarily includes maternal age. This is consistent with Erikson's (1963) assertion that adolescence involves the crisis of identity versus role confusion. For younger mothers, the task of self-discovery may take precedence over parenting. As the second factor, following Belsky and colleagues' (1984) recognition of the potential for intergenerational transmission of parenting competence, a characteristic of the mother's family of origin has been included. In accordance with Lamb and Easterbrooks' (1981) model, the third factor includes an assessment of maternal personality in the form of psychological well-being. Since 1974, no model has been complete without inclusion of the reciprocal influences of the infant on its caregiver (Lewis & Rosenblum, 1974). The child characteristic most frequently considered as influential on parenting is temperament, and it has been included as the fourth factor in the model. Finally, following the model of Belsky and colleagues (1984), a contextual factor has been added to the model. There is a tendency for single mothers to remain living within the contexts of their families of origin (Furstenberg & Crawford, 1981). Because supportive adults have the potential to influence parenting (Crockenberg, 1987), the effects of mothers' current living situations on their parenting practices need to be examined. The influence of these five factors, taken together, may become particularly evident during single mothers' early adjustments to parenting their firstborn infants.

Maternal age has been found to be positively associated with more optimal parenting within samples of adolescent mothers (Gershenson, Syc, Umeh, & Rosenberg, 1987; King & Fullard, 1982; Reis & Herz, 1987), and within samples including both adolescent and adult mothers (Coll, Hoffman, & Oh, 1987; Luster & Rhoades, 1989; Schilmoeller & Baranowski, 1985). However, when various family background, support, and child characteristics have been taken into account, contributions of maternal age to scores on the Home Observation of the Environment (HOME) have been less striking (Coll, Hoffman, Van Houten, & Oh, 1987; Philliber & Graham, 1981). Moreover, because many studies have confounded the effects of maternal age and marital status, and have failed to sufficiently account for infant age and birth order, interpretation of maternal age effects remains obscure.

Disruption in the mother's family of origin may also influence competent parenting. Evidence suggests that mothers from disrupted families of origin are more likely to have experienced extended separations from their preschool-aged children than mothers from intact families, perhaps reflecting weaker emotional bonds (Philliber & Graham, 1981). Consistent with this hypothesis, research by Hall, Pawlby, and Wolkind (1979) indicates that married mothers who grew up in single-parent or stepparent families interacted less with their 5-month-old infants than mothers originating from intact two-parent families. Children who experience marital disruption are negatively affected whether the custodial parent remarries or remains single (Allison & Furstenberg, 1989; Hetherington, Cox, & Cox, 1985). Experiences in mothers' families of origin, therefore, may influence their subsequent parenting.

Psychological characteristics of the mother are also generally believed to influence parenting such that mothers with more psychological symptoms tend to exhibit less optimal parenting (Belsky et al., 1984; Lamb & Easterbrooks, 1981). The home environments of children with depressed parents tend to be less adequate than the environments of children with nondepressed parents: Mother-infant interaction for dyads with depressed mothers is notably more negative (Cohn, Campbell, Matias, & Hopkins, 1990) and perhaps also less synchronous (Field, Healy, Goldstein, & Guthertz, 1990) than mother-infant interaction with nondepressed mothers. For adult married mothers, even subclinical depression following the birth of a baby may impact negatively on mothers' interactions with their infants (Bettes, 1988; Zekoski, O'Hara, & Wills, 1987). Likewise, within a sample of adolescent mothers, maternal emotional disturbance has been found to be associated with less optimal interactive behavior (LeResche, Strobino, Parks, Fischer, & Smeriglio, 1983).

Characteristics of the infant clearly have the capacity to influence parenting (Lamb & Easterbrooks, 1981; Thomas & Chess, 1977), although this has been assessed primarily within married samples. For example, parents of infants with difficult temperaments are particularly likely to report concerns about their infants (McKim, 1987). Recent reviews (Bates, 1987; Crockenberg, 1986) further suggest that the temperament of the infant may limit the parent's ability to be a sensitive partner and to structure an optimal caregiving environment. However, evidence on this point is inconclusive since difficult infants may elicit increased rather than decreased parental involvement and responsivity. In an assessment of the home environments of 5-month-old infants, Houldin (1987) reported no relation between infant temperament and HOME scores.

Parenting may also be affected by environmental context in terms of the people with whom single mothers live. For example, the presence of the grandmother in the homes of black adolescent mothers has been found to be beneficial (Stevens, 1984) and seeking help from extended family has been associated with more optimal parenting (Stevens, 1988). However, Wise and Grossman (1980) reported that at 6 weeks postpartum, adolescent mothers who were more independent of their own families exhibited more positive adjustment to parenthood than adolescent mothers who continued to live with their parents. Although research indicates that adolescent mothers who receive more assistance and support behave more appropriately with their young children than adolescent mothers who receive less support (see Crockenberg, 1987, for a review), too much assistance may stand in the way of mothers' opportunities to get to know their infants and thereby adapt to the parenting role (Lamb & Easterbrooks, 1981).

Assessments of parenting frequently rely on Caldwell and Bradley's (1984) Home Observation for Measurement of the Environment (HOME), and such assessments have been found to be related to children's later intellectual performance (see Caldwell & Bradley, 1984, for a review). Recently, Coll and colleagues (1987) noted that, although the physical properties of the home environment did not appear to be influenced by maternal age, the two subscales of the HOME reflecting maternal responsiveness and maternal involvement were clearly different in younger as compared with older mothers, even after controlling for socioeconomic status. This suggests that these two subscales represent particularly appropriate assessments of variation in maternal behavior, and indeed, Coll and colleagues (1987) suggest that these are particularly related to intellectual outcomes for children. Because the HOME was designed rather broadly for assessments of infants from birth to 3 years, two supplementary subscales were developed for this study to capture the age-appropriateness of maternal activities and toys particularly for 4-month-old infants.

This article examines the possible determinants of optimal parenting in single mothers of 4-month-old infants. The 4-month age was selected because it represents a period of relative stability for young infants (Thomas & Chess, 1977) following shifts in infant behavior during the third month (Emde, Gaensbauer, & Harmon, 1976) and possible changes associated with diminishing infant colic (Farran, 1983). Equipped with an established repertoire of social behavior, the 4-month-old infant is prepared to play an active role in reciprocal mother-infant exchange (Stern, 1985). Only Caucasian mothers were selected; considerable research already exists on black single mothers (e.g., Field, Widmayer, Stringer, & Ignatoff, 1980) although there are numerically more Caucasian than black single mothers. Consistent with Coll and colleagues (Coll, Vohr, Hoffman, & Oh, 1986), this investigation involves a previously little researched, relatively homogeneous group of single Caucasian mothers. Following the models of Belsky et al. (1984) and Lamb and Easterbrooks (1981), family of origin, maternal age, and psychological symptoms have been selected as representative characteristics of the mother, difficult temperament has been selected as a characteristic of the infant, and current residence has been selected as a contextual variable. For each of the five predictor variables, relations are sought between the predictor and parenting measures. In addition, to determine the viability of the complete five-factor model, the relation between the five predictor variables *as a set* and parenting measures is also examined.

METHOD

Subjects

Fifty-three single primary-caregiving mothers and their 4-month-old infants were recruited from Madison, WI and the surrounding county. Mothers were identified through a school-age Maternity Program; preparation for childbirth classes; Women, Infants, and Children programs (WIC); and public notices such as newspaper announcements. A special effort was made to include adolescent mothers in the sample. The median age was 19.5 years and the mean age was 21.4 years (range 15 to 37 years). All of the mothers were Caucasian and single at the birth of their first child, although three had been divorced, one long ago. All infants were firstborn. Educational levels of the mothers ranged from completion of 8 years of schooling to completion of a Master's degree (X = 11.9 years). Because the younger mothers were not old enough to have completed advanced schooling or even high school and because many of the subjects were themselves from single-parent families, the educational level of the mothers' mothers was also examined: The mean was 12.8 years (range 8–19 years). Thirty-five of the 53 mothers lived in households in which at least one person was employed full-time or at least two people were employed half-time.

Procedures

Two female interviewers together visited the homes of each mother and infant. Mothers were interviewed to obtain demographic and background information and to complete Caldwell and Bradley's (1984) HOME Inventory including supplementary scales designed to assess the provision of age-appropriate toys and activities for 4-month-old infants. Mothers also completed questionnaires assessing their psychological symptoms (Derogatis & Spencer, 1982) and their infants' temperament characteristics (Bates, Freeland, & Lounsbury, 1979).

Measures

Home Observation for Measurement of the Environment. Caldwell and Bradley's (1984) HOME Inventory contains 45 observational/interview items designed to assess the quality of the environment of young children from birth to age 3 years. This instrument has an overall internal consistency coefficient of .89; validity is demonstrated by significant relations between all six of the home environment variables and the socioeconomic status (SES) variables of mother's education, father's presence, father's education, and father's occupation (Caldwell & Bradley, 1984). Maternal responses were recorded independently by the two interviewers during an unstructured interview; the mean ratings of the two interviewers were used for all data analyses. To best characterize *maternal* caregiving, only experiences specifically provided by the mother and toys or equipment available in the mother's home were tallied. Following the recommendations of Block

(1978) for estimating reliabilities, part-whole correlations between the scores of the individual interviewers and the mean ratings as well as Spearman-Brown estimates of the interrater reliabilities of the subscales are included in Table 1.

Infant four-month supplement. Developed specifically for this study and administered jointly with the HOME were two subscales designed to assess particularly appropriate toys and activities for 4-month-old infants. The first subscale included six items reflecting maternal involvement in age-appropriate activities: encouraging rolling over, scooting, and sitting; playing hiding games; roughhouse play; and observed face-to-face interaction. The second subscale assessed the availability of five age-appropriate toys: squeak toy, cradle gym, busy box, toy with a mirror, and toy with musical sound. Construct validity is suggested by correlations with the total HOME score of .50 for the subscale of maternal activities and .48 for the subscale assessing age-appropriate toys. Interrater reliability for these subscales is also reported in Table 1.

Family of origin. Disruption in the family of origin was identified when the subject grew up either in a single-parent or stepparent family. That is, mothers whose families of origin included mothers who never married, mothers who were separated or divorced, and families with one or more deceased parents were coded as having single-parent families of origin.

Current residence. Mothers who were at the time of the visits living with their own mothers, fathers, aunts, uncles, or grandparents were classified as living with adult relatives.

Table 1

Means, Standard Deviations, and Interrater Reliabilities for Parenting Measures

			Interrater Reliability	
	Mean		Part-Whole	Spearman-
Parenting Measures	(N = 53)	SD	Correlations	Brown
Home Observation for Measurement of the Environment				
I. Emotional & verbal responsivity	8.25	1.83	.91	.66
II. Avoidance of restriction & punishment	6.76	.69	.89	.72
III. Organization of physical & temporal environment	4.79	.87	.94	.84
IV. Provision of appropriate play materials	6.15	1.30	.92	.77
V. Maternal involvement with child	4.31	1.15	.94	.87
VI. Opportunities for variety in daily stimulation	2.53	1.23	.96	.91
Four-Month Supplement				
Toys	2.92	1.31	.96	.73
Activities	2.78	1.19	.92	.90

Psychological symptoms. The psychological functioning of mothers was examined using Derogatis and Spencer's (1982) Brief Symptom Inventory (BSI). Mothers indicted the extent to which they were distressed by each of 53 psychological symptoms (0 = *not at all*, 4 = *extremely*). The mean score across the individual items was used as the assessment of psychological symptoms. The instrument included nine subscales: somatization, obsessive-compulsive, interpersonal sensitivity, depression, anxiety, hostility, phobic anxiety, paranoid ideation, and psychoticism. Reported internal consistency reliability coefficients (α) were .71 to .85; test-retest reliabilities were .68 to .91. In the present study, internal consistency reliability (α) for the entire scale was .96. Convergent validity is supported by considerable overlap between the BSI and the Minnesota Multiphasic Personality Inventory (MMPI). Predictive validity, a particularly useful measure for clinicians, is supported by the instrument's high sensitivity to factors effecting changes in psychological status (Derogatis & Spencer, 1982).

Infant difficulty. Infant temperament characteristics were assessed using Bates et al. (1979) Infant Characteristics Questionnaire (ICQ). This instrument was developed for the assessment of infants between 4 and 7 months of age and was primarily intended as a means of assessing "difficulty" in infant temperament. For each of 24 items, mothers were asked to indicate on a 7-point scale the description that was most characteristic of their infants. The mean score across the individual items was used as the assessment of infant difficulty. The instrument includes four subscales: fussiness, unadaptability, dullness, and unpredictability. Reported internal consistency reliability coefficients (α) were .39 to .70; test-retest reliabilities were .47 to .70 (Hubert, Wachs, Peters-Martin, & Gandour, 1982). In the present study, internal consistency reliability (α) for the entire scale was .83. Convergent validity is supported by moderately high correlations between mother and father ICQ factor scores; predictive validity is supported by analyses indicating that infants rated by the mother as more difficult on the ICQ were more fussy and unsoothable during observations (Bates et al., 1979).

Analyses

Relations between the parenting measures and each of the individual predictor variables were analyzed according to the type of data available. For the dichotomous measures of family of origin and current residence, *t* tests were used. For the continuous measures of maternal age, psychological symptoms, and infant difficulty, correlations were used. In order to assess the viability of this five-factor model, the simultaneous association between the five predictor variables from the model and each of the parenting measures was examined using multiple regression analyses.

RESULTS

Contributors to Parenting

Means, standard deviations, and interrater reliability for each of the parenting measures as presented in Table 1.

Family of origin. The effects of family of origin on parenting are displayed in Table 2. As compared with single mothers who experienced disruption in their families of origin, single mothers who grew up in intact two-parent families exhibited greater emotional and verbal responsivity, greater involvement with their infants, and provision of more age-appropriate toys and activities as assessed by the 4-month supplement measures.

Current residence. Comparisons of single mothers' provisions of quality caregiving environments for their young infants on the basis of their current resi-

dence patterns are also presented in Table 2. *T* tests indicate that single mothers living apart from their own parents or other adult relatives exhibited more emotional and verbal responsivity and greater involvement with their infants than did single mothers who were currently living with their adult relatives.

Maternal age. Pearson correlations between maternal age and each of the parenting measures are presented in Table 3. The results indicate positive associations between maternal age and three of the Caldwell and Bradley (1984) subscales: emotional and verbal responsivity, organization of the physical and temporal environment, and maternal involvement with the child.

Psychological symptoms. The extent to which mothers' psychological symptoms relate to their provisions of a quality caregiving environment for their young infants are also presented in Table 3. Psychological symptoms were significantly linked to single mothers' provisions of caregiving environments. Significant negative correlations were found between psychological symptoms and mothers' organization of the physical and temporal environment, maternal involvement with the child, and the 4-month supplement measure of age-appropriate toys; thus, less optimal parenting was associated with more psychological symptoms.

Infant difficulty. Correlations between the summary rating of infant difficulty and measures of mothers' provision of a caregiving environment are also presented in Table 3. Significant negative associations were found between infant difficulty and emotional and verbal

Table 2

Comparison of Parenting Measures by Family of Origin and Current Residence Patterns

Parenting Measures	Family of Origin			Current Residence		
	Two-Parent (n = 29)	Single or Step-parent (n = 24)	t	Apart from Adult Relatives (n = 32)	Living with Adult Relatives (n = 21)	t
Home Observation for Measurement of the Environment						
I. Emotional & verbal responsivity	8.71	7.69	2.08*	8.69	7.57	2.25*
II. Avoidance of restriction & punishment	6.76	6.75	.04	6.69	6.86	.87
III. Organization of physical & temporal environment	4.88	4.69	.80	4.89	4.64	1.02
IV. Provision of appropriate play materials	6.24	6.04	.55	6.19	6.10	.25
V. Maternal involvement with child	4.69	3.85	2.80**	4.58	3.90	2.16*
VI. Opportunities for variety in daily stimulation	2.55	2.50	.15	2.50	2.57	.20
Four-Month Supplement						
Toys	3.24	2.52	2.06*	2.94	2.88	.15
Activities	3.07	2.43	2.02*	3.02	2.40	1.89

*$p < .05$. **$p < .01$.

responsivity, organization of the physical and temporal environment, and the 4-month supplement measure of age-appropriate maternal activities. Thus, less optimal parenting was associated with greater infant difficulty.

RELATIVE EFFECTS OF CONTRIBUTORS TO PARENTING

The multiple regression analyses included an F-test to assess the simultaneous association between the five predictor variables and each of the parenting outcome measures (see Table 4). The five predictor variables included disruption in the family of origin, current residence, maternal age, psychological symptoms, and infant difficulty. R^2 represents the proportion of the overall variance in each parenting variable that is accounted for

by the five predictor variables. Accordingly, F and R^2 assess the usefulness of the five-factor model. Using these five variables, significant predictions were made for three of the HOME subscales and for both of the 4-month supplement subscales assessing age-appropriate toys and activities. The five predictor variables necessarily overlap so that the contribution of each individual variable, measured by the beta coefficients, is minimized when regressions are used to examine the five variables as a set. With the exception of maternal age, beta coefficients indicated that each of the five predictor variables related to at least one of the parenting measures.

Because SES may influence HOME scores (Caldwell & Bradley, 1984), regression results may reflect only an underlying effect of family background. To

Table 3

Correlations with Parenting Measures

Parenting Measures	Maternal Age	Psychological Symptoms	Infant Difficulty
Home Observation for Measurement of the Environment			
I. Emotional & verbal responsivity	.30*	−.02	−.27*
II. Avoidance of restriction & punishment	.03	−.19	−.18
III. Organization of physical & temporal environment	.37**	−.33*	−.35**
IV. Provision of appropriate play materials	.06	−.10	.12
V. Maternal involvement with child	.41**	−.32*	−.22
VI. Opportunities for variety in daily stimulation	−.20	−.19	.13
Four-Month Supplement			
Toys	.11	−.40**	.02
Activities	.18	−.03	−.28*

*p < .05. **p < .01.

examine this possibility, two separate hierarchical regression analyses were performed. In the first analysis, the level of education of the mothers' mothers was used as a reflection of the environment in which the mother herself grew up and first learned about parenting. For the hierarchical regression, the mothers' mother's level of education was entered on the first step and the five predictor variables were entered as a block on the second step. Controlling for educational background in this way did not significantly change the results: Significant predictions were still found for the same three HOME subscores and the supplemental activities subscale; the age-appropriate toy subscale approached significance. In the second analysis, to control approximately for the effects of family income, households were dichotomized into the 35 with the equivalent of a full-time worker and the 18 without. As above, this variable was included as the first step in a hierarchical regression analysis and the five predictor variables were entered as a block on the second step. The addition of the employment control variable did not change the regression results.

DISCUSSION

The data presented in this article illustrate the importance of considering disruption in the family of origin, maternal mental health, infant difficulty, and current patterns of residence together with maternal age when explaining parenting outcomes for single Caucasian mothers of 4-month-old infants. Although a variety of intervention programs have been shown to benefit adolescent parenting (see Panzarine, 1988 for a review), few interventions have focused specifically on single mothers (Lutzker, Lutzker, Braunling-McMorrow, & Eddleman, 1987).

Consistent with a growing body of literature (e.g., Brooks-Gunn & Furstenberg, 1986), maternal age, when examined independently in this study, was found to be a significant contributor to mothers' caregiving, including their emotional and verbal responsivity and their involvement with their infants. However,

Table 4

Predictions of Parenting Measures—Beta Coefficients and Multiple Regression Statistics

Parenting Measures	Family of Origin[a]	Current Residence[b]	Maternal Age	Psychological Symptoms	Infant Difficulty	R	R²	F
Home Observation for Measurement of the Environment								
I. Emotional & verbal responsivity	.25	−.31*	.04	.08	−.26	.49	.24	3.04*
II. Avoidance of restriction & punishment	−.07	.13	.05	−.16	−.14	.27	.07	.75
III. Organization of physical & temporal environment	−.07	−.04	.29	−.23	−.26*	.52	.27	3.51**
IV. Provision of appropriate play materials	.07	−.02	.03	−.12	.16	.20	.04	.39
V. Maternal involvement with child	.27*	−.26	.13	−.23	−.13	.57	.33	4.62**
VI. Opportunities for variety in daily stimulation	.11	−.11	−.31	−.27	.14	.36	.13	1.39
Four-Month Supplement								
Toys	.25	−.07	−.07	−.40**	.13	.48	.23	2.78*
Activities	.29*	−.33*	−.11	.05	−.29*	.47	.22	2.71*

[a]0 = single-parent or stepparent family, 1 = two-parent family.
[b]0 = living apart from adult relatives, 1 = living with adult relatives.
*$p < .05$. **$p < .01$.

when age effects were assessed within the constellation of factors potentially associated with parenting, no independent contribution of maternal age was evident. This supports the finding of Philliber and Graham (1981) within a married sample including slightly older children as well as findings for adolescent mothers (Hayes, 1987; McAnarney, Lawrence, Aten, & Iker, 1984) indicating that the effects of maternal age may be mediated by other factors. Because of considerable overlap between age and the other independent variables, evidence indicates that adolescent mothers are not necessarily deficient in their parenting by virtue of their age.

The correlational analyses also support an intergenerational transmission perspective which suggests that parenting may be influenced by the mothers' experiences within their own families of origin. Specifically, effects of disruption in the family of origin may become evident when mothers, particularly single mothers, begin parenting their own firstborn infants. Consistent with the Hall et al. (1979) findings from married mothers, the present results indicate that mothers from single-parent or stepparent families of origin exhibit significantly less involvement with their young infants than mothers from intact two-parent families. The results further indicate that mothers from single-parent or stepparent families of origin exhibit less emotional and verbal responsivity and provide fewer age-appropriate toys and activities than do mothers from two-parent intact families. Although these effects may be mediated by other factors, such as the greater likelihood of poverty in single-parent families (McLanahan & Booth, 1989), the link between experience in the family of origin and subsequent parenting is nevertheless documented by these results. Moreover, research indicating that at 2 years of age the children of mothers from disrupted families of origin exhibit delays in speech and language development (Pawlby & Hall, 1980) strengthens concern for the intergenerational transmission of the effects of family disruption.

Examination of the independent effects of mothers' psychological symptoms on their parenting suggests that mental health contributes significantly to maternal parenting. Mothers with more psychological symptoms exhibited less structuring of their infants' environments including less satisfactory organization of the physical and temporal environment, less involvement with their infants, and provision of fewer age-appropriate toys. Presumably, an egocentrism associated with impaired mental health, albeit subclinical, may interfere with these mothers' abilities to make optimal choices for their infants.

Infant difficulty likewise was associated with mothers' structuring of their infants' environments. Indeed, mothers who perceived their infants to be more difficult exhibited less emotional and verbal responsivity, less involvement, and fewer age-appropriate activities than mothers who perceived their infants to be less difficult. Even among the constellation of other factors, infant difficulty was a critical contributor to the organization of the physical and temporal environment. Although the observed links between infant difficulty and maternal structuring of the caregiving environment could also be mediated by other factors, these results confirm that infant temperament characteristics must not be overlooked.

In line with considerable research on the positive effects of social supports on the parenting of adolescent mothers (see Crockenberg, 1987), more optimal parenting might have been expected in single mothers who were living with their own parents or extended families. Yet, living with adult relatives was instead associated with *less* optimal parenting including less emotional and verbal responsivity to these 4-month-old infants. Crockenberg (1987) notes that mothers do not necessarily receive support from those with whom they associate, indeed, some mothers may experience abuse in their homes (Butler & Burton, 1990). Adult relatives living with the single mother and her infant may interfere with the development of the mothers' parenting skills or may offer assistance in such a way as to imply the mothers' incompetence. Remaining in the family of origin for single mothers, therefore, may interfere with adoption of the mothering role, whereas residence away from the family origin may reflect a higher level of maturity that coincides with the development of sensitive parenting.

In summary, optimal parenting was linked with older maternal age, fewer maternal psychological symptoms, and less difficult infant temperament. Less optimal parenting was characteristic of mothers from disrupted families of origin and mothers who currently lived with adult relatives. The viability of the complete five-factor model was investigated with multiple regression analyses. Although conclusions may be somewhat limited, the five factors, as a set, were useful predictors of parenting outcomes for these single mothers. These effects were evident even after controlling for family background effects. Assessments were limited to the quality of parenting provided by the mothers themselves rather than the quality of care received by the child from other care providers. Clearly grandmothers, fathers, or other child care providers may provide experiences that compensate for possible maternal deficiencies. As a result, the mother's own parenting may reflect an arrangement the mother and those around her have implicitly negotiated rather than the mother's actual parenting capabilities. Subsequent research must necessarily investigate the caregiving provided by others in the child's social world.

IMPLICATIONS FOR PRACTICE

Of particular interest to family policy specialists may be the finding that living with adult relatives was not associated with optimal parenting. Financial and emotional resources may allow the particularly competent single mother to move away from her family, or the single mother's competence may develop through opportunities to interact with her infant out of the reach of close relatives. Effects of the living situation may well be mediated by other factors. Thus, the goal of public policy must be to remain responsive to individual needs; policies should neither restrict nor encourage the single mother's move to independence.

Counselors should be aware of identified psychological risk factors. Mothers who grew up in single-parent or stepparent families were identified in this study as less competent than mothers who grew up in intact two-parent families. In addition, mothers with more numerous psychological symptoms did not perform optimally in parenting their young infants. Research indicates that adolescent mothers are more likely to be depressed than older mothers (Reis, 1989). At least one intervention program that included a therapeutic relationship during pregnancy and the infant's first year was successful at reducing maternal depression and enhancing the caregiving environment (Barnard et al., 1988), although a similar intervention program indicated that the effects were no longer evident by the time the child reached 3 years of age (Landy, Grey, & Walker, 1988). Perhaps psychological symptomatology may need to be given special attention during intervention, and referrals for therapy or counseling may need to be considered. Interview or pencil and paper assessments of the psychological characteristics identified in this study might help identify those mothers particularly at risk for less competent parenting.

Educators may be guided by the finding that mothers who reported their infants as having more difficult temperaments were less competent in parenting their infants than mothers who reported their infants as having less difficult temperaments. In research with married mothers, evidence for a link between infant difficulty and parenting is not entirely conclusive (Bates, 1987; Crockenberg, 1986), particularly for younger infants (Houldin, 1987). However, the results reported here indicate that the interactive aspects of parenting by single mothers were clearly compromised when mothers reported that their infants' temperaments were difficult. Therefore, although educators probably would not target populations for intervention on the basis of temperament characteristics, intervention curriculum could be enhanced by recognizing that single mothers may require particular assistance in becoming involved with and responding to infants they perceive as difficult.

Traditionally, adolescent single mothers have been primary targets for intervention, and indeed the present study found an association between maternal age and parenting competence. However, age effects tend to be mediated by other factors. Tremendous variability exists among adolescent mothers and consequently it is difficult to explain or predict parenting outcomes (Landy, Cleland, & Schubert, 1984; Osofsky, Culp, & Ware, 1988). Targeting mothers for intervention solely on the basis of their youth ignores the fact that, as Roosa and Vaughan (1984) suggested, some adolescent mothers are quite competent. More important, overlooking the other factors identified in this study may mean that assistance to those parents who need it most may not be provided. Future research must be designed to identify factors that may be associated with parenting competence in order to target parents at potential risk.

In summary, the five predictor variables investigated in this study accounted for a significant amount of the variance in parenting by single mothers. In fact, the two subscales of Caldwell and Bradley's (1984) HOME that emphasized maternal behavior (i.e., emotional and verbal responsivity and maternal involvement) together with the supplementary scale developed to assess particularly appropriate maternal activities for 4-month-old infants, represented the parenting measures most likely to be predicted by the factors in the model. The importance of mothers' direct interactions with their infants as opposed to their structuring of the infants' physical environment is underscored by evidence suggesting that early parenting influences infant cognitive (Coll et al., 1986) and socio-emotional outcomes (Lamb, Hopps, & Elster, 1987), and is further supported by evidence indicating that at least one intervention program designed to teach maternal responsiveness has achieved some success (Baskin, Umansky, & Sanders, 1987).

Clearly, the final evaluation of optimal parenting must include assessment of the caregiving provided by others in the infant's social world as well as outcomes for children (Clewell, Brooks-Gunn, & Benasich, 1989), including abuse and neglect (Olds, Henderson, Chamberlin, & Tatelbaum, 1986; Siegel, Bauman, Schaefer, Saunders, & Ingram, 1980). Evidence from the Furstenberg, Brooks-Gunn, and Morgan (1987) follow-up study of adolescent mothers suggests that effects noted during the early months may diminish later. Mothers faced with considerable adversity will not necessarily become incompetent parents and children faced with considerable adversity will not necessarily fail. The present findings provide clues for identifying those single mothers who might benefit from early intervention and guide the provision of appropriate programming.

REFERENCES

Allen, D. A., Affleck, G., McGrade, B. J., & McQueeney, M. (1984). Effects of single-parent status on mothers and their high-risk infants. *Infant Behavior and Development, 7,* 347–359.

Allison, P. D., & Furstenberg, F. F. (1989). How marital dissolution affects children: Variations by age and sex. *Developmental Psychology*, **25**, 540–549.

Barnard, K. E., Magyary, D., Sumner, G., Booth, C. L., Mitchell, S. K., & Spieker, S. (1988). Prevention of parenting alterations for women with low social support. *Psychiatry*, **51**, 248–253.

Baskin, C., Umansky, W., & Sanders, W. (1987). Influencing the responsiveness of adolescent mothers to their infants. *Zero to Three*, **2**, 7–11.

Bates, J. E. (1987). Temperament in infancy. In J. D. Osofsky (Ed.), *Handbook of Infant development* (pp. 1101–1149). New York: Wiley.

Bates, J. E., Freeland, C. A. B., & Lounsbury, M. L. (1979). Measures of infant difficulties. *Child Development*, **50**, 794–803.

Belsky, J., Robins, E., & Gamble, W. (1984). The determinants of parental competence: Toward a contextual theory. In M. Lewis (Ed.), *Beyond the dyad* (pp. 251–279). New York: Plenum Press.

Bettes, B. A. (1988). Maternal depression and motherese: Temporal and intonational features. *Child Development*, **59**, 1089–1096.

Block, J. (1978). *The Q-Sort method in personality assessment and psychiatric research*. Palo Alto, CA: Consulting Psychologists Press.

Bradley, R. H., Elardo, R., Rosenthal, D., & Friend, J. H. (1984). A comparative study of the home environments of infants from single-parent and two-parent black families. *Acta Paedologica*, **1**, 33–46.

Brooks-Gunn, J., & Furstenberg, F. F. (1986). The children of adolescent mothers: Physical, academic, and psychological outcomes. *Developmental Review*, **6**, 224–251.

Butler, J. R., & Burton, L. M. (1990). Rethinking teenage childbearing: Is sexual abuse a missing link. *Family Relations*, **39**, 73–80.

Caldwell, B. M., & Bradley, R. H. (1984). *Home observation for measurement of the environment* (rev. ed.). Unpublished manuscript, University of Arkansas, Little Rock.

Clewell, B. C., Brooks-Gunn, J., & Benasich, A. A. (1989). Evaluating child-related outcomes of teenage parenting programs. *Family Relations*, **38**, 201–209.

Cohn, J. F., Campbell, S. B., Matias, R., & Hopkins, J. (1990). Face-to-face interactions of postpartum depressed and nondepressed mother-infant pairs at 2 months. *Developmental Psychology*, **26**, 15–23.

Coll, C. G., Vohr, B. R., Hoffman, J., & Oh, W. (1986). Maternal and environmental factors affecting developmental outcome of infants of adolescent mothers. *Developmental and Behavioral Pediatrics*, **7**, 230–236.

Coll, C. T., Hoffman, J., & Oh, W. (1987). The social ecology and early parenting of Caucasian adolescent mothers. *Child Development*, **58**, 955–963.

Coll, C. T. G., Hoffman, J., Van Houten, L. J., & Oh, W. (1987). The social context of teenage childbearing: Effects on the infant's care-giving environment. *Journal of Youth and Adolescence*, **16**, 345–360.

Crockenberg, S. B. (1986). Are temperamental differences in babies associated with predictable differences in caregiving. In J. V. Lerner & R. M. Lerner (Eds.), *Temperament and social interaction in infants and children: Vol. 31. New directions for child development* (pp. 53–73). San Francisco, CA: Jossey-Bass.

Crockenberg, S. (1987). Support for adolescent mothers during the postnatal period: Theory and research. In C. F. Boukydis (Ed.), *Research on support for parents and infants in the postnatal period* (pp. 3–24). Norwood, NJ: Ablex.

Derogatis, L. R., & Spencer, P. M. (1982). *The Brief Symptom Inventory (BSI): Administration, scoring, and procedures manual*. Towson, MD: Clinical Psychometric Research.

Eiduson, B. T., Kornfein, M., Zimmerman, I. L., & Weisner, T. S. (1982). Comparative socialization practices in traditional and alternative families. In M. E. Lamb (Ed.), *Nontraditional families: Parenting and child development* (pp. 315–346). Hillsdale, NJ: Erlbaum.

Emde, R. N., Gaensbauer, T. J., & Harmon, R. J. (1976). Emotional expression in infancy: A behavioral study. *Psychological Issues Monograph Series*, **10**, (1, Serial No. 37). New York: International Universities Press.

Erikson, E. H. (1963). *Childhood and society*. New York: Norton.

Farran, C. (1983). *Infant colic*. New York: Scribner.

Field, T., Healy, B., Goldstein, S., & Guthertz, M. (1990). Behavior-state matching and synchrony in mother-infant interactions of nondepressed versus depressed dyads. *Developmental Psychology*, **26**, 7–14.

Field, T. M., Widmayer, S. M., Stringer, S., & Ignatoff, E. (1980). Teenage, lower class, black mothers and their pre-term infants: An intervention and developmental follow up. *Child Development*, **51**, 426–436.

Furstenberg, F. F., Brooks-Gunn, J., & Morgan, S. P. (1987). *Adolescent mothers in later life*. Cambridge: Cambridge University Press.

Furstenberg, F. F., & Crawford, A. G. (1981). Family support: Helping teenage mothers to cope. In F. F. Furstenberg, Jr., R. Lincoln, & J. Menken (Eds.), *Teenage sexuality, pregnancy, and childbearing* (pp. 280–300). Philadelphia: University of Pennsylvania Press.

Gershenson, H. P., Syc, S., Umeh, B., & Rosenberg, D. (1987, April). *Social correlates of child development in children of white adolescent mothers*. Paper presented at the meetings of the Society for Research in Child Development, Baltimore, MD.

Hall, F., Pawlby, S. J., & Wolkind, S. (1979). Early life experiences and later mothering behavior: A study of mothers and their 20-week old babies. In D. Shaffer & J. Dunn (Eds.), *The first year of life* (pp. 153–174). New York: Wiley.

Hayes, C. D. (Ed.). (1987). *Risking the future: Adolescent sexuality, pregnancy, and childbearing* (Vol. 1). Washington, DC: National Academy Press.

Heath, P. A. (1987). Developing parent education courses: A review of resources. *Family Relations, 36,* 209–214.

Hetherington, E. M., Cox, M., & Cox, R. (1985). Long-term effects of divorce and remarriage on the adjustment of children. *Journal of the American Academy of Psychiatry, 24,* 518–530.

Houldin, A. D. (1987). Infant temperament and the quality of the childrearing environment. *Maternal-Child Nursing Journal, 16,* 131–143.

Hubert, N. C., Wachs, T. D., Peters-Martin, P., & Gandour, M. J. (1982). The study of early temperament: Measurement and conceptual issues. *Child Development, 53,* 571–600.

Kimball, W. H., Stewart, R. B., Conger, R. D., & Burgess, R. L. (1980). A comparison of family interaction in single- versus two-parent abusive, neglectful, and control families. In T. Field (Ed.), *High risk infants and children* (pp. 43–59). New York: Academic Press.

King, T., & Fullard, W. (1982). Teenage mothers and their infants: New findings on the home environment. *Journal of Adolescence, 5,* 333–346.

Lamb, M. E., & Easterbrooks, M. A. (1981). Individual differences in parental sensitivity: Origins, components, and consequences. In M. E. Lamb & L. R. Sherrod (Eds.), *Infant social cognition: Empirical and theoretical considerations* (pp. 127–153). Hillsdale, NJ: Erlbaum.

Lamb, M. E., Hopps, K., & Elster, A. B. (1987). Strange situation behavior of infants with adolescent mothers. *Infant Behavior and Development, 10,* 39–48.

Landy, S., Cleland, J., & Schubert, J. (1984). The individuality of teenage mothers and its implication for intervention strategies. *Journal of Adolescence, 7,* 171–190.

Landy, S., Grey, R., & Walker, A. (1988). Moderator influences of informal experimenter support. *Infant Mental Health Journal, 9,* 255–271.

LeResche, L., Strobino, D., Parks, P., Fischer, P., & Smeriglio, V. (1983). The relationship of observed maternal behavior to questionnaire measures of parenting knowledge, attitudes, and emotional state in adolescent mothers. *Journal of Youth and Adolescence, 12,* 19–31.

Lewis, M., & Rosenblum, L. A. (Eds.). (1974). *The effects of the infant on its caregiver.* New York: Wiley.

Luster, T., & Rhoades, K. (1989). The relation between childrearing beliefs and the home environment in a sample of adolescent mothers. *Family Relations, 38,* 317–322.

Lutzker, S. Z., Lutzker, J. R., Braunling-McMorrow, D., & Eddleman, Jr. (1987). Prompting to increase mother-baby stimulation with single mothers. *Journal of Child and Adolescent Psychotherapy, 4,* 3–12.

McAnarney, E. R., Lawrence, R. A., Aten, M. J., & Iker, H. P. (1984). Adolescent mothers and their infants. *Pediatrics, 73,* 358–362.

McKim, M. K. (1987). Transition to what? New parents' problems in the first year. *Family Relations, 36,* 22–26.

McLanahan, S., & Booth, K. (1989). Mother-only families: Problems, prospects, and politics. *Journal of Marriage and the Family, 51,* 557–580.

Moore, K. A., Wenk, D., Hofferth, S. L., & Hayes, C. D. (1987). Statistical Appendix: Trends in adolescent sexual and fertility behavior. In S. L. Hofferth & C. D. Hayes (Eds.), *Risking the future: Adolescent sexuality, pregnancy, and childbearing* (Vol. 2, pp. 353–520). Washington, DC: National Academy Press.

National Center for Health Statistics. (1987). *Number and percentage distribution of live births* (Table 1–46, p. 78). Washington, DC: U.S. Government Printing Office.

Olds, D. L., Henderson, C. R., Chamberlin, R., & Tatelbaum, R. (1986). Preventing child abuse and neglect: A randomized trial of nurse home visitation. *Pediatrics, 78,* 65–78.

Osofsky, J. D., Culp, A. M., & Ware, L. M. (1988). Intervention challenges with adolescent mothers and their infants. *Psychiatry, 51,* 236–241.

Panzarine, S. (1988). Teen mothering: Behavior and interventions. *Journal of Adolescent Health Care, 9,* 443–448.

Parke, R. D., & Tinsley, B. J. (1987). Family interaction in infancy. In J. D. Osofsky (Ed.), *Handbook of infant development* (pp. 579–641). New York: Wiley.

Pawlby, S. J., & Hall, F. (1980). Early interactions and later language development of children whose mothers come from disrupted families of origin. In T. Field (Ed.), *High risk infants and children* (pp. 61–75). New York: Academic Press.

Pearlin, L. J., & Johnson, J. S. (1977). Marital status, life-strains and depression. *American Sociological Review, 42,* 704–715.

Philliber, S. G., & Graham, E. H. (1981). The impact of age of mother on mother-child interaction patterns. *Journal of Marriage and the Family, 43,* 109–115.

Reis, J. S. (1989). The structure of depression in community based young adolescent, older adolescent, and adult mothers. *Family Relations, 38,* 164–168.

Reis, J. S., & Herz, E. J. (1987). Correlates of adolescent parenting. *Adolescence, 22,* 599–609.

Roosa, M. W., & Vaughan, L. (1984). A comparison of teenage and older mothers with preschool children. *Family Relations, 33,* 259–265.

Schilmoeller, G. L. & Baranowski, M. D. (1985). Childrearing of firstborns by adolescent and older mothers. *Adolescence, 20,* 805–822.

Siegel, E., Bauman, K. E., Schaefer, E. S., Saunders, M. M., & Ingram, D. D. (1980). Hospital and home support during infancy: Impact on maternal attachment, child abuse and neglect, and health care utilization. *Pediatrics, 66,* 183–190.

Stern, D. N. (1985). *The interpersonal world of the infant.* New York: Basic Books.

Stevens, J. H., Jr. (1984). Black grandmothers' and black adolescent mothers' knowledge about parenting. *Developmental Psychology, 20,* 1017–1025.

Stevens, J. H., Jr. (1988). Social support, locus of control, and parenting in three low-income groups of mothers: Black teenagers, black adults, and white adults. *Child Development, 59,* 635–642.

Thomas, A., & Chess, S. (1977). *Temperament and development.* New York: Brunner/Mazel.

Wise, S., & Grossman, F. K. (1980). Adolescent mothers and their infants: Psychological factors in early attachment and interaction. *American Journal of Orthopsychiatry, 50,* 454–468.

Zekoski, E. M., O'Hara, M. W., & Wills, K. E. (1987). The effects of maternal mood on mother-infant interaction. *Journal of Abnormal Child Psychology, 15,* 361–378.

NO

Andrew L. Yarrow

PARENTS OF ANOTHER ERA

One of the most obvious facts about grown-ups to a child is that they have forgotten what it is like to be a child.

—Randall Jarrell

A COLD FAMILY CLIMATE

"Older parents probably have more psychological barriers to expressing their feelings," said a northern California marriage counselor who was a child of older parents. "They're more likely to be tightly defended, which may make them less sensitive to their child's needs and vulnerabilities. My parents' tendency was to invalidate my feelings, because I think they were more defended against remembering their own childhood feelings. If a child's feelings aren't seen or heard by their parents, there will be bruises on the heart."

Later-born children often lamented that their parents were emotionally distant, serious, and formal. There may have been considerable love and warmth at one level, but at another, many remembered a relative lack of humor and physical affection compared with the norm in other families.

"My mother was never 'Mom,'" recalled Mary, from Virginia, whose parents were forty when she was born. "She was always 'Mother.' Other parents seemed to joke with their kids more. Although she wasn't devoid of a sense of humor, there was no horsing around. She was very dignified, and I'd never be embarrassed by things she did—unlike other mothers—but she was never a pal."

Spontaneity, too, frequently seemed to be missing. There might have been planned evenings at the theater or summertime trips. But many later-born children felt that they had fewer spur-of-the-moment, fun outings with their parents—going to a movie on a Saturday afternoon or for an ice-cream cone on a summer night.

"We took a lot of vacations at Christmas and in the summers," said Mindy, from Milwaukee. "But my parents seldom took me to a movie or played with me in the yard like other parents did. I always thought it would be neat if

From Andrew L. Yarrow, *Latecomers: Children of Parents Over 35* (Macmillan, 1991). Copyright © 1991 by Andrew L. Yarrow. Reprinted by permission of Macmillan Publishing Company, a division of Simon & Schuster, Inc. Notes omitted.

my parents went dancing. Other parents seemed more festive and to like to party."

"It would have been nice to have had a little more humor in my childhood," recalled Carla, an only child who grew up in New York. "Once in awhile we'd go to the zoo or circus, and we had a ritual on Saturday of going to a late-afternoon movie and dinner. But it would have been more balanced if I could have had more of these more-frivolous types of outings."

Children of older parents often contrasted the more reserved emotional ambiance of their own families with the informality of their friends'.

"I remember walking into a friend's house, and there was a full-fledged water fight going on," said Dean, whose mother was forty when he was born. "My friend's mother, who was in her late twenties, would be shooting away with her water pistol. I could never imagine my mother doing that. She felt it wasn't parental dignity or something. There was a formality in my house. If friends came by to drop in, it was sort of tenuous if they didn't call ahead."

On this score, many later-born children had memories similar to those of a woman from Springfield, Massachusetts. She said, "Everything was overanticipated, overplanned, and anything but spontaneous."

OLD-FASHIONED AND DATED VALUES

"When you grow up with older parents, you think older automatically," said a forty-year-old Midwestern woman. "You have the values of an older generation. I grew up during the Vietnam War era, but I couldn't identify with using pot or other drugs. My values are those of people in their fifties. I feel more of a generation gap with people my own age than with my parents."

Certainly parents' values and tastes are often transmitted to their children. But this frequently creates a dilemma for children of older parents: Rejecting their parents' tastes and values is likely to cause or exacerbate family tensions. Accepting and internalizing them may foster a sense of being out of sync with their contemporaries.

One respondent, who is a therapist, noted, for example, that many older parents of the late 1980s were "still convinced that the Rolling Stones play the only 'real' rock and roll, and that Prince is some kind of 'pervert.' They hate MTV. They need to make some big changes in attitude to deal with young children. Even the 'with-it' generation can become ossified in its attitudes."

Older parents also were seen as taking a more conservative approach to child rearing and being more restrictive about what their children may and may not do. If parents' ideas are more set, there will be less room for negotiation. Thus their children's behavior will inevitably be defined in more black-or-white terms: Either they are especially obedient "little adults" or particularly defiant. In either case, if this attitude is taken to extremes, the child ultimately loses.

Parental values, expressed in the form of rules and restrictions, were accentuated markers of the generational difference. For example, some remembered that wearing jeans or makeup was taboo or recalled that they were not permitted to go to slumber parties or junior-high dances, while "all the other kids" could go.

"I was brought up like someone born in the 1930s rather than the late 1940s or 1950s," said Christy, who was born in 1946. "My mother didn't work, and she seemed very old-fashioned. There was a subliminal strictness: 'I don't think you're old enough to spend the night with friends or go out on dates.' Or, 'Don't do this, you might get hurt.'"

"My father didn't want to accept things that had changed since his time, like people living together before marriage," added Joan, from New York. "But as much as I argued with him, I didn't rebel that much. I didn't get involved with men who weren't of our religious background, and I didn't live with anyone before I got married. I internalized his values, and that did set me apart from my friends a bit."

But Edith, whose parents were about forty when she was born, recalled the generation gap as fueling her rebellion. "My brother and I were never allowed to talk back or argue," she said. "We were raised as Orthodox Jews. We kept kosher and observed the Sabbath. There were a lot of restrictions and rules, which we both rebelled against. When I was thirteen, I refused to go to the Jewish high school, and we both started eating non-kosher."

* * *

Not only were these older parents typed as more socially conservative in their outlooks and behavior, but their children saw them as less inclined to take risks and more realistic than younger parents about the ways of the world. These qualities were believed to rub off, making their children a bit less idealistic and somewhat more cautious and conservative. This cautiousness may have beneficial, protective effects, but it also may limit children's ideas of what is possible to attain or desirable to strive for.

"Having older, more economically stable parents was a detriment," argued a thirty-seven-year-old from Minneapolis. "It discouraged me from trying harder for 'success' and made it harder to be innovative."

"I once had kicked around the idea of going into modeling," recalled Sally, a young keypunch operator from Levittown, Pennsylvania. "But my mother said, 'You should be satisfied with what you are and not try to reach for the stars.' It was an old-fashioned type of idea. Most mothers who are younger probably would have said, 'Go for it.'"

Such ideas and values, labeled "dated" by the children, led some to make a very conscious and strenuous effort to be more "modern" and "with it." Maureen, from Portland, Oregon, for example, wrote that she "devoured women's and girls' magazines, trying to learn the correct and normal way to conduct my life."

But whether or not their parents' values were shaped by a more "old-fashioned" cultural Zeitgeist, many latecomers did feel that their mothers and fathers were distinctly out of step with the times. The term *Victorian* was frequently used pejoratively by children of older parents—regardless of whether they were now in their seventies and their parents had lived during the reign of the venerable, straitlaced British queen or they were in their thirties and their parents presumably had grown up during the relatively freewheeling 1920s. In any case their parents' ideas seemed to have been formed by one era, whereas their friends' parents came of age during a very different time.

Political and cultural values, which are conditioned by both the historical and family contexts in which one lives, are an illustration of this. Later-born children, naturally, are politically socialized, at least in part, by the perspectives and terms of debate of an earlier time, when the values of their parents' cohort were formed.

Many latecomers born during the postwar baby boom specifically noted the long-term effect of the depression on their mothers' and fathers' lives and values. This experience—which the younger parents of their friends did not live through—left a mark on many of these older parents. This, in turn, often set the tone of parenting and colored the lives of their sons and daughters.

"I was a child of the 1940s, but my mother's ideas were shaped by the depression," a New York man reminisced. "The economy and population were going up, though she would insist they were going down again. I was embarrassed by her ideas and resented that she wasn't closer to my age and I couldn't share my thoughts with her. My ideas were mid-twentieth-century ideas and hers were early-twentieth-century ones."

Other later-born children of this generation spoke of their parents' strong beliefs in the goals of Franklin Roosevelt's New Deal, while their peers' parents —born ten or fifteen years later—were likely to have had their political values molded by the more conservative and conformist culture of the Eisenhower era. Likewise, forty-year-old, first-time parents of the late 1980s or early 1990s, who were youths during the 1960s, might convey more liberal social and political values to their children than twenty-five-year-old parents who came of age during the Reagan-Bush years.

"My friends tended to be more conservative, Republican types—like the government is always right—but less willing to go along with social programs,"

recalled Gina, the young woman from Holland, Pennsylvania. "My father was always very liberal—almost a socialist—economically but not socially. And my mother was a diehard New Dealer."

The sense that older parents have more dated values raises interesting questions about how the length of generations may affect political beliefs and social change. Are children of older parents more conformist, assuming that they accept their parents' values, or more rebellious, because they feel their parents represent an oppressive old regime? Of course, other factors come into play, but it is nonetheless tantalizing to speculate how parents' ages may influence the degree to which children are conformist or rebellious, conservative or liberal.

THE GAP IN ADOLESCENCE

The generation gap typically became worst during adolescence, especially as sexual issues arose. It may be difficult enough for teenagers to try to relate to parents a generation apart from them, but children of older parents often said that their parents were not one but two generations removed.

They complained that their parents did not talk with them about the "facts of life" and were less able than others to accept the changes in social mores that came with sexual revolution of the 1960s and 1970s. Their parents' more "old-fashioned" values might mean that they were not allowed to date until well into high school or that they were expressly told not to go out with people of other religious or ethnic backgrounds.

"I couldn't go out driving with boys, and my mother tried to spearhead a rule with my friends' mothers that we couldn't go in cars with guys," recalled

Lisa, a New York executive whose parents were forty-one when she was born. "My mother was very conservative about sex. She was saying things that might have been appropriate ten or fifteen years earlier. I had a slumber party one night, and she threatened to have a gun if guys came over."

"There were things that a young lady just didn't do," added Marta, a Pennsylvania nurse. "My father, who was about seventy when I was thirteen, said it was horrendous for a woman to put on nail polish or makeup. And if there were boys playing ball in front of our house, I wasn't even allowed on the front porch to watch them."

And a woman from Virginia recalled: "Other parents let us play spin the bottle, but my mother would have died! She wasn't very modern in her thinking. I remember when I had been going steady with a guy, she said, 'You haven't let him kiss you?'"

The coincidence of a mother reaching menopause and a daughter entering puberty could also accentuate the generational divide. One woman recalled, "When I first got my period, my mother stopped having hers."

But because the gap in communication and understanding was so wide, it allowed some latecomers to "get away with" more than children of "hipper," younger parents.

"Older parents are more gullible," said a woman from Wisconsin. "I used to be able to hide things behind their backs, like smoking cigarettes and doing drugs."

Yet others found it harder to rebel against their parents because they were older. Whether it was because their mothers and fathers were more mature, tolerant, and experienced as parents or seemingly more fragile and grandparent-like, a surprising number of children of older parents said that they never experienced—or acted out—the usual Sturm and Drang of adolescence, with its attendant parent-child conflicts. It was not uncommon for them to recall trying to rein in emotions so as not to upset their apparently-more-vulnerable older parents.

"The strongest effect" of having a mother who was forty-six and a father who was fifty-one when she was born, wrote Jeanette, "was to keep me from getting angry at them openly in normal teenage fashion." She did not want to upset them because she constantly worried that they might die, she said; thus, "I kept everything inside."

Some degree of psychological distance between parent and child, of course, is crucial for an adolescent trying to discover and assert his or her independent identity. A very young parent may be less able than an older parent to provide that emotional space. For example, a young father may try too hard to act like his son's best friend, or a mother may try to dress like her teenage daughter or inadvertently flirt with her daughter's boyfriend.

Conversely, a greater age difference is more likely to provide needed distance and spell less competition between parent and child during adolescence, as a woman from Austin, Texas, suggested: "As a teenager, I had no problems competing with a mother facing the first fading of youth."

"I remember friends with very young parents," added a twenty-eight-year-old from Cambridge, Massachusetts. "The girls always felt they competed with their mothers in terms of appearance." ...

THE BIGGEST GAP:
MUCH-OLDER FATHERS

A thirty-five-year age difference between parent and child is one thing, but when the divide grows to a half century or more, a child can hardly help feeling that his or her parent is of another era. Biology and culture conspire to make such circumstances exceedingly rare.

Nonetheless, whereas menopause imposes an upper limit on women's childbearing years, men can become fathers at virtually any time. Certainly there have always been men who were twenty, thirty, forty, even fifty years older than their wives, and the ranks of celebrated or well-known men who became fathers after sixty have included such disparate figures as Pablo Picasso and Senator Strom Thurmond; authors Kurt Vonnegut, Jr., Leon Uris, and Budd Schulberg; and cartoonist Jules Feiffer. Of the hundreds of children of older parents surveyed, 15 percent were born when their fathers were fifty or older.

"May-December" unions have rarely been looked upon favorably, however, and continue to make many people uncomfortable. "It touches upon one of the profound unsettled issues of biological difference between men and women," said Dr. Donald A. Bloch, director of New York's Ackerman Institute of Family Therapy. "It tests the issues of envy and distress in both directions. Women live to be widows, but men are reproductive into their 60's and 70's and more."

And a television talk-show host addressing a group of men who became fathers between the ages of forty-two and sixty wondered rhetorically if a "double standard" exists. "Is it OK for men to have kids at sixty, but not for women at forty?" she asked.

Much-older fathers still remain comparatively rare in the United States. Only 19,026 American babies born in 1987, or 0.6 percent of those whose fathers' ages were known, had fathers over fifty. Of these fathers, 11,945 were between fifty and fifty-four, and 7,081 were fifty-five or older.

When the questionnaire responses of children of much-older fathers were compared with those of people who were born when their fathers were thirty-five to forty-nine years old, some striking differences emerged. Surprisingly, those born when their fathers were fifty or older consistently had more positive recollections. These feelings were particularly strong concerning their fathers' impact on their personalities, maturity, and social skills.

Children of fifty-plus fathers much more often said that their fathers were helpful to them and that their relationships were closer during childhood and adolescence than did children of the younger fathers. A greater proportion also saw their fathers as role models and denied that there was a generation gap.

Consistent with these differences were their evaluations of the positive effects their fathers had on their personalities. Forty-six percent of children of fifty-or-older fathers recalled their fathers' influence as positive, and just 31 percent said the effect was negative. By contrast, 34 percent of those whose fathers were thirty-five to forty-nine years old cited their fathers' positive influence during adolescence, whereas 36 percent expressed negative feelings.

A Connecticut woman whose father was fifty-two when she was born recalled her intense pride in him. "He was so dignified," she said. As the president of the PTA and a church elder, he was "looked up to by everyone."

These more-positive feelings of children of much older fathers even carried over into perceptions of their fathers' appearance. Thirty-two percent recalled their fathers' appearance in positive terms, compared with only 17 percent of the children of thirty-five-to-forty-nine-year-old fathers.

At first the reasons for these feelings seem hard to fathom. Yet much-older fathers are clearly a very unusual breed. Since they are almost all men who have married considerably younger women, one may assume that most of them are highly successful or charismatic. Indeed, as many children of such fathers reported, and the examples of famous older fathers illustrate, many of these men *are* "stars" of one sort or another. Whether their success is in business, politics, or entertainment, they seem to have impressed their children as well as the world. In both society and family, their individual personalities appear far more important than age.

Nevertheless, children of fifty-plus fathers did feel that their fathers' age set them off from their peers, and the age difference between parents often stood out in their minds. As a Minneapolis woman whose father was thirteen years older than his wife said, "I always felt like I was living with a mother and a grandfather."

"The wide gap between my mom and dad made me realize a lot of problems between them," added a young woman from Hong Kong, whose father was sixty and mother was thirty-five when she was born. "I decided I'd never marry someone much older than I am."

A significant age gap between parents is inevitable if a father is over fifty when a child is born, but not all much-older fathers are part of May-December unions. In some of these families, in which the parents have already had many children, the marital relationship might be better described as July-October. These much-older fathers are becoming less common today, as couples tend to have fewer children, yet a sizable minority of those interviewed did come from such a background.

Bernice's father, who was fifty-five when she was born, was a farmer in eastern South Dakota, and she was the last of five children. But her memories were of a charismatic father who seemed to defy the expected course of aging. "My father was never an old person," she said. "He made his own food and drove his car and went on vacations. He never was decrepit or wrinkled. He was in good health until he died, after an accident, at eighty-three."

Interestingly, children of much-older fathers also expressed more positive feelings about their mothers. This appeared in their evaluations of their mothers' energy and health, as well as feelings of closeness and recollections of sharing experiences with their mothers. Even those born when their mothers were in their forties were generally more upbeat about their mothers than were children of thirty-five- to thirty-nine-year-old women.

All too frequently, however, these last-born children of much-older fathers had less-than-happy experiences. In fact, they often scarcely knew their fathers.

Pam, a Florida woman who was born when her father was fifty-one, had three siblings eleven to fifteen years older. Her father died when she was seven, and her only cryptic memories were of a man with "old-fashioned values, who was a strict disciplinarian."

The specter of death early in a child's life is an inevitable concomitant of becoming a father after fifty. Albert, a student in Boston, was adopted when his father—a successful investor and art collector—was sixty-seven. Barely six years later, his father died, and because his mother remained a distant figure he spent his childhood and adolescence being ministered to by three governesses.

The positive picture of much-older fathers certainly all but vanishes by the time their children reach adulthood. When asked about their feelings as young adults concerning their fathers, 53 percent of those born to fifty-plus fathers responded negatively, compared with only 33 percent of those who had younger fathers.

These oldest fathers clearly age, ail, and die sooner in their sons' and daughters' lives than the 99-plus percent of American fathers who have children before turning fifty. Emotional scars and practical difficulties associated with fathers' medical problems were much more often reported by children of much-older fathers. Even in childhood they more frequently recalled fears that their fathers would die.

Thus much-older fathers are a sort of exaggerated version of older parents in general. Their children are frequently the recipients of a bounty of love and attention during childhood. The benefits of their maturity and the force of their personalities appear to leave a strong, positive impression on their children. But age catches up with them, leaving their children worried about their health and, all too often, fatherless early in life....

NO GENERATION GAP

Although they may have felt a generation gap, many later-born children also felt strongly that, at least in part because of their ages, their parents had had a good effect in shaping their values. Overwhelming majorities said that their parents influenced their beliefs positively. For example, 63 percent said that the values transmitted to them were good, whereas only 8 percent rejected their parents' values.

Moreover, even if they felt distant from their parents during childhood, adolescence, or young adulthood, many said that there was anything but a gap as they moved into their mid-twenties and thirties. They spoke of being especially close to their parents by this time, and said that they were able to relate well with them as adults and as friends. In many instances, relationships with their mothers and fathers, in fact, had become better than those of their friends with younger parents.

"There was a generation gap a mile wide between my mother and me," wrote Rebecca, a forty-three-year-old from Berkeley, California. "During the sixties, many of my friends with considerably younger parents felt as estranged as I did, and to this day are not particularly close to their parents." Rebecca, however, said that she became quite close to her mother after the turmoil of the 1960s had subsided.

Many also said that there was no greater generation gap in their families and that their experiences were no different from those of other teenagers. Some asserted that they had helped keep their parents young in spirit. And others argued that they experienced less of a "gap" than that which divided younger, less-patient, and less-reflective parents from their children.

"My parents were very concerned that they not be perceived as old fogeys who were behind the times," said a woman who was born when her father was fifty and mother was forty-one.

"My friends adore my parents and find them quite hip," added June, whose parents were well into their forties when she was born. "They often comment that they wish their own parents were as 'with it.'"

And one woman from Connecticut proudly enclosed with her letter an old local newspaper clipping reporting her third-grade open house. It spoke of "a sweet little girl and her dad... a handsomely dressed businessman [who] seemed enchanted with the world of 'little people,' and particularly that of his daughter.... The silver-grayness of his hair seemed to shine, as did his eyes. The 'generation gap' seemed to have sprung a leak! This father and daughter, though separated by many years, proved once more that love, mutual trust and understanding can and do tighten the string on the generation gap."

POSTSCRIPT

Do Older Parents Provide a More Nurturing Environment for Children?

Barratt, Roach, and Colbert found that maternal age, when examined by itself, contributed positively to the mother's caregiving: older maternal age was related to being more involved and being more verbally and emotionally responsive to the infant. The authors note, though, that when maternal age was combined with other factors, age was not very important in determining the mother's parenting style. Maternal age, fewer maternal psychological problems, and less difficult infant temperament were associated with optimal parenting.

Yarrow, in his argument against older parents, states that the children of older parents felt they "grew up old." They were always around older people, and they frequently feared their parents would die. These children felt that they were forced to act emotionally mature and that they never got a chance to be "just a kid."

In his book *Latecomers: Children of Parents Over 35,* Yarrow provides the following guidelines for older parents to follow in order to minimize problems with their children: (1) Older parents need to make an extra effort to understand their children's world, as it will be very different from the world they experienced; (2) Older parents should balance their lives between their children and other activities, so as not to put undue pressure on the children to meet all of the parents' needs; and (3) Parents should find substitute adults to participate in those physical activities their children want to pursue, but which the parents may not be able to.

With biomedical advances and social changes making it easier for adults to become parents in their 40s and 50s, the issue of older parents' effects on children will become more visible. How will children adapt to having older parents? Will they be at a disadvantage as compared to other children? Or will it be beneficial for children to have parents who have experienced more of the world?

SUGGESTED READINGS

Daniels, P., & Weingarten, K. (1982). *Sooner or later: Timing of parenthood in adult lives.* New York: W.W. Norton.

Harris-Adler, R. (1991, November). Late parenthood. *Chatelaine, 64,* 46.

Siegel, M. (1992, September). Having babies after 40. *Good Housekeeping, 215,* 184, 224.

ISSUE 3

Is Transracial Adoption Harmful to a Child's Development?

YES: Charlotte Goodluck, from "Mental Health Issues of Native American Transracial Adoptions," in Pamela V. Grabe, ed., *Adoption Resources for Mental Health Professionals* (Transaction, 1993)

NO: Christopher Bagley, from "Transracial Adoption in Britain: A Follow-up Study, With Policy Considerations," *Child Welfare* (May/June 1993)

ISSUE SUMMARY

YES: Charlotte Goodluck, a professor at Northern Arizona University, discusses the experiences of Native American children to show how minority children differ substantially from Anglo American children in how they are reared. She argues that putting a child into a family with a different racial and ethnic background can lead to problems in identity development, loss of cultural values, and problems in dating and mate selection.

NO: Christopher Bagley, a professor of social work at the University of Calgary, cites several studies that support transracial adoption. He concludes that these adoptions can meet the psychosocial and developmental needs of the children involved.

Our society has long embraced the notion that children do much better when they are adopted into loving homes rather than placed in institutions and orphanages. At its best, the family unit socializes a child and also provides a child with nurturance, a sense of security, and unconditional love. Unfortunately, there are hundreds of thousands of children in our society who, for various reasons, are not with their biological families. They, like all children, are in need of and entitled to loving families. Although there is agreement that a family setting is best for a child and preferable to institutionalization, not every professional who works with children agrees that every adoption situation is *always* in the best interest of the child. For example, there is considerable debate surrounding transracial adoption, where the question arises: Should a child be placed for adoption with a family whose racial and ethnic background is different from that of the child's?

Transracial adoption is a term that typically refers to an adoption in which a minority child (e.g., Asian American, Native American, African American, or Latino) or a child with a mixed racial background is adopted by an Anglo

American couple. This type of adoption has become more commonplace in the United States since the late 1940s.

A common opinion among adoption professionals today is that eligible children should be placed in adoptive homes without delay. However, whenever possible, children should be raised by people of their own culture and heritage. Leora Neal, executive director of the Association of Black Social Workers Child Adoption, Counseling, and Referral Service, outlines several problems experienced by transracial adoptees:

- Children may feel unaccepted by both the Anglo American community and the minority community from which they came.
- In a racist society, children need to learn coping skills. Since white parents have never had to deal with racism, they are often ill equipped to help their adopted children understand and deal with it effectively.
- Children lose contact with the fullness of their culture of origin. Adopting family members do not always realize this because they are now part of a mixed race family.

As you read the following two selections, consider the issue from both the adoptive parents' point of view and the child's. What are the critical issues that come to mind for you that would cause you to support one point of view over the other?

YES

Charlotte Goodluck

MENTAL HEALTH ISSUES OF NATIVE AMERICAN TRANSRACIAL ADOPTIONS

BACKGROUND

The U.S. census reports that there are 1.4 million Native Americans, 0.6% of the total population. Approximately half reside on reservations. Children under the age of eighteen make up 45% of the American Indian population. There are over 300 federally recognized tribes in 27 states.

The American Indian is at greater risk of poverty, alcoholism, low education, high dropout rate, unemployment, homicide, suicide, and mental health problems such as depression than the rest of Americans. The list of potential mental health problems is lengthy. Many of these problems result from a long history of conflict between cultures, and federal policies of eradicating Indian cultures and assimilating the Indian people into the mainstream. However, these policies have not always been successful. Many tribal people have serious difficulty responding to these policies and coping with today's life. However, there are strengths in tribal communities, such as the extended family, clan relationships, tribal identity, spiritual life, and tribal sovereignty. Too, there are positive role models and leaders for youth to identify with and emulate, but often these leaders are not in the public view.

INDIAN CHILD WELFARE

During the mid-1970's there were national efforts by Indian leaders to let Congress know about the widespread systematic breakup of Indian families by state foster-care systems and private agencies. The documented foster-care placement rates were alarming. As a result of these efforts legislation was drafted to protect Indian tribes, families, and children. The public law was called the "Indian Child Welfare Act of 1978 (ICWA) (P.L. 95–608)"; it was signed into law by President Carter in November of 1978. This public law has made monumental changes in the decision-making procedures of state social services and court systems.

From Charlotte Goodluck, "Mental Health Issues of Native American Transracial Adoptions," in Pamela V. Grabe, ed., *Adoption Resources for Mental Health Professionals* (Transaction, 1993). Copyright © 1993 by Transaction Publishers. Reprinted by permission. Notes omitted.

The law brought three major changes: 1) tribes must be notified of any state foster care and/or adoption proceeding involving Indian children, 2) tribes can intervene at any time during a proceeding when Indian children are involved, and 3) Indian parents and Indian custodians must be given due process in the action. Another significant aspect is that tribes can request a transfer of jurisdiction from state court to tribal court. These major legal changes have returned major decision-making roles to tribal authorities in order to promote and protect the Indian family and child and the tribal culture.

ICWA has been implemented for over seven years and case law has developed from different court decisions involving both state and tribal viewpoints. Many Indian children are returning from various state foster and adoptive placements to many different tribes. These tribes often have had to provide mental health and reunification services to the children in question and their families.

Mental health services are delivered in three major ways on reservations. The first major source of mental health services for a family is the support and caring from an intact functioning extended family and nuclear family system. Children, siblings, cousins and other relatives are looked after by the informal helping network including advice seeking from spiritual leaders within a tribal environment.

When this structure is not available for various reasons then external, formal structures are sought. With the inclusion of Indian Health Services, a public health hospital system on reservations during the early 40's they became the major source of health care provision for Indian families. The second source of mental health services comes via the Indian Health Service, either directly within the particular hospital setting or by contract with social workers, psychologists, or psychiatrist. Each IHS service area has its own mental health budget and its own mental health priorities so attention to different needs is seen in each geographic area. Services may include: prevention, education, counseling, assessment, evaluation and follow-up depending on the need of the particular case. Placement into foster care, group home and other institutional settings may be required depending on the severity of the mental health problem. Placement into state hospitals is a complex jurisdictional matter involving state and tribal issues and beyond the scope of this paper.

The third major source of services is available off reservation. Eligible Indian clients have access to Indian health services (if geographically available, like in a major city) similar to on reservation clients plus access to the state, private, and county resources regarding mental health services. Also, employed Indian clients have access to third party providers through employee fringe benefit policies but this is dependent on the employer's health insurance program. Services for mental health are dependent on various eligibility criteria, access to services, funding sources, and severity of problem.

There are various research studies on ICWA such as the one by the American Indian Law Center entitled "Indian Child Welfare Impact and Improvements under P.L. 95–608 and P.L. 96–272." Comprehensive questionnaires were sent to all tribes and states to assess the impact of the Indian Child Welfare Act of 1978 and the Adoption Assistance and Child Welfare Act of 1980 on their child welfare systems.

The answers point to problems with the implementation of ICWA, such as inadequate federal funding to tribes for preventive and rehabilitative programs, the high turnover of tribal staff, and inadequate training, all of which are detrimental to the maintenance of programs at the tribal level. Ultimately children suffer.

ADOPTION ISSUES

With regard to child-care practices, tribes for centuries have parented and cared for their children in both nuclear-family and extended-family structures. Native Americans differ from Anglos in that out-of-home placements are open: that is, children are generally not placed with strangers outside the tribal kinship network and thus remain known to the birth family. One important value in tribal ethics is that a child who loses a parent is accepted and cared for by other relatives in the tribal system. There was no concept of legal termination of parental rights before the Americanization of the tribal court systems which followed the Wheeler-Howard Reorganization Act of 1934. In fact, the words "adoption" and "termination" are not found in many native languages except where they are borrowed from English words.

However, due to numerous factors such as the impact of relocation, removal to "government and mission boarding schools," and the decrease of the indigenous tribal teaching systems, many Indian children were being raised away from their own families and tribes. In the 1950's, numerous tribal children were being raised in cities in the east and midwest after being placed for adoption by state, Bureau of Indian Affairs, and private agencies. The history of these transracial placements (Indian children with Anglo parents) is discussed by Fanshel, and the mental health risks of the children (emotional problems, identity confusion, depression) are analyzed by Berlin.

Adoption of an Indian child into a family system from another culture and race will promote a double identity problem; first a loss and separation from the tribal parent (biological parent) and second, a loss from the tribal culture. In addition a child must contend with the issues of adoption itself and searching for tribal identity as a young adult and reunification with tribe. These various attachments and separations are multiple and will promote identity confusion (self and culture) and serious mental health problems. Then add to this the dynamics of foster care placements and adoption disruptions are to be expected. The effects of disruption (principally Indian children running away) are painful for the child, the adoptive parents, and siblings. Grief reactions from the separation and loss are frequently seen in the total family system.

Federal policy has been affected by changes in popular attitudes toward the concept and practice of transracial adoption, with the result that Indian children have been made victims of the cycle of changing policy. During the 1960's advocacy movements, such as Black social workers denouncing transracial placements, forced agencies to make changes in recruitment practices, home study policies, and agency hiring practices. This approach began to affect American Indian child welfare, when in the early 1970's a private agency in Arizona started a program to place Indian children with Indian adoptive families. Within seven years over 100 children were placed into Indian adoptive families. Children were returned to their tribes after spending many years in non-Indian state foster care. This program included infants as well as older and special-needs children. Tribal resources were contacted and made available to children and their parents once again. There are many current programs in the nation focusing on recruiting Indian families for Indian children. Issues related to who may adopt Indian children and how state and tribal social services can work together to continue to implement the Indian Child Welfare Act are discussed in Louise Zokan de los Reyes' "Adoption and the American Indian Child." Effective recruitment of Indian families and development of appropriate tribal child-care standards are a critical part of minimizing mental health problems.

There are Indian children who were placed in adoptive homes outside their own culture and race. The psychological literature demonstrates a child's need for a nurturing and stable environment to enhance a stable identity. The impact of transracial adoption on a child creates a developmental crisis and one has to come to terms with it during the process of growing up. This crisis impacts one's sense of self-esteem and identity, and culture attachment and acceptance. Adoption itself is a crisis and implies a life-long developmental process of accepting one's history and different familial relationships. The dynamics of adoption are complex and impact emotional and psychological well-being throughout life.

The adoption field has made many systematic changes since the early 1970's. Current adoption policy should be a life-long commitment by all the parties serving the biological parents, adoptee, and adoptive parents. Post-adoption services such as mental health services for the entire triad are appropriate and necessary particularly in cases when Indian children have been raised in homes outside their own culture.

Due to the preceding factors earlier, mental health professionals across the country have come into contact with children living in various familial situations including transracial adoption. They need to understand the complex issues facing the Native American child and incorporate approaches that address these issues.

INFORMAL SURVEY

The next section of this paper is in "question and answer" format. The questions were posed to child welfare professionals with experience in foster care, adoption, and Indian affairs. The theme was adoption practice as it relates to American Indian children and culture.

What does the term "transracial placement" and "transracial adoption" mean in your work with American Indian children and families?

- A child is placed outside the community; a child loses his tribal identity.
- Placement (adoption or foster care) of an American Indian child with non-Indian parents. Caucasian parents who already have Indian children are counted as "middle ground." Placement of an Indian child with such a family is still a transracial placement, but not quite as transracial as it would be if a child were the only Indian family member.
- Placing Indian children in families where the lifestyle is different from their own culture. The child may look Indian but be acculturated internally to the family's culture. Such placement may set up confusion and nonaccep-

tance by the Indian culture as well as rejection by the adoptive family's culture in the long run; in other words, the child runs the risk of being rejected by both worlds.

- Placement of an Indian child in a non-Indian family. Usually it is assumed that both of the parents are non-Indian; however, these terms would also apply in cases where one parent is an Indian and the other parent is not. This is especially pertinent when the Indian parent is not of the same tribe as the child.

What are the positive aspects of a transracial placement?

- Gives a family a special child; it can provide a family for a child who otherwise might not have one.
- There may be positive aspects for the adoptive parent (they can raise a child), but from a child's point of view there can be too many negative aspects.
- Professionally and morally, children should be members of families who are of their own racial, ethnic, and cultural background, unless there are circumstances that do not permit it. Dealing with the issues of placement and adoption for children and families is difficult enough without the additional burden created by transracial placement or adoption.
- I fail to see any positive aspects and would support such placements only when it has been determined that no tribal or Indian resources exist for this child.

What are the negative aspects of transracial placements?

- The native language is not learned, nor are cultural skills such as weaving, silver smithing, herding sheep. An Indian child traditionally learns the importance of the land, learns the ethos of moral and spiritual lessons from elders, participates in a complex tribal religious system, and learns the significance of living in a relative/clan family system from a tribal point of view. A transracially-adopted child loses this source of a feeling of identity.

- Loss of tribal community and erosion of the tribal community system.
- The child runs a high risk of making a bad bargain: trading his culture and heritage for a new family.
- Poor identity foundation of adoptees; loss of support networks and extended family; drain of human resources for target groups; fulfilling the needs of adoptive parents, not the children.
- Places the child at higher risk of serious mental health problems during adolescence, such as difficulties with dating and selection of mate, and with having children themselves ("Who am I and where do I belong?")

How does the Indian Child Welfare Act affect your decision-making regarding children in foster care and adoption? Have you had any children who were placed for adoption in non-Indian families and then had to be replaced with an Indian family? Discuss what happened.

- From a tribal standpoint, all efforts are made to keep children within the family or at least within the community. If that is not possible, then an outside resource is sought. In that situation it is essential that the non-tribal guardians or adoptive parents become involved in the child's tribal community, in order to sensitize them to the environment from which the child comes and keep some form of meaningful relationship with the specific tribe.

- We are careful to follow the letter (not always the intent of the ICWA). There was a case where a child was placed with a non-Indian family without having the tribe participate in planning. The agency said the tribe didn't respond, but the tribe moved to overturn the adoption, saying they weren't given an opportunity to respond. After lengthy court maneuvering they won the right to move the child. The tribe decided to let the adoption stand, because their goal was to make the point about the importance of including the tribe in planning, not to disrupt a placement that was working well.
- ICWA is a federal law and it does affect decision-making regarding Indian children in state foster and adoptive placements. There are times however, when the workers are finding loopholes in the law such as allowing "voluntary placements" and not contacting the tribes, varies considerably. Because private adoptions are legal in some states, Indian parents voluntarily place children outside the tribe without notifying the tribe when these adoptions are finalized.
- Our philosophy and approach to placement of Indian children with Indian families preceeded ICWA, so that ICWA in that aspect did not affect our decision-making process in placement. Problems with ICWA have more to do with having Indian "parents' rights" and "confidentiality." Several adolescents who have been placed with non-Indian families in infancy have come to our attention because of problems related to transracial placement superimposed on adoption issues of adolescence.

- When workers follow the spirit and intent of ICWA it works best. When workers, lawyers, and judges are ignorant of or opposed to the concept, children suffer. In one case, a child adopted by a non-Indian family had to be returned after the tribe learned that ICWA regulations had not been followed. The decision was the right one, but the child suffered needlessly because of the lawyer's mistake. One case involved a young Apache teenager who had been adopted by non-Indian parents in the early 60's in the East. She became pregnant by an Indian youth and she placed the baby with a private agency for voluntary foster care. Her parents wanted her to relinquish her rights and since she did not want to the state became involved. They filed a Petition to terminate her rights as her parents claimed neglect, emotional instability and abuse. The state had to notify the tribe and the tribe intervened and requested transfer to tribal court. The tribal social services department has given services to the mother and are helping mother and child remain together with close supervision of the child. . . .

There were many American Indian children placed into non-Indian adoptive families years ago. Have you worked with these children as adults or teenagers? What problems or positive reactions did they express about their experiences? How have the tribes integrated these adults into their community?

- I have worked with two cases, one positive and one negative. In the first, the non-Indian family was stable and sensitive to the boy's cultural background, giving positive support, accepting the need to search for biological parents, encouraging his development of a positive self-esteem and image. They eventually helped their son locate his Indian parents. He now moves freely between the two families and two worlds.

In the other case, the adoptive family was dysfunctional and the young girl exhibited low and negative self-esteem, self-destructive behavior such as drug/alcohol abuse, and eating disorders. She had poor personal interaction skill, was often depressed and disliked any association with Indian culture and held a low opinion of her own Indian identity. She tended to over-identify with the non-Indian culture. The young girl was eventually placed in a residential treatment center. Contact has since been made with her birth father and a reunion was completed. It seems vital to this young lady (age 19) to have someone from her tribal birth family to show some interest in her development and growth.

- One adolescent placed with non-Indian adoptive parents wants to contact her tribe because of tribal benefits. The tribe is willing to help with her college support, but no contact is planned with birth parents.

- Unfortunately, the bonds of affectional ties and sense of permanency that this project (BIA/CWLA) sought to develop did not bear fruit. Instead the children who were the subjects of this project have experienced lives of severe identity confusion. Many of these people are now in their thirties and forties and experience severe problems of abuse of alcohol and other drugs. Some of the families have financial resources to afford private psychiatric resources for their children but find that, even with the best of help

these adult children remain severely troubled.

In the book *Far from the Reservation*, Fanshel reviewed 97 families of Indian children raised in non-Indian families. This number is low because it deals with only one research project. Another report cited at the Indian Senate Select Committee hearings estimates at least $1/4$ of Indian children placed were placed into non-Indian homes. The total number of Indian children affected by some sort of non-Indian placement is high. A significant number of these Indian children have subsequently been seen in mental health settings across the country.

- I have had numerous calls from non-Indian adoptive parents wanting to know how to provide their Indian children with a sense of Indian identity and culture. External means such as attending pow-wows and visiting museums don't give a child a whole sense of "being Indian" or "having a tribal identity." In fact they may leave him with a sense of confusion, since Indian children represent numerous tribal backgrounds, different histories, and different values and beliefs. Being exposed to a stereotyped "pan-Indian" cannot provide a person with positive self-esteem and positive tribal group identity nor the unique tribal survival skills (e.g. coping with racism, learning about inter-tribal differences, understanding tribal-cultural-spiritual ways) related to belonging to a particular tribal group and community.

Mental health services need to be available during the entire life of the children who were adopted in this project to help them with their sense of alienation, rejection, and separation from traditional tribal identity. Daily contact with positive Indian role models in the community will help deal with the acceptance and identity issues. Universities, colleges, and urban Indian centers have Indian clubs and activities to help encourage connections with other members of the tribal community.

One helpful Indian-oriented mental health approach is the "Talking Circle", where Indian elders, parents, and children can come together in a 'circle' and help heal one another by talking about their issues and accepting one another. The "Talking Circle" is a form of group therapy within a cultural framework. The circle has special meaning to Indian people as a symbol and function. The techniques included are listening, sensitivity to the group, spiritual focus, sharing strengths and problems, and the use of informal helping networks. (For more information, contact the Native American Rehabilitation Association, an Indian alcohol program in Portland, Oregon. It has been in operation since 1981.)

- We have had some Indian clients who as children were placed in non-Indian adoptive families and are now young adults who have come back to the agency. A number of them were pregnant young women wanting to place their expected babies for adoption. These young women express a positive adoptive experience, and are rejecting their Indian background, wanting their children to be placed in a non-Indian family. This may be a "double whammy" for the child in dealing with adoption issues later on: "Why didn't my parents want me, and what is so bad about my Indian heritage?"

- The cases I have heard about have had major identity problems in adolescence. The placements fall apart during these critical years of development as the Indian youths start searching and yearning for their Indian birth parents and tribal identity. The tribes are contacted, and positive or negative reunions may occur; but still there is a sense of emptiness, loss of relatives and ties to a tribal community, and lowered self-esteem. Higher incidence of alcoholism and attempted suicide are seen in this population of Indian adults. Professional counseling in tandem with Indian healers may provide the necessary bridge between the two worlds.

What is the most critical issue you want others in human services to know about American Indian adoption and the special issue of transracial adoption?

- Transracial adoption should only be considered after all tribal resources are exhausted. It should be a very rare option for tribal children. The development of urban, non-reservation resources is a critical issue because many of the Indian parents are living in fractured families already. The crisis nursery concept can prevent the breakup of young Indian families by providing preventive child protective services to both the young Indian mother and father and the high risk newborn or young child.
- If one ignores ICWA it will be at considerable risk to the child's stability.
- Children who consider themselves to be "Indian" should be treated that way, even if they don't fit the letter of ICWA eligibility. If they aren't eligible for enrollment, or had been voluntarily relinquished, they should still be placed with Indian families. We

do that with Black children when no law requires it—why not with Indian children?

- Indian children can be placed into Indian foster and adoptive homes when tribal and state policies and practices concerning staff hiring, recruitment, and home studies are changed to advocate same-race-and-culture families for Indian children. There are existing programs which can be models for other social service programs. ICWA is a federal law on which other countries are now modeling their own child welfare laws and policies to achieve tribal independence and sovereignty. The mental health problems of transracial adoption can be prevented by not placing Indian children in transracial adoptive families and by not continuing previous transracial placements. Then Indian tribal communities and families can be developed at the local level as a resource for special needs children needing placement.
- It must be clearly understood that each of us has the requirement of ensuring the integrity of the family. Continued separation of Indian children from their families and tribes ensures the destruction of Indians as a people. The underlying racism involved in these practices must be reckoned with. There are many ways to assist Indian families and their children. Removal of these children is a most destructive practice....

SUMMARY

The Indian Child Welfare Act of 1978, now the law of the land, mandates that Indian children needing families be placed within their own tribal community if at all possible, and that transracial adop-

tions are to be avoided. The placement preference section of the ICWA considers only immediate family members and then other tribal members as a source for the child; placement with another culture is only a last alternative. Recent casework experience with the results of transracial adoptions of Indian children and with the implementation of ICWA demonstrate the wisdom of the principles on which ICWA was based. Transracial adoptions tend to result in more mental health problems than same-culture or same-race adoptions, although it must also be said that some transracial adoptions have been successful from the viewpoint of the child and the adoptive parents, if not from the viewpoint of a tribe which has lost a member. However, much remains to be done before it can be said that ICWA has been fully implemented. In many areas there is an urgent need to develop a pool of Indian foster and adoptive parents in order to achieve more fully the goal of same-culture placement, and to develop reservation and urban-Indian resources such as guardianship programs that will minimize the mental health consequences.

In conclusion, Indian children who are placed in non-Indian adoptive homes need sensitive caring adoptive parents who will advocate and address the child's need for a tribal-cultural identity as well as address the special issues of adoption itself. Adoptive parents can provide for positive Indian role models to be present in their child's life and to allow for a spiritual based healer to give a ceremony for acknowledgement of Indian heritage and identity. Providing an Indian hero from music, recreation, sports, literature and the arts allows for a positive Indian image and self-esteem to grow and develop. When an Indian child and his family request mental health services, a number of options have been demonstrated to be effective. Individual, peer and group counseling are particularly helpful with older children. For younger children, the use of play therapy using Indian dolls and objects for Indian and non-Indian culture (hogan-house, horses, dancing, drums, eagle) enable the child to begin to understand his own connections to an Indian heritage. The use of these symbols can foster the ability to balance and integrate the best from both worlds. The child has a better chance to achieve acceptance of one's own self and background when both cultures are presented in a positive, constructive manner. The Indian child needs help to acknowledge the reality from both cultures and how not to become self-destructive, hateful, bitter or stuck in loss and rage. He or she must learn to move past these negative emotions and on to acceptance and integration of his Indian origins.

NO

Christopher Bagley

TRANSRACIAL ADOPTION IN BRITAIN: A FOLLOW-UP STUDY, WITH POLICY CONSIDERATIONS

Long-term British follow-up study of 27 Afro-Caribbean and mixed-race children adopted by Caucasian parents, and 25 Caucasian children adopted by same race parents, is reported. The adoptees were studied in the late 1970s, and 12 years later when they were, on average, 19 years old. Outcomes for both groups in terms of a number of measures of adjustment and identity were generally excellent. Some 10% of both groups, however, had poor adjustment. Although the outcomes for the transracially adopted group are likely to be different in identity terms from Afro-Caribbean children brought up in same-race families, there is no evidence from this and other studies that such an intercultural identity leads to unfavorable adjustment. On the contrary, these children seem well prepared by transracial adoption to participate effectively in a multicultural, multiracial society. Transracial adoption should be considered for all children (Afro-Caribbean or Caucasian) who cannot be placed inracially.

Transracial adoption is defined in this article as the adoption by parents (usually of white, European origin) of an ethnically different child (usually of Afro-Caribbean origin). This article is concerned with adoptions of minority-group children born in the country in which they are adopted. Intercountry adoptions are often also interethnic adoptions, with the added complication of adaptations of language and culture, especially for older adopted children. Research studies by the authors have treated intercountry adoptions as a special case, to be considered separately from other interethnic adoptions [Bagley and Young 1981; Bagley 1990]. The development of a sense of identity in children of ethnically mixed marriages is yet another interesting parenting issue, the literature on which is relevant to, but should be considered separately from, that on interethnic adoption [Bagley and Young 1984; Bagley 1991a].

From Christopher Bagley, "Transracial Adoption in Britain: A Follow-up Study, With Policy Considerations," *Child Welfare*, vol. 72, no. 3 (May/June 1993). Copyright © 1993 by Transaction Publishers. Reprinted by permission. References omitted.

Earlier writers on transracial adoption have pointed to mixed but generally favorable outcomes in follow-ups of preadolescents in transracial or interethnic adoptions. In Britain, Tizard [1977] has written enthusiastically about the benefits of adoption for children who would otherwise grow up in institutional or unstable care, but also points to the potentially negative impact upon black children of Caucasian parents (hereafter "parents") who ignore black culture, and have no contact with black people and their institutions. Gill and Jackson [1983], however, in another British study, have shown that 60% of Caucasian adoptive parents with black, adolescent children had no black friends, and their children likewise had few contacts with other black adolescents. Nevertheless, the majority of the adopted children had good levels of self-esteem, and few signs of behavioral maladjustment.

In the United States, Ladner [1977], who studied 136 transracial adoptions, argued that "love is not enough"—although it is essential that parents love and care for their children, they should also hold in esteem and interact with black culture if they are to fully meet their black child's identity needs. As in the British research, a minority (but a crucially important minority) of Caucasian adoptive parents had failed in the task of integrating themselves and their black child with black social institutions and culture.

Since these earlier studies were undertaken, the practice of placing black children with Caucasian parents has slowed or ceased altogether in many regions. In part, this has happened because social workers have been using more culturally appropriate models, supporting minority-group families under stress rather than removing children on grounds of alleged neglect or abuse [Bagley 1990]; in part, it is because social agencies have become more active and adept in finding black families for black children [Sandven and Resnick 1987]; and in part, for political reasons, since vocal members of the minority community have attacked the idea of black children being brought up in Caucasian families [Simon and Alstein 1987; Stubbs 1987]. Nevertheless, black and other minority-group children are still being placed transracially in Canada and the United States when their special needs, such as physical and mental disability, make them difficult to place in the still-limited pool of black or minority group adopters.

Another policy dilemma concerns the status of mixed-race children who have one Caucasian and one black biological parent. Advocates of mixed-race families, such as the British Harmony group [described by White 1988], argue that mixed-race children are neither black nor Caucasian, but both, and form a special ethnic or cultural group [Bagley and Young 1984]: Why should a child with one Caucasian biological parent not be placed with an adoptive Caucasian family, or with a family of a mixed marriage?

Further research from the United States has indicated the rather successful outcomes for transracial adoptions. Thus, McRoy and Zurcher [1983] compared 30 African American children placed with Caucasian parents and 30 African American children adopted inracially. A standardized measure of self-concept (the Tennessee scale) indicated no differences between the two adopted groups, and no statistically significant differences in comparison with normative groups for the test. Feigelman and Silverman [1984] studied... adoptive families with children from a variety of ethnic groups, and found that "the adolescent and school-aged transracial adoptees were no more poorly adjusted than their inracially adopted counterparts."

Confirmatory evidence comes from the study by Simon and Altstein [1987] of 98 transracial adoptions. Success rates (about 80%) in the adolescent years were similar to success rates from research on outcomes of both inracial adoption and ordinary parenting. Put another way, about 10% of the children from ordinary, nonadoptive families will have marked psychological problems, about 10% will have an intermediate level of problems, and 80% will be well adjusted. These figures are the benchmark for evaluating outcomes of adoption, and a large number of studies [reviewed by Brodzinsky and Schecter 1990] suggest that outcomes for children without handicap or disability placed for adoption in infancy (including black children placed with Caucasian parents) are close to the 80% benchmark figure of good adjustment. Indeed, if adoptive families can achieve a 70% or 80% level of good adjustment with children who were adopted past infancy, and have experienced many earlier traumas, including neglect, abuse, and early neurological and physical problems [Cadoret 1990], then adoptive parenting will have been particularly successful.

It is a paradox of transracial adoption, in terms of the assumed problems of black children in Caucasian families in achieving satisfactory levels of ethnic self-esteem, that many black children brought up in black families appear to have problems in this regard. In various projective tests (e.g., using photographs of black and Caucasian people, and black and white colors and figures), black children in both the United States and Britain have tended to devalue blackness and black people, and have preferred white figures, even to the extent of denying and sometimes denigrating their own blackness [Milner 1973; Weinreich 1979; Davey 1982; Williams and Morland 1976]. Although the situation is changing in the direction of a more positive evaluation of self-characteristics by black children [Milner 1983; Bagley and Young 1988], 20% of the black Jamaican children studied in Toronto in 1987 identified with white children, implicitly rejecting their own black identity, compared with 40% of the black Jamaican children in Britain described 11 years earlier by Bagley and Young [1979] and 53% of the African American children studied by Williams and Morland in 1976, using the same projective test.

This research evidence is ironic in the sense that despite negative assertions of some black political leaders about the effects of transracial adoption [Simon and Altstein 1987], black and mixed-race children adopted by Caucasian parents actually have levels of ethnic identity and evaluations of black people similar to or better than those of black children growing up in black families. This is brought out in studies of self-esteem in black adoptees reviewed by Silverman and Feigelman 1990, and most clearly by Johnson et al. [1987], who used the Clark Doll Test [1950] in their study of 42 black children adopted by Caucasian parents and 45 black children adopted by black parents. Eighty percent of the group of inracially adopted black children identified themselves as black, compared with 73% of the transracial group (which contained more children who were mixed race or fair skinned). As Feigelman and Silverman [1983] point out, agencies have tended to place light-skinned black children and mixed-race children with Caucasian families; this has complicated comparisons of ethnic identity between transracial and inracial adopted children, since fair-skinned children might be more likely to identify themselves as Caucasian.

However, Simon and Altstein [1977], who also used the Clark Doll Test as well as the Williams and Morland [1976] projective tests, reported

It appears that black children reared in the special setting of a multiracial family do not acquire the ambivalence toward their own race reported in all other studies involving young black children. Our results also show that white children do not consistently prefer white to other groups, and that there are no significant differences in the racial attitudes of any category of children. Our findings do not offer any evidence that black children reared by white parents acquire a preference for white over black. They show only that black children perceive themselves as black as accurately as white children perceive themselves as white. [158]

TRANSRACIAL ADOPTIONS: RESULTS OF THE EARLIER BRITISH STUDY

An earlier British study [Bagley et al. 1979] reported on the current adjustment of 114 adopted and nonadopted children in Southern England. Thirty were of black or mixed-race origin and had been adopted by Caucasian parents. These 30 children were compared with 30 Caucasian children adopted by same-race parents, 30 black and mixed-race children in foster or group care who had not been adopted, and 24 children in a nonsepa-

rated comparison group obtained from school sources. The authors concluded from this work that the black and mixed-race adopted children, then between six and eight years of age, had generally good psychological outcomes in terms of a number of standardized measures of adjustment, although some Caucasian parents had few black friends and were unable or unwilling to transmit to their children any consciousness or pride in the heritage of being black.

The study examined various measures of adjustment against a number of background characteristics: racial awareness in adoptive parents was associated with higher social status, parental age, and existing children in the family. In effect this meant that parents who already had children of their own and who made a conscious decision to adopt a mixed-race child were more racially aware than parents who adopted a child because of infertility. Twelve of the 30 couples had adopted because they couldn't have children of their own; only three of these had intended from the outset to adopt a mixed-race child. The remaining nine had originally wanted to adopt a Caucasian baby but eventually approached agencies with a mixed-race child in mind when it became clear that no such children were available.

These 30 couples, whatever their original motivation, were mature, kind people and appeared to make excellent parents. This was reflected in the good adjustment of the children they had adopted. But these adopted children, according to the racial identification measures we used, often tended to identify themselves as white (as frequently as black children in black families). The optimistic surmise in this early research was that since the foundations of good mental health and feelings of self-worth were laid during a crucial period of development, the transracially adopted children would possess the basic ego strength to incorporate within their identity framework, at some later stage, positive concepts of their ethnic identity. The authors of the study supposed, in Hauser's [1971] phrase, that there would not be any "premature foreclosure" of identity in these children.

In the first study the mixed-race adopted children were considered as a group by themselves and in combination with the Caucasian adopted children to see if any background factors could predict current adjustment. Sex of child and early health history (including birth weight and minor congenital malformations), were not systematically related to later adjustment. Age of child at placement with adoptive parents (average age 23 months, range one month to four years), age at separation from biological mother, and factors related to previous foster care (including a history of abuse or neglect in five cases) also bore no relationship to the children's current adjustment when they were, on average 7.3 years old. A possible reason for this finding was that, as in the 1972 study of Seglow et al., the excellent care provided by the adoptive parents had counteracted the negative effects of early environmental and physical handicaps.

METHODS IN THE SECOND FOLLOW-UP OF TRANSRACIAL ADOPTEES

This study was able to locate 27 of the 30 black and mixed-race children adopted by Caucasian parents, and 25 of the 30 Caucasian children adopted by same-race parents some 12 years after the first follow-up study. These young people completed a number of measures of mental health and adjustment, including the Middlesex Hospital Questionnaire [Bagley 1980]; the Coopersmith [1981] self-esteem scale revised for use with adults and older adolescents [Bagley 1989a]; Weinreich's measure of identity [1979, 1986]; and two measures used by Stein and Hoopes [1985] in their follow-up study of adoptees—the Tan et al. [1979] ego identity scale, and the Offer et al. [1988] Self-Image Questionnaire. A questionnaire was also developed that asked the adoptees to reflect on the process of their adoption and the degree of satisfaction it had yielded them. Questions about ethnic identity were addressed to the black adoptees only.

These instruments were chosen in order to address the measurement of identity and self-esteem, which previous writers on adoption have shown to be important [Stein and Hoopes 1985; Hoopes 1990; Brodzinsky 1990]. The hypothesis, based on the previous findings of McRoy and Zurcher [1983] and Simon and Alstein [1987], was that there would be no differences in self-esteem, identity, and adjustment between the two types of adoptees, black and Caucasian, both adopted by Caucasian parents.

The mean age of the 27 black and mixed-race adoptees at follow-up was 19.0 years; 14 were male. The Caucasian adoptees were on average 19.2 years old, with an age range (similar to that of the black adoptees) of 17 to 20 years. Twelve of these Caucasian adoptees were male. Eighty-one percent of the transracially adopted children came from families where one or both parents were in upper-level professional and white-collar occupations, compared with 72% of the Caucasian adoptees.

RESULTS

Using a variety of dependent measures (psychoneurosis, self-esteem, and identity development in the adoptees) the study tried to predict, from the earlier data collected on the adoptive parents of the transracial adoptees and on the adoptees themselves, the outcomes for these young people when they were in their late teens. None of the potential predictors examined—social status and educational level of parents, presence of biological and adopted siblings, age at which child was placed, parents' motives for adopting, attitudes of parents toward black culture and contact with black friends, child's self-esteem, and ethnic identity in the earlier period—predicted later outcome. When problems did emerge in the adolescent years, no apparent cause for this appeared in the previously collected data on the adoptive families.

In table 1 the two adopted groups (black and mixed-race children adopted by Caucasian parents, and Caucasian children adopted by same-race parents) are compared. The two groups are similar in parental age and social class profiles, and in the number of adopted and biological siblings in the adoptive families. The clinical profiles of the two groups of adoptees are similar too. Profiles of psychoneurosis, depression, and anxiety derived from the Middlesex Hospital Questionnaire have been expressed in terms of the quartiles for the combined groups. Although Caucasian adoptees tend to be more anxious, this difference did not reach the 5% level of significance.

Normative data from a large Canadian sample of young adults [Bagley 1991a] has allowed calculation of cutoff points on the Middlesex Hospital Questionnaire that indicate scores typical of those with a formal psychiatric diagnosis. Some 11.5% of the adoptees were within this clinical range, a proportion similar to that observed in the nonadopted, normative sample. Of the other measures, self-esteem and identity orientation were similar between the two groups of adoptees, with no significant deviation from the available Canadian, U.S., and European norms for these measures [Bagley 1989a; Offer et al. 1988]. In other words, the clinical profiles of the two adopted groups are similar, and do not appear to differ from those that would be expected of an unselected population of similar age.

The educational achievements of the two adopted groups are rather high, and reflect the advantaged, middle-class status of most of the adoptive families. What is clear,... however, is that the black and mixed-race adoptees move in a predominantly Caucasian milieu: the majority of their close friends, both female and male, are Caucasian (but 41% of the black adoptees have a "best girlfriend/boyfriend" who is black, mixed-race, Chinese, or Indian, compared with 24% of the Caucasian adoptees). There is no reason, however, for lament in the fact that these black and mixed-race teenagers do have dating relationships with Caucasian boys and girls. What is clear from our data is that neither group of adoptees has any trouble in finding friends of either sex.

Both groups are largely positive about their adoption experiences. Combining the information from the clinical tests and the interview data, we can say that three of the 25 Caucasian adoptees and two of the 25 black and mixed-race adoptees have ongoing psychological and adjustment problems, marked self-

Table 1

Proportions of Contrasted Adopted Adolescents in Mental Health and Identity Groupings

	Lowest (25%) (Excellent mental health)	Mid (50%)	Highest (25%) (Poorer mental health)	Significance
Total scale score—				
Psychoneurosis				
Black adoptees (27)	22.2%	55.5%	22.2%	NS
Caucasian adoptees (25)	28.0%	44.0%	28.0%	
Both groups (52)	25.0%	50.0%	25.0%	
Depression				
Black adoptees (27)	25.9%	48.1%	25.9%	NS
Caucasian adoptees (25)	24.0%	52.0%	24.0%	
Both groups (52)	25.0%	50.0%	25.0%	
Free-floating anxiety				
Black adoptees (27)	22.2%	63.0%	14.8%	NS
Caucasian adoptees (25)	28.0%	36.0%	36.0%	
Both groups (52)	25.0%	50.0%	25.0%	

Problems in range of normative clinical group			
Black adoptees (27)	11.1% (3 individuals)		
Caucasian adoptees (25)	12.0% (3 individuals)		
Self-Esteem Scale (Coopersmith—Revised)			
Black adoptees (27)	Mean: 32.88	SD: 9.78	NS
Caucasian adoptees (25)	Mean: 30.49	SD: 10.50	
Identity Measure: Percent with Fixated or Fragmented Identity			
Black adoptees (27)	7.4% (2 individuals)		
Caucasian adoptees (25)	8.0% (2 individuals)		NS
Tan Ego Identity Scale			
Black adoptees (27)	Mean: 72.36	SD: 8.05	NS
Caucasian adoptees (25)	Mean: 74.81	SD: 8.73	
Offer Self-Image Questionnaire			
Black adoptees (27)	Mean: 49.85	SD: 11.69	NS
Caucasian adoptees (25)	Mean: 53.79	SD: 13.04	

doubt, and some identity problems. But in none of these cases could we adduce factors in the adoption or in the fact of being a black child in a Caucasian family as having any causal significance in this maladjustment. As Tizard and Phoenix [1987] have argued, transracial adoption may be qualitatively different from inracial adoption in terms of identity outcomes, but it is by no means inferior in terms of identity and adjustment. It is appropriate to draw a parallel between "mixed adoptions" and "mixed marriages"—both appear to have generally successful outcomes in terms of the adjustment and identity development of the children involved. It would be reactionary to criticize the mixing of races in marriage; likewise, it is reactionary to criticize mixed adoptions simply on the grounds that somehow the identity of the partners in this relationship will be changed.

CONCLUSIONS

The findings of the present study underscore those from previous American research on transracial adoption [Silverman and Feigelman 1990]. Transracial adoption, despite the lack of black consciousness on the part of many of the Caucasian parents involved, does appear to meet the psychosocial and developmental needs of the large majority of the children involved, and can be just as successful as inracial adoption.

Despite this optimistic finding, the practice of transracial adoption in meeting the needs of black children has greatly diminished in both Britain and the United States, for both positive and negative reasons. It is likely that in Britain (as in Canada), families of Caribbean origin are stabilizing and becoming upwardly mobile, achieving the original goals of their migration [Thomas-Hope 1982; Bagley and Young 1988]. Growing economic stability is paralleled by family stability, leading to far fewer black children of Caribbean families coming into care for any reason. Thus, other things being equal (for example, the absence of racist practice by social workers), the actual need for adoptive homes for black children will decline.

There seems to be a marked contrast, however, between the stable, upwardly mobile pattern of family life that is a feature of most migrants from the Caribbean to the United States, Canada,

and Europe, and the degree of instability in the family life of a number of African Americans. As Silverman and Feigelman have observed, despite the demonstrable success of transracial adoption, it is only atypically considered as an option for the number of black children entering out-of-home care in America:

> Perhaps the most disturbing part of our review of the transracial adoption literature is the extent to which it is ignored in formulating adoption policy. We are not recommending transracial placements as a panacea for the problems of family disintegration among non-white minorities in the United States. But their success suggests that they may at least be a useful resource. The effort to expand intraracial placement for minority children, however, does not require the cessation of transracial placements. At a time when few black leaders are sanguine about the deplorably low income and employment levels found among minority underclasses, as the rates of adolescent out-of-wedlock pregnancy continue to mount, transracial placement is a resource that cannot easily be ignored. [Silverman and Feigelman 1990: 200]

In Britain the situation seems to be different, with a trend in black families toward releasing fewer children: stable, prosperous black families are more able to accept roles as foster and adoptive parents. Nevertheless, it appears that a significant number of black children in Britain remain in out-of-home care because of the blanket prohibition of many local authorities against transracial placements for black children, or placement of mixed-race children with Caucasian couples [Jarvis 1990; Bennett and Mostyn 1991]. The advocacy group Children First argues that if the child's individual needs are to be met, transracial adoption should be considered as a serious possibility for many black and mixed-race children in long-term, local authority care [Tubbs 1986].

The failure of many local authorities in Britain to consider this option is puzzling, and is clearly not based on good psychological or research evidence on the outcomes of transracial adoption [Tizard and Phoenix 1987]. Indeed, some local authority practice may be based on a naive, absurd antiracist policy, which assumes that keeping black children separated from white families will somehow serve their interests, or protect them from racism. It is clear that despite the existence of both institutional and personal racism in Britain, about 20% of the white British population do hold marked nonprejudiced and accepting views of black people and their culture [Bagley et al. 1979]. It is this sector of the population that is particularly likely to enter into the growing number of racially mixed marriages in Britain and in Canada [Bagley 1991a]. It is this sector of the population, too, that should be considered, after appropriate home studies by social workers, as transracial adoptive parents. Not only are these members of the British population educated and, usually, enlightened, with many black friends and colleagues and intercultural interests and contacts, they also express an interest in transracial adoption, an interest often frustrated by current local authority policy in Britain [Bennett and Mostyn 1991].

The movement toward *interculturalism* [defined and discussed in the British context by Verma and Bagley 1984] is one of the most positive signs in ethnic relations today. In Canada, this concept is known as *multiculturalism*, the sharing and interrelationship of cultures, the importance and integrity of which are generously supported by federal and provincial governments. This policy has, for example, led to the rapid absorption and upward social mobility of immigrants from Jamaica [Bagley 1989b; Bagley et al. 1989]. Multicultural adoption is part of this optimistic blending and sharing of ethnic group cultures and heritages. Transracial adoption, like transracial marriage, could be part of that growth. About one-fifth of all marriages in Britain involving a black person are between black and white partners. Could we hope for a similar ratio in transracial adoptions?[1]

NOTES

1. In an ideal society, not divided on grounds of race or skin color, physical features should be no more relevant in adoption placement than, say, hair or eye color. What is crucial is that there should be an essential match between the *psychological* needs and commitments of adoptive parents and child. This is entirely compatible with the adoption of white children by members of other ethnic groups, and such practice does occur, for example, in the Northwest Territory and the Yukon province of Canada, regions where Caucasians are a small minority of the total population, and where white children are adopted by Native and Inuit families.

POSTSCRIPT

Is Transracial Adoption Harmful to a Child's Development?

There are many more minority children in need of adoptive homes than can be accommodated intraracially. Is there a place in our society for transracial adoption? Can transracial adoption be handled such that it is effective for children yet satisfies the concerns of those who are opposed to it? Perhaps if the prospective adoptive family were screened to determine the parents' commitment to some of the problems enumerated in the introduction to this debate and in each selection, then transracial adoption could be successful in maximizing the child's ethnic and psychological development.

From the parental perspective, consider the plight of suitable white adoptive parents. Many of them feel that the system is unjust in that they may wait years for a child, regardless of race, while suitable black adoptive parents, for example, rarely wait as long. Often these frustrated white parents look toward foreign adoptions. This does nothing to help address the problem of American children who need adoptive parents.

The concept of transracial adoption continues to be intensely debated. However, there may be some common ground upon which those on both sides of the issue can agree: (1) There should be increased efforts in the area of family planning. This would help diminish the growing numbers of children in need of adoption. (2) Our society must be creative in developing interventions that strengthen all types of families so that we can reduce the number of children removed from them in the first place.

SUGGESTED READINGS

Andujo, E. (1988). Ethnic identity of transracially adopted Hispanic adolescents. *Social Work, 33,* 531–535.

Hayes, P. (1993). Transracial adoption: Politics and ideology. *Child Welfare, 72* (3), 301–310.

Kallgren, C. A., & Caudill, P. J. (1993). Current transracial adoption practices: Racial dissonance or racial awareness? *Psychological Reports, 72,* 551–558.

National Association of Black Social Workers. (1994, April). *Position statement: Preserving African-American families.* Detroit, MI: National Association of Black Social Workers.

Wheeler, D. L. (1993, September 15). Black children, white parents: The difficult issue of transracial adoption. *Chronicle of Higher Education, 40* (4), pp. A6, A8.

ISSUE 4

Are Gender Differences Rooted in the Brain?

YES: Doreen Kimura, from "Sex Differences in the Brain," *Scientific American* (September 1992)

NO: Carol Tavris, from *The Mismeasure of Woman* (Simon & Schuster, 1992)

ISSUE SUMMARY

YES: Doreen Kimura, a neuropsychologist, believes that biological differences at birth in the male and female brain explain the subsequent differences in behavior between boys and girls.

NO: Carol Tavris, a social psychologist, concludes that there is no scientific evidence that the brains of males and females are different.

Nature versus nurture? Heredity or environment? Biology or behavior? The debate over how to explain human behavior has been going on for years. Generally speaking, researchers have concluded that the question is *not* whether environment or heredity explain behavior. Instead, the question has become: To what extent is each responsible for behavior? In the recent past, it was thought that environment had more to do with human behavior than genetics. Currently, many studies are concluding that heredity plays a larger role in development than environment.

Classic studies conducted to get answers to the nature versus nurture debate have used identical twins and adopted children for the research. If identical twins, who have the same genetic makeup, are reared apart, will they have similar behavior or personality traits? If so, researchers say, then heredity must account for behavior. Conversely, if identical twins are reared together but still have different personalities or cognitive abilities, then the implication is that environment accounts for behavior. Adoption studies operate on a similar premise. Children from impoverished biological parents who were adopted by middle-class families have been studied to determine the effects that environment had on their development.

Researchers have studied a number of personality traits, diseases, and abilities in their attempts to determine the role that genetics plays in shaping human behavior. For example, there is evidence that shyness or being inhibited has a biological basis. And there have been some reports suggesting that alcoholism may be heritable. But researchers caution that biology is not destiny. Shy children brought up in supportive homes could well overcome their predisposition to shyness. And there may be social, psychological, and economic influences that shape a person's drinking to a greater extent than any genetic predisposition.

In the following debate, researcher Doreen Kimura argues that sex hormones affect the brain prenatally and cause it to become organized differently for each gender. But Carol Tavris, a well-known social psychologist, attacks the studies that conclude that the brain is different for males and females. She argues that some scientists ignore the facts about brain research in their eagerness to prove that men are intellectually superior to women.

YES   Doreen Kimura

SEX DIFFERENCES IN THE BRAIN

Women and men differ not only in physical attributes and reproductive function but also in the way in which they solve intellectual problems. It has been fashionable to insist that these differences are minimal, the consequence of variations in experience during development. The bulk of the evidence suggests, however, that the effects of sex hormones on brain organization occur so early in life that from the start the environment is acting on differently wired brains in girls and boys. Such differences make it almost impossible to evaluate the effects of experience independent of physiological predisposition.

Behavioral, neurological and endocrinologic studies have elucidated the processes giving rise to sex differences in the brain. As a result, aspects of the physiological basis for these variations have in recent years become clearer. In addition, studies of the effects of hormones on brain function throughout life suggest that the evolutionary pressures directing differences nevertheless allow for a degree of flexibility in cognitive ability between the sexes.

* * *

Major sex differences in intellectual function seem to lie in patterns of ability rather than in overall level of intelligence (IQ). We are all aware that people have different intellectual strengths. Some are especially good with words, others at using objects—for instance, at constructing or fixing things. In the same fashion, two individuals may have the same overall intelligence but have varying patterns of ability.

Men, on average, perform better than women on certain spatial tasks. In particular, men have an advantage in tests that require the subject to imagine rotating an object or manipulating it in some other way. They outperform women in mathematical reasoning tests and in navigating their way through a route. Further, men are more accurate in tests of target-directed motor skills —that is, in guiding or intercepting projectiles.

Women tend to be better than men at rapidly identifying matching items, a skill called perceptual speed. They have greater verbal fluency, including the ability to find words that begin with a specific letter or fulfill some other constraint. Women also outperform men in arithmetic calculation and in

From Doreen Kimura, "Sex Differences in the Brain," *Scientific American* (September 1992). Copyright © 1992 by Scientific American, Inc. All rights reserved. Reprinted by permission.

recalling landmarks from a route. Moreover, women are faster at certain precision manual tasks, such as placing pegs in designated holes on a board.

Although some investigators have reported that sex differences in problem solving do not appear until after puberty, Diane Lunn, working in my laboratory at the University of Western Ontario, and I have found three-year-old boys to be better at targeting than girls of the same age. Moreover, Neil V. Watson, when in my laboratory, showed that the extent of experience playing sports does not account for the sex difference in targeting found in young adults. Kimberly A. Kerns, working with Sheri A. Berenbaum of the University of Chicago, has found that sex differences in spatial rotation performance are present before puberty.

Differences in route learning have been systematically studied in adults in laboratory situations. For instance, Liisa Galea in my department studied undergraduates who followed a route on a tabletop map. Men learned the route in fewer trials and made fewer errors than did women. But once learning was complete, women remembered more of the landmarks than did men. These results, and those of other researchers, raise the possibility that women tend to use landmarks as a strategy to orient themselves in everyday life. The prevailing strategies used by males have not yet been clearly established, although they must relate to spatial ability.

Marion Eals and Irwin Silverman of York University studied another function that may be related to landmark memory. The researchers tested the ability of individuals to recall objects and their locations within a confined space—such as in a room or on a tabletop. Women were better able to remember whether an item had been displaced or not. In addition, in my laboratory, we measured the accuracy of object location: subjects were shown an array of objects and were later asked to replace them in their exact positions. Women did so more accurately than did men.

It is important to place the differences described above in context: some are slight, some are quite large. Because men and women overlap enormously on many cognitive tests that show average sex differences, researchers use variations within each group as a tool to gauge the differences between groups. Imagine, for instance, that on one test the average score is 105 for women and 100 for men. If the scores for women ranged from 100 to 110 and for men from 95 to 105, the difference would be more impressive than if the women's scores ranged from 50 to 150 and the men's from 45 to 145. In the latter case, the overlap in scores would be much greater.

One measure of the variation of scores within a group is the standard deviation. To compare the magnitude of a sex difference across several distinct tasks, the difference between groups is divided by the standard deviation. The resulting number is called the effect size. Effect sizes below 0.5 are generally considered small. Based on my data, for instance, there are typically no differences between the sexes on tests of vocabulary (effect size 0.02), nonverbal reasoning (0.03) and verbal reasoning (0.17).

On tests in which subjects match pictures, find words that begin with similar letters or show ideational fluency—such as naming objects that are white or red— the effect sizes are somewhat larger: 0.25, 0.22 and 0.38, respectively. As discussed above, women tend to outperform men on these tasks. Researchers have reported the largest effect sizes for certain tests measuring spatial rotation (effect size 0.7) and targeting accuracy (0.75). The large effect size in these tests means there are many more men at the high end of the score distribution.

* * *

Since, with the exception of the sex chromosomes, men and women share genetic material, how do such differences come about? Differing patterns of ability between men and women most probably reflect different hormonal influences on their developing brains. Early in life the action of estrogens and androgens (male hormones chief of which is testosterone) establishes sexual differentiation. In mammals, including humans, the organism has the potential to be male or female. If a Y chromosome is present, testes or male gonads form. This development is the critical first step toward becoming a male. If the gonads do not produce male hormones or if for some reason the hormones cannot act on the tissue, the default form of the organism is female.

Once testes are formed, they produce two substances that bring about the development of a male. Testosterone causes masculinization by promoting the male, or Wolffian, set of ducts and, indirectly through conversion to dihydrotestosterone, the external appearance of scrotum and penis. The Müllerian regression factor causes the female, or Müllerian, set of ducts to regress. If anything goes wrong at any stage of the process, the individual may be incompletely masculinized.

Not only do sex hormones achieve the transformation of the genitals into male organs, but they also organize corresponding male behaviors early in life. Since we cannot manipulate the hormonal environment in humans, we owe much of what we know about the details of behavioral determination to studies in other animals. Again, the intrinsic tendency, according to studies by Robert W. Goy of the University of Wisconsin, is to develop the female pattern that occurs in the absence of masculinizing hormonal influence.

If a rodent with functional male genitals is deprived of androgens immediately after birth (either by castration or by the administration of a compound that blocks androgens), male sexual behavior, such as mounting, will be reduced. Instead female sexual behavior, such as lordosis (arching of the back), will be enhanced in adulthood. Similarly, if androgens are administered to a female directly after birth, she displays more male sexual behavior and less female behavior in adulthood.

Bruce S. McEwen and his co-workers at the Rockefeller University have shown that, in the rat, the two processes of defeminization and masculinization require somewhat different biochemical changes. These events also occur at somewhat different times. Testosterone can be converted to either estrogen (usually considered a female hormone) or dihydrotestosterone. Defeminization takes place primarily after birth in rats and is mediated by estrogen, whereas masculinization involves both dihydrotestosterone and estrogen and occurs for the most part before birth rather than after, according to studies by McEwen. A substance called alpha-fetoprotein may protect female brains from the masculinizing effects of their estrogen.

The area in the brain that organizes female and male reproductive behavior is the hypothalamus. This tiny structure at the base of the brain connects to the pituitary, the master endocrine gland. Roger A. Gorski and his colleagues at the University of California at Los Angeles have shown that a region of the pre-optic area of the hypothalamus is visibly larger in male rats than in females. The size increment in males is promoted by the presence of androgens in the immediate postnatal, and to some extent prenatal, period. Laura S. Allen in Gorski's laboratory has found a similar sex difference in the human brain.

Other preliminary but intriguing studies suggest that sexual behavior may reflect further anatomic differences. In 1991 Simon LeVay of the Salk Institute for Biological Studies in San Diego reported that one of the brain regions that is usually larger in human males than in females—an interstitial nucleus of the anterior hypothalamus—is smaller in homosexual than in heterosexual men. LeVay points out that this finding supports suggestions that sexual preference has a biological substrate.

Homosexual and heterosexual men may also perform differently on cognitive tests. Brian A. Gladue of North Dakota State University and Geoff D. Sanders of City of London Polytechnic report that homosexual men perform less well on several spatial tasks than do heterosexual men. In a recent study in my laboratory, Jeff Hall found that homosexual men had lower scores on targeting tasks than did heterosexual men; however, they were superior in ideational fluency—listing things that were a particular color.

This exciting field of research is just starting, and it is crucial that investigators consider the degree to which differences in life-style contribute to group differences. One should also keep in mind that results concerning group differences constitute a general statistical statement; they establish a mean from which any individual may differ. Such studies are potentially a rich source of information on the physiological basis for cognitive patterns.

* * *

The lifelong effects of early exposure to sex hormones are characterized as organizational, because they appear to alter brain function permanently during a critical period. Administering the same hormones at later stages has no such effect. The hormonal effects are not limited to sexual or reproductive behaviors: they appear to extend to all known behaviors in which males and females differ. They seem to govern problem solving, aggression and the tendency to engage in rough-and-tumble play—the boisterous body contact that young males of some mammalian species display. For example, Michael J. Meaney of McGill University finds that dihydrotestosterone, working through a structure called the amygdala rather than through the hypothalamus, gives rise to the play-fighting behavior of juvenile male rodents.

Male and female rats have also been found to solve problems differently. Christina L. Williams of Barnard College has shown that female rats have a greater tendency to use landmarks in spatial learning tasks—as it appears women do. In Williams's experiment, female rats used landmark cues, such as pictures on the wall, in preference to geometric cues, such as angles and the shape of the room. If no landmarks were available, however, females used geometric cues. In contrast, males did not use landmarks at all, preferring geometric cues almost exclusively.

Interestingly, hormonal manipulation during the critical period can alter these behaviors. Depriving newborn males of testosterone by castrating them or administering estrogen to newborn females results in a complete reversal of sex-typed behaviors in the adult animals. (As mentioned above, estrogen can have a masculinizing effect during brain development.) Treated females behave like males, and treated males behave like females.

Natural selection for reproductive advantage could account for the evolution of such navigational differences. Steven J. C. Gaulin and Randall W. FitzGerald of the University of Pittsburgh have suggested that in species of voles in which a male mates with several females rather than with just one, the range he must traverse is greater. Therefore, navigational ability seems critical to reproductive success. Indeed, Gaulin and FitzGerald found sex differences in laboratory maze learning only in voles that were polygynous, such as the meadow vole, not in monogamous species, such as the prairie vole.

Again, behavioral differences may parallel structural ones. Lucia F. Jacobs in Gaulin's laboratory has discovered that the hippocampus—a region thought to be involved in spatial learning in both birds and mammals—is larger in male polygynous voles than in females. At present, there are no data on possible sex differences in hippocampal size in human subjects.

Evidence of the influence of sex hormones on adult behavior is less direct in humans than in other animals. Researchers are instead guided by what may be parallels in other species and by spontaneously occurring exceptions to the norm in humans.

One of the most compelling areas of evidence comes from studies of girls exposed to excess androgens in the prenatal or neonatal stage. The production of abnormally large quantities of adrenal androgens can occur because of a genetic defect called congenital adrenal hyperplasia (CAH). Before the 1970s, a similar condition also unexpectedly appeared when pregnant women took various synthetic steroids. Although the consequent masculinization of the genitals can be corrected early in life and drug therapy can stop the overproduction of androgens, effects of prenatal exposure on the brain cannot be reversed.

Studies by researchers such as Anke A. Ehrhardt of Columbia University and June M. Reinisch of the Kinsey Institute have found that girls with excess exposure to androgens grow up to be more tomboyish and aggressive than their unaffected sisters. This conclusion was based sometimes on interviews with subjects and mothers, on teachers' ratings and on questionnaires administered to the girls themselves. When ratings are used in such studies, it can be difficult to rule out the influence of expectation either on the part of an adult who knows the girls' history or on the part of the girls themselves.

Therefore, the objective observations of Berenbaum are important and convincing. She and Melissa Hines of the University of California at Los Angeles observed the play behavior of CAH-affected girls and compared it with that of their male and female siblings. Given a choice of transportation and construction toys, dolls and kitchen supplies or books and board games, the CAH girls preferred the more typically masculine toys—for example, they played with cars for the same amount of time that normal boys did. Both the CAH girls and the boys differed from unaffected girls in their patterns of choice. Because there is every reason to think that parents would be at least as likely to encourage feminine preferences in their CAH daughters as in their unaffected daughters, these findings suggest that the toy preferences were actually altered in some way by the early hormonal environment.

Spatial abilities that are typically better in males are also enhanced in CAH girls. Susan M. Resnick, now at the National Institute on Aging, and Berenbaum and their colleagues reported that affected girls were superior to their unaffected sisters in a spatial manipulation test, two spatial rotation tests and a disembedding test—that is, the discovery of a simple figure hidden within a more complex one. All these tasks are usually done better by males. No differences existed between the two groups on other perceptual or verbal tasks or on a reasoning task.

* * *

Studies such as these suggest that the higher the androgen levels, the better the spatial performance. But this does not seem to be the case. In 1983 Valerie J. Shute, when at the University of California at Santa Barbara, suggested that the relation between levels of androgens and some spatial capabilities might be nonlinear. In other words, spatial ability might not increase as the amount of androgen increases. Shute measured androgens in blood taken from male and female students and divided each into high- and low-androgen groups. All fell within the normal range for each sex (androgens are present in females but in very low levels). She found that in women, the high-androgen subjects were better at the spatial tests. In men the reverse was true: low-androgen men performed better.

Catherine Couchie and I recently conducted a study along similar lines by measuring testosterone in saliva. We added tests for two other kinds of abilities: mathematical reasoning and perceptual speed. Our results on the spatial tests were very similar to Shute's: low-testosterone men were superior to high-testosterone men, but high-testosterone women surpassed low-testosterone women. Such findings suggest some optimum level of androgen for maximal spatial ability. This level may fall in the low male range.

No correlation was found between testosterone levels and performance on perceptual speed tests. On mathematical reasoning, however, the results were similar to those of spatial ability tests for men: low-androgen men tested higher, but there was no obvious relation in women.

Such findings are consistent with the suggestion by Camilla P. Benbow of Iowa State University that high mathematical ability has a significant biological determinant. Benbow and her colleagues have reported consistent sex differences in mathematical reasoning ability favoring males. These differences are especially sharp at the upper end of the distribution, where males outnumber females 13 to one. Benbow argues that these differences are not readily explained by socialization.

It is important to keep in mind that the relation between natural hormonal levels and problem solving is based on correlational data. Some form of connection between the two measures exists, but how this association is determined or what its causal basis may be is unknown. Little is currently understood about the relation between adult levels of hormones and those in early life, when abilities appear to be organized in the nervous system. We have a lot to learn about the precise mechanisms underlying cognitive patterns in people.

Another approach to probing differences between male and female brains is to examine and compare the functions of particular brain systems. One noninvasive way to accomplish this goal is to study people who have experienced damage to a specific brain region. Such studies indicate that the left half of the brain in most people is critical for speech, the right for certain perceptual and spatial functions.

It is widely assumed by many researchers studying sex differences that the two hemispheres are more asymmetrically organized for speech and spatial functions in men than in women. This idea comes from several sources. Parts of the corpus callosum, a major neural system connecting the two hemispheres, may be more extensive in women; perceptual techniques that probe brain asymmetry in normal-functioning people sometimes show smaller asymmetries in women than in men, and damage to one brain hemisphere sometimes has a lesser effect in women than the comparable injury has in men.

In 1982 Marie-Christine de Lacoste, now at the Yale University School of Medicine, and Ralph L. Holloway of Columbia University reported that the back part of the corpus callosum, an area called the splenium, was larger in women than in men. This finding has subsequently been both refuted and confirmed. Variations in the shape of the corpus callosum that may occur as an individual ages as well as different methods of measurement may produce some of the disagreements. Most recently,

Allen and Gorski found the same sex-related size difference in the splenium.

The interest in the corpus callosum arises from the assumption that its size may indicate the number of fibers connecting the two hemispheres. If more connecting fibers existed in one sex, the implication would be that in that sex the hemispheres communicate more fully. Although sex hormones can alter callosal size in rats, as Victor H. Denenberg and his associates at the University of Connecticut have demonstrated, it is unclear whether the actual number of fibers differs between the sexes. Moreover, sex differences in cognitive function have yet to be related to a difference in callosal size. New ways of imaging the brain in living humans will undoubtedly increase knowledge in this respect.

The view that a male brain is functionally more asymmetric than a female brain is long-standing. Albert M. Galaburda of Beth Israel Hospital in Boston and the late Norman Geschwind of Harvard Medical School proposed that androgens increased the functional potency of the right hemisphere. In 1981 Marian C. Diamond of the University of California at Berkeley found that the right cortex is thicker than the left in male rats but not in females. Jane Stewart of Concordia University in Montreal, working with Bryan E. Kolb of the University of Lethbridge in Alberta, recently pinpointed early hormonal influences on this asymmetry: androgens appear to suppress left cortex growth.

Last year de Lacoste and her colleagues reported a similar pattern in human fetuses. They found the right cortex was thicker than the left in males. Thus, there appear to be some anatomic reasons for believing that the two hemispheres might not be equally asymmetric in men and women.

Despite this expectation, the evidence in favor of it is meager and conflicting, which suggests that the most striking sex differences in brain organization may not be related to asymmetry. For example, if overall differences between men and women in spatial ability were related to differing right hemispheric dependence for such functions, then damage to the right hemisphere would perhaps have a more devastating effect on spatial performance in men.

My laboratory has recently studied the ability of patients with damage to one hemisphere of the brain to rotate certain objects mentally. In one test, a series of line drawings of either a left or a right gloved hand is presented in various orientations. The patient indicates the hand being depicted by simply pointing to one of two stuffed gloves that are constantly present.

The second test uses two three-dimensional blocklike figures that are mirror images of one another. Both figures are present throughout the test. The patient is given a series of photographs of these objects in various orientations, and he or she must place each picture in front of the object it depicts (These nonverbal procedures are employed so that patients with speech disorders can be tested.)

As expected, damage to the right hemisphere resulted in lower scores for both sexes on these tests than did damage to the left hemisphere. Also as anticipated, women did less well than men on the block spatial rotation test. Surprisingly, however, damage to the right hemisphere had no greater effect in men than in women. Women were at least as affected as men by damage to the right hemisphere. This result suggests that the normal differences between men and women on such rotational tests are not the result of differential dependence on the right hemisphere. Some other brain systems must be mediating the higher performance by men.

Parallel suggestions of greater asymmetry in men regarding speech have rested on the fact that the incidence of aphasias, or speech disorders, are higher in men than in women after damage to the left hemisphere. Therefore, some researchers have found it reasonable to conclude that speech must be more bilaterally organized in women. There is, however, a problem with this conclusion. During my 20 years of experience with patients, aphasia has not been disproportionately present in women with right hemispheric damage.

* * *

In searching for an explanation, I discovered another striking difference between men and women in brain organization for speech and related motor function. Women are more likely than men to suffer aphasia when the front part of the brain is damaged. Because restricted damage within a hemisphere more frequently affects the posterior than the anterior area in both men and women, this differential dependence may explain why women incur aphasia less often than do men. Speech functions are thus less likely to be affected in women not because speech is more bilaterally organized in women but because the critical area is less often affected.

A similar pattern emerges in studies of the control of hand movements, which are programmed by the left hemisphere. Apraxia, or difficulty in selecting appropriate hand movements, is very common after left hemispheric damage. It is also strongly associated with difficulty in organizing speech. In fact, the critical functions that depend on the left hemisphere may relate not to language per se but to organization of the complex oral and manual movements on which human communication systems depend. Studies of patients with left hemispheric damage have revealed that such motor selection relies on anterior systems in women but on posterior systems in men.

The synaptic proximity of women's anterior motor selection system (or "praxis system") to the motor cortex directly behind it may enhance fine-motor skills. In contrast, men's motor skills appear to emphasize targeting or directing movements toward external space—some distance away from the self. There may be advantages to such motor skills when they are closely meshed with visual input to the brain, which lies in the posterior region.

Women's dependence on the anterior region is detectable even when tests involve using visual guidance—for instance, when subjects must build patterns with blocks by following a visual model. In studying such a complex task, it is possible to compare the effects of damage to the anterior and posterior regions of both hemispheres because performance is affected by damage to either hemisphere. Again, women prove more affected by damage to the anterior region of the right hemisphere than by posterior damage. Men tend to display the reverse pattern.

Although I have not found evidence of sex differences in functional brain asymmetry with regard to basic speech, motor selection or spatial rotation ability, I have found slight differences in more abstract verbal tasks. Scores on a vocabulary test, for instance, were affected by

damage to either hemisphere in women, but such scores were affected only by left-sided injury in men. This finding suggests that in reviewing the meanings of words, women use the hemispheres more equally than do men.

In contrast, the incidence of non-right-handedness, which is presumably related to lesser left hemispheric dependence, is higher in men than in women. Even among the right-handers, Marion Annett, now at the University of Leicester in the U.K., has reported that women are more right-handed than men—that is, they favor their right hand even more than do right-handed men. It may well be, then, that sex differences in asymmetry vary with the particular function being studied and that it is not always the same sex that is more asymmetric.

Taken altogether, the evidence suggests that men's and women's brains are organized along different lines from very early in life. During development, sex hormones direct such differentiation. Similar mechanisms probably operate to produce variation within sexes, since there is a relation between levels of certain hormones and cognitive makeup in adulthood.

*   *   *

One of the most intriguing findings is that cognitive patterns may remain sensitive to hormonal fluctuations throughout life. Elizabeth Hampson of the University of Western Ontario showed that the performance of women on certain tasks changed throughout the menstrual cycle as levels of estrogen went up or down. High levels of the hormone were associated not only with relatively depressed spatial ability but also with enhanced articulatory and motor capability.

In addition, I have observed seasonal fluctuations in spatial ability in men. Their performance is improved in the spring when testosterone levels are lower. Whether these intellectual fluctuations are of any adaptive significance or merely represent ripples on a stable baseline remains to be determined.

To understand human intellectual functions, including how groups may differ in such functions, we need to look beyond the demands of modern life. We did not undergo natural selection for reading or for operating computers. It seems clear that the sex differences in cognitive patterns arose because they proved evolutionarily advantageous. And their adaptive significance probably rests in the distant past. The organization of the human brain was determined over many generations by natural selection. As studies of fossil skulls have shown, our brains are essentially like those of our ancestors of 50,000 or more years ago.

For the thousands of years during which our brain characteristics evolved, humans lived in relatively small groups of hunter-gatherers. The division of labor between the sexes in such a society probably was quite marked, as it is in existing hunter-gatherer societies. Men were responsible for hunting large game, which often required long-distance travel. They were also responsible for defending the group against predators and enemies and for the shaping and use of weapons. Women most probably gathered food near the camp, tended the home, prepared food and clothing and cared for children.

Such specializations would put different selection pressures on men and women. Men would require long-distance route-finding ability so they could recognize a geographic array from varying orientations. They would also need targeting skills. Women would require short-range navigation, perhaps using landmarks, fine-motor capabilities carried on within a circumscribed space, and perceptual discrimination sensitive to small changes in the environment or in children's appearance or behavior.

The finding of consistent and, in some cases, quite substantial sex differences suggests that men and women may have different occupational interests and capabilities, independent of societal influences. I would not expect, for example, that men and women would necessarily be equally represented in activities or professions that emphasize spatial or math skills, such as engineering or physics. But I might expect more women in medical diagnostic fields where perceptual skills are important. So that even though any one individual might have the capacity to be in a "nontypical" field, the sex proportions as a whole may vary.

NO

Carol Tavris

MEASURING UP

BRAIN: DISSECTING THE DIFFERENCES

In recent years the sexiest body part, far and away, has become the brain. Magazines with cover stories on the brain fly off the newsstands, and countless seminars, tapes, books, and classes teach people how to use "all" of their brains. New technologies, such as PET scans, produce gorgeous photographs of the brain at work and play. Weekly we hear new discoveries about this miraculous organ, and it seems that scientists will soon be able to pinpoint the very neuron, the very neurotransmitter, responsible for joy, sadness, rage, and suffering. At last we will know the reasons for all the differences between women and men that fascinate and infuriate, such as why men won't stop to ask directions and why women won't stop asking men what they are feeling.

In all this excitement, it seems curmudgeonly to sound words of caution, but the history of brain research does not exactly reveal a noble and impartial quest for truth, particularly on sensitive matters such as sex and race differences. Typically, when scientists haven't found the differences they were seeking, they haven't abandoned the goal or their belief that such differences exist; they just moved to another part of the anatomy or a different corner of the brain.

A century ago, for example, scientists tried to prove that women had smaller brains than men did, which accounted for women's alleged intellectual failings and emotional weaknesses. Dozens of studies purported to show that men had larger brains, making them smarter than women. When scientists realized that men's greater height and weight offset their brain-size advantage, however, they dropped this line of research like a shot. The scientists next tried to argue that women had smaller frontal lobes and larger parietal lobes than men did, another brain pattern thought to account for women's intellectual inferiority. Then it was reported that the parietal lobes might be associated with intellect. Panic in the labs—until anatomists suddenly found that women's parietal lobes were *smaller* than they had originally believed. Wherever they looked, scientists conveniently found evidence of

From Carol Tavris, *The Mismeasure of Woman* (Simon & Schuster, 1992). Copyright © 1992 by Carol Tavris. Reprinted by permission of Simon & Schuster, Inc. Notes omitted.

female inferiority, as Gustave Le Bon, a Parisian, wrote in 1879:

> In the most intelligent races, as among the Parisians, there are a large number of women whose brains are closer in size to those of gorillas than to the most developed male brains. This inferiority is so obvious that no one can contest it for a moment; only its degree is worth discussion.

We look back with amusement at the obvious biases of research a century ago, research designed to prove the obvious inferiority of women and minorities (and non-Parisians). Today, many researchers are splitting brains instead of weighing them, but they are no less determined to find sex differences. Nevertheless, skeptical neuroscientists are showing that biases and values are just as embedded in current research—old prejudices in new technologies.

The brain, like a walnut, consists of two hemispheres of equal size, connected by a bundle of fibers called the corpus callosum. The left hemisphere has been associated with verbal and reasoning ability, whereas the right hemisphere is associated with spatial reasoning and artistic ability. Yet by the time these findings reached the public, they had been vastly oversimplified and diluted. Even the great neuroscientist Roger Sperry, the grandfather of hemispheric research, felt obliged to warn that the "left-right dichotomy ... is an idea with which it is very easy to run wild." And many people have run wild with it: Stores are filled with manuals, cassettes, and handbooks that promise to help people become fluent in "whole-brain thinking," to beef up the unused part of their right brain, and to learn to use the intuitive right brain for business, painting, and inventing.

The fact that the brain consists of two hemispheres, each characterized by different specialties, provides a neat analogy to the fact that human beings consist of two genders, each characterized by different specialties. The analogy is so tempting that scientists keep trying to show that it is grounded in physical reality. Modern theories of gender and the brain are based on the idea that the left and right hemispheres develop differently in boys and girls, as does the corpus callosum that links the halves of the brain.

According to one major theory, the male brain is more "lateralized," that is, its hemispheres are specialized in their abilities, whereas females use both hemispheres more symmetrically because their corpus callosum is allegedly larger and contains more fibers. Two eminent scientists, Norman Geschwind and Peter Behan, maintained that this sex difference begins in the womb, when the male fetus begins to secrete testosterone —the hormone that will further its physical development as a male. Geschwind and Behan argued that testosterone in male fetuses washes over the brain, selectively attacking parts of the left hemisphere, briefly slowing its development, and producing right-hemisphere dominance in men. Geschwind speculated that the effects of testosterone on the prenatal brain produce "superior right hemisphere talents, such as artistic, musical, or mathematical talent."

Right-hemisphere dominance is also thought to explain men's excellence in some tests of "visual-spatial ability"— the ability to imagine objects in three-dimensional space (the skill you need for mastering geometry, concocting football formations, and reading maps). This is apparently the reason that some men won't stop and ask directions when they are lost; they prefer to rely on their right brains, whereas women prefer to rely on a local informant. It is also supposed to be the reason that men can't talk about their feelings and would rather watch television or wax the car. Women have interconnected hemispheres, which explains why they excel in talk, feelings, intuition, and quick judgments. Geschwind and Behan's theory had tremendous scientific appeal, and it is cited frequently in research papers and textbooks. *Science* hailed it with the headline "Math Genius May Have Hormonal Basis."

The theory also has had enormous popular appeal. It fits snugly, for example, with the Christian fundamentalist belief that men and women are innately different and thus innately designed for different roles. For his radio show "Focus on the Family," James Dobson interviewed Donald Joy, a professor of "human development in Christian education" at Asbury Theological Seminary, who explained Geschwind and Behan's theory this way:

> JOY: ... this marvelous female brain, is a brain that's not damaged during fetal development as the male brain is, but the damage gives a specialization to the male brain which we don't get in the female.
>
> DOBSON: I want to pick up on that concept of us brain-damaged males. [laughter, chuckling]
>
> JOY: ... It's giving a chemical bath to the left hemisphere and this connecting link between the two hemispheres that reduced the size and number of transmission passages that exist here ... So males simply can't talk to themselves across the hemispheres in a way that a woman does.

> DOBSON: So some of the sex differences that we see in personality can be tracked back to that moment.
>
> JOY: Oh, absolutely. And when we're talking about this now, we're talking about a glorious phenomenon because these are intrinsic sex differences ... this is glorious because we are fearfully and wonderfully differentiated from each other.
>
> DOBSON: Let's look at 'em, name 'em.
>
> JOY: We're, we're mutually interdependent. Every household needs both a male brain and a female brain, for example. The woman's brain works much like a computer ... lateral transmission in her brain allows her to consult all of her past experience and give you an instant response. She can make a judgment more quickly than a male can.... [but how she arrives at it is] hidden even from her, because it is like a computer, all it gives is the answer, it doesn't give you the process.

The male brain, Joy added, is more like an "adding machine," in which facts are totaled and a logical solution presents itself. So males are good at logical reasoning, and females at intuitive judgments, because of the prenatal "chemical bath" that affects the male brain....

Now it may be true that men and women, on the average, differ in the physiology of their brains. It may even be true that this difference explains why James Dobson's wife Shirley can sum up a person's character right away, while he, with his slower, adding-machine brain, takes weeks or months to come to the same impressions. But given the disgraceful history of bias and sloppy research designed more to confirm prejudices than to enlighten humanity, I think we would all do well to be suspicious and to evaluate the evidence for these assertions closely.

This is difficult for those of us who are not expert in physiology, neuroanatomy, or medicine. We are easily dazzled by words like "lateralization" and "corpus callosum." Besides, physiology seems so *solid*; if one study finds a difference between three male brains and three female brains, that must apply to all men and women. How do I know what my corpus callosum looks like? Is it bigger than a man's? Should I care?

For some answers, I turned to researchers in biology and neuroscience who have critically examined the research and the assumptions underlying theories of sex differences in the brain. The first discovery of note was that, just like the nineteenth-century researchers who kept changing their minds about which *lobe* of the brain accounted for male superiority, twentieth-century researchers keep changing their minds about which *hemisphere* of the brain accounts for male superiority. Originally, the left hemisphere was considered the repository of intellect and reason. The right hemisphere was the sick, bad, crazy side, the side of passion, instincts, criminality, and irrationality. Guess which sex was thought to have left-brain intellectual superiority? (Answer: males.) In the 1960s and 1970s, however, the right brain was resuscitated and brought into the limelight. Scientists began to suspect that it was the source of genius and inspiration, creativity and imagination, mysticism and mathematical brilliance. Guess which sex was now thought to have right-brain specialization? (Answer: males.)

It's all very confusing. Today we hear arguments that men have greater left-brain specialization (which explains their intellectual advantage) *and* that they have greater right-brain specialization (which explains their mathematical and artistic

advantage). *Newsweek* recently asserted as fact, for instance, that "Women's language and other skills are more evenly divided between left and right hemisphere; in men, such functions are concentrated in the left brain." But [in their book *The Language of Love*, Christian fundamentalists Gary Smalley and John Trent] asserted that

> most women spend the majority of their days and nights camped out on the right side of the brain [which] harbors the center for feelings, as well as the primary relational, language, and communication skills... and makes an afternoon devoted to art and fine music actually enjoyable.

You can hear the chuckling from men who regard art museums and concert halls as something akin to medieval torture chambers, but I'm sure that the many men who enjoy art and fine music, indeed who create art and fine music, would not find that last remark so funny. Geschwind and Behan, of course, had argued that male specialization of the right hemisphere explained why men *excel* in art and fine music. But since Smalley and Trent apparently do not share these prissy female interests, they relegate them to women—to women's brains.

The two hemispheres of the brain do have different specialties, but it is far too simple-minded (so to speak) to assume that human abilities clump up in opposing bunches. Most brain researchers today believe that the two hemispheres complement one another, to the extent that one side can sometimes take over the functions of a side that has been damaged. Moreover, specific skills often involve components from both hemispheres: one side has the ability to tell a joke, and the other has the ability to laugh at one. Math abilities include both visual-spatial skills and reasoning skills. The right hemisphere is involved in creating art, but the left hemisphere is involved in appreciating and analyzing art. As neuropsychologist Jerre Levy once said, "Could the eons of human evolution have left half of the brain witless? Could a bird whose existence is dependent on flying have evolved only a single wing?"

These qualifications about the interdependence of brain hemispheres have not, however, deterred those who believe that there are basic psychological differences between the sexes that can be accounted for in the brain. So let's consider their argument more closely.

The neuroscientist Ruth Bleier ... carefully examined Geschwind and Behan's data, going back to many of their original references. In one such study of 507 fetal brains of 10 to 44 weeks gestation, the researchers had actually stated that they found *no significant sex differences* in these brains. If testosterone had an effect on the developing brain, it would surely have been apparent in this large sample. Yet Geschwind and Behan cited this study for other purposes and utterly ignored its findings of no sex differences.

Instead, Geschwind and Behan cited as evidence for their hypothesis a study of *rats'* brains. The authors of the rat study reported that in male rats, two areas of the cortex that are believed to be involved in processing visual information were 3 percent thicker on the right side than on the left. In one of the better examples of academic gobbledygook yet to reach the printed page, the researchers interpreted their findings to mean that "in the male rat it is necessary to have greater spatial orientation to interact with a female rat during estrus and to integrate that input

into a meaningful output." Translation: When having sex with a female, the male needs to be able to look around in case a dangerous predator, such as her husband, walks in on them.

Bleier found more holes in this argument than in a screen door. No one knows, she said, what the slightly greater thickness in the male rat's cortex means for the rat, let alone what it means for human beings. There is at present no evidence that spatial orientation is related to asymmetry of the cortex, or that female rats have a lesser or deficient ability in this regard. And although Geschwind and Behan unabashedly used their limited findings to account for male "superiority" in math and art, they did not specifically study the incidence of genius, talent, or even modest giftedness in their sample, nor did they demonstrate a difference between the brains of geniuses and the brains of average people.

Bleier wrote to *Science*, offering a scholarly paper detailing these criticisms. *Science* did not publish it, on the grounds, as one reviewer put it, that Bleier "tends to err in the opposite direction from the researchers whose results and conclusions she criticizes" and because "she argues very strongly for the predominant role of environmental influences." Apparently, said Bleier, one is allowed to err in only one direction if one wants to be published in *Science*. The journal did not even publish her critical Letter to the Editor.

At about the same time, however, *Science* saw fit to publish a study by two researchers who claimed to have found solid evidence of gender differences in the splenium (posterior end) of the corpus callosum. In particular, they said, the splenium was larger and more bulbous in the five female brains than in the nine male brains they examined, which had been obtained at autopsy. The researchers speculated that "the female brain is less well lateralized—that is, manifests less hemispheric specialization—than the male brain for visuospatial functions." Notice the language: The female brain is *less specialized* than, and by implication inferior to, the male brain. They did not say, as they might have, that the female brain was *more integrated* than the male's. The male brain is the norm, and specialization, in the brain as in academia, is considered a good thing. Generalists in any business are out of favor these days.

This article, which also met professional acclaim, had a number of major flaws that, had they been part of any other research paper, would have been fatal to its publication. The study was based on a small sample of only fourteen brains. The researchers did not describe their methods of selecting the brains in that sample, so it is possible that some of the brains were diseased or otherwise abnormal. The article contained numerous unsupported assumptions and leaps of faith. For example, there is at present absolutely no evidence that the number of fibers in the corpus callosum is even related to hemispheric specialization. Indeed, no one knows what role, if any, the callosum plays in determining a person's mental abilities. Most damaging of all, the sex differences that the researchers claimed to have found in the size of the corpus callosum were not statistically significant, according to the scientific conventions for accepting an article for publication.

Bleier again wrote to *Science*, delineating these criticisms and also citing four subsequent studies, by her and by others, that independently failed to find gender differences of any kind in the corpus callosum. *Science* failed to publish this criticism, as it has failed to publish all studies that find no gender differences in the brain.

Ultimately, the most damning blow to all of these brain-hemisphere theories is that the formerly significant sex differences that brain theories are attempting to account for—in verbal, spatial, and math abilities—are fading rapidly. Let's start with the famed female superiority in verbal ability. Janet Hyde, a professor of psychology at the University of Wisconsin, and her colleague Marcia Linn reviewed 165 studies of verbal ability (including skills in vocabulary, writing, anagrams, and reading comprehension), which represented tests of 1,418,899 people. Hyde and Linn reported that at present in America, there simply are no gender differences in these verbal skills. They noted: "Thus our research pulls out one of the two wobbly legs on which the brain lateralization theories have rested."

Hyde recently went on to kick the other leg, the assumption of overall male superiority in mathematics and spatial ability. No one disputes that males do surpass females at the highly gifted end of the math spectrum. But when Hyde and her colleagues analyzed 100 studies of mathematics performance, representing the testing of 3,985,682 students, they found that gender differences were smallest and favored *females* in samples of the general population, and grew larger, favoring males, only in selected samples of precocious individuals.

What about spatial abilities, another area thought to reveal a continuing male superiority? When psychologists put the dozens of existing studies on spatial ability into a giant hopper and looked at the overall results, this was what they reported: Many studies show no sex differences. Of the studies that do report sex differences, the magnitude of the difference is often small. And finally, there is greater variation *within* each sex than *between* them. As one psychologist who reviewed these studies summarized: "The observed differences are very small, the overlap [between men and women] large, and abundant biological theories are supported with very slender or no evidence."

Sometimes scientists and science writers put themselves through contortions in order to reconcile the slim evidence with their belief in sex differences in the brain. The authors of a popular textbook on sexuality, published in 1990, acknowledge that "sex differences in cognitive skills have declined significantly in recent years." Then they add: "Notwithstanding this finding, theories continue to debate why these differences exist." Pardon? Notwithstanding the fact that there are few differences of any magnitude, let's discuss why there are differences? Even more mysteriously, they conclude: "If Geschwind's theory is ultimately supported by further research, we will have hard evidence of a biological basis for alleged sex differences in verbal and spatial skills." "Hard evidence" for *alleged* sex differences—the ones that don't exist!

It is sobering to read, over and over and over again in scholarly papers, the conclusions of eminent scientists who have cautioned their colleagues against generalizing about sex differences from poor data. One leader in brain-hemisphere research, Marcel Kinsbourne, observing that the evidence for sex differences "fails to convince on logical, methodological, and empirical grounds," then asked:

Why then do reputable investigators persist in ignoring [this evidence]? Because the study of sex differences is not like the rest of psychology. Under pressure from the gathering momentum of feminism, and perhaps in backlash to it, many investigators seem determined to discover that men and women "really" are different. It seems that if sex differences (e.g., in lateralization) do not exist, then they have to be invented.

These warnings have, for the most part, gone unheeded. Poor research continues to be published in reputable journals, and from there it is disseminated to the public. Many scientists and science writers continue to rely on weak data to support their speculations, like using pebbles as foundation for a castle. Because these speculations fit the dominant beliefs about gender, however, they receive far more attention and credibility than they warrant. Worse, the far better evidence that fails to conform to the dominant beliefs about gender is overlooked, disparaged, or, as in Bleier's experience, remains unpublished.

As a result, ideas enter the common vocabulary as proven facts when they should be encumbered with "maybes," "sometimes," and "we-don't-know-yets." Scientist Hugh Fairweather, reviewing the history of sex differences research in cognition, concluded: "What had before been a possibility at best slenderly evidenced, was widely taken for a fact; and 'fact' hardened into a 'biological' dogma."

Now, it is possible that reliable sex differences in the brain will eventually be discovered. Will it then be all right for Dobson to go on the air to celebrate how delightfully but innately different men and women are? Should we then all make sure we have a male brain and a female brain in every household? Should we then worry about the abnormality of households like mine, in which the male is better at intuitive judgments and the female has the adding-machine mentality?

The answers are no, for three reasons. First, theories of sex differences in the brain cannot account for the complexities of people's everyday behavior. They cannot explain, for instance, why, if women are better than men in verbal ability, so few women are auctioneers or diplomats, or why, if women have the advantage in making rapid judgments, so few women are air-traffic controllers or umpires. Nor can brain theories explain why abilities and ambitions change when people are given opportunities previously denied to them. Two decades ago, theorists postulated biological limitations that were keeping women out of men's work like medicine and bartending. When the external barriers to these professions fell, the speed with which women entered them was dizzying. Did everybody's brain change? Today we would be amused to think that women have a brain-lateralization deficiency that is keeping them out of law school. But we continue to hear about the biological reasons that keep women out of science, math, and politics. For sex differences in cognitive abilities to wax and wane so rapidly, they must be largely a result of education, motivation, and opportunity, not of innate differences between male and female brains.

Second, the meanings of terms like "verbal ability" and "spatial reasoning" keep changing too, depending on who is using them and for what purpose. For example, when conservatives like Dobson speak of women's verbal abilities, they usually mean women's interest in and willingness to talk about relationships and feelings. But in studies of total talking time in the workplace, men far exceed women in the talk department. In everyday life, men interrupt women more than vice versa, dominate the conversation, and are more successful at introducing new topics and having their comments remembered in group discussions. What does this mean for judgments of which sex has the better "verbal ability"?

Third, the major key problem with biological theories of sex differences is that they deflect attention from the far more substantial evidence for sex similarity. The finding that men and women are more alike in their abilities and brains than different almost never makes the news. Researchers and the public commit the error of focusing on the small differences—usually of the magnitude of a few percentage points—rather than on the fact that the majority of women and men overlap. For example, this is what the author of a scientific paper that has been widely quoted as *supporting* sex differences in brain hemispheres actually concluded:

> Thus, one must not overlook perhaps the most obvious conclusion, which is that basic patterns of male and female brain asymmetry seem to be more similar than they are different.

Everyone, nevertheless, promptly overlooked it.

The habit of seeing women and men as two opposite categories also leads us to avoid the practical question: How much ability does it take to do well in a particular career? When people hear that men are better than women in spatial ability, many are quick to conclude that perhaps women, with their deficient brains, should not try to become architects or engineers. This reaction is not merely unfortunate; it is cruel to the women who *do* excel in architectural or engineering ability. The fields of math and science are losing countless capable women because girls keep hearing that women aren't as good as men in these fields.

None of this means that biology is irrelevant to human behavior. But whenever the news trumpets some version of "biology affects behavior," it obscures the fact that biology and behavior form a two-way street. Hormones affect sexual drive, for instance, but sexual activity affects hormone levels. An active brain seeks a stimulating environment, but living in a stimulating environment literally changes and enriches the brain. Fatigue and boredom cause poor performance on the job, but stultifying job conditions produce fatigue and boredom. Scientists and writers who reduce our personalities, problems, and abilities to biology thereby tell only half the story, and miss half the miracle of how human biology works.

Ruth Bleier, ... a neuroscientist, put the whole matter in perspective this way:

> Such efforts directed at the callosum (or any other particular structure in the brain, for that matter) are today's equivalent of 19th-century craniology: if you can find a bigger bump here or a smaller one there on a person's skull, if you can find a more bulbous splenium here or a more slender one there ... you will know something significant about their intelligence, their personality, their aspirations, their astrological sign, their gender and race, and their status in society. We are still mired in the naive hope that we can find something that we can *see* and *measure* and it will explain everything. It is silly science and it serves us badly.

POSTSCRIPT

Are Gender Differences Rooted in the Brain?

Kimura believes that there is substantial evidence to show that early exposure to sex hormones has permanent effects on brain functioning. She maintains that men perform better than women on spatial tasks and mathematical reasoning tests and that women perform better than men in perceptual speed and verbal fluency. She thinks that these differences are so great that they cannot be explained by socialization; they must be genetic and based on the way the brain is organized.

Tavris states that even though scientists have found no differences in the brains of men and women, they still continue to look. She cites studies that have examined hundreds of brains and found no differences based on gender. Tavris continues to refute the theory by reporting that studies do not show gender differences in verbal abilities and that females have better mathematical skills than males when they are compared to the general population. Tavris illustrates how biology and behavior form a two-way street. The brain seeks a stimulating environment, but living in a stimulating environment changes and enriches the brain.

It seems prudent to examine how nature and nurture interact to impact children. How does heredity combine with family environment and learning opportunities to affect a child's intellectual ability? If we find the answer to the nature versus nurture controversy, what do we do with it? Do adoption and twin studies provide adequate answers to the controversy?

In the spring of 1995, researchers at Yale University School of Medicine captured widespread attention when they released the results of a study that found the first definitive evidence that men and women *use* their brains differently (Shaywitz, S. E., & Shaywitz, B. A. [1995, February 16]. Sex differences in the functional organization of the brain for language. *Nature, 373,* 607–609). This study has added more fuel to the debate over sex differences in the brain.

SUGGESTED READINGS

Emde, R. (1992). Temperament, emotion, and cognition at fourteen months: The MacArthur longitudinal twin study. *Child Development, 63,* 1437–1455.

Plomin, R., Reiss, D., Hetherington, E. M., & Howe, G. (1994). Nature and nurture: Genetic contributions to measures of the family environment. *Developmental Psychology, 30,* 32–43.

Seligman, M. E. P. (1994, May/June) What you can change . . . what you cannot. *Psychology Today, 27,* 34–41, 70–74, 84.

PART 2

Early Childhood

The period of early childhood is sometimes referred to as the preschool years. It generally encompasses age two or three through age four or five. This is a time when children become much more adept at taking part in physical activities, satisfying curiosities, and learning from experience. Preschoolers play more frequently with other children, become increasingly skilled in daily tasks, and are much more reactive to people and things in their environment. Many children begin school during their preschool years, an experience that gives them their first extended contacts with a social institution other than the family. In this section we examine issues about discipline, family size, divorce, and the mass media—all of which have implications for child development during preschool years.

- Does Spanking Lead to Child Abuse and Later Violence?

- Are Only Children Less Independent Than Firstborn Children?

- Is Divorce Always Bad for Children?

- Is Television Viewing Harmful for Children?

- Should Formal Schooling Begin at an Earlier Age?

ISSUE 5

Does Spanking Lead to Child Abuse and Later Violence?

YES: Murray A. Straus, from "Discipline and Deviance: Physical Punishment of Children and Violence and Other Crime in Adulthood," *Social Problems* (May 1991)

NO: Joan McCord, from "Questioning the Value of Punishment," *Social Problems* (May 1991)

ISSUE SUMMARY

YES: Murray Straus, a social science researcher, finds a relationship between the physical punishment children experience when they are young and the violent acts they themselves commit during their teenage and adult years.

NO: Joan McCord, a professor of criminal justice, concludes that children who are rejected, neglected, and emotionally abused, not only physically abused, become violent. It is not the physical punishment that leads to later violence but the use of rewards and punishment that is problematic.

Were you spanked when you were a child? If so, what was used to spank you? Hand? Hairbrush? Ruler? Switch? Do you think the spankings affected you? Parents often use any of a number of reasons to support the ritual of spanking. They may say things such as, "Spare the rod and spoil the child." Or "I was spanked and I turned out OK." "Spankings teach children how to act." "Kids need spankings to show them who's the boss." Do any of these sound familiar to you?

James Dobson, a pediatrics professor and the author of *Dare to Discipline* (1982, Bantam Books), promotes the value of spanking as part of a parenting guidance plan that includes affection and explanation as well. On the other hand, child development professionals Lee Salk, T. Berry Brazelton, and Penelope Leach all agree that spanking is not appropriate for children, and they believe that it has too many long-term consequences to justify the short-term goal of getting children to behave.

A public opinion poll commissioned by the National Committee for the Prevention of Child Abuse in 1994 asked parents how they disciplined their children in the previous year. Denying privileges was used by 79 percent of the parents; confinement to a room was used by 59 percent; 49 percent spanked or hit their child; and 45 percent insulted or swore at their child. What was most notable about these statistics was that, for the first time, a majority of parents (51 percent) reported that they did not spank their children.

Although spanking is a popular form of guidance in the United States, five countries—Austria, Norway, Denmark, Sweden, and Finland—have banned physical punishment of children. Several states, such as Wisconsin and Maryland, have tried to pass laws related to spanking, but none to date have been passed into legislation.

The discussion over whether or not to spank is emotionally charged, and the issue presented here is whether or not childhood spanking leads to teenage and adult violence. The issue of violence is receiving overwhelming attention in the media. Violence is perceived as a social ill that has permeated our institutions and that is liable to erupt at any time. Today, violent acts by teens and adults alike are much more likely to result in death because of the ready availability of guns and people's willingness to use them.

Do children who are spanked or physically punished see spanking as an act of violence? Do they then learn to see violence as an acceptable way to solve a problem? They do something wrong and get hit for it... that's how parents solve the problem of misbehavior. When parents spank their children, are they guiding them or controlling them? If parents don't spank, how do they teach their children right from wrong? Does any kind of punishment, such as yelling or taking away privileges, lead to violent acts later on? What message are parents sending?

In the following two selections, Murray Straus and Joan McCord agree that physical punishment, such as spanking, leads to violence. However, Professor McCord takes the argument a step further in stating that all punishment, physical or not, accounts for later violence in adults.

YES

Murray A. Straus

DISCIPLINE AND DEVIANCE: PHYSICAL PUNISHMENT OF CHILDREN AND VIOLENCE AND OTHER CRIME IN ADULTHOOD

DEFINITIONS

Physical Punishment

Exploring such issues as the legitimacy of physical punishment requires some definition of terms. Physical punishment is a legally permissible physical attack on children. The most common forms are spanking, slapping, grabbing, and shoving a child "roughly"—with more force than is needed to move the child. Hitting a child with an object is also legally permissible and widespread (Wauchope and Straus 1990). Parents in the United States and most countries have a legal right to carry out these acts, as do teachers in most U.S. states and most nations; whereas, the same act is a criminal assault if carried out by someone not in a custodial relationship to the child.

The section on "General Justification" of violence in the Texas Penal Code, for example (9.61, West Publishing Company 1983), declares that the use of force, but not deadly force, against a child younger than 18 years is justified (1) when the actor is the child's parent or step-parent or is acting in *loco parentis* to the child, and (2) when and to the degree that the actor reasonably believes that force is necessary to discipline the child or to safeguard or promote welfare.

The New Hampshire Criminal Code (627.6:I, Equity Publishing 1985) similarly declares that "A parent, guardian, or other person responsible for the general care and welfare of a minor is justified in using force against such a minor when and to the extent that he reasonably believes it necessary to prevent or punish such a minor's misconduct." Both these statutes cover parents and teachers, and neither sets any limit except "not deadly."

From Murray A. Straus, "Discipline and Deviance: Physical Punishment of Children and Violence and Other Crime in Adulthood," *Social Problems*, vol. 38, no. 2 (May 1991), pp. 134–144. Copyright © 1991 by The Society for the Study of Social Problems. Reprinted by permission. References and some notes omitted.

Is Physical Punishment Violence?

Since the concept of violence is used in this paper as often as physical punishment, it also needs to be defined. Though the lack of a standard definition or consensus on its meaning results in considerable confusion, the following definition makes clear the conceptual framework of this paper, even though it will not be accepted by all readers: *Violence* is an act carried out with the intention, or perceived intention, of causing physical pain or injury to another person.

This definition and alternative definitions are examined in detail in Gelles and Straus (1979). As defined, violence is synonymous with the term "physical aggression" as used in social psychology (Bandura 1973; Berkowitz 1962). This definition overlaps with but is not the same as the legal concept of "assault." The overlap occurs because the definition of assault, like the definition of violence, refers to an *act*, regardless of whether injury occurred as a result of that act. However, the concept of assault is more narrow than that of violence because not all acts of violence are crimes, including acts of self-defense and physical punishment of children. Some violent acts are required by law—for example, capital punishment.[1]

The fact that physical punishment is legal is not inconsistent with the definition of violence just given, since, as noted, there are many types of legal violence. An examination of the definition shows that physical punishment of children fits every element of the definition of violence given. Thus, from a theoretical perspective, physical punishment and capital punishment are similar, despite the vast difference in level of severity.

PHYSICAL PUNISHMENT OF CHILDREN AS THE PRIMORDIAL VIOLENCE

Incidence of Physical Punishment by Parents

Ninety-nine percent of the mothers in the classic study of *Patterns of Child Rearing* (Sears, Maccoby, and Levin 1957) used physical punishment as defined above on at least some occasions, and 95 percent of students in a community college sample reported having experienced physical punishment at some point (Bryan and Freed 1982).... [T]he National Family Violence Surveys (Straus 1983; Wauchope and Straus 1990), studies of large and nationally representative samples of American children conducted in 1975 and 1985 ... found that almost all parents in the United States use physical punishment with young children—over 90 percent of parents of children age 3 and 4. A remarkable correspondence exists between the results of these four surveys in the near universality with which physical punishment was used on children age 2 to 6; and also between the two national surveys in showing that physical punishment was still being used on one out of three children at age 15.

Despite the widespread use of physical punishment, there is nontheless considerable variation—more than enough to enable empirical study of the correlates of physical punishment. First, we see that the percentage of people experiencing physical punishment drops off rapidly with age so that by age 13 there are nearly equal numbers of children who are and who are not punished. Second, at each age, there is enormous variation in how often a specific child experiences physical punishment (Wauchope and Straus 1990).

Incidence of Physical Punishment in Schools

In 1989 all but eleven states permitted physical punishment of children by school employees. A 1978–79 national survey of schools found an annual incidence of 2.5 instances of physical punishment per 100 children. Only five states reported no instances of physical punishment (calculated from Hyman 1990: Appendix B). These figures are probably best interpreted as "lower bound" estimates, and the reported absence of physical punishment in five states must also be regarded with some caution.

A THEORETICAL MODEL

In the light of the above incidence rates and the previously listed reasons for the importance of research on physical punishment, a framework is needed to help stimulate and guide research. This section presents such a framework in the form of a causal model. The model was created on the basis of previous theoretical and empirical research.

Cultural Spillover Theory

An important component of the theoretical model to be presented is what I have called "Cultural Spillover Theory" (Baron and Straus 1987; Baron, Straus, and Jaffee 1988; Straus 1985), which holds that violence in one sphere of life tends to engender violence in other spheres, and that *this carry-over process transcends the bounds between legitimate and criminal use of force.* Thus, the more a society uses force to secure socially desirable ends (for example, to maintain order in schools, to deter criminals, or to defend itself from foreign enemies) the greater the tendency for those engaged in illegitimate behavior to also use force to attain their own ends.

Cultural Spillover Theory was formulated as a macro-sociological theory to explain society-to-society differences in violence rates, such as the huge differences between societies in the incidence of murder and rape. My colleagues and I tested this theory using a 12 indicator index to measure the extent to which violence was used for socially legitimate purposes ranging from physical punishment of children to capital punishment of criminals. We found that the higher the score of a state on the Legitimate Violence Index, the higher the rate of criminal violence such as rape(Baron and Straus 1987, 1989; Baron, Straus, and Jaffee 1988) and murder (Baron and Straus 1988).

We must also understand the individual-level processes which underlie the macro-level relationship. These can be illustrated by considering the hypothesis that use of physical punishment by teachers tends to increase the rate of violence by children in schools. The individual level aspect of this hypothesis is based on two assumptions: (1) that children often mistreat other children, (2) that teachers are important role models. Therefore, if children frequently misbehave toward other children, and if teachers who serve as role models use violence to correct misbehavior, a larger proportion of children will use violence to deal with other children whom they perceive as having mistreated them than would be the case if teachers did not provide a model of hitting wrongdoers.

The Cultural Spillover Theory overlaps with the "Brutalization" Theory of capital punishment (Bowers 1984; Hawkins 1989), and the "Cultural Legitimation"

Theory of homicide (Archer and Gartner 1984). All three of these theories can be considered a variant of what Farrell and Swigert (1988:295) identify as "social and cultural support" theories of crime, including the Differential Association Theory, the Delinquent Subculture Theory, and the Social Learning Theory. Each of these theories seeks to show that crime is not just a reflection of individual deviance (as in psycho-pathology theories of crime) or the absence of social control (as in Social-Disorganization Theory). Rather, crime is also engendered by social integration into groups which share norms and values that support behavior which the rest of society considers to be criminal. Thus, the processes which produce criminal behavior are structurally parallel to the processes which produce conforming behavior, but the cultural content differs.[2]

The Model
The theoretical model diagramed in Figure 1 depicts the causes and consequences of physical punishment and suggests salient issues for empirical investigation. It is a "system model" because it assumes that the use of physical punishment is a function of other characteristics of the society and its members and that physical punishment in turn influences the society and its members....

Each of the blocks in Figure 1 should also have arrows between the elements within each block; except for Block II at the center of the model, they were omitted to provide a clear picture. The arrows within Box II posit a mutually reinforcing relationship between physical punishment in the schools and by parents. It seems highly plausible that a society which approves of parents hitting children will also tend to approve of teachers

doing the same, and that when physical punishment is used in the schools, it encourages parents to also hit children....

ANTECEDENTS OF PHYSICAL PUNISHMENT BY PARENTS

Block I at the left of the model identifies characteristics of the society, of the schools, of families, and of individual parents which are hypothesized to influence the extent to which physical punishment is used. This list is far from exhaustive, as are the hypotheses to be tested. Both are intended only to illustrate some of the many factors which might influence use of physical punishment.[3]

Societal Norms
Physical punishment is deeply rooted in Euro-American religious and legal traditions (Foucault 1979; Greven 1990). It would be difficult to find someone who could not recite the biblical phrase "spare the rod and spoil the child." The common law of every American state permits parents to use physical punishment. These are not mere vestiges of ancient but no longer honored principles. In addition to defining and criminalizing "child abuse," the child abuse legislation which swept through all 50 states in the late 1960s often reaffirmed cultural support for physical punishment by declaring that nothing in the statute should be construed as interfering with the rights of parents to use physical punishment. There is a certain irony to this legislation because, as will be suggested below, use of physical punishment is associated with an *increased* risk of "child abuse."[4]

Approval of physical punishment.
Attitude surveys have repeatedly demonstrated high approval of physical punish-

Figure 1
System Model of Causes and Consequences of Physical Punishment

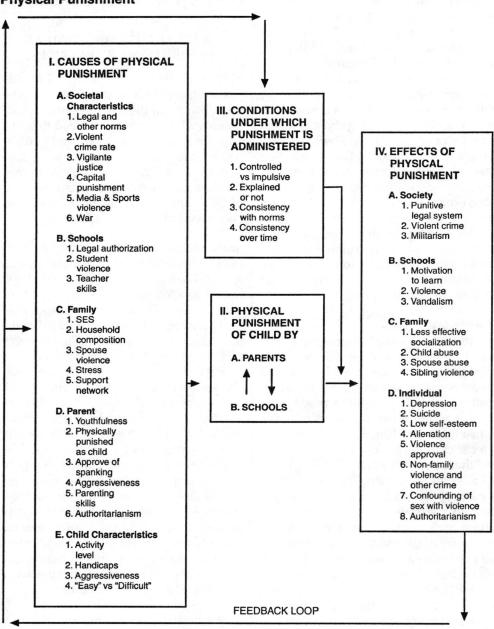

ment. Ninety percent of the parents in the 1975 National Family Violence Survey expressed at least some degree of approval of physical punishment (Straus, Gelles, and Steinmetz 1980:55). Other studies report similar percentages. For example, a 1986 NORC national survey found that 84 percent agreed or strongly agreed that "It is sometimes necessary to discipline a child with a *good, hard spanking* (italics added). Moreover, this approval does not apply only to small children. The New Hampshire Child Abuse Survey (described in the Methodological Appendix and in Moore and Straus 1987) found that less than half of the parents interviewed (47 percent) strongly disagree with the statement "Parents have a right to slap their teenage children who talk back to them." When asked whether "Spanking children helps them to be better people when they grow up," only one out of six disagreed (16.7 percent).

Approval of hitting and actual hitting.
There is evidence that, as hypothesized by the path going from Block I.D2 of the theoretical model to Block II.A, parents who approve of physical punishment do it more often. Parents who approve of slapping a teenager who talks back reported hitting their teenager an average of 1.38 times during the year, about four times more often than the average of .33 for the parents who did not approve. For younger children, the frequency of physical punishment was much greater (an average of 4.9 times for preschool children and 2.9 times for 6-12 year old children), but the relationship between approval and actual hitting was almost identical.

Role Modeling
The path in Figure 1 from I.D2 to II.A, and from II.A to IV.C2 is based on the assumption that children learn by example, and we have seen that over 90 percent of parents provide examples of physical punishment. However, as noted above, there is a great deal of variation in how long physical punishment continues to be used and in the frequency with which it is used. This variation made it possible to test the hypothesis that the more a person experienced physical punishment, the more likely such persons are to use physical punishment on their own children....

EFFECTS OF PHYSICAL PUNISHMENT BY PARENTS

Block IV on the right side of Figure 1 illustrates the hypothesized effects of physical punishment on individuals, schools, families, and the society. The empirical analyses to be reported are all derived from the proposition that the "legitimate violence" of physical punishment tends to spill over to illegitimate violence and other crime. If subsequent research supports these effects, the next step will be research to identify the processes which produce them.

Physical Punishment and Physical Abuse
The basic tenant of Cultural Spillover Theory—that legitimate violence tends to increase the probability of criminal violence—is represented by the path going from II.A (physical punishment by parents) to IV.C2 (physical abuse by parents).

Analysis of the New Hampshire Child Abuse Survey (Moore and Straus 1987) shows that parents who believe in physical punishment not only hit more often, but they more often go beyond ordinary physical punishment and assault the child in ways which carry a greater risk of injury to the child such as punching and kicking. Specifically, parents who approved of physical punishment had a child abuse rate of 99 per 1,000, which is four times the rate for parents who did not approve of physical punishment (28 per 1,000).

Assaults on Siblings and Spouses
From the 1975 National Family Violence Survey (Straus 1983), we know that children who were physically punished during the year of that survey have almost three times the rate of severely and repeatedly assaulting a sibling three or more times during the year. Though it is likely that many of these children were physically punished precisely because of hitting a sibling, it is also clear that the physical punishment did not serve to reduce the level of assaults to the rate for children who were not physically punished.

Similarly, findings from the 1975 National Family Violence Survey (Straus 1983) clearly show that for both men and women the more physical punishment a respondent experienced as a child, the higher the probability of assaulting a *spouse* during the year of the survey. These findings are consistent with the hypothesized path from Box II.A to IV.C3.

Physical Punishment and Street Crime
The theoretical model predicts that ordinary physical punishment increases the probability of "street crime" (path from Box II.A to IV.D.4). Evidence consistent with that hypothesis is presented in Figure 2 for juveniles and Figures 3 and 4 for adults.

The juvenile crime data are from a 1972 survey of 385 college students (Straus 1973, 1974, 1985) who completed

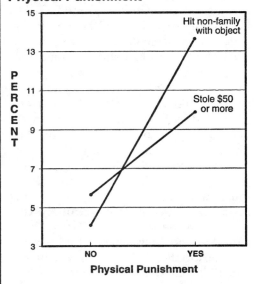

Figure 2
Juvenile Assault and Theft Rate by Physical Punishment

a questionnaire referring to events when they were high school seniors. The questionnaire included an early version of the Conflict Tactics Scales and also a self-report delinquency scale. Figure 2 shows that significantly more children who were physically punished engaged in both violent crime and property crime.

The findings on crime by adults were obtained by an analysis of covariance of the 1985 National Family Violence Survey sample, controlling for socioeconomic status. Figure 3 shows that the more physical punishment experienced by the respondent as a child, the higher the proportion who as adults reported acts of physical aggression *outside the family* in the year covered by this survey. This relationship is highly significant after controlling for SES. The results are parallel when physical punishment by the father is the independent variable.

Figure 3
Non-Family Assaults of Adults by Physical Punishment as a Teen

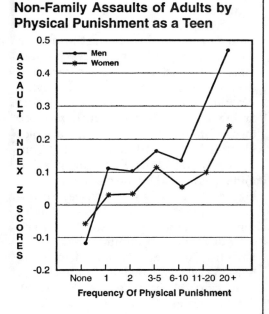

Frequency Of Physical Punishment

Although the arrest rate of respondents in the 1985 National Family Violence Survey was very low (1.1 percent or 1,100 per 100,000 population), this is very close to the 1,148 per 100,000 rate for the entire U.S. population (Federal Bureau of Investigation 1985). Consequently, despite the low rate, we examined the relationship of arrests to physical punishment experienced during the teenage years. Although the differences overall are statistically significant (F = 3.75, p < .001), the graph does not show the expected difference between those who were and were not hit as a teen. Instead, only respondents who were hit extremely often (eleven or more times during the year) had the predicted higher arrest rates. It is possible that these erratic results occur because the base rate for arrests is so low. A statistical analysis based on a characteristic which occurs in such a small percentage of the population is subject to

random fluctuations unless the sample is much larger than even the 6,002 in the 1985 survey. . . .

SUMMARY AND CONCLUSIONS

This paper formulated a theoretical model of the links between physical punishment of children and crime and also presented preliminary empirical tests of some of the paths in the model. Although the empirical findings are almost entirely consistent with the theory, they use data which cannot prove the theory because they do not establish the causal direction. Nevertheless, the fact that so many analyses which could have falsified the theory did not strengthens the case for the basic proposition of the theory: that although physical punishment may produce short term conformity, over the longer run it probably also creates or exacerbates deviance.

The Causal Direction Problem

The causal direction problem can be illustrated at the macro level by the correlation between laws authorizing physical punishment in schools and the homicide rate. It is likely that at least part of this relationship occurs because both physical punishment and crime are reflections of an underlying violent social climate. When crime and violence flourish, even ordinarily law-abiding citizens get caught up in that milieu. When crime rates are high, citizens tend to demand "getting tough" with criminals, including capital punishment and laws such as those recently enacted in Colorado and other states. These laws added protection of property to self-defense as a circumstance under which a citizen could use "deadly force." The question from the perspective of Cultural

Figure 4
Arrests Per 1,000 by Physical Punishment as a Teen

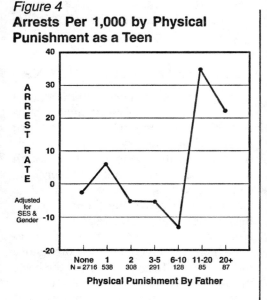

Physical Punishment By Father

Spillover Theory is whether such laws, once in effect, tend to legitimize violence and, therefore, further increase rather than reduce violent crime.

The causal direction problem in the individual-level findings is even more obvious because it is virtually certain that part of the linkage between physical punishment and crime occurs because "bad" children are hit, and these same bad children go on to have a higher rate of criminal activity than other children.[5] However, the question is not whether misbehaving children are spanked but whether spanking for misbehavior, despite immediate compliance, tends to have longer term negative effects. Research by Nagaraja (1984), Patterson (1982), and Patterson and Bank (1987) suggests that this is the case. This research found an escalating feedback loop which is triggered by attempts to use physical punishment or verbal aggression to control deviant behavior of the child. These processes together with the hypothesized

legitimation of violence are modeled in Figure 5.

It should be noted that physical punishment usually does not set in motion the deviation amplifying process just discussed, at least not to the extent that it produces seriously deviant behavior. We must understand the circumstances or branching processes which produce these different outcomes. The variables identified in Box III of Figure 1 ("Conditions Under Which Punishment is Administered") and by the diagonal path in Figure 5, are likely to be crucial for understanding this process. Three examples can illustrate this process. (1) If physical punishment is administered "spontaneously" and as a means of relieving tension, as advocated by a number of child care "experts" (e.g., Ralph 1989), it may increase the risk of producing a person who as an adult will be explosively violent, as compared to physical punishment is administered under more controlled circumstances. The latter is assumed to provide a model of controlled use of force. (2) If physical punishment is accompanied by verbal assaults, it may increase the risk of damage to the child's self-esteem compared to physical punishment administered in the context of a supportive relationship. (3) If physical punishment is administered along with reasoned explanations, the correlation between physical punishment and child's aggressiveness may be reduced. A study by Larzelere (1986) found such a reduction, but also found that despite the lowered relationship, a statistically significant relationship remains.

Research Implications

Both the overall theoretical model (Figure 1) and the micro-process model (Figure 5) can only be adequately investigated

Figure 5
Process Model of Effects of Corporal Punishment

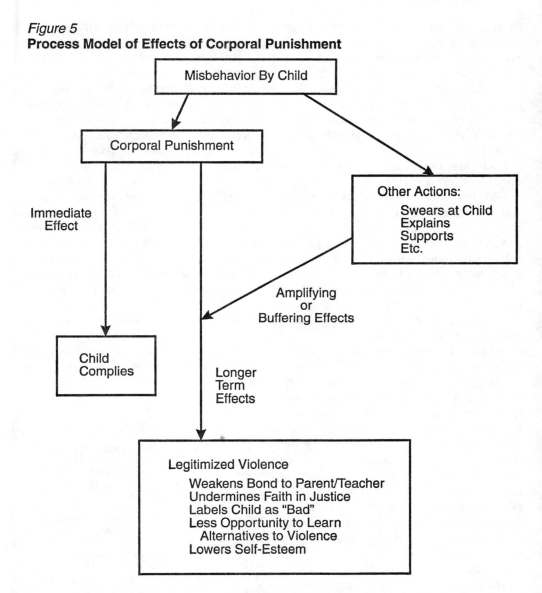

with longitudinal and experimental data. There are already examples of studies at the macro-level which meet these criteria, including the research of Archer and Gartner (1984) on the effects of war on the homicide rate and research on the "brutalization" effect of executions (Bowers 1984; Hawkins 1989). At the in-dividual level, McCord's follow up of the Cambridge-Somerville Youth Study (1988) sample illustrates what can be done with a longitudinal design. As for experiments, it would be unethical to randomly assign groups of parents to "spanking" and "no spanking" condi-tions. However, the fact that almost all parents do spank makes a number of experiments possible because the treatment can be in the form of helping parents use alternatives to spanking. One example would be an interrupted time series using volunteer parents. Another example would be a randomized field trial of a "no-spanking" parent education program.

There are hundreds of research questions that spring from the theoretical model presented in this paper. The process of transforming that model into meaningful research can be aided if criminologists and family violence researchers collaborate more than in the past to seek a full accounting of the links between physical punishment and crime outside the family. There are no serious structural or theoretical barriers to discourage such mutually informed work, but there is a set of beliefs that continues to define "family violence" in ways which inhibit research on physical punishment. Among family violence researchers, but especially those concerned with wife-beating, there has been a reluctance, and sometimes even condemnation, of considering ordinary physical punishment as part of the same continuum as wife-beating and child abuse (Breines and Gordon 1983: 505, 511). Spanking children is not seen as "real family violence." Similarly, among criminologists, physical punishment of children is not seen as important for understanding "real crime."

The theory developed in this paper and the research evidence so far available on that theory support the opposite formulation. However, there is no contradiction between the idea that all violence has something in common and the idea that there are important differences between various types of violence. Both propositions can be correct, and both approaches

are needed for research on this complex phenomenon. Whether one focuses on the common elements in all violence or on the unique aspects of a certain type of violence depends on the purpose of the study. Research intended to inform interventions designed to aid "battered women" or "abused children," or to deter "wife-beating" or "street crime" must focus on the specific situation of those specific types of victims and offenders (Straus 1990c). However, for research intended to inform programs of "primary prevention" (Caplan 1974; Cowen 1984) of violent crime such as wife beating and homicide, it is essential to understand the social structural and social psychological process by which violence becomes an integral part of both legitimate and criminal behavior. The theoretical model presented in this paper suggests that the almost universal use of physical punishment in child rearing is part of the process.

NOTES

1. This brief discussion shows that the fact of a physical assault having taken place is not sufficient for understanding violence. Several other dimensions also need to be considered. It is also important that each of these other dimensions be measured separately so that their causes and consequences and joint effects can be investigated. Other dimensions include the seriousness of the assault (ranging from a slap to shooting), whether a physical injury was produced (from none to death), the motivation (from a concern for a person's safety, as when a child is spanked for going into the street, to hostility so intense that the death of the person is desired), and whether the act of violence is normatively legitimate (as in the case of slapping a child) or illegitimate (as in the case of slapping a spouse), and which set of norms are applicable (legal, ethnic or class norms, couple norms, etc.). See Gelles and Straus (1979) for further analyses of these issues.

2. There are a number of other theories relevant to the issues discussed in this paper. The larger theoretical task will be to integrate Cultural

Spillover Theory and the theories just listed with theories such as Control Theory (Hirshi 1969), Labeling Theory (Scheff 1966; Straus 1973), Social Learning Theory (Bandura 1973; Berkowitz 1962; Eron, Walder, and Lefkowitz 1971; Gelles and Straus 1979; McCord 1988), and a variety of personality mediated theories. Although space limitations required deletion of my initial attempts to specify some of the interrelationships, the concluding theoretical discussion is a small step in that direction. I argue that physical punishment might bring about changes in personality, such as lowered self-esteem or increased powerlessness and alienation. These personality variables can, by themselves, serve as "risk factors" for violence. At the empirical level, it will require a "competing theories" research design and triangulation via several different types of research to adequately investigate these issues.

3. Moreover, due to space limitations, I will only discuss the paths for which I carried out empirical tests. However, since a reader of an earlier draft of the paper questioned the hypothesized paths and feedback loop running from use of corporal punishment back to low teacher and parental skill (I.C3 and I.D5), the reasoning needs to be summarized: It is simply that to the extent parents and teachers use corporal punishment as a means of inducing appropriate behavior, they get less practice in using other means of inducing appropriate behavior and, therefore, do not enhance their skills in those techniques, thus further increasing the probability of using corporal punishment.

4. A study of the reasons for including reaffirmation of corporal punishment in the child abuse legislation might provide important insights on American attitudes about children and violence. Such a study could be undertaken by analysis of the proceedings of state legislatures. For the moment, I would like to suggest two scenarios, both of which may have been operating. The first reason is that both spring from a concern about the welfare of children, and specifically the idea that children need to be protected from abuse but also need "strong discipline" (including physical punishment "when necessary") if they are to become responsible law-abiding citizens. The second reason is that the combination reflects a political compromise which the advocates of "child protection" needed to make in order to have the legislation pass. However, these two reasons overlap to a certain extent because conservative members of the legislatures who needed to be placated favor physical punishment because they deeply believe it is in the best interests of children.

5. I emphasize "a higher *rate*" because most "bad" children, regardless of whether they have been physically punished, do not become criminals. The theory put forth in this paper does not assert that corporal punishment is a necessary and sufficient cause of violence and other crime. On the contrary, crime is a multiply determined phenomenon, and corporal punishment is assumed to be only one of these many causes. Consequently, many individuals who have not been assaulted as children engage in crime, just as many who have been assaulted by teachers or parents avoid criminal acts.

NO

Joan McCord

QUESTIONING THE VALUE OF PUNISHMENT

The author critically examines and rejects the claim that physical punishments lead to aggression through the acceptance of norms of violence. She proposes an alternate theory to account for how children acquire norms and why they become violent. The proposed Construct Theory explains why abused, neglected, and rejected children—as well as those who are punished—tend to become anti-social.

"Spare the rod and spoil the child," many have argued. "No," say others, as they refer to evidence that physical punishment leads to, rather than prevents, violent behavior. Yet only a few, it seems, have whispered that we should question the value of every type of punishment, including psychological punishments and deprivation of privileges as well as physical punishments.

When attention has been focused only on physical punishment, critics typically note that such discipline provides a model for the use of force, thereby teaching people to use force. Murray Straus, for example, argues that corporal punishment contributes to a cycle of violence that includes violent crime, child abuse, spouse abuse, non-violent crimes, ineffective family socialization, and ineffective schooling. Straus accounts for correlations between the use of physical punishment, on the one hand, and antisocial or dysfunctional behaviors on the other by means of Cultural Spillover Theory. This theory is an amalgam of explanations that consider behavior to be learned through imitation of models and adoption of norms supported by groups with whom an individual associates. In this view, individuals come to accept the use of violence—and to be violent—because they see violence as legitimated through its use by role models, and they generalize the behavioral norm to include illegitimate uses of violence.

While Straus is correct that physical punishments tend to increase aggression and criminal behavior, I believe he takes too narrow a view about the mechanisms that account for the relationships. My conclusion is grounded in evidence from longitudinal studies about the transmission of violence from

From Joan McCord, "Questioning the Value of Punishment," *Social Problems*, vol. 38, no. 2 (May 1991), pp. 167–176. Copyright © 1991 by The Society for the Study of Social Problems. Reprinted by permission.

one generation to the next. I offer a competing theory, one that merges evidence from experimental studies designed by psychologists to understand the conditions under which children learn and that considers critical issues related to the learning of language. The competing theory, which I call the Construct Theory, suggests how the same mechanism that links physical punishment to aggression can be triggered by nonphysical punishments and neglect. Before turning to the competing theory, I present empirical evidence that physical punishment leads to aggression and criminal behavior and then show that the Cultural Spillover Theory inadequately explains the relationship.

PROBLEMS WITH THE CULTURAL SPILLOVER EXPLANATION

Much of the research to which Straus refers in his analysis of the relationship between physical punishment and misbehavior is cross-sectional. With such data, as Straus acknowledges, one cannot determine whether punishments were a cause or an effect of the behavior. Three longitudinal studies that measured discipline prior to the age serious antisocial behavior began, however, suggest temporal priority for punitive discipline. Comparing children whose parents depended on physical punishments with those whose parents did not in Finland (Pulkkinen 1983), Great Britain (Farrington 1978), and in the United States (McCord 1988), researchers found that those whose parents used harsh physical punishments had greater probabilities for subsequently committing serious crimes. Longitudinal studies of victims of child abuse, too, suggest that violence tends to increase the probability that victims will commit serious crimes (McCord 1983; Widom 1989).

The theory of Cultural Spillover, like similar theories that attempt to explain pockets of violence, postulates acceptance of norms exhibited by the subculture using violence. Although longitudinal studies suggest that violence in the family precedes violence in society, they contain data incongruent with a theory that explains the causal mechanism as socialization into norms that legitimize violence.

One incongruence is revealed in my study of long-term effects of child abuse in which I compared abused sons with neglected and rejected and loved sons (McCord 1983). The classifications were based on biweekly observations in the homes when the boys were between the ages of 8 and 16 years and living in high-crime areas. Records of major (FBI Index) crime convictions were collected thirty years after the study ended. Twenty-three percent of those reared in loving families and 39 percent of those reared in abusing families had been convicted; but the conviction rate was 35 percent for the neglected and 53 percent for the rejected boys. That is, the data show almost as much violence produced from neglect as from abuse, and greater violence from rejection without abuse than from abuse. Because neglect and rejection typically lead to socialization failure, these results raise doubts that acceptance of norms of violence account for transmission of violence. It would be an anomaly if the very conditions that undermine acceptance of other types of norms promoted norms of violence.

One might argue that Cultural Spillover Theory accounts for violence among the abused and some other theory accounts for violence among neglected and rejected children. Yet neglect and rejection have enough in common with abuse to suggest that a more parsimonious account would be desirable. Furthermore, as will be shown, when neglect is combined with abuse, the result is not increased violence as one would expect were there different causes involved.

My data from the Cambridge-Somerville Youth Study records permitted further checks on the Cultural Spillover Theory. The data include parental criminal records as well as coded descriptions of family life between 1939 and 1945. Sons' criminal records had, as noted, been collected in 1978, when the sons were middle-aged. Among the 130 families containing two natural parents, 22 included a father who had been convicted for an Index crime. Fifty-five percent (12) of their sons were convicted for an Index crime. In comparison, twenty-five percent (27) of the 108 sons of noncriminal men had been convicted ($X^2_{(1)}$ = 7.60, P = .006). The criminal fathers were more likely to use physical punishment: 73 percent compared with 48 percent ($X^2_{(1)}$ = 4.43, P = .035). Further, the combined impact of a criminal father using physical punishment appeared to be particularly criminogenic.

These data support the view that use of physical punishment increases the likelihood that sons of criminals will be criminals. Cultural Spillover Theory suggests that the increase comes about because sons adopt the norms displayed through physical punishments. If the theory were correct, then the transmission of norms of violence should be particularly effective under conditions that promote acceptance of other types of norms as well. The evidence, however, gives another picture.

Many studies have shown that warmth or affection facilitates acceptance of social norms (e.g., Austin 1978; Bandura and Huston 1961; Bandura and Walters 1963; Baumrind 1978; Bender 1947; Bowlby 1940; Glueck and Glueck 1950; Goldfarb 1945; Hirschi 1969; Liska and Reed 1985; Maccoby 1980; McCord 1979; Olson, Bates, and Bayles 1990; Patterson 1976). Parental affection for the child should increase concordance if a similar mechanism for acceptance of norms accounts for a connection between parents' and children's aggression. To test this hypothesis, the 130 families were divided into three groups: those not using physical punishment, those using physical punishment and also expressing affection for the child, and those using physical punishment and not expressing affection for the child.

The data show that parental affection did not increase acceptance of norms of violence, but the opposite. For individuals reared with physical punishment, those whose parents were affectionate were *less* likely to become criminals. This result does not easily fit an assumption that normative acquisition accounts for the violence.

Another inconsistency is apparent in a longitudinal study that at first glance might appear to support the Cultural Spillover Theory. Widom (1989) retraced children reported to have been victims of abuse or neglect prior to the age of 11. Using records from elementary schools and hospitals at birth, Widom was able to match 667 of 908 children on sex, race, and age with children not known to have been either abused or neglected. Widom's analyses, based either on aggregate data combining abuse with neglect or matched and unmatched cases, have led her to conclude that violence breeds violence.

I reanalyzed her data (Widom 1990) to differentiate effects of neglect from effects of violence.

The matched pairs were divided into those in which the child had experienced sexual abuse (85 females, 15 males), neglect but not physical abuse (205 females, 254 males), physical abuse but not neglect (14 females, 35 males), and both physical abuse and neglect (29 females, 30 males). Assuming that acceptance of a norm of violence accounts for the high rates of crime that Widom found to follow abuse, crime would be considerably more prevalent among those who had been physically abused than among those who had been neglected but not abused.

Using Widom's codes of the individuals' criminal records, I compared each case with the matched control to see which had the worse criminal record. If both had been convicted of at least one crime, the one convicted for more crimes was counted as being worse.

The data show that neglect is about as criminogenic as sexual abuse and physical abuse. Moreover, the combined effects of neglect and abuse are not worse than those of either alone as would be expected if each had separate causal impact. Comparisons of cases and controls for crimes of violence (e.g., assault, murder, attempted murder) produced similar results.

These comparisons again suggest that continuity in violence among abusing families has been mistakenly attributed to transmission of norms of violence. Among males, neglect and sexual abuse were in fact more likely than physical abuse to lead to violence. Yet if transmission of social norms accounts for violence, physical abuse should create more. The reanalysis of these data suggest that one ought to search for a common cause, for something shared by neglect and abuse that might lead to violence.

In sum, violence seems to beget violence, but studies of child abuse and of family socialization undermine the argument that violence begets violence *through acceptance of family (subcultural) norms of violence.* Because neglect, rejection, and physical abuse result in similarly high rates of crime, it seems appropriate to search for a cause in terms of what they have in common.

A sound understanding of the way children learn can explain why physical abuse, neglect, and rejection lead to antisocial behavior. Below I develop such an understanding to show that a norm of self-interest, rather than a norm of violence, underlies the education shared by those who are rejected, neglected, and abused. It is the norm of self-interest that leads to violence in some circumstances.

UNDERMINING SOME ASSUMPTIONS

Side stepping the issue of how infants learn, many psychologists have simply assumed that babies are completely self-centered. In contrast, the evidence shows that how much children care about their own pleasures and pains and what they will consider pleasurable and painful is largely a function of the way are taught.

It may, for instance, be tempting to believe that an infant "instinctively" cries for food, to be held, or to have dirty diapers removed, but evidence points to large contributions from experience. In a study of neonates, Thoman, Korner, and Benson-Williams (1977) randomly assigned primiparous healthy newborns to conditions in which one third were held when they awakened. As anticipated by the authors, the babies who were held spent more time with their eyes open and cried less vigorously while being held; unexpectedly, however, they spent more time crying during non-stimulus periods. The babies had been equated for pretrial behaviors, so the authors suggest that the infants had come to associate their crying with being picked up during the 48 hour training period.

In another study also showing that neonates learn from their environments, Riese (1990) compared 47 pairs of monozygotic twins, 39 pairs of dizygotic twins of the same sex, and 72 pairs of dizygotic twins of the opposite sex. Using standardized tests for irritability, resistance to soothing, activity level when awake, activity level when asleep, reactivity to a cold disk on the thigh and to a pin prick, and response to cuddling, she found significant correlations for the dizygotic twins (both same and opposite sex), indicating shared environmental influences, but no significantly larger correlations among the monozygotic pairs. Riese concluded that "environment appears to account for most of the known variance for the neonatal temperament variables" (1236).

Just as neonates can learn to cry in order to be picked up, children learn what to consider painful. Variability in recognizing sensations as painful has been dramatically evidenced through studies of institutionalized infants, who received serious injuries without seeming to notice (Goldfarb 1958). During the period of observation, one child caught her hand in the door, injuring a finger so severely that it turned blue; yet the child did not cry or otherwise indicate pain. Another child sat on a radiator too hot for the teacher to touch. Observed injuries also included a child who was cutting the palm of his own hand with sharp scissors and another who had removed from her cornea a steel splinter that had been imbedded for two days without any report of pain. All the children, however, gave pain responses to a pin prick, dispelling the hypotheses that they had a higher than normal threshold for pain. Goldfarb reasonably concluded: "The perception of pain and the reaction to pain-arousing stimuli are episodes far more complex than is implied in the concept of pure, unencumbered sensation" (1945: 780–781).

Often, children show no signs of pain after a fall until adults show that they expect a "pained" response. Studies with college students that feeling pain is influenced by pain exhibited by models (Craig and Theiss 1971), role playing as calm or upset (Kopel and Arkowitz 1974), and feedback from one's own responsive behavior (Bandler, Madaras, and Bem 1968). My personal experience and reports from students suggest that children whose mothers do not respond to their cuts with anxious concern do not exhibit such pain-behavior as crying when they fall.

Not only do children learn what is painful, but they attach pleasure to circumstances intended to result in pain. Solomon (1980) demonstrated that over a range of behaviors, pain-giving consequences acquire positive value through repetition (see Shipley 1987; Aronson, Carlsmith, and Darley 1963; Walster, Aronson, and Brown 1966). Studies showing that children learn to repeat behaviors that result in "reinforcement" through negative attention demonstrate that expectations are only one basis for the attraction of "pain-giving" stimuli (Gallimore, Tharp, and Kemp 1969; Witte and Grossman 1971).

Children also learn without extrinsic reinforcement. Curious about why so many young children appeared to increase their aggressiveness in experimental situations, Siegel and Kohn (1959) measured aggression both with and without an adult in the room. Only when adults were present did escalation occur. The authors drew the sensible conclusion that young children assume that what is not forbidden is permitted.

The egocentric motivational assumption that underlies classic theories of socialization has been subjected to a series of criticism, most notably by Butler (1726) and Hume (1960 [1777]). These authors pointed out that the plausibility of the egocentric assumption rests on circular reasoning. The fact that a voluntary action must be motivated is confused with an assumption that voluntary actions must be motivated by desire to benefit from them. Often the only evidence for self-interest is the occurrence of the act for which a motive is being sought.

Raising further questions about the assumption of egocentrism in children, some studies indicate that altruistic behavior is not always egoistic behavior in disguise (Batson et al. 1988; Grusec and Skubiski 1970). In fact, altruistic behavior turns up at very young ages (Rheingold and Emery 1986; Zahn-Waxler and Radke-Yarrow 1982; Zahn-Waxler et al. 1988) suggesting that even babies are not exclusively interested in themselves.

The prevalent view that children require punishment in order to learn socialized behavior rests on three erroneous assumptions. The first two—that children are motivated by self-interest and that what gives them pain is "fixed"—have been shown to lack support in empirical research. The third—that unless there are punishments rules have no power—

is addressed in my proposal of Construct Theory.

AN ALTERNATIVE: CONSTRUCT THEORY

Construct Theory states that children learn what to do and what to believe in the process of learning how to use language. In simplest form, Construct Theory claims that children learn by constructing categories organized by the structure of the language in their culture. These categories can be identified by descriptions, much as one might identify a file, for example, "accounting," "things to do," "birthdays," "Parsons, T.," "true." Some categories are collections of objects, but others are actions that can be identified by such descriptions as "to be done" or "to be believed" or "to be doubted."

Learning a language requires learning more than concepts. Children learn not only what to count as tables and chairs, cars and trucks, but also what to count as painful or pleasant, undesirable or desirable, and worth avoiding or pursuing. In learning labels, in learning how to name and to re-identify objects, children are constructing classifications. The classification systems they develop will permeate what they notice and how they act as well as what they say.

Construct Theory explains the fact that different people consider similar events to have different affective characteristics —for example, as undesirable and desirable—because individuals construct different classifications of the events. This theory can account for relations between knowledge and action that have led many theorists to conjure "pro-attitudes" as the means by which some knowledge sometimes changes behavior (e.g.,

Kenny 1963; Milligan 1980; Müller 1979; Nowell-Smith 1954). According to Construct Theory, those reasons that move one to action are classified as "reasons worth acting upon"; no special entity need also be attached to them.[1] Construct Theory also explains how language can be learned and how people can communicate, for it shows the way in which meanings can be made public through the categories that are constructed.[2]

Learning a language involves learning to formulate sentences as well as learning how to use words. At its most fundamental level, sentences involve stringing together what logicians call "predicates" (which can be thought of as classes) and functional relations among them. Perhaps no component of a sentence is so critical to understanding how punishment works as the connective "if... then," for on this connective punishments rely. This connective also gives linguistic expression to what the neonates described above learned when they cried and were picked up (if I cry, then I will be picked up), what an infant learns by pushing a ball (if I push, then it will roll), and what the child learns when discovering natural consequences in the physical world.

Both natural and artificial contingencies provide information to the child who is learning about consequences. When a child is credibly threatened with punishment, the information conveyed extends beyond the intended message that the child ought not do something. A punishment is designed to give pain. Unless the chosen event is thought by the punisher to be painful, it would not be selected as a means for controlling the child's behavior. What is selected as a punishment, then, shows what the punisher thinks to be painful.[3]

A child also perceives the intention of the punisher to give pain (and may attempt to thwart the intention by saying such things as "I didn't like the dessert anyway" or "There's nothing good on TV anyhow"). So the use of punishment shows the child that the punisher is willing to hurt the threatened or punished child. This knowledge may decrease the child's desire to be with the punisher or to care how the punisher feels, thereby reducing the socializing agent's influence.

An interesting study illustrated another feature of punishment: it conveys information about what (according to the punisher) is valuable, thus potentially enhancing the value of the forbidden. Aronson and Carlsmith (1963) asked preschool children, individually, to compare five toys until they established stable transitive preferences. The experimenter then said he had to leave the room for a few minutes and placed on a table the toy ranked second-favorite by the child. The child was told not to play with that toy but that playing with the others was permissible. Half of the 44 children were randomly assigned to each of two conditions. In the "mild threat" condition, the experimenter said he would be annoyed if the child played with the forbidden toy. In the "severe threat" condition, the experimenter said that if the child played with the forbidden toy, the experimenter would be very angry and would take all the toys and never come back. The experimenter left the child for 10 minutes. Approximately 45 days later, the children were again asked to rank the five toys. For this ranking, 4 of the children from the mild threat condition ranked the forbidden toy as a favorite whereas 14 of those in the severe threat condition regarded the forbidden toy as the favorite. Conversely, 8 of those who were merely told that the experimenter would be annoyed had decreased their preference for the forbidden toy whereas none of the children who were threatened with punishment had they played with the toy decreased their preference for it.

In a near replication, Lepper (1973) found that, two weeks later, children from his stronger threat condition were more likely to cheat in a game. There are two explanations for this. Lepper explained the findings by suggesting that the children who resisted with severe threat reasoned: "I am the sort of person who would break the rules except for the fact that I would be punished." In contrast, according to this self-referential theory, the children under mild threat defined themselves as the sorts of people who generally conform to rules and requests.

I suggest an alternative explanation: The different exposures in the experiment taught the children something about the world and about other people—not primarily something about themselves. The more severe threats taught the children that they ought to orient their behavior around estimates of consequences *to themselves*. In the process of assessing their self-interests, the children looked for attractive features of that which had been forbidden. The "mild threat" condition in both experiments, however, implied only that the child should be concerned about how the experimenter might feel.

Punishments are invoked only when rules are disobeyed, so that telling a child about rules in conjunction with information about punishments for infractions informs a child that he or she has a choice: obey, or disobey-and-accept-the-consequences named as punishment.

Negative correlations between a parent's use of punishments and insistence that rules be followed were so strong in their study of misbehavior that Patterson, Dishion, and Bank (1984) could not use both measures in their model. Believing that punishments were more important, they dropped the follow-through measure. The data, however, show equally that a parent who insists that rules be followed need not use punishments to socialize children.

It might be tempting to argue that rewards circumvent the unwanted effects of punishment as a means for teaching norms. That would be a mistake. Although using rewards does not hazard rejection of the purveyor, rewarding shares many of the characteristics of punishing. Rewards as well as punishments employ the "if . . . then" relationship. Laboratory studies have demonstrated, as predicted from the Construct Theory, that contingent reinforcements sometimes interfere with the discovery of general rules (Schwartz 1982). Studies have demonstrated, also as predicted from Construct Theory, that incentives larger than necessary to produce an activity sometimes result in devaluation of the activity being rewarded (Greene and Lepper 1974; Lepper, Greene, and Nisbett 1973; Lepper et al. 1982; Ross 1975; Ross, Karniol, and Rothstein 1976).

Like those involved in punishments, contingencies that use rewards convey more information than intended when a socializing agent uses them to convince a child to do something. A reward is designed to be attractive, so rewards contain information about what the rewarder believes to be valuable. When a reward is clearly a benefit to the person being promised the reward, rewarding teaches the child to value his or her own benefit.[4]

In addition to learning that whatever requires reward is probably considered unpleasant, children learn that the reward is something considered valuable by the reward-giver. That children *learn* to perceive rewards as valuable has been demonstrated in the laboratory (Lepper et al. 1982). Children were told a story about a mother giving her child two supposed foods; children in the study were asked which the child in the story would prefer: "hupe" or "hule." Children in the experimental group were told that the mother explained to her child that (s)he could have one ("hupe" or "hule" for different children) if (s)he ate the other. In this condition, the contingent relation led the children to suppose that the second food was a reward for eating the first. The children overwhelmingly thought the second food would be preferred—and gave grounds for the choice in terms of its tasting better. The experiment showed that the continguent relation, rather than the order of presentation, influenced preference because children in the control condition who were told only that the child's mother gave the child first one and then the other food either refused to make a choice or gave no reason for a selection (which they equally distributed between the two). In other experiments with preschool children, play objects have been manipulated similarly, showing that an activity that is arbitrarily selected as the one to be rewarded will be "discounted" whereas the arbitrarily selected inducement gains value (e.g., Lepper et al. 1982; Boggiano and Main 1986). These studies show that children learn what to value as well as how to act from perceiving the ways in which rewards are used.[5]

The Construct Theory explains why punishments tend to increase the attraction of activities punished—and why extrinsic rewards tend to reduce the value of activities rewarded. The categorizing that children learn as they learn sentences in a language can be schematically represented by formal logic. When children become aware of the logical equivalence between the conditional (if x then y) and the disjuctive (either not-x or y), they learn that *rewards and punishments weaken the force of a rule by introducing choices.* If rewards are designed to give pleasure to the child and punishments are designed to give the child pain, then their use teaches children that they ought to value their own pleasure and to attempt to reduce their own pain.

CONCLUSION

Rewards and punishments are used to manipulate others. They often result in short-term gains, but their use teaches children to look for personal benefits. Like rewards and punishments, neglect and rejection teach egocentrism. Children brought up among adults who do not attend to their well-being are given no grounds for learning to consider the welfare of others.

Using punishment seems particularly short-sighted. Punishments may increase the attraction of forbidden acts. They also risk desensitizing children both to their own pains and to the pains of others (Cline, Croft, and Courrier 1973; Pearl 1987; Thomas et al. 1977). Although severe penalties may force compliance in specific instances, the behavior being punished is actually more likely to occur at a time or place when opportunities for detection are reduced (Bandura and Walters 1959).

No increase in punishment or in reward can guarantee that children will make the choices adults wish them to make. Several studies show, however, that children are more likely to want to do what an adult wishes if the adult generally does as the child desires. In one study, randomly selected mothers of preschoolers were trained to respond to their children's requests and to avoid directing them during a specified period of time each day for one week. Their children complied with more of the mother's standardized requests in the laboratory than the comparison group of children whose mothers used contingency training (Papal and Maccoby 1985). The results are mirrored in a natural setting with the discovery that children reared at pre-school age in a consensual environment were among the most likely to value autonomy, intellectual activity, and independence as well as to have high educational aspirations ten years later (Harrington, Block, and Block 1987).

In another study, mothers and children were observed at home for three months when the children were between 9 and 12 months in age. Mothers were rated for their sensitivity to their babies, a rating based on their perceived ability to see things from the baby's perspective, positive feelings expressed toward the baby, and adaptations favoring the baby's arrangements of his or her own behavior. Discipline was rated for verbal commands as well as for frequency of any physical interventions. The baby's compliance was a simple measure of the proportion of verbal commands the baby obeyed without further action by the mother. Compliance turned out to be practically unrelated to discipline, although it was strongly related to the mother's responsiveness. The authors note: "The findings suggest that a disposition toward obedience emerges in a responsive, accommodating social environment without extensive training, discipline or other massive attempts to shape the infant's course of development" (Stayton, Hogan, and Ainsworth 1971:1065).

Punishments—nonphysical as well as physical—teach children to focus on their own pains and pleasures in deciding how to act. If parents and teachers were to substitute non-physical punishments for physical ones, they might avoid teaching children to hit, punch, and kick; yet, they would nevertheless perpetuate the idea that giving pain is a legitimate way to exercise power. If the substitute for physical punishment were to be non-physical punishments, the consequences could be no less undermining of compassion and social interests.

Children do not require punishments if their teachers will guide them consistently, and they do not require rewards if intrinsic values of what they ought to do are made apparent to them. I am not suggesting that a child will be constantly obedient or agree completely with the values of those who do not punish. No techniques will guarantee a clone. Rather, I do suggest that children can be taught to follow reasonable rules and to be considerate—and that the probabilities for their learning these things are directly related to the use of reason in teaching them and to the consideration they see in their surroundings.

Straus turns a spotlight on physical punishment, suggesting that by using violence to educate, adults legitimize the use of violence. I paint a broader canvas, suggesting that by using rewards and punishments to educate, adults establish self-interest as the legitimate grounds for choice.

NOTES

1. This interpretation of language provides a modification of the Aristotelian notion that action is the conclusion of a practical syllogism; it adds a proviso that the syllogism must correctly represent the classification system of the actor, and then "straightway action follows." The interpretation also reflects the Humean claim that reason alone cannot account for action. It does so by including motivational classifications as separate from purely descriptive classifications.

2. Wittgenstein (1958) demonstrated the implausibility of accounting for language through private identification of meanings.

3. Thus, there is the irony that when teachers use school work, parents use performing chores, and both use being by oneself as punishments, they are likely to create distaste for learning, doing chores, and being alone.

4. One could, of course, reward a child by permitting some action beneficial to others or by permitting the child a new challenge.

5. The phenomenon is well enough known to have produced several theories, ranging from balance theory (Heider 1946) and Theory of Cognitive Dissonance (Festinger 1957) to Psycholoical Reactance (Brehm 1966; Brehm and Brehm 1981). None to my knowledge has tied the phenomenon with language.

REFERENCES

Aronson, Elliot, and J. Merrill Carlsmith 1963 "Effect of the severity of threat on the devaluation of forbidden behavior." Journal of Abnormal and Social Psychology 66:584–588.

Aronson,Elliot, J. Merrill Carlsmith, and John M. Darley 1963 "The effects of expectancy on volunteering for an unpleasant experience." Journal of Abnormal and Social Psychology 6:220–224.

Austin, Roy L. 1978 "Race, father-absence, and female delinquency." Criminology 15:487–504.

Bandler, Richard J., George R. Madaras, and Daryl J. Bem 1968 "Self-observation as a source of pain perception." Journal of Personality and Social Psychology 9:205–209.

Bandura, Albert and Aletha C. Huston 1961 "Identification as a process of incidental learning." Journal of Abnormal and Social Psychology 63:311–318.

Bandura, Albert and Richard H. Walters 1959 Adolescent Aggression. New York: Ronald. 1963 Social Learning and Personality Development. New York: Holt, Rinehart, and Winston.

Batson, C. Daniel, Janine L. Dyck, J. Randall Brandt, Judy G. Batson, Anne L. Powell, M. Rosalie McMaster, and Cari Griffitt 1988 "Five studies testing two new egoistic alternatives to the empathy-altruism hypothesis." Journal of Personality and Social Psychology 55:52–77.

Baumrind, Diana 1978 "Parental disciplinary patterns and social competence in children." Youth and Society 9:239–276.

Bender, Loretta 1947 "Psychopathic behavior disorders in children." In Handbook of Correctional Psychology, ed. R. Lindner and R. Seliger, 360–377. New York: Philosophical Library.

Boggiano, Ann K., and Deborah S. Main 1986 "Enhancing children's interest in activities used as rewards: The bonus effect." Journal of Personality and Social Psychology 31:1116–1126.

Bowlby, John 1940 "The influence of early environment on neurosis and neurotic character." International Journal of Psychoanalysis 21:154–178.

Brehm, Jack W. 1940 A Theory of Psychological Reactance. New York: Academic Press.

POSTSCRIPT

Does Spanking Lead to Child Abuse and Later Violence?

Both Straus and McCord agree that physical punishment of children contributes to a cycle of violence, yet their explanations as to how this happens differs. Straus found that children whose parents spanked them, when compared to unspanked peers, were more aggressive, had higher rates of juvenile delinquency, had higher rates of spouse abuse, had lower economic achievement, and showed higher drug and alcohol abuse rates. By spanking, he argues, parents modeled the norm of violence and legitimized it as a way to solve problems.

On the other hand, McCord theorizes that punishment in general accounts for increased violent acts. Neglected, abused, rejected, as well as physically punished children tend to become antisocial. When parents use a system of reward and punishment, they are modeling the norm of self-interest verses the welfare of others. Because these children work for rewards and are punished for failure, they do not learn the value of intrinsic reward and the need to care for others. Because these children are more concerned about themselves than others, McCord concludes, they are more prone to violence.

McCord cites a study of criminals and the type of child-rearing they received. The fewest number of criminals came from nonpunitive homes, the next highest number came from punitive but affectionate homes, and the largest number of criminals came from punitive, unaffectionate homes.

If spanking and any kind of punishment leads to increased violence in children and adults, what form of guidance can parents use? Many child development experts feel that reasoning, talking, and listening to children works well in teaching right from wrong and that these techniques preserve a child's self-concept. They admit that this child-rearing approach takes more time, but the benefits outweigh the costs.

SUGGESTED READINGS

Brown, C. (1994, April 22–24). To spank or not to spank. *USA Weekend*, pp. 4–7.

Dobson, J. (1992). *The new dare to discipline*. Wheaton, Illinois: Tyndale.

Ellison, C., & Sherkat, D. (1993, February). Conservative Protestantism and support for corporal punishment. *American Sociological Review, 58,* 131–144.

Leach, P. (1994). *Children first*. New York: Alfred A. Knopf.

Straus, M. (1994). *Beating the devil out of them: Corporal punishment in American families and its effects on children*. Boston: Lexington Books/Macmillan.

ISSUE 6

Are Only Children Less Independent Than Firstborn Children?

YES: Barbara Byrd, Arnold P. DeRosa, and Stephen S. Craig, from "The Adult Who Is an Only Child: Achieving Separation or Individuation," *Psychological Reports* (August 1993)

NO: Steven Mellor, from "How Do Only Children Differ from Other Children?" *The Journal of Genetic Psychology* (June 1990)

ISSUE SUMMARY

YES: Barbara Byrd, Arnold DeRosa, and Stephen Craig, professors at Seton Hall University, conclude from a study of college students that only children are less autonomous than firstborn children.

NO: Steven Mellor, a psychology professor at Pennsylvania State University, reports that only children are similar to firstborns as well as children from two-child families in terms of their developmental path.

For many years research on the birth order, or ordinal position of children in a family, has suggested that there are certain personality traits that can be attributed to oldest, middle, and youngest children. Only children and firstborns had been thought to be very similar in personality characteristics. Researchers define as *firstborn* the first child in a family, the last child born if there is a significant time lapse between siblings' births, or the only child in a one-child family. Only children and firstborns have been labeled perfectionists, high achievers, and conformists. Almost all of the original astronauts and many of the world's leaders, for example, were firstborn or only children.

But some contemporary researchers believe that only children are significantly different from firstborns in terms of their ability to separate from their families. These scientists posit that only children get more attention from their parents for the duration of their childhoods than do firstborns. Moreover, only children can become more dependent on their parents for emotional support than children who have siblings. Consequently, these factors might slow the rate at which only children individuate from their families as compared to children from families with more than one child. Similarly, researchers argue that firstborns may have more success individuating from their parents due in part to the "dethroning process" that takes place within the family system upon the arrival of the second child. This process, which is briefly discussed by Barbara Byrd and her colleagues, refers to the firstborn's loss of exclusive parental attention with the addition of a sibling and the ways in which the firstborn adjusts to the change.

The debate that follows presents two studies that investigate whether or not being an only child can impact a person's ability to achieve independence from the family system. As you read them, think about your own family. Where are you in terms of ordinal position? Do you think birth order influences the development of self-sufficiency or individuation from one's family of origin?

YES

Barbara Byrd, Arnold P. DeRosa, and Stephen S. Craig

THE ADULT WHO IS AN ONLY CHILD: ACHIEVING SEPARATION OR INDIVIDUATION

Summary.—60 women and 60 men between the ages of 18 and 45 years ($M = 30.5$, $SD = 9.6$) were categorized by sex, age, and birth order (only child, firstborn, lastborn) to assess the differences among the adult only-child, the youngest child, and the oldest child in autonomous characteristics and cohesiveness in family interaction. Analysis of the responses on a biographical data sheet, the California Psychological Inventory, and the Family Adaptability Cohesion Scales III showed that main effects for birth order and sex are significant in the process of separation-individuation and that the only child is less autonomous than the oldest child.

Family Systems and Differentiating Influences

Maintaining relatedness, yet allowing independence of its members is a primary task that challenges the well functioning family throughout the life cycle. There has been increased interest on the part of family theorists and researchers in recent years concerning issues of differentiation, autonomy, and individuation (Bowen, 1978; Grotevant & Cooper, 1986; Haley, 1980; Minuchin, 1974; Sabatelli & Mazor, 1985). Of particular relevance to issues of autonomy is Bowen's construct of differentiation of self. Bowen uses this formulation to define the functioning and experience both of individuals and of family relationships. In Bowenian theory, individual and family functioning are seen as a direct consequence of the differentiation achieved between emotionality and intellect. Individuals with low differentiation are unable to separate themselves from their family system. From this perspective, the farther a person is along the continuum toward differentiation, the healthier is that person. A family's differentiation influences how interpersonal distances are regulated among the family members. For Bowen (1976) the "triangle" is the basic foundation of any family emotional system. Ideally, a family should

From Barbara Byrd, Arnold P. DeRosa, and Stephen S. Craig, "The Adult Who Is an Only Child: Achieving Separation or Individuation," *Psychological Reports*, vol. 73, no. 1 (August 1993), pp. 171–177. Copyright © 1993 by *Psychological Reports*. Reprinted by permission.

consist of differentiated individuals; however, since one-to-one relationships are difficult to maintain, parents will typically triangulate around a child. The concept of triangulation is especially relevant to the only-child family wherein this natural threesome may be particularly vulnerable to fusion of this kind.

Researchers interested in the process of leaving home have demonstrated ways that dysfunctional parent-adolescent relationships curtail the successful attainment of autonomy. Stierlin, Levi, and Savard (1971) stress issues concerning families that are too tightly bound together. He found that this binding mode keeps the adolescent locked within the parental orbit and thwarts opportunities for individuation. Haley (1980), focusing on a population of dysfunctional young adults with psychosomatic illnesses who were unable to leave home, posited complex parent-child dynamics that prevent healthy separation. These formulations coincide with the earlier work of Masterson (1976), who studied borderline adolescents and attributed certain family interactions to the disrupted individuation of these teenagers. While these theorists have concentrated on a clinical population, elements of similar family dynamics may be in operation in modified forms in most family units.

Blos (1979), as a corollary to Mahler, Pine, and Bergman's (1975) work, has proposed that the transition from adolescence into adulthood requires a second separation-individuation. While Josselson (1980) views individuation as a life-long process, she stresses that there is a prominent acceleration during adolescence. For identity formation to proceed, the main tasks of individuation during adolescence involve (1) psychological separation from the "reality" parents and

(2) the separation from the introjected parents (Josselson, 1980, p. 193). Consistent with this is the relational perspective of Grotevant and Cooper (1986), who proposed that there is a co-occurrence of individuality and connectedness in family relationships that contribute to the adolescent's ability to explore identity-related choices (p. 96). From these perspectives, issues of personal autonomy cannot be understood apart from the family as a whole, since it is only relative and reciprocally shared by all.

Siblings and Issues of Separation-Individuation

Bank and Kahn (1975) view the sibling relationship as a life-long process, influential throughout the life cycle which often is overlooked when studying family functioning. Both authors view identification as the "glue" of the sibling relationship. "Identification with brothers and sisters are more abundant than the possibilities for parent-child identification, but the motivation (love, protection, relief of guilt) may be less" (p. 320). This implies that sibling identifications are apt to be more spontaneous and less encumbered than parent-child identifications. Bank and Kahn (1975) also point out that the sibling experience helps foster differentiations, which can serve as an inhibitor against fusion within a family. This mutually regulatory process is common among brothers and sisters, which can provide an "observing ego" for siblings that is not present in most parent-child relationships.

Neubauer (1982, 1983), in his studies on the importance of siblings' interaction, makes many of the same observations and further adds that, because siblings often share a similar psychic organization, they are responsive to one another with respect to drive manifestations and fluctuations between progression and regression. "Experimentation, sexual curiosity, and displacement of aggression can provide special, shared nontraumatic experiences that go far beyond the identification with the parents they share" (1983, p. 334). Neubauer views issues of rivalry, jealousy, and envy among siblings in nonpathological or traumatic settings as a positive contribution to emotional development. He sees these dynamics as an expression of the interactions of all psychic structural components, facilitating comparisons promoting the differentiation of object and self.

METHOD

Subjects
Subjects, 552 undergraduate and graduate students at a private university, were sampled from which 120 were randomly drawn for inclusion in the study. Among the original 552, 284 were firstborn, 200 lastborn, and 68 only children. Of the 284 firstborn, 171 were younger (18 to 30 years old) firstborn, and 113 older (31 to 45 years old) firstborn. Of the 68 only children, 38 were younger and 30 older only children. Of the 200 lastborn, 112 were younger and 88 older lastborn. Twenty subjects (10 men and 10 women) were randomly selected from each of the six categories so defined for inclusion in the study. Subjects whose childhood included either divorce or death of a parent were eliminated from the pool from which the final sample were selected.

Procedure
Biological data sheets, the California Psychological Inventory (30 items of the Independence scale) and the Family Adaptability and Cohesion Evaluation Scales (FACES III) were distributed in packets to 200 subjects. Each completed packet was assigned a number from 1 to 200. Subjects ($N = 120$) were placed into subgroups based on age, sex, and birth-order categories, placing 20 men and 20 women in each of the three categories.

Biographical data sheet. The biographical data sheet was devised to provide information about each subject's birth-order position, family status, age, sex, and number of members in the family.

The Family Adaptability Cohesion Evaluation Scales III (Olson, Portner, & Lavee, 1985). Family Adaptability Cohesion Evaluation Scales (FACES III) is a 20-item instrument used to measure cohesion and adaptability. The instrument is designed to assess how family members see their family (perceived) and how they would like it to be (ideal) (Olson, et al., 1985). The instrument addresses four levels of family cohesion, namely, disengaged, separated, connected, and enmeshed (Minuchin, 1974).

Each item of the FACES III has a five-point response option. The subject is asked to describe his family as it is or was and how ideally he would like it to be or have been. The difference between the two should give an inverse estimate of one's family satisfaction (Olson, et al., 1985). The higher the cohesion scores the more enmeshed is a family. Reliability ($N = 242$) was reported as .77 for the 10-item cohesion scale, and .68 for the Total FACES III scores.

California Psychological Inventory (Gough, 1987). From the California Psychological Inventory the Independence Scale was used to measure autonomy, higher independence (55 to 70T) indicating self-sufficiency, resourcefulness, and detachment, lower independence (30 to 45T) indicating lack of self-confidence and support-seeking behavior. Reliability coefficients for the Independence Scales were .69 for men and .67 for women.

RESULTS

A completely randomized factorial analysis of variance was used to investigate the differences in autonomy, as measured by the Independence Scale, across the three birth orders and two genders. The analysis indicated significant main effects for both birth order ($F_{2,114} = 2.93$, $p = .06$) and gender ($F_{1,114} = 5.13$, $p = .03$) but no significant interaction for birth order × gender. Effect sizes based on formulas suggested by Cohen (1988) and Rosnow and Rosenthal (1988) for both birth order, .3, and gender, .4, were rather low. The effect size of .4 for gender indicates that variable accounted for approximately 4% of the variance in autonomy while the effect size of .3 for birth order indicates that variable accounted for approximately 3% of the variance in autonomy.

Post hoc analysis using Tukey's test indicated that men evidenced higher autonomy than did women and oldest siblings evidenced higher autonomy than did only children.. . .

Scores on the Cohesion scale of FACES III were used to classify subjects' families as disengaged, separated, connected, or enmeshed. Chi-squared analysis indicated that among the only children more subjects rated their families of origin as enmeshed than would be expected by chance ($x^2 = 8.33$, $p < .05$).

DISCUSSION

The purpose of the present investigation was to examine the relationship between birth order and autonomous functioning. The position advanced was based on the orientation that there is a continuous interplay between individuality and connectedness in family relationships. Differences in scores on autonomy, as measured on the California Psychological Inventory's Independence Scale, were significantly associated with birth order. The results, therefore, show that only children were less independent than oldest children. In addition, men exhibited greater independence than women.

The present data showed that firstborn children were significantly more independent than only children. While lastborn children had a higher mean independence score than only children, this difference was not significantly greater. It might be hypothesized that the "dethronement process," in which the firstborn must relinquish only-child status at the birth of a sibling, is instrumental in fostering independence. Unique to the oldest child is the status of having been first and foremost, a rank which may produce a sense of entitlement and even superiority. It is also likely that the loss of exclusive parental attention reduces the later tendency for dependent and potentially guilt-producing relationships. Taylor and Kogan (1973) observed that mothers may withdraw emotionally from a first child in anticipation of and immediately following the birth of their second child so the firstborn's relationship to the parents must be redefined. There is a repeated "rapprochement crisis" when there is another birth in the family. However, it may be that for the firstborn the resolution of the crisis is a more individuated state characterized by greater autonomous functioning. Furthermore, it may be that with the birth of a sibling assertive behavior becomes necessary and even reinforced, and the firstborn is propelled to achieve independence from his parents. One might suggest that for the oldest child the inevitable dethronement process can be a positive and useful adaptation in the attainment of autonomy.

The data indicated that youngest children were more independent than only children and that only children were significantly less independent than firstborns. Adler (Ansbacher & Ansbacher, 1984) described the youngest child as " . . . a pampered child . . . all the family spoils them. A spoiled child can never be independent" (p. 381). Adler's comments are consistent with findings of Blane and Barry (1973) who reported heightened conflict between dependency and independent striving in lastborn males.

The data showed only children to be less independent than firstborns. This finding is consistent with the observations of both Feldman (1981) and Forer (1977) who attribute a prolonged Oedipal triangle as an obstacle that created a fixated dependent relationship for the only child and his parents. An important aspect of the separation-individuation phase is the ability to neutralize aggression towards the parental objects. The only child would seem to have greater difficulty with this task because the parent-child relationship is exclusive. Sibling aggression is adaptive in nature and is an integral part of the give and take relationship of siblings, as well as a healthy avenue for the expression of conflict and frustration. Minuchin (1974) views sibling rivalry as a stabilizing force in the system of many families. Clearly, the only child is lacking in this experience, a factor which could contribute to greater anxiety with aggressive feelings and increased dependency.

REFERENCES

Ansbacher, H. L., & Ansbacher, R. (Eds.) (1984) *The individual psychology of Alfred Adler: a systematic presentation in selections from his writings.* New York: Basic Books.

Bank, S. P., & Kahn, M. D. (1975) Sisterhood-brotherhood is powerful: sibling subsystems and family therapy. *Family Process,* 14, 317–319.

Blane, H. T., & Barry, H. III. (1973) Birth order and alcoholism. *Quarterly Journal of Studies on Alcohol,* 34, 837–852.

Blos, P. (1979) *The adolescent passage: developmental issues.* New York: International Universities Press.

Bowen, M. (1976) Theory and practice in psychotherapy. In P. J. Guerin (Ed.), *Family therapy: theory and practice in psychotherapy.* New York: Gardner Press. Pp. 42–90.

Bowen, M. (1978) *Family therapy in clinical practice.* New York: Jason Aronson.

Cohen, J. (1988) *Statistical power analysis for the behavioral sciences.* (2nd ed.) Hillsdale, NJ: Erlbaum.

Feldman, G. C. (1981) Three's company: family therapy with only child families. *Journal of Marital and Family Therapy,* 7, 43–46.

Forer, L. K. (1977) Use of birth order information in psychotherapy. *Journal of Individual Psychology,* 33, 105–118.

Gough, H. G. (1987) *California Psychological Inventory.* Palo Alto, CA: Consulting Psychologists Press.

Grotevant, H. D., & Cooper, C. R. (1986) Individuation in family relationship. *Human Development,* 29, 82–100.

Haley, J. (1980) *Leaving home: the therapy of disturbed young people.* New York: McGraw-Hill.

Josselson, R. L. (1980). Ego development in adolescence. In J. Adelson (Ed.), *Handbook of adolescent psychology.* New York: Wiley, Pp. 188–210.

Mahler, M. (1968) *On human symbiosis and the vicissitudes of individuation.* Vol. 1. *Infantile psychosis.* New York: International Universities Press.

Mahler, M., Pine, F., & Bergman, A. (1975) *The psychological birth of the human infant.* New York: Basic Books.

Masterson, J. (1976) *Psychotherapy of the borderline adult: a developmental approach.* New York: Brunner/Mazel.

Minuchin, S. (1974) *Families and family therapy.* Cambridge, MA: Harvard Univer. Press.

Neubauer, P. B. (1982) Rivalry, envy and jealousy. In A. J. Solnit (Ed.), *Psychoanalytic study of the child.* Vol. 37. New Haven, CT: Yale Univer. Press, Pp. 121–142.

Neubauer, P. B. (1983) The importance of the sibling experience. In A. J. Solnit (Ed.), *Psychoanalytic study of the child.* Vol. 38. New Haven, CT: Yale Univer. Press. Pp. 325–336.

Olson, D., Portner, J., & Lavee, Y. (1985) *FACES III.* St. Paul, MN: Family Social Science.

Rosnow, R. L., & Rosenthal, R. (1988) Focused tests of significance and effect size estimates in counseling psychology. *Journal of Counseling Psychology,* 59, 217–224.

Sabatelli, R. M., & Mazor, A. (1985) Differentiation, individuation and identity formation: the integration of family system and individual developmental perspectives. *Adolescence,* 20, 619–633.

Stierlin, H., Levi, L., & Savard, R. (1971) Parental perceptions of separating children. *Family Process,* 10, 411–427.

Taylor, L., & Kogan, K. (1973) Effects of birth of a sibling on mother-child interactions. *Child Psychiatry and Human Development,* 4(1), 53–58.

NO
Steven Mellor

HOW DO ONLY CHILDREN DIFFER FROM OTHER CHILDREN?

ABSTRACT. Developmental outcomes of only and non-only children, categorized by birth order and by family size, were investigated. Multiple hypotheses based on meta-analyses of the only-child literature (Falbo & Polit, 1986) were tested with independent comparison techniques. Results indicated that developmental outcomes of only children were similar to outcomes for firstborns and children from two-child families but dissimilar to outcomes for later borns and children from larger families. Furthermore, outcomes were more positive for only children, firstborns, and children from two-child families than for all other comparison groups. In agreement with Falbo and Polit, only-child deprivation and only-child uniqueness explanations for outcome differences were not supported in favor of an explanation that emphasizes qualities of the parent–child relationship. Results suggest that future comparisons to only-child outcomes should preserve the independence of contrast results and expand the only-child category to include data from firstborns and others from two-child families.

How do only children differ from other children? Falbo and Polit (1986) reported the results of six meta-analyses of the research literature on the only child since 1925 and concluded that several of the developmental outcomes of only children were similar to the outcomes for firstborn children and children from two-child families but dissimilar to outcomes for children from three- or four-child families and children from five- or more child families. Despite dissimilarities between only children and a group of non-only children, Falbo and Polit ruled out explanatory mechanisms relating to only-child deprivation and only-child uniqueness in favor of theoretical propositions that emphasized qualities of the parent–child relationship. Although Falbo and Polit are probably correct in their conclusion that the developmental paths of only children have more in common with the paths of children from smaller families, we believe that theoretical propositions based on meta-analyses are

From Steven Mellor, "How Do Only Children Differ from Other Children?" *The Journal of Genetic Psychology*, vol. 151, no. 2 (June 1990), pp. 221–230. Copyright © 1990 by The Helen Dwight Reid Educational Foundation. Reprinted by permission of Heldref Publications, 1319 18th Street, NW, Washington, DC 20036-1802. Some notes omitted.

tenuous at best and require support from independent comparison techniques designed to test multiple hypotheses.

Falbo and Polit (1986) searched through the sibling relationship, birth order, and family size literature for studies that included only-child comparison groups. These studies variously defined the only child as firstborn, last born or as a one-child family. Of 200 studies reviewed for inclusion in the meta-analyses, 115 survived a 6-point quality rating system based on sample size, controls for extraneous variables, and other indices of methodological rigor. Other studies were omitted because effect sizes (based on Cohen's d) could not be computed from reported correlations or because data for only borns were combined with data for firstborns or others from small families. On the basis of included studies, with total sample sizes ranging from 50 to over 600,000, Falbo and Polit formed a series of contrasts between only children and a non-only comparison group (anyone who had a sibling), and between only children and comparison groups defined in terms of birth order (firstborns or later borns from multichild families) and family size—small (two-child), medium (three- or four-child), or large (five- or more child) families.

A broad variety of developmental outcomes found in the literature were classified into 14 categories (e.g., academic progress/grades, self-esteem, personal control/autonomy, IQ/standardized ability tests, and affiliation need/extraversion). Because of the uneven number of studies represented by these categories, outcomes were grouped into five general developmental categories: achievement, adjustment, character, intelligence, and sociability. The outcome groups were used as dependent variable measures

for five separate meta-analyses involving contrasts between only children and non-only children and comparison groups defined by birth order and by family size.[1] Mean effect sizes reliably differed from zero (based on nonorthogonal t tests) for achievement, character, and intelligence outcomes. For achievement and intelligence, only children had more desirable outcomes than comparison groups of all non-only borns, children from medium and large families, and later borns, but had similar outcomes to groups of firstborns and children from small families. In the character area, only children had more desirable outcomes than groups of all non-only borns and groups of children from medium and large families but similar outcomes to all other comparison groups. None of the mean effect sizes for sociability and adjustment outcomes were reliably different from zero ($p < .05$).

Meta-analysis results were used by Falbo and Polit (1986) to suggest that only borns had higher levels of achievement and intelligence than children from medium and large families, had more desirable personalities, and were as sociable and adjusted as peers with siblings. Because no data were uncovered that revealed a single significant disadvantage for only borns across developmental outcomes, and because only borns were not found to be reliably different from all other comparison groups, Falbo and Polit argued that explanatory mechanisms that employ only-child deprivation and uniqueness were less feasible than a mechanism that emphasizes the parent–child relationship. Indirect support for this mechanism came from the finding that, across all meta-analyses, comparison between only borns and firstborns, and comparisons between only borns and children from small families, never yielded reliable outcome differences. Falbo and Polit suggested that, because both only borns and firstborns were their parents' first child, at least for awhile, both were only borns, and concluded that the parent–child mechanism that produces only child outcomes was probably at work in producing similar firstborn and small-family outcomes.

Our central concern was with Falbo and Polit's (1986) theoretical proposition that two explanatory mechanism have been excluded in favor of one that can explain how only children differ from others on general developmental outcomes. At the very least, Falbo and Polit's use of nonorthogonal t tests (36 at $p < .05$) to evaluate contrasts between comparison groups (when independent mean comparison tests are preferable) calls for replication; a task we address with a new sample in our study. But, we also believed that theoretical propositions ruling out other mechanisms must find support from procedures designed to test multiple hypotheses and preserve outcome probability levels. Thus, our study was designed to retest hypotheses that follow from Falbo and Polit's meta-analyses and to further clarify a number of the similar and dissimilar developmental outcomes of only and non-only borns.

METHOD

Subjects
The sample consisted of 434 students (239 males and 195 females) recruited from six junior and senior high schools and one community college in the Los Angeles area. Subjects' ages ranged from 11 to 19 years, with a mean age of 15.9 years. Adolescents and young adults were targeted as subjects to approximate the mean age

of subjects (16.6 years) and the majority of age groups (56%) included in Falbo and Polit's (1986) sample. Seventy-nine percent were Caucasian, 11% were Black, 8% were Hispanic, and 2% were Asian, an ethnic mix proportional to current national percentages ("The Nation," 1988).

Subjects were first categorized by birth order and then by family size. Eight percent were only borns, 32% were firstborns, and 60% were later borns. In terms of family size, 8% percent were from one-child families, 38% were from small (two-child) families, 38% were from medium (three- or four-child) families, and 15% were from large (five- or more child) families. The distribution of gender within categories for birth order and family size was proportional to the distribution in the total sample, and mean ages did not significantly differ from one category to the next ($p < .05$).

Procedure
Measures were administered in random order to students in "home" classrooms by undergraduates earning course credits. Informed consent forms were used to brief subjects on the nature of the project, to request voluntary participation, and to assure subjects of anonymity. Completed measures were received from 89% of the students contacted. Feedback on group results were sent to subjects through their home classroom instructors.

Measures
The Erikson Psychosocial Stage Inventory (EPSI; Rosenthal, Gurney, & Moore, 1981) was selected to measure general developmental outcomes included in Falbo and Polit's (1986) meta-analyses. The EPSI is a measure of negative and positive resolutions to identity crises as defined by Erikson, and many of the res-

olutions are thought to play a critical role in influencing the outcomes grouped by Falbo and Polit. For example, outcomes related to affiliation need, personal control/autonomy, and academic progress/grades overlap with resolutions to the crises of trust versus mistrust, autonomy versus shame, and industry versus inferiority (cf. Hamachek, 1988). One important shortcoming for this claim is in the area of intelligence. The EPSI does not include standardized items designed to measure ability per se, but arguments can be launched that suggest that achievement and intelligence are highly correlated with respect to developmental outcomes (cf. Fitzgerald & Mellor, 1988).

The EPSI is a 72-item self-report inventory consisting of six 12-item subscales that assess degrees of negative to positive resolutions to six of Erikson's identity crises in childhood, adolescence, and early adulthood (trust vs. mistrust, autonomy vs. shame, initiative vs. guilt, industry vs. inferiority, identity vs. identity confusion, and intimacy vs. isolation). Items are rated on a 5-point scale ranging from *hardly ever true* (1) to *almost always true* (5). Subscale scores are represented by mean item scores. High mean scores for each subscale indicate positive resolutions to crises. Rosenthal et al. (1981) reported internal reliability (alpha) coefficients for subscales ranging from .57 to .81. Alpha coefficients for the present sample ranged from .74 to .86. Supportive validity can be found in Rosenthal, Moore, and Taylor (1983), and further subscale uses can be found in Moore and Rosenthal (1984), Pickar and Tori (1986), and Mellor (1989).[2]

Sociobiographic measures also were included to assess subject gender, age, educational level (indexed by grade level), ethnic mix, vocabulary, and socioeco-

nomic status (SES). A variety of other measures were used to determine birth order and family size. Form Z of the Basic Word Vocabulary Test (BWVT; Dupey, 1974) was used as the measure of vocabulary, and SES was based on Hollingshead's (1975) Four-Factor Index of Social Status, adjusting for combined parental income. Along with age and educational level, the latter two measures were given to check for covariation affects on birth-order and family-size differences reported in the only-child literature (cf. Claudy, 1984; Falbo, 1984; Gecas & Pasley, 1983; Mednick, Baker, & Hocevar, 1985).

RESULTS

The results of primary interest are the outcomes of sets of orthogonal planned comparisons computed on the data of all subjects. Comparison sets were constructed within Gender × Birth Order (only borns, firstborns, later borns) and Gender × Family Size (one-child, small, medium, large), analyses of variance. Analyses were repeated for EPSI subscales as separate dependent variable measures. Weights were assigned to birth-order and family-size groups to ensure that contrast results were independent within sets, despite the fact that some contrast results were redundant within analyses.

Four sets of contrasts (two per analysis) were performed to retest contrasts indicated by Falbo and Polit (1986)....

Comparison results indicated that only predicted contrasts within sets yielded reliable differences between group means or group mean combinations on dependent variable measures. All other group contrasts failed to reach significance ($p < .05$). Furthermore, reliable mean differences were consistent with high-low predictions. Within the first contrast set for birth–order groups, reliable differences were not found between only borns and firstborns, but differences were found between only borns and later borns on autonomy, $F(1,411) = 4.84$, $p < .03$, initiative, $F(1,405) = 5.00$, $p < .03$, and industry, $F(1,413) = 3.79$, $p < .05$. Mean differences for these groups indicated that only borns had significantly higher mean scores (4.12, 3.93, 3.88) than later borns (3.87, 3.69, 3.64). Within the second set for birth–order groups, group combination differences were not detected between means for only borns and average means for firstborns and later borns, but differences were detected between average means for only borns and first-borns and means for later borns on autonomy, $F(1,411) = 4.26$, $p < .04$, initiative, $F(1,405) = 3.86$, $p < .05$, industry, $F(1,413) = 5.36$, $p < .02$, and identity, $F(1,404) = 3.97$, $p < .05$. Mean differences for these latter contrasts indicated that mean scores for only borns and firstborns were significantly higher (4.02, 3.82, 3.82, 3.84) than mean scores for later borns (3.87, 3.69, 3.64, 3.69).

For the third and fourth contrast sets, we noted a consistent pattern of comparison results. Within the third contrast set for family-size groups, only contrasts between only-child and medium family groups, and between only-child and large family groups, yielded reliable differences on dependent variable measures. Significant mean differences between only-child and medium family groups were recorded on autonomy, $F(1,409) = 4.03$ $p < .04$, and initiative, $F(1,403) = 4.26$ $p < .04$. Mean differences for these contrasts indicated that only-child scores were significantly higher (4.12, 3.93) than medium-family scores (3.88, 3.70). Reliable mean differences between only-child and large-family groups were recorded on initiative, $F(1,403) = 3.75$, $p < .05$, and identity, $F(1,402) = 6.20$, $p < .01$. Mean differences for the latter contrasts indicated that only-child scores were significantly higher (3.93, 3.88) than large-family scores (3.57, 3.53).

The most reliable differences between comparison groups occurred with the fourth set for family size. Although no other contrasts between group combinations were significant, average means for only-child and small-family groups were reliably different from average means for medium- and large-family groups on trust, $F(1,404) = 3.99$, $p < .05$, autonomy, $F(1,409) = 5.95$, $p < .01$, initiative, $F(1,403) = 7.92$, $p < .005$, industry, $F(1,411) = 7.39$, $p < .007$, and identity, $F(1,402) = 4.54$, $p < .03$. Mean differences for these combined groups indicated that only-child and small-family mean scores were significantly higher (3.55, 4.02, 3.83, 3.82, 3.82) than medium- and large-family mean scores (3.39, 3.83, 3.63, 3.59, 3.65).

Within all contrast sets, we also found reliable differences between male and female groups on intimacy, $F(1,408) = 27.28$, $p < .001$. Mean differences for these groups indicated that females' mean scores were significantly higher (3.86) than males' mean scores (3.52). In addition, we repeated analyses for all sets, controlling for the influence of age, grade level, SES, and vocabulary. Results for separate and multiple analyses of covariance with adjusted probability levels ($p < .05$) produced similar results, and reported significant effects were unchanged. Furthermore, across all analyses, we failed to find a single significant interaction effect between gender and birth order or gender and family size.

DISCUSSION

The data of this study support Falbo and Polit's (1986) conclusion that the developmental paths of only children are similar to the paths of firstborns and children from two-child families but dissimilar to paths of children from larger families. In fact, on the basis of developmental outcomes related to resolutions of developmental crises in childhood, adolescence, and early adulthood, the crucial outcome differences appear precisely between the only child, whether defined as only born or firstborn, and the later-born child on the birth-order variable, and precisely between children from two-child families and three-child families on the family-size variable.

We believe that our results provide much clearer support for the hypotheses revealed in Falbo and Polit's meta-analyses. Although the procedures they used to construct the analyses appeared sound, the use of non-orthogonal *t* tests to test comparison group differences failed to preserve the independence of contrast results and protect against inflated outcome probability levels. As such, the theoretical propositions offered by Falbo and Polit were tenuous at best.

In contrast with techniques used by Falbo and Polit (1986), we retested multiple hypotheses related to only-child uniqueness and deprivation, and the parent–child relationship, with orthogonal contrasts that ensured that comparison results were independent and outcome probability levels were fixed as stated. The only-child uniqueness hypothesis was not supported. Only-children resolution outcomes were not reliably different from outcomes for all non-only comparison groups, whether defined by birth order or by family size.

Comparisons revealed that, across outcomes, the positive-negative resolutions of only children did not significantly differ from the resolutions of firstborns or children from small families.

The only-child deprivation hypothesis also was not supported. Only children had significantly higher positive outcomes to crises than did later borns and children from medium and large families. Furthermore, group means indicated that the positive outcomes of only borns were higher across the board than the positive outcomes for all other comparison groups, including first-borns and children from small families.

Our findings were consistent with the parent–child hypothesis simply because we failed to find significant outcome differences between group combinations of only children and firstborns or between group combinations of only children and children from small families. In contrast, we did find significant outcome differences between combinations of only children and later borns and others from medium and large families. Although we did not directly test the parent–child hypothesis, qualities of the parent–child relationship are apparently similar for only children, firstborns, and children from two-child families but dissimilar to qualities of the parent–child relationship for later borns and others from larger families. On the basis of the outcome differences found in this study, we would suggest that the definition of the only child be expanded to include firstborns and others from two-child families in future studies that use the parent–child mechanism to explain the outcome differences of only children.

We found differences in resolution outcomes between birth-order groups and between family-size groups. Findings that suggest that only children, compared with non-only children, are generally more autonomous in terms of personal control, have higher levels of initiative or personal aspiration or motivation, are more industrious in terms of educational or occupational achievement, and have stronger identities (as indexed by self-esteem or adjustment levels) are not new in the only-child literature (cf. Falbo, 1984, 1987 for reviews). Inconsistencies often appear with respect to each of these findings, however, and a consensus of thought about only-child outcome advantages and disadvantages is far from established. We suggest that profitable meta-analyses for future research include sets of orthogonal comparisons of developmental outcomes of an only-child group (defined as only borns, first-borns, and others from two-child families) with outcomes of various non-only child groups. We believe that outcome differences will be consistent with the present results and that a stronger consensus can be reached in terms of the similarities and dissimilarities of the developmental paths of the only child.

NOTES

1. A sixth meta-analysis was conducted on 19 studies that included various ratings of the quality of the parent–child relationship (keyed toward more positive relationships). Results indicated mean effect sizes reliably different from zero (based on multiple t tests) for comparisons between only children and all non-only borns, and between only children and children from large families. Because mean effect sizes were positive, Falbo and Polit suggested that only children had more positive relationships with their parents than did other children.

2. Additional psychometric information on the EPSI, including factor structure results and inter-subscale correlations may be found in Rosenthal (1982).

3. A detailed explanation for male-female outcome differences relating to intimacy may be found in Mellor (1989).

REFERENCES

Claudy, J. G. (1984). The only child as a young adult: Results from Project Talent. In T. Falbo (Ed.), *The single-child family* (pp. 211–252). New York: Guilford Press.

Dupey, H. J. (1974). The rationale, development, and standardization of the Basic Word Vocabulary Test. *Vital and Health Statistical Series 2, 60*, 1–71.

Falbo, T. (1984). Only children: a review. In T. Falbo (Ed.)., *The single-child family* (pp. 1–24). New York: Guilford Press.

Falbo, T. (1987). Only children in the United States and China. In S. Oskamp (Ed.), *Annual social psychology* (Vol. 7, pp. 159–183). Beverly Hills: Sage.

Falbo, T., & Polit, D. F. (1986). Quantitative review of the only child literature: Research evidence and theory development. *Psychological Bulletin, 100*, 176–189.

Fitzgerald, J. M., & Mellor, S. (1988). How do people think about intelligence? *Multivariate Behavioral Research, 23*, 143–157.

Gecas, V., & Pasley, K. (1983). Birth order and self-concept in adolescence. *Journal of Youth and Adolescence, 12*, 521–535.

Hamachek, D. E. (1988). Evaluating self-concept and ego development within Erikson's framework: A formulation. *Journal of Counseling and Development, 66*, 354–360.

Hollingshead, A. B. (1975). *Four-Factor Index of Social Status.* Unpublished manuscript, Department of Sociology, Yale University, New Haven, CT.

Mednick, B. R., Baker, R. L., & Hocevar, D. (1985). Family size and birth order correlates of intellectual, psychosocial, and physical growth. *Merrill-Palmer Quarterly, 31*, 67–84.

Mellor, S. (1989). Gender differences in identity formation as a function of self-other relationships. *Journal of Youth and Adolescence, 18*, 361–375.

Moore, S. M., & Rosenthal, D. A. (1984). Balance versus main effects androgyny: Their relationship to adjustment in three ethnic groups. *Psychological Reports, 54*, 823–831.

Pickar, D. B., & Tori, C. D. (1986). The learning disabled adolescent: Eriksonian psychological development, self-concept, and delinquent behavior. *Journal of Youth and Adolescence, 15*, 429–440.

Rosenthal, D. A., (1982). *The Erikson Psychosocial Stage Inventory.* Unpublished manuscript. University of Melbourne, Department of Psychology, Victoria, Australia.

Rosenthal, D. A., Gurney, R. M., & Moore, S. M. (1981). From trust to intimacy: A new inventory for examining Erikson's stages of psychosocial development. *Journal of Youth and Adolescence, 10,* 525–537.

Rosenthal, D. A., Moore, S. M., & Taylor, M. J. (1983). Ethnicity and adjustment: A study of the self-image of Anglo-, Greek-, and Italian-Australian working class adolescents. *Journal of Youth and Adolescence, 12,* 117–135.

The Nation. (1988, September). *The Chronicle of Higher Education Almanac,* p. 3.

POSTSCRIPT

Are Only Children Less Independent Than Firstborn Children?

Byrd, DeRosa, and Craig measured college students' level of self-sufficiency and resourcefulness and found that firstborn children, as well as youngest children, were more independent than only children. Additionally, men displayed greater individuation than women. The researchers speculated that only children have less need for assertive behavior than firstborns who have brothers and sisters. Not only do firstborns adapt to the family by developing more autonomy, but parents support their independent behavior by reinforcing it. Because only children have an exclusive relationship with their parents and do not have to compete with anyone for their attention, they do not achieve the same level of independence as firstborns.

Mellor studied the way that children aged 11 to 19 responded to psychoanalyst Erik Erikson's identity crises. Children were rated on their reactions to developmental crises such as autonomy versus shame and identity versus identity confusion. He found that firstborn children and only children responded similarly and had more positive outcomes to the crises than laterborn children or children from medium and large families. Only children and firstborns were also similar to children from two-child families in their responses to Erikson's developmental crises.

Although research continues on the effects of birth order on personality, there are societal influences that may change future results on the subject, such as smaller family size, more employed mothers, increased use of day care for children, and a greater incidence of stepfamily situations. Today families in the United States have fewer children than families in the past. As a result, parents often spend as much time with the younger children as with the older ones. Will this increased attention from adults create the same personality characteristics in younger children as firstborns?

More mothers are working outside the home than ever before; thus, more children are spending their early years in child-care centers. Not only are these children less likely to spend time with adults, but they are also being socialized by other children. Will this decrease in adult interaction and increase in child interaction change the personality characteristics previously assigned to firstborns and only children?

What about the stepfamily effect? When parents remarry and families blend together, ordinal positions in the family change. In the original family, for example, a child could have been the firstborn or an only child. Now, with the addition of a stepparent and an older sibling, the child is neither the firstborn nor the only child. While previous research on this subject has been useful in understanding children's development, future studies will likely reflect these changes in our society.

SUGGESTED READINGS

Bernstein, L. (1994, February). What's new about the oldest child? *Working Mother, 17,* 60–64.

Bohmer, P., & Sitton, S. (1993, Summer). The influence of birth order and family size on notable American women's selection of careers. *The Psychological Record, 43,* 375–380.

Falbo, T. (1984). Only children: A review. In T. Falbo (Ed.), *The single-child family* (pp. 1–24). New York: Guilford Press.

Hudson, V. (1990, September). Birth order of world leaders: An exploratory analysis of effects on personality and behavior. *Political Psychology, 11,* 583–601.

Leman, K. (1985). *The birth order book.* New York: Dell.

Marzollo, J. (1990, December). What birth order means. *Parents, 65,* 84–91.

Segal, J. (1992, May). The firstborn child. *Parents, 67,* 219.

ISSUE 7

Is Divorce Always Bad for Children?

YES: Barbara Dafoe Whitehead, from "Dan Quayle Was Right," *The Atlantic Monthly* (April 1993)

NO: David Gately and Andrew I. Schwebel, from "Favorable Outcomes in Children After Parental Divorce," *Journal of Divorce and Remarriage* (vol. 18, nos. 3–4, 1992)

ISSUE SUMMARY

YES: Barbara Whitehead, a researcher and journalist, argues that children of divorce are more likely than children from intact families to live in poverty, drop out of school, and commit criminal acts.

NO: David Gately and Andrew Schwebel, both university educators, contend that children of divorce show enhanced levels of maturity, self-esteem, empathy, and androgyny.

How many people whose parents are divorced do you know? Do they perceive the divorce as having had a positive or negative effect on them? What would their lives be like if their parents had not divorced? How would their lives be different if they had grown up in an unhappy, intact home (with both parents)? These are the sorts of questions that need to be answered when studying the effects of divorce on children.

As rates of divorce increased in the 1960s and 1970s, research began to be conducted to determine its effects on children. Children whose parents divorce are not involved in the decision, but they are involved in the aftermath of the divorce. Statistics on the number of children who have experienced divorce are quite varied. Some research indicates that 26 percent of American children live in single-parent families; other research shows that over 1 million children a year experience divorce. Some futurists predict that in the 1990s, 40 to 50 percent of all children in the United States will experience the divorce of their parents.

What often causes problems for children in divorced families is that the parents split up legally but not emotionally. Such families might ride an emotional roller coaster for years after the initial divorce decree. One parent pitted against the other with the children in the middle is not uncommon for these families. This family turmoil may result in children doing poorly in school, beginning to have sex at an early age, and displaying delinquent behavior.

On the other hand, there is some evidence that children from divorced families reap positive benefits as a consequence of their experience of the divorce, particularly if the parents model responsible coping skills. Some children do better when no longer faced with the constant tension and fighting that can exist in an unhappy, intact home. These children appear to be more mature, are more realistic about life, and are more flexible.

In the following two selections, arguments are made about the negative and positive consequences of divorce for children. Barbara Whitehead quotes many of the classic studies of divorce and children to make her point that parents are more concerned about their own freedom than about their children's sense of stability and family structure. David Gately and Andrew Schwebel also cite classic studies of divorce and children, but their interpretations of the results and methods of those studies and their conclusions are opposed to those of Whitehead.

YES
Barbara Dafoe Whitehead

DAN QUAYLE WAS RIGHT

Divorce and out-of-wedlock childbirth are transforming the lives of American children. In the postwar generation more than 80 percent of children grew up in a family with two biological parents who were married to each other. By 1980 only 50 percent could expect to spend their entire childhood in an intact family. If current trends continue, less than half of all children born today will live continuously with their own mother and father throughout childhood. Most American children will spend several years in a single-mother family. Some will eventually live in stepparent families, but because stepfamilies are more likely to break up than intact (by which I mean two-biological-parent) families, an increasing number of children will experience family breakup two or even three times during childhood.

According to a growing body of social-scientific evidence, children in families disrupted by divorce and out-of-wedlock birth do worse than children in intact families on several measures of well-being. Children in single-parent families are six times as likely to be poor. They are also likely to stay poor longer. Twenty-two percent of children in one-parent families will experience poverty during childhood for seven years or more, as compared with only two percent of children in two-parent families. A 1988 survey by the National Center for Health Statistics found that children in single-parent families are two to three times as likely as children in two-parent families to have emotional and behavioral problems. They are also more likely to drop out of high school, to get pregnant as teenagers, to abuse drugs, and to be in trouble with the law. Compared with children in intact families, children from disrupted families are at a much higher risk for physical or sexual abuse.

Contrary to popular belief, many children do not "bounce back" after divorce or remarriage. Difficulties that are associated with family breakup often persist into adulthood. Children who grow up in single-parent or stepparent families are less successful as adults, particularly in the two domains of life —love and work—that are most essential to happiness. Needless to say, not all children experience such negative effects. However, research shows that many children from disrupted families have a harder time achieving intimacy in a relationship, forming a stable marriage, or even holding a steady job....

From Barbara Dafoe Whitehead, "Dan Quayle Was Right," *The Atlantic Monthly* (April 1993). Copyright © 1993 by Barbara Dafoe Whitehead. Reprinted by permission.

[I]t is... risky to ignore the issue of changing family structure. In recent years the problems associated with family disruption have grown. Overall child well-being has declined, despite a decrease in the number of children per family, an increase in the educational level of parents, and historically high levels of public spending. After dropping in the 1960s and 1970s, the proportion of children in poverty has increased dramatically, from 15 percent in 1970 to 20 percent in 1990, while the percentage of adult Americans in poverty has remained roughly constant. The teen suicide rate has more than tripled. Juvenile crime has increased and become more violent. School performance has continued to decline. There are no signs that these trends are about to reverse themselves.

If we fail to come to terms with the relationship between family structure and declining child well-being, then it will be increasingly difficult to improve children's life prospects, no matter how many new programs the federal government funds. Nor will we be able to make progress in bettering school performance or reducing crime or improving the quality of the nation's future work force—all domestic problems closely connected to family breakup. Worse, we may contribute to the problem by pursuing policies that actually increase family instability and breakup....

In the 1960s the rate of family disruption suddenly began to rise. After inching up over the course of a century, the divorce rate soared. Throughout the 1950s and early 1960s the divorce rate held steady at fewer than ten divorces a year per 1,000 married couples. Then, beginning in about 1965, the rate increased sharply, peaking at twenty-three divorces per 1,000 marriages by 1979. (In 1974 divorce passed death as the leading cause of family breakup.) The rate has leveled off at about twenty-one divorces per 1,000 marriages—the figure for 1991. The out-of-wedlock birth rate also jumped. It went from five percent in 1960 to 27 percent in 1990. In 1990 close to 57 percent of births among black mothers were nonmarital, and about 17 percent among white mothers. Altogether, about one out of every four women who had a child in 1990 was not married. With rates of divorce and nonmarital birth so high, family disruption is at its peak. Never before have so many children experienced family breakup caused by events other than death. Each year a million children go through divorce or separation and almost as many more are born out of wedlock.

Half of all marriages now end in divorce. Following divorce, many people enter new relationships. Some begin living together. Nearly half of all cohabiting couples have children in the household. Fifteen percent have new children together. Many cohabiting couples eventually get married. However, both cohabiting and remarried couples are more likely to break up than couples in first marriages. Even social scientists find it hard to keep pace with the complexity and velocity of such patterns. In the revised edition (1992) of his book *Marriage, Divorce, Remarriage*, the sociologist Andrew Cherlin ruefully comments: "If there were a truth-in-labeling law for books, the title of this edition should be something long and unwieldy like *Cohabitation, Marriage, Divorce, More Cohabitation, and Probably Remarriage.*"...

Given its dramatic impact on children's lives, one might reasonably expect that this historic level of family disruption would be viewed with alarm, even regarded as a national crisis. Yet this has not been the case. In recent years some people have argued that these trends pose a serious threat to children and to the nation as a whole, but they are dismissed as declinists, pessimists, or nostalgists, unwilling or unable to accept the new facts of life. The dominant view is that the changes in family structure are, on balance, positive.

A SHIFT IN
THE SOCIAL METRIC

There are several reasons why this is so, but the fundamental reason is that at some point in the 1970s Americans changed their minds about the meaning of these disruptive behaviors. What had once been regarded as hostile to children's best interests was now considered essential to adults' happiness. In the 1950s most Americans believed that parents should stay in an unhappy marriage for the sake of the children. The assumption was that a divorce would damage the children, and the prospect of such damage gave divorce its meaning. By the mid-1970s a majority of Americans rejected that view. Popular advice literature reflected the shift. A book on divorce published in the mid-1940s tersely asserted: "Children are entitled to the affection and *association* of two parents, not one." Thirty years later another popular divorce book proclaimed just the opposite: "A two-parent home is not the only emotional structure within which a child can be happy and healthy.... The parents who take care of themselves will be best able to take care of their children." At about the same time, the long-standing taboo against out-of-wedlock childbirth also collapsed. By the mid-1970s three fourths of Americans said that it was not morally wrong for a woman to have a child outside marriage.

Once the social metric shifts from child well-being to adult well-being, it is hard to see divorce and nonmarital birth in anything but a positive light. However distressing and difficult they may be, both of these behaviors can hold out the promise of greater adult choice, freedom, and happiness. For unhappy spouses, divorce offers a way to escape a troubled or even abusive relationship and make a fresh start. For single parents, remarriage is a second try at marital happiness as well as a chance for relief from the stress, loneliness, and economic hardship of raising a child alone. For some unmarried women, nonmarital birth is a way to beat the biological clock, avoid marrying the wrong man, and experience the pleasures of motherhood. Moreover, divorce and out-of-wedlock birth involve a measure of agency and choice; they are man- and woman-made events. To be sure, not everyone exercises choice in divorce or nonmarital birth. Men leave wives for younger women, teenage girls get pregnant accidentally—yet even these unhappy events reflect the expansion of the boundaries of freedom and choice.

This cultural shift helps explain what otherwise would be inexplicable: the failure to see the rise in family disruption as a severe and troubling national problem. It explains why there is virtually no widespread public sentiment for restigmatizing either of these classically disruptive behaviors and no sense— no public consensus—that they can or should be avoided in the future. On the contrary, the prevailing opinion is that we should accept the changes in family structure as inevitable and devise new forms of public and private support for single-parent families. . . .

No one would claim that two-parent families are free from conflict, violence, or abuse. However, the attempt to discredit the two-parent family can be understood as part of what Daniel Patrick Moynihan has described as a larger effort to accommodate higher levels of social deviance. "The amount of deviant behavior in American society has increased beyond the levels the community can 'afford to recognize,'" Moynihan argues. One response has been to normalize what was once considered deviant behavior, such as out-of-wedlock birth. An accompanying response has been to detect deviance in what once stood as a social norm, such as the married-couple family. Together these responses reduce the acknowledged levels of deviance by eroding earlier distinctions between the normal and the deviant. . . .

[T]he popular portrait of family life does not simply reflect the views of a cultural elite, as some have argued. There is strong support at the grass roots for much of this view of family change. Survey after survey shows that Americans are less inclined than they were a generation ago to value sexual fidelity, lifelong marriage, and parenthood as worthwhile personal goals. Motherhood no longer defines adult womanhood, as everyone knows; equally important is the fact that fatherhood has declined as a norm for men. In 1976 less than half as many fathers as in 1957 said that providing for children was a life goal. The proportion of working men who found marriage and children burdensome and restrictive more than doubled in the same period. Fewer than half of all adult Americans today regard the idea of sacrifice for others as a positive moral virtue.

DINOSAURS DIVORCE

It is true that many adults benefit from divorce or remarriage. According to one study, nearly 80 percent of divorced women and 50 percent of divorced men say they are better off out of the marriage. Half of divorced adults in the same study report greater happiness. A competent self-help book called *Divorce and New Beginnings* notes the advantages of single parenthood: single parents can "develop their own interests, fulfill their own needs, choose their own friends and engage in social activities of their choice. Money, even if limited, can be spent as they see fit." Apparently, some women appreciate the opportunity to have children out of wedlock. "The real world, however, does not always allow women who are dedicated to their careers to devote the time and energy it takes to find—or be found by—the perfect husband and father wanna-be," one woman said in a letter to *The Washington Post*. . . .

[A] telling glimpse into the meaning of family disruption can be found in the growing children's literature on family dissolution. Take, for example, the popular children's book *Dinosaurs Divorce: A Guide for Changing Families* (1986), by Laurene Krasny Brown and Marc Brown. This is a picture book, written for very young children. The book begins with a short glossary of "divorce words" and encourages children to "see if you can find them" in the story. The words include "family counselor," "separation agreement," "alimony," and "child custody." The book is illustrated with cartoonish drawings of green dinosaur parents who fight, drink too much, and break up. One panel shows the father dinosaur, suitcase in hand, getting into a yellow car.

The dinosaur children are offered simple, straightforward advice on what to do about the divorce. *On custody decisions:* "When parents can't agree, lawyers and judges decide. Try to be honest if they ask you questions; it will help them make better decisions." *On selling the house:* "If you move, you may have to say good-bye to friends and familiar places. But soon your new home will feel like the place you really belong." *On the economic impact of divorce:* "Living with one parent almost always means there will be less money. Be prepared to give up some things." *On holidays:* "Divorce may mean twice as much celebrating at holiday times, but you may feel pulled apart." *On parents' new lovers:* "You may sometimes feel jealous and want your parent to yourself. Be polite to your parents' new friends, even if you don't like them at first." *On parents' remarriage:* "Not everyone loves his or her stepparents, but showing them respect is important."

These ... books point to an uncomfortable and generally unacknowledged fact: what contributes to a parent's happiness may detract from a child's happiness. All too often the adult quest for freedom, independence, and choice in family relationships conflicts with a child's developmental needs for stability, constancy, harmony, and permanence in family life. In short, family disruption creates a deep division between parents' interests and the interests of children.

One of the worse consequences of these divided interests is a withdrawal of parental investment in children's well-being. As the Stanford economist Victor Fuchs has pointed out, the main source of social investment in children is private. The investment comes from the children's parents. But parents in disrupted families have less time, attention, and money to devote to their children. The single most important source of disinvestment has been the widespread withdrawal of financial support and involvement by fathers. Maternal investment, too, has declined, as women try to raise families on their own and work outside the home. Moreover, both mothers and fathers commonly respond to family breakup by investing more heavily in themselves and in their own personal and romantic lives.

Sometimes the tables are completely turned. Children are called upon to invest in the emotional well-being of their parents. Indeed, this seems to be the larger message of many of the children's books on divorce and remarriage. *Dinosaurs Divorce* asks children to be sympathetic, understanding, respectful, and polite to confused, unhappy parents. The sacrifice comes from the children: "Be prepared to give up some things." In the world of divorcing dinosaurs, the children rather than the grown-ups are the exemplars of patience, restraint, and good sense.

THREE SEVENTIES ASSUMPTIONS

As it first took shape in the 1970s, the optimistic view of family change rested on three bold new assumptions. At that time, because the emergence of the changes in family life was so recent, there was little hard evidence to confirm or dispute these assumptions. But this was an expansive moment in American life.

The first assumption was an economic one: that a woman could now afford to be a mother without also being a wife. There were ample grounds for believing this. Women's work-force participation had been gradually increasing in the postwar period, and by the beginning of the 1970s women were a strong presence in the workplace. What's more, even though there was still a substantial wage gap between men and women, women had made considerable progress in a relatively short time toward better-paying jobs and greater employment opportunities. More women than ever before could aspire to serious careers as business executives, doctors, lawyers, airline pilots, and politicians. This circumstance, combined with the increased availability of child care, meant that women could take on the responsibilities of a breadwinner, perhaps even a sole breadwinner. This was particularly true for middle-class women....

Feminists, who had long argued that the path to greater equality for women lay in the world of work outside the home, endorsed this assumption. In fact, for many, economic independence was a stepping-stone toward freedom from both men and marriage. As women began to earn their own money, they were less dependent on men or marriage, and marriage diminished in importance. In Gloria Steinem's memorable words, "A woman without a man is like a fish without a bicycle." ...

The second assumption was that family disruption would not cause lasting harm to children and could actually enrich their lives. *Creative Divorce: A New Opportunity for Personal Growth*, a popular book of the seventies, spoke confidently to this point: "Children can survive any family crisis without permanent damage—and grow as human beings in the process...." Moreover, single-parent and stepparent families created a more extensive kinship network than the nuclear family. This network would envelop children in a web of warm and supportive relationships. "Belonging to a stepfamily means there are more people in your life," a children's book published in 1982 notes. "More sisters and brothers, including the step ones. More people you think of as grandparents and aunts and uncles. More cousins. More neighbors and friends.... Getting to know and like so many people (and having them like you) is one of the best parts of what being in a stepfamily... is all about."

The third assumption was that the new diversity in family structure would make America a better place. Just as the nation has been strengthened by the diversity of its ethnic and racial groups, so it would be strengthened by diverse family forms. The emergence of these brave new families was but the latest chapter in the saga of American pluralism.

Another version of the diversity argument stated that the real problem was not family disruption itself but the stigma still attached to these emergent family forms. This lingering stigma placed children at psychological risk, making them feel ashamed or different; as the ranks of single-parent and stepparent families grew, children would feel normal and good about themselves.

These assumptions continue to be appealing, because they accord with strongly held American beliefs in social progress. Americans see progress in the expansion of individual opportunities for choice, freedom, and self-expression. Moreover, Americans identify progress with growing tolerance of diversity. Over the past half century, the pollster Daniel Yankelovich writes, the United States has steadily grown more open-minded and accepting of groups that were previously perceived as alien, untrustworthy, or unsuitable for public leadership or social esteem. One such group is the burgeoning number of single-parent and stepparent families.

THE EDUCATION OF SARA MCLANAHAN

In 1981 Sarah McLanahan, now a sociologist at Princeton University's Woodrow Wilson School, read a three-part series by Ken Auletta in *The New Yorker*. Later published as a book titled *The Underclass*, the series presented a vivid portrait of the drug addicts, welfare mothers, and school dropouts who took part in an education-and-training program in New York City. Many were the children of single mothers, and it was Auletta's clear implication that single-mother families were contributing to the growth of an underclass. McLanahan was taken aback by this notion. "It struck me as strange that he would be viewing single mothers at that level of pathology." ...

One of the leading assumptions of the time was that single motherhood was economically viable. Even if single mothers did face economic trials, they wouldn't face them for long, it was argued, because they wouldn't remain single for long: single motherhood would be a brief phase of three to five years, followed by marriage. Single mothers would be economically resilient: if they experienced setbacks, they would recover quickly. It was also said that single mothers would be supported by informal networks of family, friends, neighbors, and other single mothers. As McLanahan shows in her study [on single motherhood, published in 1986], the evidence demolishes all these claims.

For the vast majority of single mothers, the economic spectrum turns out to be narrow, running between precarious and desperate. Half the single mothers in the United States live below the poverty line. (Currently, one out of ten married couples with children is poor.) Many others live on the edge of poverty. Even single mothers who are far from poor are likely to experience persistent economic insecurity. Divorce almost always brings a decline in the standard of living for the mother and children.

Moreover, the poverty experienced by single mothers is no more brief than it is mild. A significant number of all single mothers never marry or remarry. Those who do, do so only after spending roughly six years, on average, as single parents. For black mothers the duration is much longer. Only 33 percent of African-American mothers had remarried within ten years of separation. Consequently, single motherhood is hardly a fleeting event for the mother, and it is likely to occupy a third of the child's childhood. Even the notion that single mothers are knit together in economically supportive networks is not borne out by the evidence. On the contrary, single parenthood forces many women to be on the move, in search of cheaper housing and better jobs. This need-driven restless mobility makes it more difficult for them to sustain supportive ties to family and friends, let alone other single mothers. ...

McLanahan cites three reasons why single-mother families are so vulnerable economically. For one thing, their earnings are low. Second, unless the mothers are widowed, they don't receive public subsidies large enough to lift them out of poverty. And finally, they do not get much support from family members—especially the fathers of their children. In 1982 single white mothers received an average of $1,246 in alimony and child support, black mothers an average of $322. Such payments accounted for about 10 percent of the income of single white mothers and for about 3.5 percent of the income of single black mothers. These amounts were dramatically smaller than the income of the father in a two-parent family and also smaller than the income from a second earner in a two-parent family. Roughly 60 percent of single white mothers and 80 percent of single black mothers received no support at all.

Until the mid-1980s, when stricter standards were put in place, child-support awards were only about half to two-thirds what the current guidelines require. Accordingly, there is often a big difference in the living standards of divorced fathers and of divorced mothers with children. After divorce the average annual income of mothers and children is $13,500 for whites and $9,000 for nonwhites, as compared with $25,000 for white nonresident fathers and $13,600 for nonwhite nonresident fathers. Moreover, since child-support awards account for a smaller portion of the income of a high-earning father, the drop in living standards can be especially sharp for mothers who were married to upper-level managers and professionals.

Unwed mothers are unlikely to be awarded any support at all, partly because the paternity of their children may not have been established. According to one recent study, only 20 percent of unmarried mothers receive child support.

Even if single mothers escape poverty, economic uncertainty remains a condition of life. Divorce brings a reduction in income and standard of living for the vast majority of single mothers. One study, for example, found that income for mothers and children declines on average about 30 percent, while fathers experience a 10 to 15 percent increase in income in the year following a separation. Things get even

more difficult when fathers fail to meet their child-support obligations. As a result, many divorced mothers experience a wearing uncertainty about the family budget: whether the check will come in or not; whether new sneakers can be bought this month or not; whether the electric bill will be paid on time or not. Uncertainty about money triggers other kinds of uncertainty. Mothers and children often have to move to cheaper housing after a divorce. One study shows that about 38 percent of divorced mothers and their children move during the first year after a divorce. Even several years later the rate of moves for single mothers is about a third higher than the rate for two-parent families. It is also common for a mother to change her job or increase her working hours or both following a divorce. Even the composition of the household is likely to change, with other adults, such as boyfriends or babysitters, moving in and out.

Sara McLanahan's investigation and others like it have helped to establish a broad consensus on the economic impact of family disruption on children. Most social scientists now agree that single motherhood is an important and growing cause of poverty, and that children suffer as a result. (They continue to argue, however, about the relationship between family structure and such economic factors as income inequality, the loss of jobs in the inner city, and the growth of low-wage jobs.) By the mid-1980s, however, it was clear that the problem of family disruption was not confined to the urban underclass, nor was its sole impact economic. Divorce and out-of-wedlock childbirth were affecting middle- and upper-class children, and these more privileged children were suffering negative consequences as well. It appeared that the problems associated with family breakup were far deeper and far more widespread than anyone had previously imagined.

THE MISSING FATHER

Judith Wallerstein is one of the pioneers in research on the long-term psychological impact of family disruption on children. The California Children of Divorce Study, which she directs, remains the most enduring study of the long-term effects of divorce on children and their parents. . . .

When, in 1971, Wallerstein and her colleagues set out to conduct clinical interviews with 131 children from the San Francisco area, they thought they were embarking on a short-term study. Most experts believed that divorce was like a bad cold. There was a phase of acute discomfort, and then a short recovery phase. According to the conventional wisdom, kids would be back on their feet in no time at all. Yet when Wallerstein met these children for a second interview more than a year later, she was amazed to discover that there had been no miraculous recovery. In fact, the children seemed to be doing worse.

The news that children did not "get over" divorce was not particularly welcome at the time. Wallerstein recalls, "We got angry letters from therapists, parents, and lawyers saying we were undoubtedly wrong. They said children are really much better off being released from an unhappy marriage. Divorce, they said, is a liberating experience." One of the main results of the California study was to overturn this optimistic view. In Wallerstein's cautionary words, "Divorce is deceptive. Legally it is a single event, but psychologically it is a chain—sometimes a never-ending chain—of events, relocations, and radically shifting relationships strung through time, a process that forever changes the lives of the people involved."

Five years after divorce more than a third of the children experienced moderate or severe depression. At ten years a significant number of the now young men and women appeared to be troubled, drifting, and underachieving. At fifteen years many of the thirtyish adults were struggling to establish strong love relationships of their own. In short, far from recovering from their parents' divorce, a significant percentage of these grownups were still suffering from its effects. In fact, according to Wallerstein, the long-term effects of divorce emerge at a time when young adults are trying to make their own decisions about love, marriage, and family. Not all children in the study suffered negative consequences. But Wallerstein's research presents a sobering picture of divorce. "The child of divorce faces many additional psychological burdens in addition to the normative tasks of growing up," she says.

Divorce not only makes it more difficult for young adults to establish new relationships. It also weakens the oldest primary relationship: that between parent and child. According to Wallerstein, "Parent-child relationships are permanently altered by divorce in ways that our society has not anticipated." Not only do children experience a loss of parental attention at the onset of divorce, but they soon find that at every stage of their development their parents are not available in the same way they once were. "In a reasonably happy intact family," Wallerstein observes, "the child gravitates first to one parent and then to the other, using skills and attributes from each in climbing the developmental ladder." In a divorced family, children find it "harder to find the needed parent at needed times." This may help explain why very young children suffer the most as the result of family disruption. Their opportunities to engage in this kind of ongoing process are the most truncated and compromised.

The father-child bond is severely, often irreparably, damaged in disrupted families. In a situation without historical precedent, an astonishing and disheartening number of American fathers are failing to provide financial support to their children. Often, more than the father's support check is missing. Increasingly, children are bereft of any contact with their fathers. According to the National Survey of Children, in disrupted families only one child in six, on average, saw his or her father as often as once a week in the past year. Close to half did not see their father at all in the past year. As time goes on, contact becomes even more infrequent. Ten years after a marriage breaks up, more than two thirds of children report not having seen their father for a year....

Even for fathers who maintain regular contact, the pattern of father-child relationships changes. The sociologists Andrew Cherlin and Frank Furstenberg, who have studied broken families, write that the fathers behave more like other relatives than like parents. Rather than helping with homework or carrying out a project with their children, nonresidential fathers are likely to take the kids shopping, to the movies, or out to dinner. Instead of providing steady advice and guidance, divorced fathers become "treat" dads.

Apparently—and paradoxically—it is the visiting relationship itself, rather than the frequency of visits, that is the real source of the problem. According to Wallerstein, the few children in the California study who reported visiting with their fathers once or twice a week over a ten-year period still felt rejected. The need to schedule a special time to be with the child, the repeated leave-takings, and the lack of connection to the child's regular, daily schedule leaves many fathers adrift, frustrated, and confused. Wallerstein calls the visiting father a parent without portfolio....

LONG-TERM EFFECTS

Since most children live with their mothers after divorce, one might expect that the mother-child bond would remain unaltered and might even be strengthened. Yet research shows that the mother-child bond is also weakened as the result of divorce. Only half of the children who were close to their mothers before a divorce remained equally close after the divorce. Boys, particularly, had difficulties with their mothers. Moreover, mother-child relationships deteriorated over time. Whereas teenagers in disrupted families were no more likely than teenagers in intact families to report poor relationships with their mothers, 30 percent of young adults from disrupted families have poor relationships with their mothers, as compared with 16 percent of young adults from intact families. Mother-daughter relationships often deteriorate as the daughter reaches young adulthood. The only group in society that derives any benefit from these weakened parent-child ties is the therapeutic community. Young adults from disrupted families are nearly twice as likely as those from intact families to receive psychological help.

... Obviously, not all children in two-parent families are free from emotional turmoil, but few are burdened with the troubles that accompany family breakup. Moreover, as the sociologist Amitai Etzioni explains in a new book, *The Spirit of Community*, two parents in an intact family make up what might be called a mutually supportive education coalition. When both parents are present, they can play different, even contradictory, roles. One parent may goad the child to achieve, while the other may encourage the child to take time out to daydream or toss a football around. One may emphasize taking intellectual risk, while the other may insist on following the teacher's guidelines. At the same time, the parents regularly exchange information about the child's school problems and achievements, and have a sense of the overall educational mission. ...

THE BAD NEWS ABOUT STEPPARENTS

Perhaps the most striking, and potentially disturbing, new research has to do with children in stepparent families. Until quite recently the optimistic assumption was that children saw their lives improve when they became part of a stepfamily. When Nicholas Zill and his colleagues began to study the effects of remarriage on children, their working hypothesis was that stepparent families would make up for the shortcomings of the single-parent family. Clearly, most children are better off economically when they are able to share in the income of two adults. When a second adult joins the household, there may be a reduction in the time and work pressures on the single parent.

The research overturns this optimistic assumption, however. In general the evidence suggests that remarriage neither reproduces nor restores the intact family structure, even when it brings more income and a second adult into the household. Quite the contrary. Indeed, children living with stepparents appear to be even more disadvantaged than children living in a stable single-parent family. Other difficulties seem to offset the advantages of extra income and an extra pair of hands. However much our modern sympathies reject the fairy-tale portrait of stepparents, the latest research confirms that the old stories are anthropologically quite accurate. Stepfamilies disrupt established loyalties, create new uncertainties, provoke deep anxieties, and sometimes threaten a child's physical safety as well as emotional security.

Parents and children have dramatically different interests in and expectations for a new marriage. For a single parent, remarriage brings new commitments, the hope of enduring love and happiness, and relief from stress and loneliness. For a child, the same event often provokes confused feelings of sadness, anger, and rejection. Nearly half the children in Wallerstein's study said they felt left out in their stepfamilies. The National Commission on Children, a bipartisan group headed by Senator John D. Rockefeller, of West Virginia, reported that children from stepfamilies were more likely to say they often felt lonely or blue than children from either single-parent or intact families. Children in stepfamilies were the most likely to report that they wanted more time with their mothers. When mothers remarry, daughters tend to have a harder time adjusting than sons. Evidently, boys often respond positively to a male presence in the household, while girls who have established close ties to their mother in a single-parent family often see the stepfather as a rival and an intruder. According to one study, boys in remarried families are less likely to drop out of school than boys in single-parent families, while the opposite is true for girls. . . .

One of the most severe risks associated with stepparent-child ties is the risk of sexual abuse. As Judith Wallerstein explains, "The presence of a stepfather can raise the difficult issue of a thinner incest barrier." The incest taboo is strongly reinforced, Wallerstein says, by knowledge of paternity and by the experience of caring for a child since birth. A stepfather enters the family without either credential and plays a sexual role as the mother's husband. As a result, stepfathers can pose a sexual risk to the children, especially to daughters. According to a study by the Canadian researchers Martin Daly and Margo Wilson, preschool children in stepfamilies are forty times as likely as children in intact families to suffer physical or sexual abuse. (Most of the sexual abuse was committed by a third party, such as a neighbor, a stepfather's male friend, or another nonrelative.) Stepfathers discriminate in their abuse: they are far more likely to assault nonbiological children than their own natural children.

Sexual abuse represents the most extreme threat to children's well-being. Stepfamilies also seem less likely to make the kind of ordinary investments in the children that other families do. Although it is true that the stepfamily household has a higher income than the single-parent household, it does not follow that the additional income is reliably available to the children. To begin with, children's claim on stepparents' resources is shaky. Stepparents are not legally required to support stepchildren, so their financial support of these children is entirely voluntary. Moreover, since stepfamilies are far more likely to break up than intact families, particularly in the first five years, there is always the risk —far greater than the risk of unemployment in an intact family—that the second income will vanish with another divorce. The financial commitment to a child's education appears weaker in stepparent families, perhaps because the stepparent believes that the responsibility for educating the child rests with the biological parent. . . .

DIMINISHING INVESTMENTS

There are several reasons for [stepparents'] diminished interest and investment [in their stepchildren]. In the law, as in the children's eyes, stepparents are shadowy figures. According to the legal scholar David Chambers, family law has pretty much ignored stepparents. Chambers writes, "In the substantial majority of states, stepparents, even when they live with a child, have no legal obligation to contribute to the child's support; nor does a stepparent's presence in the home alter the support obligations of a noncustodial parent. The stepparent also has . . . no authority to approve emergency medical treatment or even to sign a permission slip. . . ." When a marriage breaks up, the stepparent has no continuing obligation to provide for a stepchild, no matter how long or how much he or she has been contributing to the support of the child. In short, Chambers says, stepparent relationships are based wholly on consent, subject to the inclinations of the adult and the child. The only way a stepparent can acquire the legal status of a parent is through adoption. Some researchers also point to the cultural ambiguity of the stepparent's role as a source of diminished interest, while others insist that it is the absence of a blood tie that weakens the bond between stepparent and child....

In short, as Andrew Cherlin and Frank Furstenburg put it, "Through divorce and remarriage, individuals are related to more and more people, to each of whom they owe less and less." Moreover, as Nicholas Zill argues, weaker parent-child attachments leave many children more strongly exposed to influences outside the family, such as peers, boyfriends or girlfriends, and the media. Although these outside forces can sometimes be helpful, common sense and research opinion argue against putting too much faith in peer groups or the media as surrogates for Mom and Dad....

THE TWO-PARENT ADVANTAGE

All this evidence gives rise to an obvious conclusion: growing up in an intact two-parent family is an important source of advantage for American children. Though far from perfect as a social institution, the intact family offers children greater security and better outcomes than its fast-growing alternatives: single-parent and stepparent families. Not only does the intact family protect the child from poverty and economic insecurity; it also provides greater noneconomic investments of parental time, attention, and emotional support over the entire life course. This does not mean that all two-parent families are better for children than all single-parent families. But in the face of the evidence it becomes increas-

ingly difficult to sustain the proposition that all family structures produce equally good outcomes for children.

[T]he case against the two-parent family is remarkably weak. It is true that disaggregating data can make family structure less significant as a factor, just as disaggregating Hurricane Andrew into wind, rain, and tides can make it disappear as a meteorological phenomenon. Nonetheless, research opinion as well as common sense suggests that the effects of changes in family structure are great enough to cause concern. Nicholas Zill argues that many of the risk factors for children are doubled or more than doubled as the result of family disruption. "In epidemiological terms," he writes, "the doubling of a hazard is a substantial increase... the increase in risk that dietary cholesterol poses for cardiovascular disease, for example, is far less than double, yet millions of American have altered their diets because of the perceived hazard."

The argument that family conflict, rather than the breakup of parents, is the cause of children's psychological distress is persuasive on its face. Children who grow up in high-conflict families, whether the families stay together or eventually split up, are undoubtedly at great psychological risk. And surely no one would dispute that there must be societal measures available, including divorce, to remove children from families where they are in danger. Yet only a minority of divorces grow out of pathological situations; much more common are divorces in families unscarred by physical assault. Moreover, an equally compelling hypothesis is that family breakup generates its own conflict. Certainly, many families exhibit more conflictual and even violent behavior as a consequence of divorce than they did before divorce.

Finally, it is important to note that clinical insights are different from sociological findings. Clinicians work with individual families, who cannot and should not be defined by statistical aggregates. Appropriate to a clinical approach, moreover, is a focus on the internal dynamics of family functioning and on the immense variability in human behavior. Nevertheless, there is enough empirical evidence to justify sociological statements about the causes of declining child well-being and to demonstrate that despite the plasticity of human response, there are some useful rules of thumb to guide our thinking about and policies affecting the family.

For example, Sara McLanahan says, three structural constants are commonly associated with intact families, even intact families who would not win any "Family of the Year" awards. The first is economic. In intact families, children share in the income of two adults. Indeed, as a number of analysts have pointed out, the two-parent family is becoming more rather than less necessary, because more and more families need two incomes to sustain a middle-class standard of living.

McLanahan believes that most intact families also provide a stable authority structure. Family breakup commonly upsets the established boundaries of authority in a family. Children are often required to make decisions or accept responsibilities once considered the province of parents. Moreover, children, even very young children, are often expected to behave like mature adults, so that the grown-ups in the family can be free to deal with the emotional fallout of the failed relationship. In some instances family disruption creates a complete vacuum in authority; everyone invents his or her own rules. With lines of authority disrupted or absent, children find it much more difficult to engage in the normal kinds of testing behavior, the trial and error, the failing and succeeding, that define the developmental pathway toward character and competence. McLanahan says, "Children need to be the ones to challenge the rules. The parents need to set the boundaries and let the kids push the boundaries. The children shouldn't have to walk the straight and narrow at all times."

Finally, McLanahan holds that children in intact families benefit from stability in what she neutrally terms "household personnel." Family disruption frequently brings new adults into the family, including stepparents, live-in boyfriends or girlfriends, and casual sexual partners. Like stepfathers, boyfriends can present a real threat to children's, particularly to daughters', security and well-being. But physical and sexual abuse represents only the most extreme such threat. Even the very best of boyfriends can disrupt and undermine a child's sense of peace and security. McLanahan says. "It's not as though you're going from an unhappy marriage to peacefulness. There can be a constant changing until the mother finds a suitable partner."

McLanahan's argument helps explain why children of widows tend to do better than children of divorced or unmarried mothers. Widows differ from other single mothers in all three respects. They are economically more secure, because they receive more public assistance through Survivors Insurance, and possibly private insurance or other kinds of support from family members. Thus widows are less likely to leave the neighborhood in search of a new or better job and a cheaper house or apartment. Moreover, the death of a father is not likely to disrupt the authority structure radically. When a father dies, he is no longer physically present, but his death does not dethrone him as an authority figure in the child's life. On the contrary, his authority may be magnified through death. The mother can draw on the powerful memory of the departed father as a way of intensifying her parental authority: "Your father would have wanted it this way." Finally, since widows tend to be older than divorced mothers, their love life may be less distracting.

Regarding the two-parent family, the sociologist David Popenoe, who has devoted much of his career to the study of families, both in the United States and in Scandinavia, makes this straightforward assertion:

Social science research is almost never conclusive. There are always methodological difficulties and stones left unturned. Yet in three decades of work as a social scientist, I know of few other bodies of data in which the weight of evidence is so decisively on one side of the issue: on the whole, for children, two-parent families are preferable to single-parent and stepfamilies.

NO

David Gately and
Andrew I. Schwebel

FAVORABLE OUTCOMES IN CHILDREN AFTER PARENTAL DIVORCE

SUMMARY. The present paper is based on a review of the literature that considers the short- and long-term effects parental divorce has on children. Most studies in this literature have identified unfavorable outcomes that develop in many areas of children's lives as they struggle to cope with their changed family situations. However, as children adjust to the challenges they face before, during, and after parental divorce, neutral and favorable outcomes are also possible in one or more areas of their lives. In fact, the literature review indicated that many investigators have identified certain strengths in children who had experienced parental divorce. In particular they have observed that following the divorce of their parents some children, in comparison to peers or their own pre-divorce development, have shown enhanced levels of functioning in four areas: maturity, self-esteem, empathy, and androgyny.

Over ten million divorces were granted in the United States during the 1980s (U.S. Bureau of the Census, 1990). The great number of people affected by divorce in the second half of the 20th century stimulated scholarly interest in this area. One topic that received considerable attention is the effects of parental divorce on children, a group affected at a rate of about one million per year since the mid 1970s (U.S. Bureau of Census, 1990).

Findings consistently show that children experience distress during the process of parental separation and divorce and that it is associated with a variety of short- and long-term negative outcomes (see reviews by Anthony, 1974; Fry & Addington, 1985; Kelly, 1988; Kurdek, 1981; Long & Forehand, 1987; Lopez, 1987; Santrock, 1987). Wallerstein and Blackeslee (1989) stated, "Almost all children of divorce regard their childhood and adolescence as having taken place in the shadow of divorce. . . . Almost half of the children entered adulthood as worried, underachieving, self-deprecating, and sometimes angry young men and women" (pp. 298–299).

From David Gately and Andrew I. Schwebel, "Favorable Outcomes in Children After Parental Divorce," *Journal of Divorce and Remarriage*, vol. 18, nos. 3–4, (1992), pp. 57–63, 66–78. Copyright © 1992 by The Haworth Press, Inc. Reprinted by permission.

In fact, studies indicate that children may experience difficulties in interpersonal relationships, school behavior, academic achievement, self-esteem, in future life outlook, etc. Besides delineating the wide range of unfavorable outcomes that can develop in children before, during, and after the divorce, the literature also identifies factors that can moderate and exacerbate the problems children face.

Although much of the literature discusses children's struggle to cope with parental divorce and the unfavorable outcomes they may experience in one or more aspects of their lives, some children in adjusting to their changed circumstances before, during, and after parental divorce may also become strengthened in one or more areas. These individuals develop competencies or grow psychologically because of what they learn while undertaking the divorce-related challenges they face and/or because of the changes they experience in self-view as a result of successfully meeting the challenges.

Decades ago Bernstein and Robey (1962) suggested that successful coping with the demands presented by parental divorce can spur emotional and personality growth in children. Since then a number of investigators have found these favorable outcomes in youngsters relative either to their pre-divorce status or to matched peers from intact family backgrounds. (These include: Grossman, Shea, & Adams, 1980; Hetherington, 1989; Kelly & Wallerstein, 1976; Kurdek & Siesky, 1979, 1980a, 1980b, 1980c; MacKinnon, Stoneman & Brody, 1984; Reinhard, 1977; Richmond-Abbott, 1984; Rosen, 1977; Santrock & Warshak, 1979; Slater, Stewart, & Linn, 1983; Springer & Wallerstein, 1983; Wallerstein, 1984, 1985a, 1987; Wallerstein & Kelly, 1974, 1976, 1980b; Warshak & Santrock, 1983; Weiss, 1979).

The present paper is based on a comprehensive review of the literature that investigated post-divorce outcomes in children. The review included literature generated from computer searches of the Psychological Abstracts and Family Resources and Educational Resources Information Center data bases. Manual searches of the Psychological Abstracts, The Inventory of Marriage and Family Literature, and the Social Sciences Index bases were conducted to supplement the computer searches. Finally, empirical and theoretical contributions published in books, chapters, and Dissertation Abstracts were reviewed. Following a brief assessment of this body of literature, the present paper focuses on those studies that reported favorable outcomes in children following parental divorce.

Most of the earliest investigations used a pathogenic model that viewed the divorced family as a deviation from the traditional 2-parent family, and attempted to link this "inferior" family structure to negative effects on children's adjustment and psychosocial development (Levitin, 1979). The picture of the effects of parental divorce on children were further colored in a negative way because these projects typically employed clinical samples and studied the crisis period immediately following divorce (Bernstein & Robey, 1962; Kalter, 1977; McDermott, 1968; Westman, 1972).

Later studies employing non-clinical samples showed that, although divorce is associated with an initial crisis reaction in most children, long-term consequences are variable (Hetherington, Cox, & Cox, 1982; Hetherington, 1989). While longitudinal studies demonstrated that parental divorce may have long-term negative effects on the social, emotional, and cognitive functioning of children (Guidubaldi & Cleminshaw, 1985; Hetherington, Cox, & Cox, 1985), they also showed that children may escape long-term negative outcomes if the crisis of divorce is not compounded by multiple stressors and continued adversity (Hetherington, 1979, 1989; Hetherington et al., 1982, 1985).

The finding that divorce does not necessarily result in long-term dysfunction led to a search for individual, family, and environmental factors that moderate children's adjustment. Researchers found the quality of adjustment related to: the child's gender and age at the time of separation/divorce (Guidubaldi & Perry, 1985; Hetherington et al., 1982, 1985; Kalter & Rembar, 1981; Wallerstein & Kelly, 1980a); the child's temperament, locus of control, interpersonal knowledge, and level of coping resources (Ankerbrandt, 1986; Hetherington, 1989; Kurdek & Berg, 1983; Kurdek, Blisk, & Siesky, 1981; Kurdek & Siesky, 1980a); the amount of interparental conflict prior to, during, and following separation/divorce (Emery, 1982; Hetherington et al., 1982; Jacobson, 1978; Wallerstein & Kelly, 1980b); the quality of parent-child relationships (Hess & Camara, 1979; Hetherington, Cox, & Cox, 1982; Wallerstein & Kelly, 1980a); the parents' mental and physical health (Guidubaldi & Cleminshaw, 1985; Guidubaldi & Perry, 1985); the type of custody arrangement (Ambert, 1984; Lowery & Settle, 1985; Santrock & Warshak, 1979; Santrock, Warshak, & Elliot, 1982; Warshak & Santrock, 1983; Wolchik, Braver, & Sandler, 1985); parental remarriage (Clingempeel & Segal, 1986; Hetherington et al., 1982; Santrock, Warshak, Lindbergh & Meadows, 1982); the number of major life changes experienced following divorce

(Hetherington et al., 1985; Stolberg, Camplair, Currier, & Wells, 1987), including the amount of financial decline experienced by the post-divorce family (Desimone-Luis, O'Mahoney, & Hunt, 1979); and the social support available to both the parents and children (Isaacs & Leon, 1986).

Drawing upon the concept of stress, Wallerstein (1983a) and Peterson, Leigh, & Day (1984) developed models that could account for the absence of negative outcomes in children. For example, Wallerstein conceived of divorce as an acute social stressor that had consequences and made unique demands on children (differing from those associated with stressors like the death of a parent). Although families experiencing divorce and the loss of a parent pass through similar transitional stages (Schwebel, Fine, Moreland & Prindle, 1988), studies comparing the short- and long-term effects on children of separation/divorce and death of a parent support Wallerstein's contention (Boyd & Parish, 1983; Felner, Stolberg, & Cowen, 1975; Hetherington, 1972; Mueller & Cooper, 1986; Rozendal, 1983).

Wallerstein (1983a, 1983b) described the sequence of adjustments a child must make: (1) acknowledge the marital disruption, (2) regain a sense of direction and freedom to pursue customary activities, (3) deal with loss and feelings of rejection, (4) forgive the parents, (5) accept the permanence of divorce and relinquish longings for the restoration of the pre-divorce family, and (6) come to feel comfortable and confident in relationships. The successful completion of these tasks, which allows the child to stay on course developmentally, depends on the child's coping resources and the degree of support available to help in dealing with the stressors. Of course, the divorce process also may include pre-separation distress, family conflict, and compromised parenting which both place children at risk and call for them to make adjustments well before the time when the legal divorce is granted (Block, Block & Gjerde, 1986).

Reports describing protective factors that could mitigate negative outcomes for children following parental divorce complemented findings being described in stress research. More specifically, several authors (Garmezy, 1981, Rutter, 1987; Werner, 1989; Werner & Smith, 1982) found that some children, although exposed to multiple stressors that put them at risk, did not experience negative outcomes. Protective factors diminished the impact of these stressors. Although these investigators studied different stressors, their findings were remarkably similar and suggested that the factors which produce "resilience" in children-at-risk fit into three categories: (1) positive personality dispositions (e.g., active, affectionate, socially responsive, autonomous, flexible, intelligent; possessing self-esteem, an internal locus of control, self-control, and a positive mood); (2) a supportive family environment that encourages coping efforts; and (3) a supportive social environment that reinforces coping efforts and provides positive role models (Garmezy, 1981).

These protective factors reduce the likelihood of negative outcomes by means such as: decreasing exposure to or involvement with risk factors; opening of opportunities for successful task accomplishment and growth; and promoting self-esteem and self-efficacy through secure, supportive personal relationships (Rutter, 1987). Besides helping children avoid short-term harm, these resiliency-building factors strengthen children so they will cope more effectively with and master the stressful life events they will encounter in the future. This "steeling" effect is a favorable outcome that develops after an exposure to stressors of a type and degree that is manageable in the context of the child's capacities and social situation (Rutter, 1987).

The number of studies that identify favorable outcomes of any type of children following parental divorce is small in contrast to the number of studies that have reported unfavorable outcomes. To state the obvious, this difference in the volume of research reports primarily reflects the reality of what children face before, during, and after their parents' divorce. However, a small yet significant part of the difference may be due to the way science has addressed the question of children's outcomes. Specifically, the content of the literature has certainly been shaped, in part, by the fact that neither the pathological nor the stress models heuristically guide researchers to search for favorable outcomes (Kanoy & Cunningham, 1984; McKenry & Price, 1984, 1988; Scanzoni, Polonko, Teachman, & Thompson, 1988) and the fact that the research methods which have been typically employed are more likely to detect negative consequences than positive ones (Blechman, 1982; Kanoy & Cunningham, 1984). For instance, the wide use of measures that identify weaknesses (Blechman, 1982; Kanoy & Cunningham, 1984) and of subjects drawn from clinical samples, who are more maladjusted than their peers (Isaacs, Leon, & Donohue, 1987), makes the likelihood of detecting favorable outcomes unlikely (Kanoy & Cunningham, 1984).

A similar issue is presented by the tendency among researchers to neglect children as a source of data while, at the same time electing to use informants (eg., parents, teachers, clinicians) aware of children's family status (Kanoy & Cunningham, 1984). Although parents' ratings of their elementary school children's adjustment is not related to the children's assessment of the emotional support they are receiving, the children's self-rating of their adjustment are significant (Cowen, Pedro-Carroll & Alpert-Gillis, 1990). Teachers hold more negative expectations for children from divorced families than for their counterparts from intact families (Ball, Newman, & Scheuren, 1984) while parents and clinicians, in contrast to the children, tend to overestimate the negative effects of the divorce (Forehand, Brody, Long, Slotkin, & Fauber, 1986; Wolchik, Sandler, Braver, & Fogas, 1985). In fact, correlations between children's ratings of their own post-divorce adjustment and their parent's ratings are typically low (Kurdek & Siesky, 1980b), a finding consistent with correlations found between children's self-ratings and the ratings of adult informants in other areas of the literature (Achenbach, McConaughy & Howell, 1987)....

The review of... the divorce-adjustment literature suggested four areas, in particular, in which children may experience favorable outcomes following their parents' divorce: in maturity, self-esteem, empathy, and androgyny. Each is discussed below.

Maturity

Intact families have an "echelon structure" in which parents form the executive unit. In the single-parent home this structure is replaced by a parent-child partnership that encourages children to assume more self and family responsibility and to participate more fully in important family decisions (Weiss, 1979). Such involvement fosters maturity which is evidenced by increased levels of responsibility, independence, and awareness of adult values and concerns.

Studies employing nonclinical samples have supported Weiss's conclusions. Kurdek and Siesky (1980a) reported that about 80% of the 132 5–19 year-old children they sampled (four years post-separation) believed they had assumed increased responsibilities after the divorce and learned to rely on themselves more. Their parents agreed, with about 75% of the 74 parents sampled rating their children as more mature and independent (Kurdek & Siesky, 1980b). Similar findings were reported by Rosen (1977), who assessed children 6–10 years after parental divorce, and by Reinhard (1977), who surveyed 46 adolescents three years post-divorce.

Children from single-parent families spend more time working in the home and taking care of siblings (Amato, 1987; Bohannon & Erikson, 1978; Hetherington, 1989; Zakariya, 1982). These chores can foster maturity in children, if they are age-appropriate and if the children receive adequate support. The maturity may exhibit itself in the form of an increased level of independence, realism, or identity development (Grossman et al., 1980). Single-parents further foster maturity when they (1) involve children in appropriate decision making and in a healthy range of other responsibilities in the post-divorce family (Bohannon & Erickson, 1978; Devall, Stoneman, & Brody, 1986; Hetherington, 1989; Kurdek & Siesky, 1979, 1980a; Reinhard, 1977; Wallerstein, 1985a; Weiss, 1979; Zakariya, 1982), and (2) allow children appropriate access to feelings that they, the adult caretakers, have as vulnerable individuals who may not always be able to meet the children's needs (Springer & Wallerstein, 1983; Wallerstein & Kelly, 1974).

Finally, a distinction is needed between pseudomaturity, a precocious adoption of adult roles and responsibilities, and maturity, an adaptive development that helps individuals cope more effectively. Pseudomaturity is seen in females from divorced families who display flirtatious and attention-seeking behavior with male interviewers (Hetherington, 1972), who engage in earlier and more frequent sexual activity (Boss, 1987; Hetherington, 1972; Kinnaird & Gerard, 1986) and who possess a greater likelihood of premarital pregnancy (Boss, 1987) than counterparts from intact families. Pseudomaturity is also found in both males and females from divorced families who engage in earlier and more frequent dating activity (Booth, Brinkerhoff & White, 1984; Hetherington, 1972) and marry earlier (Boss, 1987; Glenn & Kramer, 1987) than peers from intact families.

Self-Esteem

Children may experience increased self-esteem in the aftermath of parental divorce because they cope effectively with changed circumstances, are asked to assume new responsibilities, successfully perform new duties, and so forth. Santrock and Warshak (1979) studied 6–11 year-old children, three years after their parents' divorce, and matched youngsters from intact, mother-custody and father-custody families. Father-custody boys demonstrated higher levels of self-esteem and lower levels of anxiety than intact family boys, while the opposite was true for girls. Slater et al. (1983) studied matched adolescents and found that boys from divorced family backgrounds possessed significantly higher levels of self-esteem than boys from intact and girls from both intact and divorced family backgrounds. Girls from divorced family backgrounds had lower levels of self-esteem than their counterparts from intact families. These results are consistent with Wallerstein and Kelly's (1980a).

One circumstance that appears to foster boys' increased self-esteem in post-divorce families is that they may be more heavily relied upon by custodial parents (most of whom are women) than girls, and as a result may gain a new position of increased responsibility and status. A study of children raised during the Great Depression indicated that older children were strengthened by assuming domestic responsibilities and part-time work (Elder, 1974).

Besides developing as a result of an individual's accomplishments, feelings of self-efficacy may also evolve from vicarious experience, verbal persuasion, and a reduction in the level of fear associated with performing particular behaviors (Bandura, Adams, and Beyer, 1977). Concretely, this suggests that divorcing parents benefit their children by modeling adaptive coping behavior (Kaslow & Hyatt, 1982) and by persuading children to be less fearful and to cope more effectively. Children are most likely to develop hardiness in facing post-divorce challenges if the demands upon them are moderate, if their parents support their efforts to perform new responsibilities, and if family members hold a positive view of divorce-related changes (Maddi & Kobasa, 1984).

Empathy

Some children in divorced and single-parent families show increased concern for the welfare of family members (Kurdek & Siesky, 1980b; Reinhard, 1977; Weiss, 1979). For example, Hetherington (1989) found older girls in divorced families, in contrast to peers, are more often involved in supportive and nurturing teaching, play, and caretaking activities with younger sisters and tend to help and share more frequently. Likewise, about 25% of Rosen's (1977) South African children sample reported they had gained a greater understanding of human emotions as a result of their parent's divorce 6 to 10 years earlier.

Although Wallerstein (1985b) suggested that children's increase in empathy does not extend beyond the parent-child relationship, Hetherington (1989) believes the increased empathy and sensitivity may reflect a more general orientation. The conditions prevalent during children's adjustment may determine the extent to which empathy develops and generalizes. If children are encouraged to provide age-appropriate emotional and practical support to family members, they may be able to extend themselves, gaining an understanding of others' feelings and, in this way, practice and refine their role- and perspective-taking skills. Hetherington and Parke (1979) suggested that more advanced role-taking skills are related to increased altruism, prosocial behavior, communication skills, moral standards, and empathetic understanding.

Androgyny

Necessity, encouragement from others, and the observation of models are among the factors that can lead children to shift away from stereotypical sex-role thinking and behavior and toward androgyny. This shift, in turn, can result in increased cognitive and behavioral flexibility (Bem,

1975; Bem & Lenney, 1976; Bem, Martyna, & Watson, 1976).

MacKinnon et al. (1984) investigated the effects of marital status and maternal employment on sex-role orientations in matched groups of mothers and children between 3 and 6 years old. While employment influenced mother's sex-role views, divorce appeared related to children's sex-role views. These authors suggested that the more androgynous sex-role views of the children in the post-divorce homes may stem from the mothers modeling more generalized sex-role behavior, or from the children assuming more nontraditional responsibilities.

Kurdek & Siesky (1980c) investigated the sex-role self-concepts of divorced single parents and their 10 to 19 year-old children, approximately four years post-separation. They found that custodial and noncustodial parents and their children possessed higher levels of self-reported androgyny, when compared to published norms, and that the boys and girls possessed more androgynous sex-role self-concepts than a comparison group of children from intact family backgrounds.

Richmond-Abbott (1984) found that the sex-role attitudes of children, ages 8 to 14, tended to reflect the liberal ones of their divorced, single-parent mothers. However, although the mothers stated that they wanted their children to behave in nontraditional ways, children were encouraged to pursue and tended to prefer sex-stereotyped chores and activities. This fits with the failure of others to find an effect of divorce on preadolescent female's sex-role orientation (Kalter, Riemer, Brickman & Chen, 1985; Hetherington, 1972). Another finding, that the girls in the sample did foresee themselves engaging in nontraditional behaviors and occupations in the future, supports a conclusion that clear post-divorce increases in androgynous attitudes and behaviors may not emerge until children cope with adolescent identity issues.

Stevenson and Black (1988) conducted a meta-analysis of 67 studies that compared the sex-role development of children in father-present and father-absent homes. The applicability of their findings to the present issue are limited, however, by the fact that father absence because of divorce was not treated separately from father absence because of death or other reasons. Nonetheless, some conclusions they drew fit well with points made above. Specifically, father-absent female adolescents and young adults were slightly but consistently less feminine than their father-present peers in measures of traditionally feminine characteristics such as nurturance and expressiveness. Similarly, father-absent preschool boys, compared to their father-present peers, made fewer stereotypically sex-typed choices in picking toys and activities. However, older father-absent boys were more stereotypical than their father-present peers in their overt behavior, particularly in the expression of aggression. This latter difference could be reflecting the fact that in a mother-headed household an older boy may be asked to assume "man-of-the-house" duties.

In conclusion, the literature suggests that increased androgyny in children may develop following divorce if parents model nontraditional attitudes and behaviors or if children, by necessity and/or with parental encouragement, engage in nontraditional activities following divorce. While children in adolescence may struggle with androgynous thoughts, feelings, and behaviors, by their late teens and early twenties many will have worked through the issues. For example, two studies used by Stevenson and Black (1988) showed that college men who had experienced father absence reported fewer stereotypical vocational preferences. Finally, methodology has affected findings: While data collected from parents and teachers suggests that father-absent boys' behavior is more stereotypical than father-present boys', self-report measures indicate the opposite. In this connection, teachers' assessments have differed depending on whether they thought they were rating a child from a divorced or an intact home (Ball et al., 1984; Santrock & Tracy, 1978).

RESEARCH AND TREATMENT IMPLICATIONS

Research is needed to identify a full list of favorable outcomes that can emerge following children's adjustment to parental divorce. Longitudinal studies would be desirable, especially those using matched comparison groups of intact family children while controlling for possible confounding variables, including parental conflict and family SES.

Hurley, Vincent, Ingram, and Riley (1984) categorize interventions designed to cope with unfavorable consequences in children following parental divorce as either therapeutic or preventative. The therapeutic approaches, which include psychodynamic and family systems interventions, focus on treating psychopathology, while the preventative approaches help healthy children avoid significant dysfunction by coping effectively with the normal post-divorce crisis reaction. Preventative interventions take the form of school-based support groups for children (Cantor, 1977; Gwynn & Brantley, 1987; Moore & Sumner, 1985;

Pedro-Carroll & Cowen, 1985) or school and community-based support groups for parents (Davidoff & Schiller, 1983; Omizo & Omizo, 1987) and families (Magid, 1977; Stolberg, & Cullen, 1983). Outcome studies show that parents, children, and group leaders believe support groups decrease distress and dysfunction in children (Cantor, 1977; Freeman, 1984; Gwynn & Brantly, 1987; Magid, 1977; Omizo & Omizo, 1987; Pedro-Carroll & Cowen, 1985). At this point, mental health workers could draw from the literature and design a third type of intervention: ones aimed at promoting favorable outcomes in children who must adjust to their parents' divorce.

REFERENCES

Achenbach, T. M., McConaughy, S. H., & Howell, C. T. (1987). Child/adolescent behavioral and emotional problems: Implications of cross-informant correlations for situational specificity. *Psychological Bulletin, 101,* 213–232.

Amato, P. R. (1987). Family processes in one-parent, stepparent, and intact families: The child's point of view. *Journal of Marriage and the Family, 49,* 327–337.

Ambert, A. M. (1984). Longitudinal changes in children's behavior toward custodial parents. *Journal of Marriage and the Family,* (May), 463–467.

Ankenbrandt, M. J. (1986). Learned resourcefulness and other cognitive variables related to divorce adjustment in children. *Dissertation Abstracts International, 47* B, DA8628750, 5045.

Anthony, E. J. (1974). Children at risk from divorce: A review. In E. J. Anthony & C. Koupernik (Eds.) *The child in his family: Children at psychiatric risk* (Vol. 3), 461–478. N.Y. John Wiley & Sons.

Ball, D. W., Newman, J. M., Scheuren, W. J. (1984). Teachers' generalized expectations of children of divorce. *Psychological Reports, 54,* 347–352.

Bandura, A., Adams, N. E., & Beyer, J. (1977). Cognitive processes mediating behavioral changes. *Journal of Personality and Social Psychology, 35,* 125–139.

Bem, S. L. (1975). Sex-role adaptability: One consequence of psychological androgyny. *Journal of Personality and Social Psychology, 31,* 634–643.

Bem, S. L. & Lenney, E. (1976). Sex typing and the avoidance cross-sex behavior. *Journal of Personality and Social Psychology, 33,* 48–54.

Bem, S. L., Martyna, W., & Watson, C. (1976). Sex typing and androgyny: Further explorations of the expressive domain. *Journal of Personality and Social Psychology, 34,* 1016–1023.

Bernstein, N., & Robey, J. (1962). The detection and management of pediatric difficulties created by divorce. *Pediatrics, 16,* 950–956.

Blechman, E. A. (1982). Are children with one parent at psychiatric risk? A methodological review. *Journal of Marriage and the Family, 44,* 179–195.

Block, J. H., Block, J., & Gjerde, P. F. (1986). The personality of children prior to divorce: A prospective study. *Child Development, 57,* 827–840.

Bohannon, P., & Erickson, R. (1978, Jan.) Stepping in. *Psychology Today, 11,* 53–59.

Booth, A., Brinkerhoff, D. B., White, L. K. (1984). The impact of parental divorce on courtship. *Journal of Marriage and the Family, 46,* 85–94.

Boss, E. R. (1987). The demographic characteristics of children of divorce. *Dissertation Abstracts International, 48* 1026A, DA8714900.

Boyd, D. A. & Parish T. (1983). An investigation of father loss and college students' androgyny scores. *The Journal of Genetic Psychology, 145,* 279–280.

Cantor, D. W. (1977). School based groups for children of divorce. *Journal of Divorce, 1,* 183–187.

Clingempeel, W. G., & Segal, S. (1986). Stepparent-stepchild relationships and the psychological adjustment of children in stepmother and stepfather families. *Child Development, 57,* 474–484.

Cowen, E., Pedro-Carroll, J., & Alpert-Gillis, L. (1990). Relationships between support and adjustment among children of divorce. *Journal of Child Psychology and Psychiatry, 31,* 727–735.

Davidoff, I. F. & Schiller, M. S. (1983). The divorce workshop as crisis intervention: A practical model. *Journal of Divorce, 6,* 25–35.

Desimone-Luis, J., O'Mahoney, K., & Hunt, D. (1979). Children of separation and divorce: Factors influencing adjustment. *Journal of Divorce, 3,* 37–41.

Devall, E., Stoneman, Z., & Brody, G. (1986). The impact of divorce and maternal employment on pre-adolescent children. *Family Relations, 35,* 153–159.

Elder, G. H. (1974). *Children of the great depression.* Chicago: University of Chicago Press.

Emery, R. E. (1982). Interparental conflict and the children of discord and divorce, *Psychological Bulletin, 92,* 310–330.

Felner, R. D., Stolberg, A., & Cowen, E. L. (1975). Crisis events and school mental health referral patterns of young children. *Journal of Consulting and Clinical Psychology, 3,* 305–310.

Forehand, R., Brody, G., Long, N., Slotkin, J., & Fauber, R. (1986). Divorce/divorce potential and interparental conflict: The relationship to early adolescent social and cognitive functioning. *Journal of Adolescent Research*, 1, 389–397.

Freeman, R. (1984). Children in families experiencing separation and divorce: An investigation of the effects of brief intervention. Family Service Association of Metropolitan Toronto (Ontario).

Fry, P. S. & Addington, J. (1985). Perceptions of parent and child adjustment in divorced families. *Clinical Psychology Review*, 5, 141–157.

Garmezy, N. (1981). Children under stress: Perspective on antecedents and correlates of vulnerability and resistance to psychopathology. In A. I. Rabin, J. Arnoff, A. N. Barclay, & R. A. Zucker (Eds.), *Further explorations in personality* (pp. 196–269). N.Y.: Wiley.

Glenn, N. D. & Kramer, K. B. (1987). The marriage and divorce of children of divorce. *Journal of Marriage and the Family*, 49, 811–825.

Grossman, S. M., Shea, J. A. & Adams, G. R. (1980). Effects of parental divorce during early childhood on the ego development and identity formation of college students. *Journal of Divorce*, 3, 263–271.

Guidubaldi, J. & Cleminshaw, H. (1985). Divorce, family health, and child adjustment. *Family Relations*, 34, 35–41.

Guidubaldi, J. & Perry, J. D. (1985). Divorce and mental health sequelae for children: A two-year follow-up of a nationwide sample. *Journal of American Academy of Child Psychiatry*, 24 (5), 531–537.

Gwynn, C. A. & Brantley, H. T. (1987). Effects of a divorce group intervention for elementary school children. *Psychology in the Schools*, 24, 161–164.

Hess, R. D. & Camara, K. A. (1979). Post-divorce family relationships as mediating factors in the consequences of divorce for children. *Journal of Social Issues*, 35 (4), 79–95.

Hetherington, E. M. (1972). Effects of father absence on personality development in adolescent daughters. *Developmental Psychology*, 7, 313–326.

Hetherington, E. M. (1979). Divorce a child's perspective. *American Psychologist*, 34, 851–858.

Hetherington, E. M. (1989). Coping with family transitions: Winners, losers, and survivors. *Child Development*, 60, 1–14.

Hetherington, E. M., Cox, M., & Cox, R. (1982). Effects of divorce on parents and children. In M. Lamb (Ed.), *Nontraditional families: Parenting and child development* (233–288). Hillsdale, N.J.: Erlbaum.

Hetherington, E. M., Cox, M., & Cox, R. (1985). The long-term effects of divorce and remarriage on the adjustment of children. *Journal of the American Academy of Child Psychiatry*, 24 (5), 518–530.

Hetherington, E. M. & Parke, R. D. (1979). *Child psychology: A contemporary viewpoint*. New York: McGraw-Hill Inc.

Hurley, E. C., Vincent, L. T., Ingram, T. L., & Riley, M. T. (1984). Therapeutic interventions for children of divorce. *Family Therapy*, 9, 261–268.

Isaacs, M. B. & Leon, G. (1986). Social networks, divorce, and adjustment: A tale of three generations. *Journal of Divorce*, 9, 1–16.

Isaacs, M. B., Leon, G., & Donohue, A. M. (1987). Who are the "normal" children of divorce? On the need to specify population. *Journal of Divorce*, 10, 107–119.

Jacobson, D. S. (1978). The impact of marital separation/divorce on children: II. Interparental hostility and child adjustment. *Journal of Divorce* 2(1), 3–19.

Kalter, N. (1977). Children of divorce in an outpatient psychiatric population. *American Journal of Orthopsychiatry*, 47, 40–51.

Kalter, N., & Rembar, J. (1981). The significance of a child's age at the time of divorce. *American Journal of Orthopsychiatry*, 51, 85–100.

Kalter, N., Riemer, B., Brickman, A., & Chen, J. W. (1985). Implications of parental divorce for female development. *Journal of the American Academy of Child Psychiatry*, 24, 538–544.

Kanoy, K. W. & Cunningham, J. L. (1984). Consensus or confusion in research on children and divorce: Conceptual and methodological issues. *Journal of Divorce*, 74, 45–71.

Kaslow, F. & Hyatt, R. (1982). Divorce: A potential growth experience for the extended family. *Journal of Divorce*, 6, 115–126.

Kelly, J. B. (1988). Longer-term adjustment in children of divorce: Converging findings and implications for practice. *Journal of Family Psychology*, 2, 119–140.

Kelly, J. B. & Wallerstein, J. S. (1976). The effects of parental divorce: Experiences of the child in early latency. *American Journal of Orthopsychiatry*, 46, 20–32.

Kinnaird, K. L. & Gerrard, M. (1986). Premarital sexual behavior and attitudes toward marriage and divorce among young women as a function of their mothers' marital status. *Journal of Marriage and the Family*, 48, 757–765.

Kurdek, L. A. (1981). An integrative perspective on children's divorce adjustment. *American Psychologist*, 36, 856–866.

Kurdek, L. A. & Berg, B. (1983). Correlates of children's adjustment to their parents' divorce. In L. A. Kurdek (Ed.). *Children and Divorce* (pp. 47–60). San Francisco: Jossey-Bass Inc., Publishers.

Kurdek, L. A., Blisk, D., & Siesky, A. E. (1981). Correlates of children's long-term adjustment to their parents' divorce. *Developmental Psychology*, 17, 565–579.

Kurdek, L. A. & Sieksy, A. E. (1979). An interview study of parents' perceptions of their children's reactions and adjustment to divorce. *Journal of Divorce, 3*, 5–17.

Kurdek, L. A. & Siesky, A. E. (1980a). Children's perceptions of their parents' divorce. *Journal of Divorce, 3*, 339–379.

Kurdek, L. A. & Siesky, A. E. (1980b). Effects of divorce on children: The relationship between parent and child perspectives. *Journal of Divorce, 4*, 85–99.

Kurdek, L. A. & Siesky, A. E. (1980c). Sex-role self-concepts of single divorced parents and their children. *Journal of Divorce, 3*, 249–261.

Levitin, T. E. (1979). Children of divorce. *Journal of Social Issues, 35*, 1–25.

Long, N. & Forehand, R. (1987). The effects of parental divorce and parental conflict on children: An overview. *Developmental and Behavioral Pediatrics, 8*, 292–296.

Lopez, F. G. (1987). The impact of parental divorce on college student development. *Journal of Counseling and Development, 65*, 484–486.

Lowery, C. R. & Settle, S. A. (1985). Effects of divorce on children: Differential impact of custody and visitation patterns. *Family Relations, 34*, 455–463.

MacKinnon, C. E., Stoneman, Z., & Brody, G. H. (1984). The impact of maternal employment and family form on children's sex-role stereotypes and mothers' traditional attitudes. *Journal of Divorce, 8*, 51–60.

Maddi, S. R. & Kobasa, S. C. (1984). *The hardy executive: Health under stress.* Chicago: Dorsey Professional Books.

Magid, K. M. (1977). Children facing divorce: A treatment program. *Personnel and Guidance Journal, 55*, 534–536.

McDermott, J. F. (1968). Parental divorce in early childhood. *American Journal of Psychiatry, 124*, 1424–1432.

McKenry, P. C. & Price, S. J. (1984). The present state of family relations research. *Home Economics Journal, 12*, 381–402.

McKenry, P. C. & Price, S. J. (1988). Research bias in family science: Sentiment over reason. *Family Science Review, 1*, 224–233.

Moore, N. E. & Sumner, M. G. (1985). *Support group for children of divorce: A family life enrichment group model.* Paper presented at Annual Meeting of the National Association of Social Workers, New Orleans.

Mueller, D. & Cooper, P. W. (1986). Children of single parent families: How they fare as young adults. *Family Relations, 35*, 169–176.

Omizo, M. M. & Omizo, S. A. (1987). Effects of parents' divorce group participation on child-rearing attitudes and children's self-concepts. *Journal of Humanistic Education and Development, 25*, 171–179.

Pedro-Carroll, J. L. & Cowen, E. L. (1985). The children of divorce intervention program: An investigation of the efficacy of a school based prevention program. *Journal of Consulting and Clinical Psychology, 53*, 603–611.

Peterson, G., Leigh, G. K., & Day, R. D. (1984). Family stress theory and the impact of divorce on children. *Journal of Divorce, 7*, 1–20.

Reinhard, D. (1977). The reaction of adolescent boys and girls to the divorce of their parents. *Journal of Clinical Child Psychology, 6*, 21–23.

Richmond-Abbott, M. (1984). Sex-role attitudes of mothers and children in divorced, single-parent families. *Journal of Divorce, 8*, 61.

Rosen, R. (1977). Children of divorce: What they feel about access and other aspects of the divorce experience. *Journal of Clinical Child Psychology, 6*, 24–27.

Rozendal, F. G. (1983). Halos vs. stigmas: Long-term effects of parent's death or divorce on college students' concepts of the family. *Adolescence, 18*, 948–955.

Rutter, M. (1987). Psychosocial resilience and protective mechanisms. *American Journal of Orthopsychiatry, 57*, 316–331.

Santrock, J. W. (1987). The effects of divorce on adolescence: Needed Research perspectives. *Family Therapy, 14*, 147–159.

Santrock, J. W. & Tracy, R. L. (1978). Effects of children's family structure status on the development of stereotypes by teachers. *Journal of Educational Psychology, 70*, 754–757.

Santrock, J. W. & Warshak, R. A. (1979). Father custody and social development in boys and girls. *Journal of Social Issues, 35*, 112–125.

Santrock, J. W., & Warshak, R. A., & Elliot, G. L. (1982). Social development and parent child interactions in father-custody and stepmother families. In M. Lamb (Ed.), *Nontraditional families: Parenting and child development.* Hillsdale, N.J.: Erlbaum, 289–314.

Santrock, J. W., Warshak, R. A., Lindbergh, C., & Meadows, L. (1982). Children's and parents' observed social behavior in stepfamilies. *Child Development, 53*, 472–480.

Scanzoni, J., Polonko, K., Teachman, J. T., & Thompson, L. (1988). *The sexual bond: Rethinking families and close relationships.* Newbury Park, CA: Sage Publications Inc.

Schwebel, A. I., Fine, M., Moreland, J. R., & Prindle, P. (1988). Clinical work with divorced and widowed fathers: The adjusting family model. In P. Bronstein & C. Cowen (Eds.), *Fatherhood today: Men's changing role in the family.* New York: Wiley, 299–319.

Slater, E. J., Stewart, K., & Linn, M. (1983). The effects of family disruption on adolescent males and females. *Adolescence, 18*, 933.

Springer, C. & Wallerstein, J. S. (1983). Young adolescents' responses to their parents' divorce. In L. A. Kurdek (Ed.), *Children and divorce.* San Francisco: Jossey-Bass, 15–27.

Stevenson, M. R. & Black, K. N. (1988). Paternal absence and sex-role development: A meta-analysis. *Child Development, 59,* 795–814.

Stolberg, A., Camplair, C., Currier, K., & Wells, M. (1987). Individual, familial, and environmental determinants of children's post-divorce adjustment and maladjustment. *Journal of Divorce, 11,* 51–70.

Stolberg, A. L. & Cullen, P. M. (1983). Preventive interventions for families of divorce: The divorce adjustment project. *New Directions for Child Development, 19,* 71–81.

U.S. Bureau of the Census (1990). *Statistical abstract of the U.S.: 1990.* Washington, D.C.

Wallerstein J. (1983a). Children of divorce: Stress and developmental tasks. In N. Garmezy and M. Rutter (Eds.), *Stress, coping, and development.* New York: McGraw-Hill Inc., 265–302.

Wallerstein, J. (1983b). Children of divorce: The psychological tasks of the child. *American Journal of Orthopsychiatry, 53,* 230–243.

Wallerstein, J. (1984). Children of divorce: Preliminary report of a ten-year follow-up of young children. *American Journal of Orthopsychiatry, 54*(3), 444–458.

Wallerstein, J. (1985a). Children of divorce: Preliminary report of a ten-year follow-up of older children and adolescents. *Journal of American Academy of Child Psychiatry, 24*(5), 545–553.

Wallerstein, J. (1985b). The overburdened child: Some long-term consequences of divorce. *Social Work, 30*(2), 116–123.

Wallerstein, J. (1987). Children of divorce: Report of a ten-year follow-up of early latency-age children. *American Journal of Orthopsychiatry, 57,* 199–211.

Wallerstein, J. & Blackeslee, S. (1989). *Second chances.* New York: Ticknor & Fields.

Wallerstein, J., & Kelly, J. (1974). The effects of divorce: The adolescent experience. In J. Anthony & C. Koupernik (Eds.), *The child in his family: Children at psychiatric risk* (Vol. 3). N.Y.: Wiley.

Wallerstein, J., & Kelly, J. (1976). The effects of divorce: Experiences of the child in later latency. *American Journal of Orthopsychiatry, 46*(2), 256–269.

Wallerstein, J., & Kelly, J. (1980a). *Surviving the Breakup.* New York: Basic Books Inc.

Wallerstein, J., & Kelly, J. (1980b, Jan.) California's children of divorce. *Psychology Today,* 67–76.

Warshak, R. & Santrock, J. W. (1983). The impact of divorce in father-custody and mother-custody homes: The child's perspective. In L. Kurdek (Ed.), *Children and divorce,* San Francisco: Jossey-Bass Inc., Publishers, 29–45.

Weiss, R. (1979). Growing up a little faster: The experience of growing up in a single-parent household. *Journal of Social Issues, 35*(4), 97–111.

Werner, E. E. (1989). High-risk children in young adulthood: A longitudinal study from birth to 32 years. *American Journal of Orthopsychiatry, 59,* 72–81.

Werner, E. E. & Smith, B. S. (1982). *Vulnerable but invincible: A study of resilient children.* New York: McGraw-Hill Inc.

Westman, J. C. (1972). Effect of divorce on child's personality development. *Medical Aspects of Human Sexuality, 6,* 38–55.

Wolchik, S. A., Braver, S., Sandler, I. (1985). Maternal versus joint custody: Children's postseparation experiences and adjustment. *Journal of Clinical Child Psychology, 14,* 5–10.

Wolchik, S. A., Sandler, I., Braver, S., & Fogas, B. (1985). Events of parental divorce: Stressfulness ratings by children, parents, and clinicians. *American Journal of Community Psychology, 14,* 59–74.

Zakariya, S. B. (1982, Sept.). Another look at the children of divorce: Summary report of school needs of one-parent children. *Principal, 62,* 34–38.

POSTSCRIPT

Is Divorce Always Bad for Children?

Whitehead provides support for her belief that parents get divorced to liberate themselves from the ties of a family structure that does not work for them. Parents fail to consider what this does to the child's sense of security and need for both parents. Parents who rebel against the notion of "staying together for the sake of the children" are ripping their children apart, Whitehead finds. She attributes a number of social problems to increased divorce rates, including juvenile crime, teen pregnancy, and poor school performance. Whitehead concludes that children who were thought to recover after several years from the trauma of divorce got worse, not better, over time.

Gately and Schwebel find that studies of children and divorce have focused on negative outcomes. However, they also feel that much of the available research is based on methodology that tends to produce negative results. Many of the researchers conducting these studies, for example, did not question the children themselves but instead asked parents or teachers to provide their perceptions of what a child was experiencing. Others' perceptions of children's well-being may not always be accurate and may be clouded by other factors. Furthermore, many of the studies did not have a control group of children who were being raised in unhappy but nevertheless intact homes to which children from divorced families could be compared. Instead, children of divorce are often compared to children from intact homes that are presumed to be happy.

Although the number of studies that show negative divorce effects outweigh studies with positive results, Gately and Schwebel use this research to illustrate the resilience that children of divorce display. These children develop self-protective skills, such as positive personality traits, self-control, self-reliance, and empathy for others. Gately and Schwebel consider these traits a result of the divorce situation.

Is it divorce that creates problems for children? Or is it the poverty, family disorganization, and unmet needs, which so often go along with divorce, that create problems? Is it divorce that produces negative effects on children, or is it living in a single-parent family? Is it best to have two parents to meet children's needs? If one parent is not available or is too stressed out to help the child, then the other parent can take over. If this is true, why stop with two parents? Why not have three, four, or five parents? The more adults available to the child, the more likely the child will have his or her needs met. A common complaint of children is that there is no adult in their lives to whom they can confide their problems.

In addition to the ways divorce may affect the development of any one child, this debate over the impact of divorce on children has implications for society as a whole. Many social critics, including Whitehead, identify divorce and the breakup of the two-parent family as the primary cause of many of today's social problems: increases in poverty and crime, for example, and more and more children failing in school or unprepared to join the world of work. Do you think that is an accurate assessment? Could there be other explanations to account for these social problems? What, if anything, could or should be done about national rates of divorce? How have these selections changed your opinion about divorce?

SUGGESTED READINGS

Cherlin, A. (1993, Winter). Nostalgia as family policy (emotional and economic effects of divorce on children). *The Public Interest, 110,* 77–85.

Gill, R. (1992, Spring). For the sake of the children (effects of divorce on children). *The Public Interest, 108,* 81–97.

Jones, S. (1993, May). The two-parent heresy (divorce and single parent families can adversely affect children). *Christianity Today, 37,* 20–22.

Jost, K., & Robinson, M. (1991, June 7). Children and divorce. *The Congressional Quarterly Researcher, 1,* 351–367.

Lehrman, K. (1993, May). Growing up with divorce. *Vogue, 183,* 182–186.

Wallerstein, J., & Blakeslee, S. (1989). *Second chances: Men, women, and children a decade after divorce—who wins, who loses, and why.* New York: Ticknor and Fields.

ISSUE 8

Is Television Viewing Harmful for Children?

YES: Brandon S. Centerwall, from "Television and Violent Crime," *The Public Interest* (Spring 1993)

NO: Brian Siano, from "Frankenstein Must Be Destroyed: Chasing the Monster of TV Violence," *The Humanist* (January/February 1994)

ISSUE SUMMARY

YES: Brandon S. Centerwall, an epidemiologist, explains that children have an instinctive desire to imitate behavior. However, they do not possess the instinct for determining the appropriateness of the behavior—for determining whether or not a given behavior should be imitated. As a consequence, children act out the violence they see on television shows and carry the violent behaviors into adulthood. This is one reason why violent crimes such as homicide, rape, and assault have been increasing.

NO: Brian Siano, a writer and researcher, says that while we should constantly strive for quality programming, we should not attempt to indiscriminately eliminate all violence from television. He argues that children with non-nurturing parents and those who least identify with their parents tend to be the most aggressive. These variables are more influential than TV violence in affecting aggression in children.

Ask any group of people you meet today about violence in contemporary society and the responses you get will likely be remarkably similar: "Violence is epidemic"; "there is a lot more violence out on the streets now than when I was a kid"; "it's just not safe to be out anymore"; "we live in such violent times." The anecdotes we hear about violence and the nostalgia that people express for a more peaceful past seem to be commonplace. However, the unison with which society decries the rise in violence begins to disintegrate once the discussion turns to the causes for the increase in violence.

Television, particularly television programming for children, is regularly targeted as a key contributor to the rise in violence in U.S. society. There is considerable debate over whether or not television is too violent. It has been suggested, for example, that a child will witness in excess of 100,000 acts of simulated violence on television before graduating from elementary school. Poor children may view even more. Many researchers suggest that television violence is at least partly responsible for the climbing rates of violent crime because children tend to imitate in life what they observe on television. On the other side, critics argue that it is not what is on television that bears responsibility for the surge in violence. Programming is merely reflective of the level of violence in contemporary society. The argument is that while television watching may be associated with violence, it does not mean that it causes violence. For example, some social scientists have suggested that aggressive children tend to watch more aggressive television programming than their relatively passive counterparts. But does the aggressive nature of the child predispose the child to be interested in aggressive programming, or does the programming *cause* the aggression? This is a question that has sparked hotly contested debates.

Those who believe television viewing is at least partly responsible for aggressive behavior in children want the United States Congress to take action and regulate the amount of violence shown on television and the time slots within which programs containing violence can be broadcast. Those on the other side of the issue point out that such legislation would be an infringement on First Amendment rights of freedom of expression.

The two selections that follow are typical of the debate that surrounds violence and television and its effects on children. Brandon Centerwall presents a compelling argument, documented with carefully selected research, that violence in children's television programming must be limited. Brian Siano suggests that although adults who seek to regulate television are well intentioned, they are missing the mark by misinterpreting research on the topic and seeing the issue through adult eyes rather than those of a child.

YES

Brandon S. Centerwall

TELEVISION AND VIOLENT CRIME

Children are born ready to imitate adult behavior. That they can, and do, imitate an array of adult facial expressions has been demonstrated in newborns as young as a few hours old, before they are even old enough to know that they have facial features. It is a most useful instinct, for the developing child must learn and master a vast repertoire of behavior in short order.

But while children have an instinctive desire to imitate, they do not possess an instinct for determining whether a behavior ought to be imitated. They will imitate anything, including behavior that most adults regard as destructive and antisocial. It may give pause for thought, then, to learn that infants as young as fourteen months demonstrably observe and incorporate behavior seen on television.

The average American preschooler watches more than twenty-seven hours of television per week. This might not be bad if these young children understood what they were watching. But they don't. Up through ages three and four, most children are unable to distinguish fact from fantasy on TV, and remain unable to do so despite adult coaching. In the minds of young children, television is a source of entirely factual information regarding how the world works. There are no limits to their credulity. To cite one example, an Indiana school board had to issue an advisory to young children that, no, there is no such thing as Teenage Mutant Ninja Turtles. Children had been crawling down storm drains looking for them.

Naturally, as children get older, they come to know better, but their earliest and deepest impressions are laid down at an age when they still see television as a factual source of information about the outside world. In that world, it seems, violence is common and the commission of violence is generally powerful, exciting, charismatic, and effective. In later life, serious violence is most likely to erupt at moments of severe stress—and it is precisely at such moments that adolescents and adults are most likely to revert to their earliest, most visceral sense of the role of violence in society and in personal behavior. Much of this sense will have come from television.

From Brandon S. Centerwall, "Television and Violent Crime," *The Public Interest,* no. 111 (Spring 1993), pp. 56–71. Copyright © 1993 by National Affairs, Inc. Reprinted by permission.

THE SEEDS OF AGGRESSION

In 1973, a remote rural community in Canada acquired television for the first time. The acquisition of television at such a late date was due to problems with signal reception rather than any hostility toward TV. As reported in *The Impact of Television* (1986), Tannis Williams and her associates at the University of British Columbia investigated the effect of television on the children of this community (which they called "Notel"), taking for comparison two similar towns that already had television.

The researchers observed forty-five first- and second-graders in the three towns for rates of inappropriate physical aggression before television was introduced into Notel. Two years later, the same forty-five children were observed again. To prevent bias in the data, the research assistants who collected the data were kept uninformed as to why the children's rates of aggression were of interest. Furthermore, a new group of research assistants was employed the second time around, so that the data gatherers would not be biased by recollections of the children's behavior two years earlier.

Rates of aggression did not change in the two control communities. By contrast, the rate of aggression among Notel children increased 160 percent. The increase was observed in both boys and girls, in those who were aggressive to begin with an in those who were not. Television's enhancement of noxious aggression was entirely general and not limited to a few "bad apples."

In another Canadian study, Gary Granzberg and his associates at the University of Winnipeg investigated the impact of television upon Indian communities in northern Manitoba. As described in *Television and the Canadian Indian* (1980), forty-nine third-, fourth-, and fifth-grade boys living in two communities were observed from 1973, when one town acquired television, until 1977, when second town did as well. The aggressiveness of boys in the first community increased after the introduction of television. The aggressiveness of boys in the second community, which did not receive television then, remained the same. When television was later introduced in the second community, observed levels of aggressiveness increased there as well.

In another study conducted from 1960 to 1981, Leonard Eron and L. Rowell Huesmann (then of the University of Illinois at Chicago) followed 875 children living in a semirural U.S. county. Eron and Huesmann found that for both boys and girls, the amount of television watched at age eight predicted the seriousness of criminal acts for which they were convicted by age thirty. This remained true even after controlling for the children's baseline aggressiveness, intelligence, and socioeconomic status. Eron and Huesmann also observed second-generation effects. Children who watched much television at age eight later, as parents, punished their own children more severely than did parents who had watched less television as children. Second- and now third-generation effects are accumulating at a time of unprecedented youth violence.

All seven of the U.S. and Canadian studies of prolonged childhood exposure to television demonstrate a positive relationship between exposure and physical aggression. The critical period is preadolescent childhood. Later exposure does not appear to produce any additional effect. However, the aggression-enhancing effect of exposure in pre-adolescence extends into adolescence and adulthood. This suggests that any interventions should be designed for children and their caregivers rather than for the general adult population.

These studies confirmed the beliefs of most Americans. According to a Harris poll at the time of the studies, 43 percent of American adults believe that television violence "plays a part in making America a violent society." An additional 37 percent think it might. But how important is television violence? What is the effect of exposure upon entire populations? To address this question, I took advantage of an historical accident—the absence of television in South Africa prior to 1975.

THE SOUTH AFRICAN EXPERIENCE

White South Africans have lived in a prosperous, industrialized society for decades, but they did not get television until 1975 because of tension between the Afrikaner- and English-speaking communities. The country's Afrikaner leaders knew that a South African television industry would have to rely on British and American shows to fill out its programming schedule, and they felt that this would provide an unacceptable cultural advantage to English-speaking South Africans. So, rather than negotiate a complicated compromise, the government simply forbade television broadcasting. The entire population of two million whites—rich and poor, urban and rural, educated and uneducated—was thus excluded from exposure to television for a quarter century after the medium was introduced in the United States.

In order to determine whether exposure to television is a cause of violence, I compared homicide rates in South Africa, Canada, and the United States. Since blacks in South Africa live under quite different conditions than blacks in the United States, I limited the comparison to white homicide rates in South Africa and the United States, and the total homicide rate in Canada (which was 97 percent white in 1951).[1] I chose the homicide rate as a measure of violence because homicide statistics are exceptionally accurate.

From 1945 to 1974, the white homicide rate in the United States increased 93 percent. In Canada, the homicide rate increased 92 percent. In South Africa, where television was banned, the white homicide rate declined by 7 percent.

CONTROLLING FOR OTHER FACTORS

Could there be some explanation other than television for the fact that violence increased dramatically in the U.S. and Canada while dropping in South Africa? I examined an array of alternative explanations. None is satisfactory:

- **Economic growth.** Between 1946 and 1974, all three countries experienced substantial economic growth. Per capita income increased by 75 percent in the United States, 124 percent in Canada, and 86 percent in South Africa. Thus differences in economic growth cannot account for the different homicide trends in the three countries.

- **Civil Unrest.** One might suspect that anti-war or civil-rights activity was responsible for the doubling of the homicide rate in the United States during this period. But the experience of Canada shows that this was not the case, since Canadians suffered a doubling of the homicide rate without similar civil unrest.

Other possible explanations include changes in age distribution, urbanization, alcohol consumption, capital punishment, and the availability of firearms. As discussed in *Public Communication and Behavior* (1989), none provides a viable explanation for the observed homicide trends.

In the United States and Canada, there was a lag of ten to fifteen years between the introduction of television and a doubling of the homicide rate. In South Africa, there was a similar lag. Since television exerts its behavior-modifying effects primarily on children, while homicide is primarily on adult activity, this lag represents the time needed for the "television generation" to come of age.

The relationship between television and the homicide rate holds *within* the United States as well. Different regions of the U.S., for example, acquired television at different times. As we would expect, while all regions saw increases in their homicide rates, the regions that acquired television first were also the first to see higher homicide rates.

Similarly, urban areas acquired television before rural areas. As we would expect, urban areas saw increased homicide rates several years before the occurrence of a parallel increase in rural areas.

The introduction of television also helps explain the different rates of homicide growth for whites and minorities. White households in the U.S. began acquiring television sets in large numbers approximately five years before minority households. Significantly, the white homicide rate began increasing in 1958, four years before a parallel increase in the minority homicide rate.

Of course, there are many factors other than television that influence the amount of violent crime. Every violent act is the result of a variety of forces coming together—poverty, crime, alcohol and drug abuse, stress—of which childhood TV exposure is just one. Nevertheless, the evidence indicates that if, hypothetically, television technology had never been developed, there would today be 10,000 fewer homicides each year in the United States, 70,000 fewer rapes, and 700,000 fewer injurious assaults. Violent crime would be half what it is.

THE TELEVISION INDUSTRY TAKES A LOOK

The first congressional hearings on television and violence were held in 1952, when not even a quarter of U.S. households owned television sets. In the years since, there have been scores of research reports on the issue, as well as several major government investigations. The findings of the National Commission on the Causes and Prevention of Violence, published in 1969, were particularly significant. This report established what is now the broad scientific consensus: Exposure to television increases rates of physical aggression.

Television industry executives were genuinely surprised by the National Commission's report. What the industry produced was at times unedifying, but physically harmful? In response, network executives began research programs that collectively would cost nearly a million dollars.

CBS commissioned William Belson to undertake what would be the largest and most sophisticated study yet, an investigation involving 1,565 teenage boys. In *Television Violence and the Adolescent Boy* (1978), Belson controlled for one hundred variables, and found that teenage boys who had watched above-average quantities of television violence before adolescence were committing acts of serious violence (e.g., assault, rape, major vandalism, and abuse of animals) at a rate 49 percent higher than teenage boys who had watched below-average quantities of television violence. Despite the large sum of money they had invested, CBS executives were notably unenthusiastic about the report.

ABC commissioned Melvin Heller and Samuel Polsky of Temple University to study young male felons imprisoned for violent crimes (e.g, homicide, rape, and assault). In two surveys, 22 and 34 percent of the young felons reported having consciously imitated crime techniques learned from television programs, usually successfully. The more violent of these felons were the most likely to report having learned techniques from television. Overall, the felons reported that as children they had watched an average of six hours of television per day—approximately twice as much as children in the general population at that time.

Unlike CBS, ABC maintained control over publication. The final report, *Studies in Violence and Television* (1976), was published in a private, limited edition that was not released to the general public or the scientific community.

NBC relied on a team of four researchers, three of whom were employees of NBC. Indeed, the principal investigator, J. Ronald Milavsky, was an NBC vice president. The team observed some 2,400 schoolchildren for up to three years to see if watching television violence increased their levels of physical aggressiveness. In *Television and Aggression* (1982), Milavsky and his associates reported that television violence had no effect upon the children's behavior. However, every independent investigator who has examined their data has concluded that, to the contrary, their data show that television violence did cause a modest increase of about 5 percent in average levels of physical aggressiveness. When pressed on the point, Milavsky and his associates conceded that their findings were consistent with the conclusion that television violence increased physical aggressiveness "to a small extent." They did not concede that television violence actually caused an increase, but only that their findings were consistent with such a conclusion.

The NBC study results raise an important objection to my conclusions. While studies have repeatedly demonstrated that childhood exposure to television increases physical aggressiveness, the increase is almost always quite minor. A number of investigators have argued that such a small effect is too weak to account for major increases in rates of violence. These investigators, however, overlook a key factor.

Homicide is an extreme form of aggression—so extreme that only one person in 20,000 committed murder each year in the United States in the mid-1950s. If we were to rank everyone's degree of physical aggressiveness from the least aggressive (Mother Theresa) to the most aggressive (Jack the Ripper), the large majority of us would be somewhere in the middle and murderers would be virtually off the chart. It is an intrinsic property of such "bell curve" distributions that small changes in the average imply major changes at the extremes. Thus, if exposure to television causes 8 percent of the population to shift from below-average aggression to above-average aggression, it follows that the homicide rate will double. The findings of the NBC study and the doubling of the homicide rate are two sides of the same coin.

After the results of these studies became clear, television industry executives lost their enthusiasm for scientific research. No further investigations were funded. Instead, the industry turned to political management of the issue.

THE TELEVISION INDUSTRY AND SOCIAL RESPONSIBILITY

The television industry routinely portrays individuals who seek to influence programming as un-American haters of free speech. In a 1991 letter sent to 7,000 executives of consumer product companies and advertising agencies, the president of the Network Television Association explained:

> Freedom of expression is an inalienable right of all Americans vigorously supported by ABC, CBS, and NBC. However, boycotts and so-called advertiser "hit lists" are attempts to manipulate our free society and democratic process.

The letter went on to strongly advise the companies to ignore all efforts by anyone to influence what programs they choose to sponsor. By implication, the networks themselves should ignore all efforts by anyone to influence what programs they choose to produce.

But this is absurd. All forms of public discourse are attempts to "manipulate" our free society and democratic process. What else could they be? Consumer boycotts are no more un-American than are strikes by labor unions. The Network Television Association is attempting to systematically shut down all discourse between viewers and advertisers, and between viewers and the television industry. Wrapping itself in patriotism,

the television industry's response to uppity viewers is to put them in their place. If the industry and advertisers were to actually succeed in closing the circle between them, the only course they would leave for concerned viewers would be to seek legislative action.

In the war against tobacco, we do not expect help from the tobacco industry. If someone were to call upon the tobacco industry to cut back production as a matter of social conscience and concern for public health, we would regard that person as simple-minded, if not frankly deranged. Oddly enough, however, people have persistently assumed that the television industry is somehow different— that it is useful to appeal to its social conscience. This was true in 1969 when the National Commission on the Causes and Prevention of Violence published its recommendations for the television industry. It was equally true in 1989 when the U.S. Congress passed an anti-violence bill that granted television industry executives the authority to hold discussions on the issue of television violence without violating antitrust laws. Even before the law was passed, the four networks stated that there would be no substantive changes in their programming. They have been as good as their word.

For the television industry, issues of "quality" and "social responsibility" are peripheral to the issue of maximizing audience size—and there is no formula more tried and true than violence for generating large audiences. To television executives, this is crucial. For if advertising revenue were to decrease by just 1 percent, the television industry would stand to lose $250 million in revenue annually. Thus, changes in audience size that appear trivial to most of us are regarded as catastrophic by the industry. For this reason, industry spokespersons have made innumerable protestations of good intent, but nothing has happened. In the more than twenty years that levels of television violence have been monitored, there has been no downward movement. There are no recommendations to make to the television industry. To make any would not only be futile but could create the false impression that the industry might actually do something constructive.

On December 11, 1992, the networks finally announced a list of voluntary guidelines on television violence. Curiously, reporters were unable to locate any network producers who felt the new guidelines would require changes in their programs. That raises a question: Who is going to bell the cat? Who is going to place his or her career in jeopardy in order to decrease the amount of violence on television? It is hard to say, but it may be revealing that when Senator Paul Simon held the press conference announcing the new inter-network agreement, no industry executives were present to answer questions.

MEETING THE CHALLENGE

Television violence is everybody's problem. You may feel assured that your child will never become violent despite a steady diet of television mayhem, but you cannot be assured that your child won't be murdered or maimed by someone else's child raised on a similar diet.

The American Academy of Pediatrics recommends that parents limit their children's television viewing to one to two hours per day. But why wait for a pediatrician to say it? Limiting children's exposure to television violence should become part of the public health agenda, along with safety seats, bicycle helmets, immunizations, and good nutrition. Part of the public health approach should be to promote child-care alternatives to the electronic babysitter, especially among the poor.

Parents should also guide what their children watch and how much. This is an old recommendation that can be given new teeth with the help of modern technology. It is now feasible to fit a television set with an electronic lock that permits parents to preset the channels and times for which the set will be available; if a particular program or time of day is locked, the set will not operate then. Time-channel locks are not merely feasible; they have already been designed and are coming off the assembly line.

The model for making them widely available comes from closed-captioning circuitry, which permits deaf and hard-of-hearing persons access to television. Market forces alone would not have made closed-captioning available to more than a fraction of the deaf and hard-of-hearing. To remedy this problem, Congress passed the Television Decoder Circuitry Act in 1990, which requires that virtually all new television sets be manufactured with built-in closed-captioning circuitry. A similar law should require that all new television sets be manufactured with built-in time-channel lock circuitry—and for a similar reason. Market forces alone will not make this technology available to more than a fraction of households with children and will exclude most poor families, the ones who suffer the most from violence. If we can make television technology available to benefit twenty-four million deaf and hard-of-hearing Americans, surely we can do no less for the benefit of fifty million American children.

A final recommendation: Television programs should be accompanied by a violence rating so that parents can judge how violent a program is without having to watch it. Such a rating system should be quantitative, leaving aesthetic and social judgments to the viewers. This approach would enjoy broad popular support. In a *Los Angeles Times* poll, 71 percent of adult Americans favored the establishment of a TV violence rating system. Such a system would not impinge on artistic freedom since producers would remain free to produce programs with high violence ratings. They could even use high violence ratings in the advertisements for their shows.

None of these recommendations would limit freedom of speech. That is as it should be. We do not address the problem of motor vehicle fatalities by calling for a ban on cars. Instead, we emphasize safety seats, good traffic signs, and driver education. Similarly, to address the problem of television-inspired violence, we need to promote time-channel locks, program rating systems, and viewer education about the hazards of violent programming. In this way we can protect our children and our society.

NOTES

1. The "white homicide rate" refers to the rate at which whites are the victims of homicide. Since most homicide is intra-racial, this closely parallels the rate at which whites commit homicide.

REFERENCES

William A. Belson, *Television Violence and the Adolescent Boy*. Westmead, England: Saxon House (1978).

Brandon S. Centerwall, "Exposure to Television as a Cause of Violence," *Public Communication and Behavior*, Vol. 2. Orlando, Florida: Academic Press (1989), pp. 1–58.

Leonard D. Eron and L. Rowell Huesmann, "The Control of Aggressive Behavior by Changes in Attitudes, Values, and the Conditions of Learning," *Advances in the Study of Aggression*. Orlando, Florida: Academic Press (1984), pp. 139–171.

Gary Granzberg and Jack Steinbring (eds.), *Television and the Canadian Indian*. Winnipeg, Manitoba: University of Winnipeg (1980).

L. Rowell Huesmann and Leonard D. Eron, *Television and the Aggressive Child*. Hillsdale, New Jersey: Lawrence Erlbaum Associates (1986), pp. 45–80.

Candace Kruttschnitt, et al., "Family Violence, Television Viewing Habits, and Other Adolescent Experiences Related to Violent Criminal Behavior," *Criminology*, Vol. 24 (1986), pp. 235–267.

Andrew N. Meltzoff, "Memory in Infancy," *Encyclopedia of Learning and Memory*. New York: Macmillan (1992), pp. 271–275.

J. Ronald Milavsky, et al., *Television and Aggression*. Orlando, Florida: Academic Press (1982).

Jerome L. Singer, et al., "Family Patterns and Television Viewing as Predictors of Children's Beliefs and Aggression," *Journal of Communication*, Vol. 34, No. 2 (1984), pp. 73–89.

Tannis M. Williams (ed.), *The Impact of Television*. Orlando, Florida: Academic Press (1986).

NO

Brian Siano

FRANKENSTEIN MUST BE DESTROYED: CHASING THE MONSTER OF TV VIOLENCE

Here's the scene: Bugs Bunny, Daffy Duck, and a well-armed Elmer Fudd are having a stand-off in the forest. Daffy the rat-fink has just exposed Bugs' latest disguise, so Bugs takes off the costume and says, "That's right, Doc, I'm a wabbit. Would you like to shoot me now or wait until we get home?"

"Shoot him now! Shoot him now!" Daffy screams.

"You keep out of this," Bugs says. "He does not have to shoot you now."

"He does *so* have to shoot me now!" says Daffy. Full of wrath, he storms up to Elmer Fudd and shrieks, "And I *demand* that you shoot me now!"

Now, if you *aren't* smiling to yourself over the prospect of Daffy's beak whirling around his head like a roulette wheel, stop reading right now. This one's for a very select group: those evil degenerates (like me) who want to corrupt the unsullied youth of America by showing them violence on television.

Wolves' heads being conked with mallets in Tex Avery's *Swing Shift Cinderella*. Dozens of dead bodies falling from a closet in *Who Killed Who?* A sweet little kitten seemingly baked into cookies in Chuck Jones' *Feed the Kitty*. And best of all, Wile E. Coyote's unending odyssey of pain in *Fast and Furrious* and *Hook, Line, and Stinker*. God, I love it. The more explosions, crashes, gunshots, and defective ACME catapults there are, the better it is for the little tykes.

Shocked? Hey, I haven't even gotten to "The Three Stooges" yet.

* * *

The villagers are out hunting another monster—the Frankenstein of TV violence. Senator Paul Simon's hearings in early August 1993 provoked a fresh round of arguments in a debate that's been going on ever since the first round of violent kids' shows—"Sky King," "Captain Midnight," and "Hopalong Cassidy"—were on the air. More recently, Attorney General Janet Reno has taken a hard line on TV violence. "We're fed up with excuses," she told

From Brian Siano, "Frankenstein Must Be Destroyed: Chasing the Monster of TV Violence," *The Humanist*, vol. 54, no. 1 (January/February 1994). Copyright © 1994 by The American Humanist Association. Reprinted by permission.

the Senate, arguing that "the regulation of violence is constitutionally permissible" and that, if the networks don't do it, "government should respond." ...

Simon claims to have become concerned with this issue because, three years ago, he turned on the TV in his hotel room and was treated to the sight of a man being hacked apart with a chainsaw.... This experience prompted him to sponsor a three-year antitrust exemption for the networks, which was his way of encouraging them to voluntarily "clean house." But at the end of that period, the rates of TV violence hadn't changed enough to satisfy him, so Simon convened open hearings on the subject in 1993....

The debate becomes even more impassioned when we ask how children might be affected. The innocent, trusting little tykes are spending hours bathed in TV's unreal colors, and their fantasy lives are inhabited by such weirdos as Wolverine and Eek the Cat. Parents usually want their kids to grow up sharing their ideals and values, or at least to be well-behaved and obedient. Tell parents that their kids are watching "Beavis and Butt-head" in their formative years and you set off some major alarms.

There are also elitist, even snobbish, attitudes toward pop culture that help to rationalize censorship. One is that the corporate, mass-market culture of TV isn't important enough or "art" enough to deserve the same free-speech protection as James Joyce's *Ulysses* or William Burrough's *Naked Lunch*. The second is that rational, civilized human beings are supposed to be into Shakespeare and Scarlatti, not Pearl Jam and "Beavis and Butt-head." Seen in this "enlightened" way, the efforts of Paul Simon are actually for *our own good*. And so we define anything even remotely energetic as "violent," wail about how innocent freckle-faced children are being defiled by such fare as "NYPD Blue," and call for a Council of Certified Nice People who will decide what the rest of us get to see. A recent *Mother Jones* article by Carl Cannon (July/August 1993) took just this hysterical tone, citing as proof "some three thousand research studies of this issue."

Actually, there aren't 3,000 studies. In 1984, the *Psychological Bulletin* published an overview by Jonathan Freedman of research on the subject. Referring to the "2,500 studies" figure bandied about at the time (it's a safe bet that 10 years would inflate this figure to 3,000), Freedman writes:

> The reality is more modest. The large number refers to the complete bibliography on television. References to television and aggression are far fewer, perhaps around 500.... The actual literature on the relation between television violence and aggression consists of fewer than 100 independent studies, and the majority of these are laboratory experiments. Although this is still a substantial body of work, it is not vast, and there are only a small number of studies dealing specifically with the effects of television violence outside the laboratory.

The bulk of the evidence for a causal relationship between television violence and violent behavior comes from the research of Leonard Eron of the University of Illinois and Rowell Huesmann of the University of Michigan. Beginning in 1960, Eron and his associates began a large-scale appraisal of how aggression develops in children and whether or not it persists into adulthood. (The question of television violence was, originally, a side issue to the long-term study.) Unfortunately, when the popular press writes about Eron's work, it tends to present his methodology in the simplest of terms: *Mother Jones* erroneously stated that his study "followed the viewing habits of a group of children for twenty-two years." It's this sort of sloppiness, and overzealousness to prove a point, that keeps people from understanding the issues or raising substantial criticisms. Therefore, we must discuss Eron's work in some detail.

* * *

The first issue in Eron's study was how to measure aggressiveness in children. Eron's "peer-nominated index" followed a simple strategy: asking each child in a classroom questions about which kids were the main offenders in 10 different categories of classroom aggression (that is, "Who pushes or shoves children?"). The method is consistent with other scales of aggression, and its one-month test/retest reliability is 91 percent. The researchers also tested the roles of four behavioral dimensions in the development of aggression: *instigation* (parental rejection or lack of nurturance), *reinforcement* (punishment versus reward), *identification* (acquiring the parents' behavior and values), and *sociocultural norms*.

Eron's team selected the entire third-grade population of Columbia County, New York, testing 870 children and interviewing about 75 to 80 percent of their parents. Several trends became clear almost immediately. Children with less nurturing parents were more aggressive. Children who more closely identified with either parent were less aggressive. And children with low parental identification who were punished tended to be *more* aggressive (an observation which required revision of the behavioral model).

Ten years later, Eron and company tracked down and re-interviewed about half of the original sample. (They followed up on the subjects in 1981 as well.) Many of the subjects—now high-school seniors—demonstrated a persistence in aggression over time. Not only were the "peer-nominated" ratings roughly consistent with the third-grade ratings, but the more aggressive kids were three times as likely to have a police record by adulthood.

Eron's team also checked for the influences on aggression which they had previously noted when the subjects were eight. The persistent influences were parental identification and socioeconomic variables. Some previously important influences (lack of nurturance, punishment for aggression) didn't seem to affect the subjects' behavior as much in young adulthood. Eron writes of these factors:

> Their effect is short-lived and other variables are more important in predicting later aggression. Likewise, contingencies and environmental conditions can change drastically over 10 years, and thus the earlier contingent response becomes irrelevant.

It's at this stage that Eron mentions television as a factor:

> One of the best predictors of how aggressive a young man would be at age 19 was the violence of the television programs he preferred when he was 8 years old. Now, because we had longitudinal data, we could say with more certainty, on the basis of regression analysis, partial correlation, path analysis, and so forth, that there indeed was a cause-and-effect relation. *Continued research, however, has indicated that the causal effect is probably bidirectional: Aggressive children prefer violent television,*

*and the violence on television causes them to
be more aggressive.* [italics added]

Before we address the last comment,
I should make one thing clear. Eron's
research is sound. The methods he used
to measure aggression are used by social
scientists in many other contexts. His
research does not ignore such obvious
factors as the parents' socioeconomic
status. And, as the above summary
makes clear, Eron's own work makes a
strong case for the positive or negative
influence of parents in the development
of their children's aggressiveness.

Now let's look at this "causal effect"
business. Eron's data reveals that aggressive kids who turn into aggressive adults
like aggressive television. But this is a
correlation; it is not proof of a causal influence. If aggressive kids liked eating
strawberry ice cream more often than the
class wusses did, that too would be a predictor, and one might speculate on some
anger-inducing chemical in strawberries.

Of course, the relation between repre-
sentational violence and its influence on
real life isn't as farfetched as that. The
problem lies in determining precisely the
nature of that relation, as we see when we
look at the laboratory studies conducted
by other researchers. Usually, the protocol of these experiments involves providing groups of individuals with entertainment calibrated for violent content, and
studying some aspect of behavior after
exposure—response to a behavioral test,
which toys the children choose to play
with, and so forth. But the results of these
tests have been somewhat mixed. Sometimes the results are at variance with
other studies, and many have methodological problems. For example, which
"violent" entertainment is chosen? Bugs
Bunny and the "Teenage Mutant Ninja
Turtles" present action in very different
contexts, and in one study, the Adam
West "Batman" series was deemed non-
violent, despite those *Pow! Bam! Sock!* fist-
fights that ended every episode.

Many of the studies report that children do demonstrate higher levels of
interpersonal aggression shortly after
watching violent, energetic entertainment. But a 1971 study by Feshbach
and Singer had boys from seven schools
watch preassigned violent and nonviolent shows for six weeks. The results were
not constant from school to school—and
the boys watching the *nonviolent* shows
tended to be more aggressive. Another
protocol, carried out in Belgium as well
as the United States, separated children
into cottages at an institutional school
and exposed certain groups to violent
films. Higher aggression was noted in *all*
groups after the films were viewed, but
it returned to a near-baseline level after a
week or so. (The children also rated the
less violent films as less exciting, more
boring, and sillier than the violent films
—indicating that maybe kids *like* a little
rush now and then.) Given the criticisms
of the short-term-effects studies, and the
alternate interpretations of the longitudinal studies, is this matter really settled?

Eron certainly thinks so. Testifying before Simon's committee in August, he declared that "the scientific debate is over"
and called upon the Senate to reduce TV
violence. His statement did not include
any reference to such significant factors
as parental identification—which, as his
own research indicates, can change the
way children interpret physical punishment. And even though Rowell Huesmann concurred with Eron in similar testimony before a House subcommittee,
Huesmann's 1984 study of 1,500 youths
in the United States, Finland, Poland, and

Australia argued that, assuming a causal influence, television might be responsible for 5 percent of the violence in society. At *most*.

This is where I feel one has to part company with Leonard Eron. He is one of the most respected researchers in his field, and his work points to an imperative for parents in shaping and sharing their children's lives. But he has lent his considerable authority to such diversionary efforts as Paul Simon's and urged us to address, by questionable means, what only *might* be causing a tiny portion of real-life violence.

Some of Eron's suggestions for improving television are problematic as well. In his Senate testimony, Eron proposed restrictions on televised violence from 6:00 AM to 10:00 PM—which would exclude pro football, documentaries about World War II, and even concerned lawperson Janet Reno's proudest moments. Or take Eron's suggestion that, in televised drama, "perpetrators of violence should not be rewarded for violent acts." I don't know what shows Eron's been watching, but all of the cop shows I remember usually ended with the bad guys getting caught or killed. And when Eron suggests that "gratuitous violence that is not necessary to the plot should be reduced or abandoned," one has to ask just *who* decides that it's "not necessary"? Perhaps most troubling is Eron's closing statement:

> For many years now Western European countries have had monitoring of TV and films for violence by government agencies and have *not* permitted the showing of excess violence, especially during child viewing hours. And I've never heard complaints by citizens of those democratic countries that their rights have been violated. If something

doesn't give, we may have to institute some such monitoring by government agencies here in the U.S.A. If the industry does not police itself, then there is left only the prospect of official censorship, distasteful as this may be to many of us.

* * *

The most often-cited measure of just how violent TV programs are is that of George Gerbner, dean of the Annenberg School of Communications at the University of Pennsylvania. Few of the news stories about TV violence explain how this index is compiled, the context in which Gerbner has conducted his studies, or even some criticisms that could be raised.

Gerbner's view of the media's role in society is far more nuanced than the publicity given the violence profile may indicate. He sees television as a kind of myth-structure/religion for modern society. Television dramas, situation comedies, news shows, and all the rest create a shared culture for viewers, which "communicates much about social norms and relationships, about goals and means, about winners and losers." One portion of Gerbner's research involves compiling "risk ratios" in an effort to discern which minority groups—including children, the aged, and women—tend to be the victims of the aggressors in drama. This provides a picture of a pecking order within society (white males on top, no surprise there) that has remained somewhat consistent over the 20-year history of the index.

In a press release accompanying the 1993 violence index, Gerbner discusses his investigations of the long-term effects of television viewing. Heavy viewers were more likely to express feelings of living in a hostile world. Gerbner adds, "Violence is a demonstration of power.

It shows who can get away with what against whom."

In a previous violence index compiled for cable-television programs, violence is defined as a "clear-cut and overt episode of physical violence—hurting or killing or the threat of hurting and/or killing —in any context." An earlier definition reads: "The overt expression of physical force against self or other compelling action against one's will on pain of being hurt or killed, or actually hurting or killing." These definitions have been criticized for being too broad; they encompass episodes of physical comedy, depiction of accidents in dramas, and even violent incidents in documentaries. They also include zany cartoon violence; in fact, the indexes for Saturday-morning programming tend to be substantially higher than the indexes for prime-time programming. Gerbner argues that, since he is analyzing cultural norms and since television entertainment is a deliberately conceived expression of these norms, his definition serves the purposes of his study.

The incidents of violence (total number = R) in a given viewing period are compiled by Gerbner's staff. Some of the statistics are easy to derive, such as the percentage of programs with violence, the number of violent scenes per hour, and the actual duration of violence, in minutes per hour. The actual violence index is calculated by adding together the following stats:

$\%P$—the *percentage* of programs in which there is violence;

$2(R/P)$—twice the number of violent episodes per program;

$2(R/H)$—twice the number of violent episodes per *hour;*

$\%V$—percentage of *leading characters* involved in violence, either as victim or perpetrator; and

$\%K$—percentage of leading characters involved in an actual *killing*, either as victim or perpetrator.

But if these are the factors used to compile the violence profile, it's difficult to see how they can provide a clear-cut mandate for the specific content of television drama. For example, two of the numbers used are averages; why are they arbitrarily doubled and then added to percentages? Also, because the numbers are determined by a definition which explicitly separates violence from dramatic context, the index says little about actual television content outside of a broad, overall gauge. One may imagine a television season of nothing but slapstick comedy with a very high violence profile.

This is why the violence profile is best understood within the context of Gerbner's wider analysis of media content. It does not lend itself to providing specific conclusions or guidelines of the sort urged by Senator Paul Simon. (It is important to note that, even though Simon observed little change in prime-time violence levels during his three-year antitrust exemption, the index for all three of those years was *below* the overall 20-year score.)

* * *

Finally, there's the anecdotal evidence— loudly trumpeted as such by Carl Cannon in *Mother Jones*—where isolated examples of entertainment-inspired violence are cited as proof of its pernicious influence. Several such examples have turned up recently. A sequence was edited out of the film *The Good Son* in which McCaulay

Culkin drops stuff onto a highway from an overhead bridge. (As we all know, nobody ever did this before the movie came out.) The film *The Program* was re-edited when some kids were killed imitating the film's characters, who "proved their courage" by lying down on a highway's dividing line. Perhaps most notoriously, in October 1993 a four-year-old Ohio boy set his family's trailer on fire, killing his younger sister; the child's mother promptly blamed MTV's "Beavis and Butt-head" for setting a bad example. But a neighbor interviewed on CNN reported that the family didn't even have cable television and that the kid had a local rep as a pyromaniac months before. This particular account was not followed up by the national media, which, if there were no enticing "Beavis and Butt-head" angle, would never have mentioned this fire at a low-income trailer park to begin with.

Numerous articles about media-inspired violence have cited similar stories —killers claiming to be Freddy Kreuger, kids imitating crimes they'd seen on a cop show a few days before, and so forth. In many of these cases, it is undeniably true that the person involved took his or her inspiration to act from a dramatic presentation in the media—the obvious example being John Hinckley's fixation on the film *Taxi Driver*. . . . But stories of media-inspired violence are striking mainly because they're so *atypical* of the norm; the vast majority of people don't take a movie or a TV show as a license to kill. Ironically, it is the *abnormality* of these stories that ensures they'll get widespread dissemination and be remembered long after the more mundane crimes are forgotten.

Of course, there are a few crazies out there who will be unfavorably influenced by what they see on TV. But even assuming that somehow the TV show (or movie or record) shares some of the blame, how does one predict what future crazies will take for inspiration? What guidelines would ensure that people write, act, or produce something that *will not upset a psychotic*? Not only is this a ridiculous demand, it's insulting to the public as well. We would all be treated as potential murderers in order to gain a hypothetical 5 percent reduction in violence.

* * *

In crusades like this—where the villagers pick up their torches and go hunting after Frankenstein—people often lose sight of what they're defending. I've read reams of statements from people who claim to know what television does to kids; but what do *kids* do with television? Almost none of what I've read gives kids any credit for thinking. None of these people seems to remember what being a kid is like.

When *Jurassic Park* was released, there was a huge debate over whether or not children should be allowed to see it. Kids like to see dinosaurs, people argued, but this movie might scare them into catatonia. . . . These objections were actually taken seriously. But kids like dinosaurs because they're big, look really weird, and scare the hell out of everything around them. Dinosaurs *kick ass*. What parent would tell his or her child that dinosaurs were *cute*? . . .

Along the same lines, what kid hasn't tried to gross out everyone at the dinner table by showing them his or her chewed-up food? Or tried using a magnifying glass on an anthill on a hot day? Or clinically inspected the first dead animal he or she ever came across? Sixty years ago, adults were terrified of *Frankenstein* and fainted at the premiere of *King Kong*. But today, *Kong* is regarded as a fantasy story, *Godzilla* can be shown without the objections of child psychologists, and there are breakfast cereals called Count Chocula and Frankenberry. Sadly, there are few adults who seem to remember how they identified more with the monsters. Who wanted to be one of those stupid villagers waving torches at Frankenstein? That's what our *parents* were like.

But it's not just an issue of kids liking violence, grossness, or comic-book adventure. About 90 percent of the cartoon shows I watched as a child were the mass-produced sludge of the Hanna-Barbera Studios—like "Wacky Races," "The Jetsons," and "Scooby Doo, Where Are You?" I can't remember a single memorable moment from any of them. But that Bugs Bunny sequence as the beginning of this article (from *Rabbit Seasoning*, 1952, directed by Chuck Jones) was done from memory, and I have no doubt that it's almost verbatim.

I know that, even at the age of eight or nine, I had some rudimentary aesthetic sense about it all. There was something hip and complex about the Warner Bros. cartoons, and some trite, insulting *sameness* to the Hanna-Barbera trash, although I couldn't quite understand it then. Bugs Bunny clearly wasn't made for kids according to some study on social-interaction development. Bugs Bunny was meant to make adults laugh as much as children. Kids can also enjoy entertainment ostensibly created for adults—in fact, that's often the most rewarding kind. I had no trouble digesting *Jaws*, James Bond, and Clint Eastwood "spaghetti westerns" in my preteen years. And I'd have no problems with showing a 10-year-old *Jurassic Park*, because I know how much he or she would love it....

I don't enjoy bad television with lots of violence, but I'd rather not lose *decent* shows that use violence for good reason. Shows like "Star Trek," "X-Men," or the spectacular "Batman: The Animated Series" can give kids a sense of adventure while teaching them about such qualities as courage, bravery, and heroism. Even better, a healthy and robust spirit of irreverence can be found in Bugs Bunny, "Ren and Stimpy," and "Tiny Toons." Some of these entertainments—like adventure stories and comic books of the past—can teach kids how to be really *alive*.

Finally, if we must have a defense against the pernicious influence of the mass media, it cannot be from the Senate's legislation or the pronouncements of social scientists. It must begin with precisely the qualities I described above—especially irreverence. One good start is Comedy Central's "Mystery Science Theater 3000," where the main characters, forced to watch horrendous movies, fight back by heckling them. Not surprisingly, children love the show, even though most of the jokes go right over their curious little heads. They recognize a kindred spirit in "MST 3000." Kids want to stick up for themselves, maybe like Batman, maybe like Bugs Bunny, or even like Beavis and Butt-head—but always against a world made by adults.

You know, *adults*—those doofuses with the torches, trying to burn up Frankenstein in the old mill.

POSTSCRIPT

Is Television Viewing Harmful for Children?

For those who think that television viewing is harmful, a simple solution to the problems that they think are associated with television watching and violence and child development would be to unplug the "boob tube." We could go back to the days when reading, listening to the radio, and swapping stories while sitting by the fireplace were the most common forms of at-home entertainment. On the other hand, there are those who argue that television is merely the next step in the evolution of communication technology and, consequently, we should just go with the flow, grin and bear it, for television is surely here to stay. We should stop worrying about watching television; after all, it is ultimately harmless.

What should be done, and by whom, to effectively address this question? Is it realistic to revert back to the days prior to the television era? Should everyone just relax and stop worrying about television? Are children resilient enough that they can eventually understand TV's impact on their lives? How much truth lies in Siano's contention that if parents were more involved with their children, especially while they are watching television, then what children watch would not be a problem? Would American society end up forfeiting quality programming if Congress were authorized to more closely censor television programming? How do you respond to Centerwall's contention that children are incapable of discriminating between what they should and should not imitate?

Critics of television do not see televised violence as the only potential harm to children. School-age children, for example, are a prime target audience for advertisers. This is evident in the fact that there are more commercial breaks per hour for children's programming than for any other. Additionally, with the growth of cable television, many children now have access to an even greater amount of adult programming. Furthermore, some research suggests that children who spend excessive amounts of time watching television tend to do poorly in school. Interestingly, research also indicates that children who spend a moderate amount of time watching television perform better scholastically than those who do not watch television at all.

Perhaps if all parents could accept the inevitable, that television is here to stay and that viewing choices are expanding almost daily, we, as a society, could move past this dichotomy of thinking that television is either good or bad. Television viewing could be thought of as an active endeavor rather than a passive one. Parents could become more involved with their children as they watch television. Through modeling, parents could teach children to be skeptical about television advertisements, point out the differences between fantasy and reality, and argue the moral values being portrayed on the tube when they differ from the values that are important to the parents.

Parents can use television watching to teach their children how to make decisions. Within limits set by the parents, children can be permitted to choose what they want to watch. Parents can discuss the programs that they watch with their children, always with an eye toward having children express their views while the parents gently challenge opinions and actions that may be different from the values they hold and want to develop in their children. To maximize choices in quality programming, parents can use VCRs (videocassette recorders) to tape-record programs and then find convenient times to watch special programs with their children.

SUGGESTED READINGS

Centerwall, B. S. (1989). Exposure to television as a cause of violence. *Public Communication and Behavior, 2,* 1–58.

Eron, L. D., & Huesmann, L. R. (1984). The control of aggressive behavior by changes in attitudes, values and the conditions of learning. *Advances in the Study of Aggression* (pp. 139–171). Orlando, FL: Academic Press.

Huesmann, L. R., & Eron, L. (1986). *Television and the aggressive child.* Hillsdale, NJ: Lawrence Erlbaum Associates.

Kolbert, E. (1994, December 14). Television gets closer look as a factor in real violence. *The New York Times (National),* D1, D20.

Kruttschnitt, C. (1986). Family violence, television viewing habits and other adolescent experiences related to violent criminal behavior. *Criminology, 24,* 235–267.

Kunkel, D. (1991, November/December). Crafting media policy. *American Behavioral Scientist, 35,* 181–202.

Kuney, J. (1992). Turn-off time? *Television Quarterly, 26,* 43–46.

Liebes, T. (1992, Fall). Television, parents and the political socialization of children. *Teacher's College Record, 94,* 73–86.

ISSUE 9

Should Formal Schooling Begin at an Earlier Age?

YES: Lawrence J. Schweinhart and David P. Weikart, from "Success by Empowerment: The High/Scope Perry Preschool Study Through Age 27," *Young Children* (November 1993)

NO: Michael F. Meyers, from "An Argument Against Educating Young Children," *Education* (Spring 1993)

ISSUE SUMMARY

YES: Lawrence Schweinhart and David Weikart, from the High/Scope Educational Research Foundation, followed a group of children from preschool to adulthood and found that a quality preschool education predicted success for the children.

NO: Michael Meyers, a professor at the University of Massachusetts–Boston, concludes on the basis of his work that preschool-age children should not have education forced on them and should not be separated from their parents to attend a formal preschool program.

The Children's Defense Fund reports that approximately 38 percent of children under age five whose mothers are employed attend preschool; 27 percent spend their days in a family-based child care home; 25 percent are cared for by relatives; and the remaining 10 percent are cared for by a nonrelative in the family's home or have some other care arrangement. Young children whose mothers work and who are receiving a preschool education are in the minority when compared to the 62 percent of children who are cared for in a family home environment. Yet, the number of young children in preschool has steadily increased over the past 20 years and is expected to continue to rise.

Is it in the best interests of children to attend school at three or four years of age? Developmentally, preschool-age children are naturally curious and enjoy playing with other children. Most preschool facilities offer children opportunities for group play, as well as an abundance of play materials that they might not have at home. On the other hand, attendance at a preschool means that children must be separated from parents and placed in a setting that is foreign to them.

There are many types of schools with programs for young children, such as Head Start, Montessori, public schools that have sessions for four-year-olds, and a host of private, commercial preschools. These schools vary in the type of curriculums they offer, the amount of freedom and structure they build into their curriculums, and the total quality of care they provide. Could it be harmful for young children with their natural curiosity to be placed in preschool settings with rules and procedures that must be followed? In this environment, could children learn to dislike school?

How can researchers study the long-term effects of preschool education on children? Once the research is completed, how could one decide whether or not the effects shown were a result of preschool or a result of numerous other factors that influence children's lives? Can researchers control for those other, competing variables? These procedural questions are as much a part of this issue as the philosophical debate on the effects of preschool on children.

In the first selection, Lawrence Schweinhart and David Weikart summarize longitudinal research that was conducted on the effects of preschool education. They attribute the achievements of the children in the experimental group to their participation in a quality preschool program. They conclude that preschool education, as a form of preventive intervention, saves society money on social programs in the long run. Professor Michael Meyers disagrees with this positive assessment of preschool, and he argues against imposing formal education on young children. He points out that perhaps preschool education meets the needs of adults rather than those of children.

YES

Lawrence J. Schweinhart
and David P. Weikart

SUCCESS BY EMPOWERMENT:
THE HIGH/SCOPE PERRY PRESCHOOL
STUDY THROUGH AGE 27

The High/Scope Perry Preschool study, now with findings through age 27, has more than ever to say about the importance to society of doing early childhood programs right. By virtue of an experimental design rarely achieved in research of this type, this study reveals that high-quality, active-learning programs for young children living in poverty return $7.16 for every dollar invested, cut in half participants' crime rate through age 27, significantly increase participants' earnings and property wealth as adults, and significantly increase participants' commitment to marriage (Schweinhart, Barnes, & Weikart with Barnett & Epstein, 1993).

Although these findings address the environmental extremes of poverty versus a high-quality early childhood program, they apply to all children and not just to children living in poverty, in demonstrating that the quality of early childhood experiences affects all children for the rest of their lives. Similarly, the findings depend on the quality of the early childhood program, not on whether it happens to be in a child care center or home or Head Start center or public school.

The evidence of the High/Scope Perry study and similar studies clarifies what we can and must achieve as early childhood teachers and advocates. As teachers, we now know what we can do to positively influence young children for the rest of their lives. As early childhood advocates, we can say, in all modesty, that we have stronger evidence of the importance of our work than do teachers at any other level or workers in any other type of social service. Because society has not yet fully recognized and acknowledged the value of high-quality early childhood programs, we must communicate the importance of our work not only in testimony for policymakers but also in day-to-day conversations with parents, supervisors, colleagues, and everyone else we encounter.

From Lawrence J. Schweinhart and David P. Weikart, "Success by Empowerment: The High/Scope Perry Preschool Study Through Age 27," *Young Children* (November 1993). Copyright © 1993 by The High/Scope Educational Research Foundation. Reprinted by permission. Notes omitted.

THE PROMISE OF SIGNIFICANT BENEFITS

The High/Scope Perry study demonstrates the power of an experimentally designed longitudinal study to reveal program effects, even decades after the program. (Figure 1 summarizes the major findings at age 27.) To conduct the Perry study, project staff

- identified 123 young African American children living in poverty and at risk for school failure;
- randomly assigned 58 of them to a program group and 65 of them to a no-program group;
- provided the program group with a high-quality, active learning program at age 3 and 4;
- collected data on both groups annually from age 3 through 11 and at age 14, 15, 19, and 27; and
- after each phase of data collection, analyzed the data and wrote reports of the study.

In *educational performance* by age 27, the program group completed a significantly higher level of schooling than did the no-program group; 71% of the program group, but only 54% of the no-program group, graduated from either regular or adult high school or received General Education Development certification. Compared to the female no-program group, the female program group had a significantly higher rate of high school graduation or the equivalent (84% vs. 35%). The finding that a preschool program has an effect on the high school graduation rate is important because graduation is a gateway to other long-term effects. The finding has been corroborated in three other studies of preschool-program effects (Monroe & McDonald, 1981; Gotts,

1989; and Fuerst & Fuerst, 1993). Previous High/Scope Perry Preschool Project findings on educational performance indicated that the program group spent fewer than half as many years in programs for educable mental impairment as did the no-program group (group means of 1.1 years vs. 2.8 years) and scored significantly higher on tests of educational performance at the ages of 4 to 7, 14, 19, and 27.

Regarding *crime prevention*, police and court records showed that program-group members averaged 2.3 arrests, half the number of 4.6 arrests averaged by no-program-group members. Only 7% of the program group had been arrested five or more times, compared to 35% of the no-program group. Only 12% of the program males had been arrested five or more times—one fourth as many compared to 49% of the no-program males. Only 7% of the program group had ever been arrested for drug dealing, significantly fewer than the 25% of the no-program group. Program-group members also spent significantly less time on probation than did no-program-group members (12% vs. 26% ever on probation). Similarly, the Syracuse University Family Development Research Program (Lally, Mangione, & Honig, 1988), a study of the effects of a program of high-quality day care and weekly home visits, showed that significantly fewer program-group than no-program-group members had been placed on probation for delinquent offenses as teens (6% vs. 22%).

Regarding *economic development*, 29% of the program group reported monthly earnings at age 27 of $2,000 or more, significantly greater than the 7% of the no-program group who reported such earnings. For males the difference resulted from better-paying jobs; 42% of

Figure 1
High/Scope Perry Preschool Project: Major Findings at Age 27

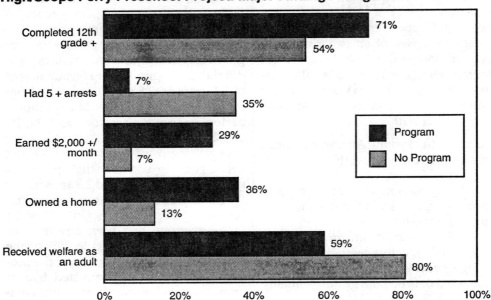

the program males, compared to only 6% of the no-program males, reported monthly earnings of $2,000 or more. For females employment rates accounted for the difference; 80% of the program females, but only 55% of the no-program females, were employed at the interview time of age 27. Significantly more of the program group than the no-program group owned their own homes (36% vs. 13%) and owned two cars (30% vs. 13%). According to social services records and interviews of study participants at age 27, significantly fewer program-group members than no-program-group members received welfare assistance or other social services in the past ten years (59% vs. 80%).

Regarding *commitment to marriage*, although the same percentages of program and no-program males were married (26%), there were differences in the length of their marriages. Among those who married, program males were married an average of 6.2 years, nearly twice as long as the average for no-program males (3.3 years). Among the females, 40% of the program group, but only 8% of the no-program group, were married at age 27. While 57% of the births to program females were out-of-wedlock, 83% of the births to no-program females were out-of-wedlock.

Return on investment was calculated in a benefit-cost analysis (reported by W. Steven Barnett in Schweinhart, Barnes, et al., 1993) that involved the estimation of the program's monetary value and its effects, in constant 1992 dollars discounted annually at three percent. Although the analysis included economic benefits to program participants, only the economic benefits to the public, as taxpayers and as potential crime victims, are presented here. The average annual cost of the program was $7,258 per participant. Forty-five of the program participants attended for two years and 13 attended for one year. The average cost of the program per participant was $12,888 before discounting and $12,356 after discounting.

Also, the average amount of public economic benefits was $88,433 per participant, from the following sources:

- savings in schooling, primarily due to reduced need for special education services and despite added college costs for preschool-program participants;
- increased taxes paid by preschool-program participants because they had higher earnings;
- savings in welfare assistance;
- savings in the criminal justice system; and
- savings on in-court and out-of-court settlements for would-be victims of crimes.

The $88,433 in benefits divided by the $12,356 in cost per participant results in a benefit-cost ratio of $7.16 returned to the public for every dollar invested in the High/Scope Perry Preschool program; thus, the program was an extremely good economic investment, better than most alternative public uses of society's resources and better than most private-sector investments.

RELEVANCE TO EXISTING PROGRAMS

The High/Scope Perry Preschool study shows what programs for young children living in poverty can achieve *if these programs are done right*. The High/Scope Perry program was developed as a model of early childhood education with substantial outreach to parents, meant to be emulated and adapted in the context of local circumstances. Head Start and similar programs are, by and large, service programs for young children living in poverty, including not only outreach to parents but meals and health care for children and social services for families. According to a national survey of High/Scope trainers, one fourth of the nation's Head Start programs use some or all elements of the High/Scope curriculum that was developed and used in the Perry program (Epstein, 1993).

A year of the High/Scope Perry program cost $7,258 per child in 1992 dollars; but this model program was an experimental prototype, not designed for cost efficiency. Run as a service program, the Perry preschool could have been as effective with eight children per teacher as it was with five to six per teacher. Adding approximately $500 per child for meals, health care, and social services, the cost would be $5,500 per child. A year in Head Start in 1992 cost $4,100 per child. Run at the recommended level of quality, Head Start too would cost $5,500 per child, with full-day programs costing somewhat more per child. Increases in Head Start funding per child to enhance program quality should go to systematic in-service curriculum training, curriculum supervision, observational assessment of programs and children, and higher staff salaries and benefits. School districts and community agencies that spend less per child are probably doing so not because of any greater efficiency but because they have sacrificed program elements that are crucial to the quality and effectiveness of the program and its economic return on investment.

Since President Clinton was elected, there has been much talk in Congress and throughout the country of full funding for Head Start. Despite increased funding of such programs in recent years, only 58% of preschoolers (three years old to kindergarten-entry age) from households with incomes less than $10,000 attend any type of preschool program, compared to 79% of preschoolers from households with incomes more than $30,000 (West, Hausken, & Collins, 1993). Full funding, however, must also mean the full funding per child that is necessary to ensure program quality.

PROGRAM QUALITY: THE KEY TO SIGNIFICANT BENEFITS

The High/Scope Perry Preschool study and similar studies suggest that high-quality programs for young children produce significant long-term benefits because they

- **empower children** by encouraging them to initiate and carry out their own learning activities,
- **empower parents** by involving them as full partners with teachers in supporting their children's development, and
- **empower teachers** by providing them with systematic in-service curriculum training and supportive curriculum supervision.

Empowering Children

The National Association for the Education of Young Children has defined developmentally appropriate practice as a basis for program quality (Bredekamp, 1987). Central to this definition is the idea that young children are active learners who can initiate their own learning activities and function as active learners, rather than mere passive recipients of information from others. Such active learning empowers children to assume a measure of control over their environment and develop the conviction that they have some control over their lives. At the same time, children are learning how to solve their everyday intellectual, social, and physical problems. Erikson (1963) pointed out that preschoolers are developing a sense of initiative, responsibility, and independence. They develop these qualities, however, as byproducts of their active learning experiences, not by memorizing self-esteem slogans that are not grounded in their actual social experience. In the High/Scope curriculum (Hohmann, Banet, & Weikart, 1979; Hohmann & Weikart, in press) that was developed during the High/Scope Perry program, children plan their learning activities, carry out these activities in a materials-rich environment, and report on their experiences afterwards. This plan-do-review process helped children in the Perry program develop their abilities and sense of control over their environment. Through home visits the parents, too, came to see their children as active learners.

The High/Scope Preschool Curriculum Comparison study (Schweinhart, Weikart, & Larner, 1986) helped identify the lasting value of developmentally appropriate practices and child-initiated learning activities. The study compared the effects of three approaches to early childhood education. Two of them, the High/Scope approach and the traditional nursery-school approach, supported child-initiated learning activities; the other, the direct-instruction approach, encouraged children to respond to fast-paced, scripted questions from the teacher. While the intellectual performance of all three groups improved substantially—an average of 27 IQ points in one year—High/Scope and nursery-school group members at age 15 reported engaging in half as many delinquent acts as did the members of the direct-instruction group, including one fifth as many property offenses. The programs that emphasized child-initiated learning activities appear to have improved children's social responsibility considerably more than did the direct instruction-program.

Early childhood teachers who want to encourage children to initiate their own learning activities often face the obstacle of *misassessment* of children's performance (Schweinhart, 1993). Most tests focus only on language and mathematics and insist that children provide the one right answer on demand. As an alternative to such assessment procedures, we developed the High/Scope Child Observation Record (COR), a process of taking notes on children's day-to-day behavior, then rating the behavior on 30 five-level developmental items representing children's initiative, social relations, creative representation, music and movement, language and literacy, and logic and mathematics. A two-year study established the High/Scope COR's reliability and concurrent validity when used by trained Head Start teachers and assistant teachers (Schweinhart, McNair, Barnes, & Larner, 1993). Widespread use of such assessment tools in early childhood programs will maintain the integrity of developmentally appropriate programs while responding to demands for accountability.

Empowering Parents

The High/Scope Perry Preschool program included weekly home visits by the teachers with the parents, as well as regularly scheduled group meetings. Each home visit lasted about an hour and a half and involved the child as well as the parent in discussion and modeling of activities like the child's activities in the classroom. The initial goal each year was to establish rapport with parents new to the program. Rather than trying to meet all of the family's needs, the home visitor's focus was on the child and the parent-child relationship. The parents came to see their children as active learners who were capable of learning. The parent component of the program empowered the parents to support their children's development of a sense of control and their intellectual, social, and physical abilities. Today, observational assessment tools like the High/Scope COR can facilitate the dialogue between teachers and parents concerning their children's development.

To develop working relationships with children's parents, teachers must surmount various obstacles, not the least of which is their own reluctance to develop such relationships. Ironically, one obstacle can be the extent of teacher contact time with children (that is, the length of class sessions). Teachers need adequate time when they are not in contact with children so that they can engage in home visits or other activities with parents and plan for activities with children and with parents. Programs in which teachers provide double half-day sessions or full-day sessions five days a week do not allow teachers any time for activities with parents. Another obstacle is the lack of parents' availability because they are otherwise occupied in work, schooling, or other activities. Teachers need to help parents become involved by using strategies such as alternative scheduling and providing child care during group meetings. Another obstacle to home visits can be the lack of safety in some communities, due to the prevalence of criminal violence and drug abuse. Early childhood program staff cannot surmount this obstacle alone, but they may reduce their anxieties somewhat by developing rapport with the parents.

Empowering Teachers

To engage in the practices that empower children and parents, teachers need to be empowered themselves through systematic in-service curriculum training and supportive curriculum supervision. Such training and supervision were key elements of the High/Scope Perry program.

The national High/Scope Training of Trainers evaluation (Epstein, 1993) indicated that such training and supervision in the High/Scope curriculum could significantly improve the effectiveness of the early childhood programs that had already achieved a high degree of quality in other ways. The evaluation found that systematic in-service curriculum training is most successful in promoting program quality when an agency has a supportive administration that includes a trained curriculum specialist on staff who provides teachers with hands-on workshops, observation and feedback, and follow-up sessions. Effective trainers focus on a coherent, validated, developmentally appropriate curriculum model, such as the High/Scope curriculum. The evaluation found that each certified High/Scope trainer worked with an average of 25 teachers and assistant teachers in 13 classrooms and that the teachers they trained scored significantly better than did comparable teachers without such training, not only in their understanding of the High/Scope curriculum but also in their implementation of the approach. The evaluation also found that children in the High/Scope classrooms scored significantly higher than did children in comparison classrooms in initiative, social relations, music and movement, and overall development.

Just as teacher-child ratio is important to program effectiveness, so is it important that early childhood program delivery systems have one curriculum trainer for every 25 teachers and assistant teachers. The High/Scope Training of Trainers evaluation found that trainers spent only eight hours a week, on the average, providing training; but, in many situations teachers do not have any access to staff trainers. Cohesive curriculum training and supervision requires the development and improvement of early childhood program delivery systems, such as Head Start, public school districts, child care agencies, and networks of family child care homes. Such training and supervision should also be backed by publicly supported evaluation, research, and product development.

As public funding of early childhood programs increases, it must go beyond full funding for children living in poverty to providing decreasing percentages of funding for children as their family household economic level increases. In this way we can begin to overcome the strong socioeconomic segregation that now characterizes publicly funded programs. Ultimately, the walls between public and private early childhood programs must become much more permeable.

REFERENCES

Bredekamp, S. (Ed.). (1987). *Developmentally appropriate practice in early childhood programs serving children from birth through age 8* (exp. ed.). Washington, DC: NAEYC.

Epstein, A. S. (1993). *Training for quality: Improving early childhood programs through systematic inservice training* (High/Scope Educational Research Foundation Monograph No. 9). Ypsilanti, MI: High/Scope Press.

Erikson, E. H. (1963). *Childhood and society* (2nd ed.). New York: W. W. Norton.

Fuerst, J. S., & Fuerst, D. (1993). *Chicago experience with early childhood programs: The special case of the Child Parent Center Programs.* Manuscript submitted for publication.

Gotts, E. E. (1989). *HOPE, preschool to graduation: Contributions to parenting and school-family relations theory and practice.* Charleston, WV: Appalachia Educational Laboratory.

Hohmann, M., & Weikart, D. P. (in press). *Young children in action: A manual for preschool educators* (rev. ed.) Ypsilanti, MI: High/Scope Press.

Hohmann, M., Banet, B., & Weikart, D. P. (1979). *Young children in action: A manual for preschool educators.* Ypsilanti, MI: High/Scope Press.

Lally, J. R., Mangione, P. L., & Honig, A. S. (1988). The Syracuse University Family Development Research Program: Long-range impact of an early intervention with low-income children and their families. In D. R. Powell (Ed.), *Parent education as early childhood intervention: Emerging directions in theory, research, and practice* (pp. 79–104). Norwood, NJ: Ablex.

Monroe, E., & McDonald, M. S. (1981). *Follow-up study of the 1966 Head Start program, Rome City Schools, Rome, Georgia.* Unpublished paper.

Schweinhart, L. J. (1993). Observing young children in action: The key to early childhood assessment. *Young Children, 48*(5), 29–33.

Schweinhart, L. J., Barnes, H. V., & Weikart, D. P. with Barnett, W. S., & Epstein, A. S. (1993). *Significant benefits: The High/Scope Perry Preschool study through age 27.* (High/Scope Educational Research Foundation Monograph No. 10). Ypsilanti, MI: High/Scope Press.

Schweinhart, L. J., McNair, S., Barnes, H., & Larner, M. (1993, Summer). Observing young children in action to assess their development: The High/Scope Child Observation Record study. *Educational and Psychological Measurement, 53,* 445–455.

Schweinhart, L. J., Weikart, D. P., & Larner, B. (1986). Consequences of three preschool curriculum models through age 15. *Early Childhood Research Quarterly, 1*(1), 15–45.

West, J., Hausken, E. G., & Collins, M. (1993). *Profile of preschool children's child care and early education program participation. National Household Education Survey statistical analysis report.* (DOE Publication No. NCES 93-133). Washington, DC: U.S. Government Printing Office.

NO

Michael F. Meyers

AN ARGUMENT AGAINST EDUCATING YOUNG CHILDREN

This article points out that many pre-school formal education programs, with apparent positive impact on youngsters, may in fact have negative, long-term educational consequences.

Research indicates the pre-school developmental time frame as being a critical period for developing the natural curious tendencies in children, and that a nurturing, stable curriculum-free home environment is usually best. This period increases the breadth of exploratory interest in naturally inquisitive children and fosters a close parent-child relationship, providing an experience that emphasizes consistency, continuity and values in a stable loving environment. Nurturing the educational interest and psychological needs that children have at this delicate imprinting stage forges the mindset and equips the child for new experiences throughout his/her life.

Americans are finding out, the painful way, that having an educated society is very important to the continued success of that society. In many ways, other countries are passing the United States in terms of technology, productivity, and breakthroughs in research. In order to try to regain their superiority, Americans have taken to educating their children at very early ages. There are many programs that involve formal education, complete with textbooks and teachers, for children between three and five years of age. Some children may be able to survive such programs, others may not. The question is whether or not they should be subjected to such programs.

Within the context of this paper, I will demonstrate the importance of allowing our children to remain children and not forcing education upon them until they are mature enough to maximize their efforts. I will introduce some of the underlying reasons for early education and why many of them are not in the best interest of the child. I will also offer possible solutions to the proponents of early education. To accomplish these objectives, there are some terms that need to be defined. Formal education is the education received in a school of some kind. There is an instructor present and there is a program

From Michael F. Meyers, "An Argument Against Educating Young Children," *Education*, vol. 113, no. 3 (Spring 1993). Copyright © 1993 by Project Innovation. Reprinted by permission. Notes omitted.

to be followed. Self-directed learning refers to the child's natural curiosity and methods of learning within their environment. The child asks questions regarding stimuli within his/her environment and develops his/her skills at a personal pace on an informal level. There are several arguments for using the self-directed method of education for the education of our children. Before we examine them, we must first look at the reasons why early education has become such an issue and how it is currently being handled.

As stated earlier, Americans appear to be sliding down the ladder of international excellence. Many countries are developing in the fields of science, medicine, and technology at a pace that is embarrassing to the United States. In order to regain what has been lost [primarily to complacency] we as a nation have turned toward our youth and their education. Some believe that if we begin to teach our children earlier than we have been that these children will develop into geniuses and put the U.S. back on top. This would be considered a political pressure. In today's society, there are more children placed in various forms of day-care due to the fact that there are more two-income households, and, due to high divorce rates, more single parents who have little choice if they are to support their children. These forms of day-care range from a formal educational setting to leaving the children with a friend. This would constitute a social pressure. One other form of pressure that David Elkind mentions in his article "Formal Education and Early Childhood Education: An Essential Difference" is economic pressure. Because more people have to leave their children to earn a living, there is a great deal of pressure from the parents for better quality out-of-home care. One solu-tion that seems to be growing in popularity is that of the full-day kindergarten or full-day nursery school. This alternative seems to put more parents at ease because their children are not wasting their time as they would at a friend's house, they are learning. As Elkind points out in his research, we should not allow social, political, or economic considerations to cloud our minds when it comes to the education of our youth.

Elkind states that there are several reasons that we should not be so quick to force education on our children. There are health reasons to consider. Children undergo a certain amount of stress when learning. Stress can be defined as "... a demand for adaptation." Related to this stress are negative physiological reactions ranging from fatigue, loss of appetite, and decreased efficiency, to headaches and stomachaches. When a child is placed in a situation where they are required to learn certain topics in a certain time frame, the possibility of stress is naturally increased. This situation opposes the child's natural learning process and the possibility for failure or negative impact on the child is increased. Adding to the detriment of the child is that in many of the accelerated programs, the child is separated from his/her parents, is in an unfamiliar place, and is required to adapt to a new set of rules and regulations. One other potentially negative consequence is the damage to the child's motivation toward learning. If a child is placed into a formal education setting and is frustrated while trying to learn, the experience may affect the child's motivation.

There are some parents, especially those with some college background, who are trying to put their children at the top of the class before classes begin.

They feel that early education is a good thing and that their child should have a jump on the rest of the class. That premise is acceptable but some of the methods they are using are not. Some points that many parents are not aware of are that young children learn differently than older children or adults do, they learn in much broader categories than those available in formal education, and they tend to want to learn more if they are allowed to learn at their own pace. One concept that is passed over concerning informal formal education is that of "reflective abstraction." When a child is given the opportunity to learn on his/her own, they can learn more by thinking about what they have just learned or, to state this more simply, they begin to answer their favorite question, WHY? One example is a child who is given 10 stones makes different shapes, a circle, a square, and although some shapes give the appearance that they have more stones, they know that they always have ten. Most formal education is simply memorization and repetition. This can be very boring to a child who, because of his/her age, is naturally curious and wants to learn about everything all at once.

Another concept that may hinder a child's motivation is the concept of right and wrong, correct and incorrect. A child suddenly becomes afraid of self-directed learning because the 'teacher' dictates what is right or wrong and the child is now in competition with other children for the praise and approval of the adult. The child now depends upon the adult for praise and for the learning process itself. The child no longer feels comfortable initiating learning on its own for fear of reprimand from the adult.

In the past, early education was handled in the home. Parents were responsible for the content of early learning and in most cases, children were ready for school by age six or seven. In fact, prior to the 20th century, most education was in the home. It was during this time that America reached its literacy peak. Coincidentally, there are many people in the field of early childhood education that believe that children should not begin their education at age 5 but should wait until age 8 or later! Some of these 'experts' contend that the most beneficial setting for a child to fully develop in terms of early education is in the home where they are able to interact one-on-one with a parent in a comfortable setting. If a child spends too much time with friends, he/she become dependent on the friends for their values, his/her education, and his/her outlook on the world around them. If they are allowed their own way, the chances for success are greatly increased. The best education a child can receive is the education he/she obtains for himself/herself.

If educating the children of our country through formal education isn't right, and if teaching formal concepts to our children at home isn't right, what is right? To achieve the maximum benefit from early education, it is important to instruct those involved with caring for children about the proper methods for letting them learn. Allow children to be children. Let them investigate the world around them at their own pace and let them ask questions. When the time comes to learn math, science, and reading, a child who has had the chance to learn and achieve success on their own is more likely to be successful in the classroom than a child who has already experienced failure in the classroom. There is little evidence to support the claim that early formal instruction has any long-term negative effects on the learning abilities of a child. It can also be suggested that the desire for early education is not being promoted from the side of the children but from the side of parents interested in either furthering their child's education or looking for some type of day-care.

There can be some long-lasting benefits from teaching children in the home. Before this century, most education was handled in the home. Unfortunately, the emphasis today is to develop young children into college graduates by the time they are 10 years old. Parents or educators must be educated in the development of learning in children and follow that process rather than trying to force education on a child who would rather be outside exploring his/her world. Anyone who has attempted to teach a child knows that the attention span given to any one project is minimal because there is so much going on that the child wants to learn. Trying to focus the child on one specific area will bore the child, or the child will have difficulty grasping the subject matter and become frustrated with the whole process. Some parents purchase 'learning tools' such as computers for their youngsters but don't know how to incorporate these tools so that they maximize its potential benefit to the child.

It's unfortunate that in today's society, many children are being deprived of parental interaction on a regular basis. The term 'quality time' has been thrown around today's society as a panacea for the collapse of the family unit. If we spend some 'quality time' with our children, they'll be fine. If we put them into formal education programs early, they'll be better off. If we buy the computers, they'll get a jump on the rest of their classmates. Nothing can take the place of parental interaction with child. Nothing can motivate a child like personal achievement. Until we can find a way to let children be children again, we may face generations of students who lack the motivation to be academically successful. We may, as has been demonstrated in certain parts of the country, face generations of youths with little or no respect for authority or law. We know what the problem is and we know what the solution is. It's up to us to put the two together for the sake of our children.

SUMMARY

One of the most important parts of a human being's life is their education. The level of a person's education can determine his/her profession, his/her vocation, their social status and his/her acceptance. Within our society, there is a question that needs to be addressed and that is when should education begin and what should it consist of? The answers we come up with as a society, will determine how far, as a society, we will go in the future. Early formal education, which many parents are supporting, may not be the best long-term solution for our children. There are several physical and psychological problems that accompany early formal education which can affect the child's future study habits and motivation toward learning.

Some of the options that we have regarding the education of our youth are: let nature take its course, informal group settings where children can interact with adults, or try to demonstrate the success of child/parent interaction in early educational development. If we let nature take its course, many children will try to learn about the world around them on their own. It can be successful if, at some point, there is some support from an adult who can answer the child's questions as they arise. Children in an informal setting can explore their environment and, through reflective abstraction, develop questions regarding their surroundings. The second suggestion, informal group settings, may introduce the concepts of incorrect and correct which implies to the student that they are either smarter or not as smart as their peers. This may have a negative impact on a child's motivation to learn. If handled extremely well by an adult in charge, it can have a positive result but the chance in this setting is too great. The third suggestion which reflects a time we may not be able to recapture, is the child-parent interaction. A parent is there to answer the child's questions and, because of the naturally existing relationship, is there to provide some continuity in the learning process. Other factors that support this choice are: the child is familiar with the parent, the child is familiar with the environment, and the child is able to be himself/herself. All of these factors are beneficial to the child's emotional state of mind and lend themselves to letting the child learn on his/her own. This promotes a sense of achievement in the child and gives them the motivation to learn.

POSTSCRIPT

Should Formal Schooling Begin at an Earlier Age?

Schweinhart and Weikart report that when compared to the control group, more of the children who attended the Perry Preschool Project in Ypsilanti, Michigan, received high school diplomas or general education degrees (GED). Children who went to the preschool also had fewer arrests, earned more money, and were less likely to have children outside of marriage than their counterparts who did not receive a preschool education. Although the authors believe that the preschool experience had a significant impact on the children's lives, they admit that the preschool experience is only one of many factors that could explain the differences between the groups.

Conversely, Michael Meyers argues that a formal preschool education causes stress in young children and may have long-term detrimental effects. Young children lose their appetites and have headaches and stomachaches as a result of the unnatural learning process imposed on them in preschool. Meyers feels that we should let children be children—they should be allowed to explore on their own and not be guided by a structured curriculum in preschool. He maintains that children would be much better off to stay in a family environment until about age eight, when they would be more developmentally ready to leave home and attend school.

Which is better for children? An informal, self-directed group setting with parents, as Meyers suggests, or a quality preschool setting like the Perry Preschool Project? Does preschool education put undue stress on children? David Elkind's book, *The Hurried Child* (Addison-Wesley, 1988), deals with the issue of pushing children to achieve too fast and too soon. Perhaps putting children in the preschool classroom, rather than their home environment, and asking them to adjust to a new adult (the teacher) is stressful.

SUGGESTED READINGS

Bracey, G. (1994, January). More on the importance of preschool. *Phi Delta Kappan, 75,* 416–417.

Bredekamp, S. (1993, March). Myths about developmentally appropriate practice: A response to Fowell and Lawton. *Early Childhood Research Quarterly, 8,* 117–119.

Canning, P. M., & Lyon, M. E. (1991). Misconceptions about early child care education and intervention. *Journal of Child and Youth Care, 5,* 1–10.

Lewis, A. C. (1993, June). The payoff from a quality preschool. *Phi Delta Kappan, 74,* 748–749.

PART 3

Middle Childhood

Middle childhood, or school age, is the period from age five through twelve. The rate of a child's growth generally slows until the later part of this stage of development. Usually, the most important experience during middle childhood is schooling. As a child progresses through this stage, new significant others, who are outside of the child's family, become part of the child's life. The peer group (especially same-sex peers), teachers, and media personalities take on increased importance for the child. This section examines issues related to schooling and self-care.

- Are Boys Better in Math Than Girls?

- Are Latchkey Children at a Disadvantage?

- Is Home Schooling an Effective Method
   of Education?

ISSUE 10

Are Boys Better in Math Than Girls?

YES: Carol J. Mills, Karen E. Ablard, and Heinrich Stumpf, from "Gender Differences in Academically Talented Young Students' Mathematical Reasoning: Patterns Across Age and Subskills," *Journal of Educational Psychology* (vol. 85, no. 2, 1993)

NO: American Association of University Women, from *How Schools Shortchange Girls: A Study of Major Findings on Girls and Education* (American Association of University Women, 1992)

ISSUE SUMMARY

YES: Carol Mills, Karen Ablard, and Heinrich Stumpf, all associates of the Center for Talented Youth Research at Johns Hopkins University, report that boys perform better than girls on tests for math reasoning ability.

NO: A report developed by the Center for Research on Women at Wellesley College for the American Association of University Women concludes that the differences in math achievement between boys and girls are not significant and are narrowing.

You may have heard the common assertion that "boys are better in math and girls are better in verbal skills." Does being born male automatically predispose a child to have a greater mathematical acuity? Are girls fated to go through life with perpetual math anxiety? Research results are divided on the question of gender and math ability. There are a number of studies that report that boys outperform girls in math. Other reports, based on analyses of over 100 studies, conclude that girls and boys perform equally on math tests.

Some of the reasons for the conflicting conclusions are due to the sample populations studied and the math skills that were tested. Some researchers argue that because boys are more likely to drop out of school than girls, the pool of boys and girls tested may be unequal. The boys left in school might be more likely to be above-average students than the girls. A boy's prior knowledge is also considered to be advantageous. For example, if boys are placed in more accelerated math courses than girls, they will probably perform better on standard math tests.

On the other hand, there are researchers who contend that there are no real differences in boys' and girls' ability or achievement in math. Math acuity could be more of a self-fulfilling prophecy issue: Boys are expected to be better in math and girls are not. So discrepancies in mathematical performance might simply be the result of children living up to expectations.

In the following selections you will read conflicting conclusions based on similar research studies. One set of authors concludes that there are clear and distinct differences in boys' and girls' math ability. The other selection draws the opposite conclusion, that there are no gender differences when it comes to mathematics.

YES
Carol J. Mills, Karen E. Ablard, and Heinrich Stumpf

GENDER DIFFERENCES IN ACADEMICALLY TALENTED YOUNG STUDENTS' MATHEMATICAL REASONING: PATTERNS ACROSS AGE AND SUBSKILLS

When a sample of academically talented students in Grades 2–6 was given a test of mathematical reasoning ability, boys performed better overall than girls. The gender differences for mathematical ability appeared as early as 2nd grade in samples tested over a 7-year period but varied somewhat according to mathematical subskills. There were no substantial gender-related differences on tasks requiring students to identify whether enough information was provided to solve a task; however, boys performed better than girls on tasks requiring application of algebraic rules or algorithms, as well as on tasks in which the understanding of mathematical concepts and number relationships was required.

Speculation and research efforts concerning gender differences in cognitive abilities appear to be a "national preoccupation" (Jacklin, 1989). This is particularly true for differences in mathematical and spatial ability, whereas few consistent gender-related differences have been found for verbal ability.

One of the reasons for the tenacious interest in gender differences in mathematical ability is the possible relationship between mathematics performance and academic or career opportunities and performance (e.g., Sells, 1980). Research results suggest that gender differences in mathematical ability may be related to mathematics attitudes (Armstrong, 1985), self-confidence (Eccles et al., 1985; Fox, Brody, & Tobin, 1985), course choices (Benbow & Stanley, 1983), persistence in a mathematics discipline (Casserly & Rock, 1985), and career choices (Subotnik, Duschl, & Selmon, 1991). It has also been suggested that gender differences in ability combined with gender differences on a variety of other variables (including interests, values, and cognitive style) may

From Carol J. Mills, Karen E. Ablard, and Heinrich Stumpf, "Gender Differences in Academically Talented Young Students' Mathematical Reasoning: Patterns Across Age and Subskills," *Journal of Educational Psychology,* vol. 85, no. 2, (1993). Copyright © 1993 by The American Psychological Association. Reprinted by permission.

represent a particularly persistent constraint on equal representation of men and women across a variety of disciplines (Lubinski & Benbow, 1992; Mills, 1992).

General statements on gender differences in mathematical reasoning ability, however, are likely to be misleading because they mask the complexity of the issue. For example, the age at which gender differences first appear and the direction of such differences differ from one study or review article to another.

In general, small but reliable gender differences in favor of boys/men in mathematical reasoning ability have been consistently noted from adolescence onward (Hyde, Fennema, & Lamon, 1990; Maccoby & Jacklin, 1974; Weiner & Robinson, 1986). Some reviewers have concluded that the differences emerge only in the last 2 or 3 years of high school (Hyde et al., 1990; Meece, Parsons, Kaczala, Goff, & Futterman, 1982; Stage, Kreinberg, Eccles, & Becker, 1985).

Studies reporting gender differences at an earlier age (elementary school) have been based primarily on findings from achievement or knowledge tests as opposed to ability tests (Dossey, Mullis, Lindquist, & Chambers, 1988; Marshall & Smith, 1987). Some of these studies with younger students also have reported girls scoring higher than boys (Hilton & Berglund, 1971; Marshall & Smith, 1987). Overall, the point at which gender differences first appear and the direction they take seem to depend on the content and cognitive demands of the items used.

The appearance and nature of gender differences may also depend on the particular characteristics of the population studied. For example, gender-related differences in favor of boys/men appear to be even more pronounced in academically talented populations. In very select but large samples tested over the past 11 years, boys have consistently scored higher as a group than girls on the mathematics section of the Scholastic Aptitude Test (SAT) as early as the seventh grade (Benbow, 1988; Benbow & Stanley, 1980; Durden, Mills, & Barnett, 1990).

Such differences in mathematical reasoning ability have not been clearly established, however, in academically talented samples at an earlier age. One of the obstacles in the past to such an endeavor has been the belief that the existing mathematical reasoning tests were inappropriate for assessing the ability in younger children (Benbow, 1988). The School and College Ability Test (SCAT), however, has been successfully used for a number of years in above-grade-level testing to identify academic talent in students of elementary school age (Durden, Mills, & Barnett, 1990). Because academically talented students, such as those tested in our study, have been shown to exhibit abstract reasoning ability and formal operational thinking at an earlier age than typically found in a general population of students (Ablard, Tissot, & Mills, 1992; Keating, 1975), gender differences may emerge earlier for these students than previous research has suggested. The nature of gender differences in mathematical reasoning ability in an elementary school population of academically talented students was, therefore, a major focus of the present study.

Another important issue surrounding gender differences in mathematical ability is the identification of subskills and the degree to which the performance of male and female students may differ on specific item types. Researchers such as Hyde et al. (1990), Marshall and Smith (1987), and Stage et al. (1985) have found that mathematical ability consists of several subskills, such as computation and problem solving, that differ in their degree of gender sensitivity.

Tests that predominantly measure computational skills are generally found to favor girls/women or show no gender-related differences at all, whereas tests involving the use of mathematical concepts or mathematical problem solving generally favor boys/men (Hyde et al., 1990). In a study of young adults, Klieme (1989) also found that tasks requiring the application of known mathematical algorithms did not show gender differences as large as did tasks requiring mathematical problem solving. These findings emphasize the need to differentiate between achievement or knowledge tests and tests of ability or aptitude. As Marshall and Smith (1987) have pointed out, it is equally important to examine gender patterns in performance on subcategories of items within a given test. This was also a focus of the present study.

The generalizability of all these findings, however, is challenged by the observation of some authors that gender-related differences in cognitive variables, such as mathematical and spatial ability, have declined during recent years (Emanuelsson & Svensson, 1986; Feingold, 1988; Hilton, 1985; Hyde et al., 1990; Linn, 1991; Rosenthal & Rubin, 1982; Stumpf & Klieme, 1989). Other recent studies (e.g., Cleary, 1991; Oosthuizen, 1991; Stanley, Benbow, Brody, Dauber, & Lupowski, 1991), however, have continued to find substantial differences between male and female students in these domains of cognitive functioning, so this matter is not as yet resolved.

In view of the research findings, three major questions were asked in the present study: (a) In a sample of academically talented elementary school children, do boys and girls differ in mathematical reasoning ability? (b) If a gender difference exists, does it differ by age or grade level? and (c) If gender differences are found for overall mathematical ability, does the pattern of results differ by subskills identified in the test of mathematical reasoning ability?

METHOD

Participants

The participants in our study were 2,586 students between 7 and 11 years of age. These students participated in eligibility testing (between 1985 and 1991) for special course work offered to elementary school children by the Center for Talented Youth at the Johns Hopkins University as part of a program introduced in 1985. Information on the racial, ethnic, and socioeconomic background of students attending the courses is obtained on a voluntary basis. Because such information is incomplete, analyses across subsamples are not reported in this article.[1]

All students had scored at or above the 97th percentile for either verbal or mathematical ability or achievement on a nationally normed test (such as the California Achievement Test) administered in their schools. Although all students could be considered academically talented, not all were talented specifically in mathematics. Therefore, we were able to obtain a sample with a relatively wide range of mathematical ability. Indeed, SCAT scores in the sample ranged across virtually all possible standard scores.

Procedure

Students identified as academically talented by their scores on a nationally normed mathematical or verbal aptitude test took the SCAT to apply for eligibility for advanced-level course work. Because the students had already shown high academic performance on a grade-appropriate test, a more challenging level of the SCAT (a level designed for students at least two grades above the participants' actual grade level) was administered to prevent ceiling effects and to make finer ability distinctions among these talented students. Testing took place in group sessions.

Two equivalent forms (X and Y) and three difficulty levels (elementary, intermediate, or advanced) of the SCAT were administered to accommodate the various age levels[2] and testing dates (Form X for fall administrations and Form Y for spring administrations). To make the scores on these forms and levels comparable, the raw scores were converted to standard scores as specified in the SCAT manual. The results reported here are predominantly based on the standard scores.

School and College Ability Test

The SCAT is a nationally normed standardized test developed by the Educational Testing Service; the SCAT Series III (Educational Testing Service, 1980) was used in this study. The test has two parts (subtests), verbal and quantitative, each of which consists of 50 items. Although students took both sections of the SCAT, only the results from the quantitative section were of interest for this article.

The quantitative subtest includes tasks covering a variety of content, such as estimation, fractions, proportions, and geometry. All items are quantitative comparison tasks: The student must decide which of two quantities is greater than the other, whether they are the same, or whether there is not enough information available to make a decision.

The questions on the SCAT III place minimum emphasis on reading and require more resourcefulness and insight than traditional computation items. Although some knowledge of arithmetic operations is necessary to answer the items correctly, no actual computations are required on the test. In fact, students who take the time to do the computations typically do less well and often do not complete the test within the time allowed. Because an "out-of-level" version (i.e., above the student's grade level) of the SCAT was administered to this group of students, thereby ensuring that most of them had not been formally exposed to many of the operations and concepts dealt with in the test, it seems reasonable to consider it a measure of high-level reasoning and problem-solving ability for this sample. Three sample items from the test are presented in the Appendix [at the end of this selection].

The SCAT Series III used in this study represents revisions of the SCAT Series II tests. It has been widely used since 1980 to assess the verbal and quantitative aptitude of 3rd- through 12th-grade students in both public and private schools (Educational Testing Service, 1980). In addition, a number of school districts currently use the SCAT to identify academically talented students for special programs.

The SCAT has been shown to predict scores on the SAT reasonably well (Educational Testing Service, 1980). In addition, the SCAT has successfully predicted how students progressed in advanced-level mathematics and humanities courses offered by the Center for Talented Youth over the past 7 years (Durden et al., 1990; Mills & Ablard, 1992). For more detailed psychometric evaluations of the SCAT, the reader is referred to Ahmann (1985) and Passow (1985).

RESULTS

Score differences for gender, grade level, and year of testing were examined for statistical significance with analyses of variance (ANOVAs). The regression approach within the Statistical Package for the Social Sciences (Norusis, 1988) was used for the ANOVAs. In this approach, all effects are assessed simultaneously, and each effect is adjusted for all other effects in the model. Given the occasionally observed difference in variance for male and female students, a test for homogeneity of variance (Cochran's test) was conducted. The results of this test indicated that the two variances were not significantly different ($C = .55, p > .001$). Because the sample was very large, a conservative criterion ($p < .001$) for classifying a difference as significant was adopted for all statistical tests.

In addition to the significance tests, the formula for unequal variances (Cohen, 1977, p. 44) was used to obtain effect-size estimates (d coefficients) for the differences between various groups. These estimates were useful for comparisons among group differences within the present study, as well as for comparisons with findings reported in the literature.

Grade Level
A 2 (gender) × 5 (grade level) ANOVA conducted for the quantitative subtest revealed significant main effects for gender and grade level, $F(1, 2576) = 99.10, p < .001$, and $F(4, 2576) = 448.62, p < .001$, respectively. The Scheffé test revealed that boys performed better than girls across all grade levels and that performance in-

creased with grade level for both boys and girls. The interaction effect for gender and grade level on mathematical reasoning performance, however, was not significant, $F(4, 2576) = 0.76, p > .05$, indicating that the gender effect did not vary across grade level.

The largest gender difference (for the fifth graders) was about one half of a standard deviation. Even among the youngest students, the second graders, the scores of the boys were higher than those for girls, as documented by means that differ by more than one third of a standard deviation. In view of the previous studies with young subjects (as summarized by Hyde et al., 1990), this finding suggests that gender differences in mathematics ability, at least in a population of highly able students, appear much earlier than thought and are relatively consistent across age levels.

Mathematical Subskills
Previous research has shown that the concept of mathematical reasoning ability can be broken down into concepts of more specific subskills required to solve mathematical problems. These subskills have been found to vary in the amount of gender-related differences they show (e.g., Hyde et al., 1990; Klieme, 1989). Higher level problem solving and understanding of mathematical concepts are believed to be more gender sensitive than computational skills, for which there is no difference at all or a slight superiority for females (Hyde et al., 1990). Factors underlying students' performance on the SCAT were examined, as well as the extent to which boys differed from girls on these factors....

Before the scores on the three factors were compared across gender (t tests), the factor structures for boys and girls (separately) were compared. Three factors were obtained for both sexes and rotated independently to an orthogonal simple structure. Coefficients of congruence (Harman, 1976, p. 344) were computed for each pair of factors from the two subgroups. These coefficients were .95, .94, and .92 for Factors 1, 2, and 3, respectively, thus indicating that the factor structures are basically the same and that it is meaningful to assume a common factor structure.

Factor 1 was characterized by high loadings of items that required the decision that not enough information was available to solve the task (seven of eight items). Although the items vary in format and content, their common element is that students must evaluate the sufficiency of the available information to solve the tasks. A sample item for this factor is provided in the Appendix as Item 1.

Factor 2 was dominated by tasks requiring the understanding of algebraic operations or handling expressions with an unknown quantity, especially when fractions and decimals were involved. A sample item for this factor is given as Item 2 in the Appendix.

Factor 3 was marked by tasks requiring the understanding of mathematical concepts (e.g., the concepts of whole numbers and even numbers) and relationships among numbers, especially when units, proportions (e.g., percentages), or simple statistics (e.g., the arithmetic mean) were to be evaluated. A sample item for this factor is given as Item 3 in the Appendix.

... [B]oys had higher scores than girls on all three factors, but only the differences on Factors 2, $t(685) = 4.18$, $p < .001$, and 3, $t(685) = 4.76$, $p < .001$, were significant; for Factor 1, $t(685) =$

2.50, $p > .01$. In terms of Cohen's (1977) classification, the differences on Factors 2 and 3 represent small effect sizes.

Although the difference of scores on Factor 1 was not significant, the "not enough information" response (Response D) was itself of interest in terms of differential responding by boys and girls. To determine whether boys and girls differed with respect to deciding whether enough information was available for solving a task, we examined gender differences for hits and false alarms.[3] ...

[B]oys had a slightly higher average of hits and a slightly smaller average of false alarms than did girls. Neither difference was statistically significant. As far as the discrimination score is concerned, however, the mean score for boys was significantly higher than that for girls, $t(685) = 3.53$, p $< .001$. Thus, boys were more accurate overall in deciding whether enough information was given to solve a problem. This male advantage for accurately choosing the not enough information response is obviously related to the slight (but nonsignificant) male advantage on Factor 1.

A final analysis was conducted to investigate a recent suggestion that gender-related differences on tests with time-limits may be related to gender differences in test-taking habits and confidence levels (Goldstein, Haldane, & Mitchell, 1990). Goldstein et al. suggested comparing conventional scores with ratio scores (number of items correctly answered divided by number of items attempted, multiplied by 100).

Using the largest subsample in our study, the students who had taken the intermediate level of SCAT Form X, we computed both the conventional and ratio scores and compared them for boys and girls. On the conventional number-correct scores, boys had a raw score mean of 28.12 (SD = 8.19) and girls had a mean of 24.19 (SD = 7.86), yielding a d coefficient of .49 for the gender-related difference. On the ratio scores, boys had a mean of 61.76 (SD = 15.76) and girls had a mean of 54.56 (SD = 16.03), which corresponds to a d value of .45. An examination of the d values reveals that the gender differences in this subsample of students are very similar according to either conventional or ratio scores, and they are consistent with the differences reported for all grade levels. Thus, only a small fraction of the gender differences found in the present study can be explained by the factors mentioned earlier and operationalized by the ratio score.

DISCUSSION

In contrast to studies that have reported a convergence in mental test scores of male and female students in recent years (Hyde et al., 1990; Linn, 1991), we found gender differences in mathematical ability.[4] We are not alone in our findings, because other recent studies have reported gender differences in mathematical ability (Cleary, 1991; Stanley et al., 1991).

The major purpose of this study, however, was not merely to revisit the gender difference issue but to help clarify and further understand such differences. Although an overall gender difference was found in our study, the more important findings are that (a) this difference was discovered as early as second grade in an academically talented population, (b) the magnitude of the gender difference was approximately the same across five grade levels, and (c) mathematical reasoning ability can be

meaningfully broken down into several subsets of skills that differ somewhat in their gender sensitivity.

A unique contribution of our study is the finding of gender differences in mathematical reasoning ability in children at a much younger age than has previously been reported. This result was accompanied by the finding that the differences did not change appreciably across age or grade level.

To understand our findings, it is important to consider several related facts. First, we tested reasoning ability, which is rarely done with young elementary school students. Generally, standardized tests before seventh grade focus on specific knowledge and computational skills (achievement tests). Second, we used equivalent forms of the same test across all age levels, which meant that the type of ability tested did not change. Studies reporting changes in gender differences across age are often plagued by changes in test content, format, or focus when testing different age groups (e.g., Hyde et al., 1990; Marshall & Smith, 1987).

It is also important to consider the advanced cognitive development of the subjects in our study. Gender differences appear to be greatest for tasks involving problem solving and understanding of mathematical concepts that require higher level thinking (Hyde et al., 1990). Such differences generally first appear around the age of 12 years, when most children begin to develop formal operational thinking. Because academically talented students have been shown to exhibit performance indicative of formal operations well before 12 years of age (Ablard et al., 1992; Keating, 1975), it is not surprising that we found gender differences in mathematical reasoning at a younger age than has typically been found.

A side benefit of studying the development of reasoning and problem-solving ability in students who are cognitively advanced may be a resulting better understanding of general developmental patterns of such abilities. With the national push for reform in mathematics instruction to include more of an emphasis on problem solving and higher level reasoning in elementary school, an understanding of when and how gender differences in such skills develop takes on immediate importance.

The results of the factor analysis indicate, once again, that mathematical reasoning is not monolithic but can be broken down into several subskills. Our classification of subskills of mathematical reasoning ability, however, is purely post hoc. It is a description of the demands of various tasks, not an identification of cognitive processes involved in these tasks. More research is needed to arrive at a delineation of the basic cognitive processes underlying the specific sub-skills that make up mathematical reasoning ability, as well as how boys/men and girls/women may or may not differ in their development and use of such processes.

Although we found gender differences in favor of boys on two of the factors identified in the SCAT, on one factor significant differences did not emerge. This factor (Factor 1) contained mainly items requiring subjects to determine whether sufficient information was present to solve the task. However, in an analysis focusing on the discrimination between hits and false alarms on all not enough information responses given by students in our study, boys were more accurate.

Clearly, an understanding of the pattern of gender differences across subskills within what is called "mathematical reasoning ability" is still incomplete. Examining differences across subskills, however, may ultimately prove to be more useful than considering overall scores for understanding the cognitive development of males and females. A similar approach (Linn & Petersen, 1985) in the area of spatial ability proved to be useful in explaining inconsistencies in the literature. In addition, as Marshall and Smith (1987) suggested, an understanding of possible gender differences in the development of different skills may lead to useful educational recommendations for the teaching of mathematics.

Finally, it has been suggested that differences in test-taking styles and attitudes may be responsible for gender differences on tests exhibiting gender sensitivity (Goldstein et al., 1990). Specifically, researchers have hypothesized that female test takers are at a disadvantage on tests, such as the SCAT, that have time limits. A comparison of conventional and ratio scores, however, revealed that only a small fraction of the gender-related differences observed in this study could be explained by such factors.

One should, of course, never generalize from a select sample such as ours to the general population. One caution discussed recently by Feingold (1992) centers around the frequent finding over the years that the scores of male students on a large number of general ability tests have a larger variance than those of female students. Gender differences in the scores of a group selected from the right tail of the distribution may, therefore, show differences in the means even when the overall means are equal, for the simple reason that more high-scoring male students are likely to be selected than high-scoring female students. This may be one of the reasons why studies with select samples (Benbow, 1988; Benbow & Stanley, 1980, 1983; Hyde et al., 1990; Stanley et al., 1991) generally have found larger gender differences than have been found in a population with a full range of ability levels.

Even when such a generalization is explicitly avoided, however, a gender-related difference among highly talented students in the area of mathematical reasoning ability is a finding that needs to be described and explained in its own right. Although such gender differences in academically talented samples are usually small to moderate in magnitude and are not consistently found for all aspects of mathematical reasoning ability, they are consistently found for overall mathematical reasoning ability. In addition, these differences appear at a relatively young age (i.e., early elementary school), and they seem to be stable across age level and year of testing within a population from which future mathematicians and scientists are most likely to come.

NOTES

1. Most students are from a White or Asian background. African Americans and other minorities constitute a small percentage of the sample. The socioeconomic status of most families is middle class, although scholarships are available for students with financial need.

2. The elementary level of the SCAT (designed for mid-3rd-grade through mid-6th-grade students) was given to 2nd-, 3rd-, and 4th-grade students; the intermediate level (designed for mid-6th-grade through mid-9th-grade students) was given to 4th- and 5th-grade students; and the advanced level (designed for mid-9th-grade through mid-12th-grade students) was given to 6th-grade students.

3. A hit was defined as correctly responding that not enough information was available to solve the problem, whereas a false alarm was defined as indicating that not enough information was available when, in fact, there was. Both scores were standardized to a mean of 0 and a standard deviation of 1.

4. A trend analysis across years was considered because the data in this study were collected over a 7-year span. Most of the data, however, were collected during the last 5 years, a span considered to be too short for such an analysis.

REFERENCES

Ablard, K. E., Tissot, S. L., & Mills, C. J. (1992). *Academically talented students' precocious cognitive development and its predictors.* Unpublished manuscript, Johns Hopkins University, Baltimore.

Ahmann, J. S. (1985). Review of School and College Ability Tests, Series III. In J. V. Mitchell (Ed.), *The ninth mental measurements yearbook* (pp. 1315–1316). Lincoln: University of Nebraska Press.

Armstrong, J. M. (1985). A national assessment of participation and achievement of women in mathematics. In S. F. Chipman, L. R. Brush, & D. M. Wilson (Eds.), *Women and mathematics: Balancing the equation* (pp. 59–94). Hillsdale, NJ: Erlbaum.

Benbow, C. P. (1988). Sex differences in mathematical reasoning ability in intellectually talented preadolescents: Their nature, effects, and possible causes. *Behavioral and Brain Science, 11*, 169–183.

Benbow, C. P., & Stanley, J. C. (1980). Sex differences in mathematical reasoning ability: Fact or artifact? *Science, 210*, 1262–1264.

Benbow, C. P., & Stanley, J. C. (1983). Sex differences in mathematical reasoning ability: More facts. *Science, 222*, 1029–1031.

Casserly, P. L., & Rock, D. (1985). Factors related to young women's persistence and achievement in advanced placement mathematics. In S. F. Chipman, L. R. Brush, & D. M. Wilson (Eds.), *Women and mathematics: Balancing the equation* (pp. 225–247). Hillsdale, NJ: Erlbaum.

Cleary, T. A. (1991, October). *Sex differences in testing.* Paper presented at the invitational conference sponsored by the Educational Testing Service, New York.

Cohen, J. (1977). *Statistical power analysis for the behavioral sciences* (Rev. ed.). San Diego, CA: Academic Press.

Dossey, J. A., Mullis, I. V., Lindquist, M. M., & Chambers, D. L. (1988). *The mathematics report card.* Princeton, NJ: Educational Testing Service.

Durden, W. G., Mills, C. J., & Barnett, L. B. (1990). Aspects of gender differentiation in the Johns Hopkins University Center for Talented Youth. In W. Wieczerkowski & T. M. Prado (Eds.), *Highly talented young women* (pp. 166–185). Bad Honnef, Germany: K. H. Bock.

Eccles, J., Adler, T. F. Futterman, R., Goff, S. B., Kaczala, C. M., Meece, J. L., & Midgely, C. (1985). Self-perception, socializing influences, and the decision to enroll in mathematics. In S. F. Chipman, L. R. Brush, & D. M. Wilson (Eds.), *Women and mathematics: Balancing the equation* (pp. 95–121). Hillsdale, NJ: Erlbaum.

Educational Testing Service. (1979). *School and College Ability Tests: Intermediate Level Form X.* Monterey, CA: CTB/McGraw-Hill.

Educational Testing Service. (1980). *School and College Ability Tests (SCAT III): Manual and technical report.* Princeton, NJ: Author.

Emanuelsson, I., & Svensson, A. (1986). Does the level of intelligence decrease? A comparison between thirteen-year-olds tested in 1960, 1966, and 1980. *Scandinavian Journal of Educational Research, 30,* 25–37.

Feingold, A. (1988). Cognitive gender differences are disappearing. *American Psychologist, 43,* 95–103.

Feingold, A. (1992). Sex differences in variability in intellectual abilities: A new look at an old controversy. *Review of Educational Research, 62,* 61–84.

Fox, L. H., Brody, L., & Tobin, D. (1985). The impact of early intervention programs upon course-taking and attitudes in high school. In S. F. Chipman, L. R. Brush, & D. M. Wilson (Eds.), *Women and mathematics: Balancing the equation* (pp. 249–274). Hillsdale, NJ: Erlbaum.

Goldstein, G., Haldane, D., & Mitchell, C. (1990). Sex differences in visual-spatial ability: The role of performance factors. *Memory & Cognition, 18,* 546–550.

Harman, H. H. (1976). *Modern factor analysis.* Chicago: University of Chicago Press.

Hilton, T. L. (1985). *National changes in spatial-visual ability from 1960 to 1980* (Report No. RR-85-27). Princeton, NJ: Educational Testing Service.

Hilton, T. L., & Berglund, G. W. (1971). *Sex differences in mathematics achievement.* Princeton, NJ: Educational Testing Service.

Hyde, J. S., Fennema, E. F., & Lamon, S. J. (1990). Gender differences in mathematics performance: A meta-analysis. *Psychological Bulletin, 107,* 139–155.

Jacklin, C. N. (1989). Female and male: Issues of gender. *American Psychologist, 44,* 127–133.

Keating, D. P. (1975). Precocious cognitive development at the level of formal operations. *Child Development, 46,* 276–280.

Klieme, E. (1989). *Mathematisches Problemloesen als Testleistung* [Mathematical problem solving as test performance]. Frankfurt: Lang.

Linn, M. C. (1991, October). *Sex differences in educational achievement.* Paper presented at the invitational conference sponsored by the Educational Testing Service, New York.

Linn, M. C., & Petersen, A. C. (1985). Emergence and characterization of sex differences in spatial ability: A meta-analysis. *Child Development, 56,* 1479–1498.

Lubinski, D., & Benbow, C. P. (1992). Gender differences in abilities and preferences among the gifted: Implications for the math-science pipeline. *Current Directions in Psychological Science, 1*(2), 61–65.

Maccoby, E. E., & Jacklin, C. N. (1974). *The psychology of sex differences.* Stanford, CA: Stanford University Press.

Marshall, S. P., & Smith, J. D. (1987). Sex differences in learning mathematics: A longitudinal study with item and error analyses. *Journal of Educational Psychology, 79,* 372–383.

Meece, J. L., Parsons, J., Kaczala, C. M., Goff, S. B., & Futterman, R. (1982). Sex differences in math achievement: Toward a model of academic choice. *Psychological Bulletin, 91,* 324–348.

Mills, C. J. (1992, March). *Gender, personality, and academic ability.* Paper presented at the 15th annual meeting of the Eastern Educational Researchers Association, Hilton Head, SC.

Mills, C. J., & Ablard, K. E. (1992). *Academically talented young students' achievement in an individually-paced mathematics program.* Unpublished manuscript, Johns Hopkins University.

Norusis, M. (1986). *SPSS/PC+ V2.0 Base manual.* Chicago: SPSS.

Oosthuizen, S. (1991). Sex-related differences in spatial ability in a group of South African students. *Perceptual and Motor Skills, 73,* 51–54.

Passow, A. H. (1985). Review of School and College Ability Tests, Series III. In J. V. Mitchell (Ed.), *The ninth mental measurements yearbook* (pp. 1317–1318). Lincoln: University of Nebraska Press.

Rosenthal, R., & Rubin, D. B. (1982). Further meta-analytic procedures for assessing cognitive gender differences. *Journal of Educational Psychology, 74,* 708–712.

Sells, L. (1980). The mathematics filter and the education of women and minorities. In L. Fox, L. Brody, & D. Tobin (Eds.), *Women and the mathematical mystique* (pp. 66–75). Baltimore, MD: Johns Hopkins University Press.

Stage, E. K., Kreinberg, N., Eccles, J. R., & Becker, B. J. (1985). Increasing the participation and achievement of girls and women in mathematics, science, and engineering. In S. S. Klein (Ed.), *Handbook for achieving sex equity through education* (pp. 237–269). Baltimore, MD: Johns Hopkins University Press.

Stanley, J. C., Benbow, C. P., Brody, L. E., Dauber, S., & Lupowski, A. E. (1991). Gender differences on eighty-six nationally standardized aptitude and achievement tests. In N. Colangelo, S. G. Assouline, & D. Ambroson (Eds.), *National Research Symposium on Talent Development* (pp. 42–65). Iowa City: University of Iowa Press.

Stumpf, H., & Klieme, E. (1989). Sex-related differences in spatial ability: More evidence for convergence. *Perceptual and Motor Skills, 69,* 915–921.

Subotnik, R. F., Duschl, R. A., & Selmon, E. H. (1991, April). *Retention and attrition of science talent: A longitudinal study of Westinghouse science talent search winners.* Paper presented at the biennial meeting of the Society for Research in Child Development, Seattle, WA.

Weiner, N. C., & Robinson, S. E. (1986). Cognitive abilities, personality and gender differences in math achievement of gifted adolescents. *Gifted Child Quarterly, 30,* 83–47.

APPENDIX:
SAMPLE ITEMS FROM THE
SCHOOL AND COLLEGE ABILITY
TEST, INTERMEDIATE LEVEL

(Instructions and items were taken verbatim from the test; Educational Testing Service, 1979, pp. 6–8.)

Each of the following questions has two parts. One part is Column A. The other part is Column B.

You must find out if one part is greater than the other, or if the parts are equal, or if not enough information is given for you to decide. Then, find the row of spaces on your answer sheet which has the same number as the question. In this row mark:

A if the part in Column A is greater,

B if the part in Column B is greater,

C if the two parts are equal,

D if not enough information is given for you to decide.

Column A

1. The number p if $p + q = 1$
2. A number, if one-half of it is 4
3. 0.11

Column B

1. The number q if $p + q = 1$
2. 5
3. $^{10}/_{11}$

NO

American Association of
University Women

ACHIEVEMENT AND PARTICIPATION: WHAT DO THE DATA SHOW?

There is considerable evidence that girls earn higher grades than boys throughout their school careers. Test scores, however, because they measure all students on exactly the same material and are available nationally, are the measures most often used to discuss sex differences in achievement. The latest work on achievement differences presents a rather different picture than much of what has been reported and accepted in the past. The traditional wisdom that girls are better in verbal areas while boys excel in quantitative skills is less true today. Data indicate a narrowing of sex differences in tested achievement on a variety of measures. However, a narrowing of differences is not an absence of differences. Important insights can be gained by looking carefully at the continuing gender gaps in educational achievement and participation. Furthermore, research that looks at sex, race, ethnicity, and socioeconomic status reveals critical vulnerabilities among various groups of girls.

VERBAL SKILLS: LANGUAGE ARTS AND READING

Research does not entirely support the still-common assumption that girls do better in verbal areas than do boys. Almost twenty years ago Eleanor Maccoby and Carol Jacklin challenged the prevailing view that girls performed better than boys on verbal measures in their early years. However, researchers continued to document that girls outscored boys on tests of verbal ability starting at grade five or six. Recent work indicates that sex differences in verbal abilities have decreased markedly. Researchers completing a meta-analysis comparing earlier studies of verbal abilities with more recent research conclude: "There are not gender differences in verbal ability at least at this time, in American culture, in the standard ways that verbal ability has been measured."

Some researchers argue that girls do have certain verbal advantages but that these are not adequately measured by most tests. Furthermore, although

From American Association of University Women, *How Schools Shortchange Girls: A Study of Major Findings on Girls and Education* (American Association of University Women, 1992). Copyright © 1992 by The American Association of University Women Educational Foundation, 1111 16th Street, NW, Washington, DC 20036, (202) 785-7700. Reprinted by permission. Notes omitted.

boys have outscored girls on the verbal section of the Scholastic Achievement Test (SAT) since 1972, some suggest this may merely reflect the inclusion of more scientifically oriented items on which boys often perform better than do girls. An additional difficulty with the SAT is that test-takers are not a nationally representative sample; they are a self-selected group.

READING

A review of three representative surveys of reading skills indicates a mixed picture. In two major surveys—the National Assessment of Educational Progress (NAEP) and the National Education Longitudinal Survey (NELS)—girls perform better than boys on reading tests. In the High School and Beyond Survey (HSB), boys perform better than girls on reading and vocabulary tests. In all three surveys, the sex differences are very small.

NAEP is the most comprehensive survey of achievement. A congressionally mandated project of the National Center for Education Statistics (NCES), it measures the proficiency of nine-year-olds, thirteen-year-olds, and seventeen-year-olds in a variety of disciplines. In all age groups, girls have consistently received higher test scores in reading and writing since the 1970s. Since 1971, however, boys have made gains relative to girls, particularly in the seventeen-year-old group.

The NELS is a longitudinal survey of eighth-graders also being conducted under the auspices of NCES. The first wave of eighth-graders were interviewed and tested in 1988. Mean test scores for girls were higher than those for boys, although the difference was modest. Girls were less likely to score below "basic" and more likely to be rated as "advanced" when compared to boys. This sex difference is found for all racial and ethnic groups.

The HSB, also sponsored by NCES, is a longitudinal study of high school sophomores and seniors begun in 1980. Contrary to the other studies, boys consistently score better than girls on the HSB reading tests. This is true of sophomores and seniors, and for whites, blacks, and Hispanics. One possible explanation for the differences in these surveys is that sex differences narrow as children grow older. This would be consistent with the very small difference found for seventeen-year-olds in the NAEP and the gains boys make relative to girls in the follow-up of the HSB cohort.

Another explanation is that these differences may reflect differences in the tests given for each survey. The HSB tests were shorter and the NAEP tests much more comprehensive. This could prove to be another case where apparent sex differences may instead reflect test differences rather than differences in the test-takers knowledge or ability.

Even within the NAEP reading test, the performance of boys relative to girls varied, depending on the type of reading exercise. Boys did as well as girls on the expository passages and were most disadvantaged relative to girls in the literary passages. This is consistent with the finding that boys read more nonfiction than girls, and girls read more fiction than boys. This is also consistent with the finding that boys do slightly better than girls on other NAEP tests in subjects requiring good skills in expository reading and writing: civics, history, and geography.

If, as some suggest, boys regard fiction as more "feminine," any advantage girls experience relative to boys in the NAEP may reflect culturally defined biases against boys' reading certain kinds of material. It has been suggested that even if the small gender difference favoring girls is *statistically significant*, it may not be *educationally significant*. Boys still do better than girls in almost every other subject tested by NAEP, and the difference in reading scores appears to narrow and possibly even favor boys in older age groups.

Finally, it has also been argued that gender differences in reading favoring girls may be more pronounced among low-achieving or low-income students. This is particularly relevant given the recent heightening of concern about the education of low-income minority boys. An examination of achievement by race, sex, and social class is presented later in this section.

WRITING

Writing skills are tested less frequently. NAEP data do indicate that girls consistently outperform boys on writing-skills assessment. Smaller studies of particular populations do not always support these national findings. A seven-year longitudinal study comparing the development of written language skills of boys and girls from kindergarten through grade six found that—at least in the population studied—neither sex had an advantage over the other.

MATHEMATICS AND SCIENCE

The past fifteen years have seen an explosion of research on the relationship between gender and mathematics. While there has been less study on the linkage of gender and science there still is sufficient information to draw preliminary

conclusions. However, the usual cautions apply. Most of the research does not break down the data by both race/ethnicity and gender. Furthermore, the interactions of race/ethnicity and gender are rarely studied, and most conclusions based on predominantly white respondents cannot be generalized to women and girls of color.

Achievement in Mathematics. Gender differences in mathematics achievement are small and declining. Recent meta-analyses have found only very small differences in female and male performance in mathematics. Furthermore, meta-analyses comparing recent research with studies done in 1974 indicate a significant decline in gender differences. The High School and Beyond study of high school sophomores and seniors also shows that gender differences favoring boys in mathematics are declining.

Gender differences in mathematics do exist but are related to the age of the sample, how academically selective it is, and which cognitive level the test is tapping. Indeed these three variables were found to account for 87 percent of the variance in one meta-analysis. For example, no gender differences were found in the problem-solving ability of elementary- and middle-school girls and boys, but moderate to small differences favoring males emerged in high school. Large research studies support these results, finding no gender differences in math performance at age nine, minimal differences at age thirteen, and a larger difference favoring males at age seventeen. The most recent National Assessment of Educational Progress (NAEP) report finds few gender-related differences in math ability in grades four and eight other than a higher average proficiency in measurement and estimation for boys. However, by grade twelve males showed a small advantage in every content area except algebra.

Larger differences are found at the higher academic and cognitive levels. For example, an earlier NAEP report stated that 8.2 percent of the males but only 4.5 percent of the females were at the highest math levels, while 54 percent of the males and 48 percent of the females could do moderately complex procedures and reasoning. The college Board reports that males in 1988 scored an average of 37 points higher than females on the Level I Math Advanced Placement Test and 38 points higher on the Level II Math Advanced Placement Test. Another study revealed that nearly all differences in math performance between girls and boys at ages eleven and fifteen could be accounted for by differences among those scoring in the top 10–20 percent, with boys more often in the top-scoring groups. However, in classroom work, girls' math grades are as high or higher than boys'.

Gender differences on the SAT-Math have decreased, although they are still large. Between 1978 and 1988 female scores increased by eleven points while male scores increased by four points. However, males still outscored females 498 to 455. The Educational Testing Service does test a demographically matched sample of girls and boys on the Preliminary Scholastic Aptitude Test (PSAT) each year. From 1960 through 1983 gender differences in math from this group declined, although males still slightly outscored females.

A smaller body of research tying both gender and ethnicity to math achievement indicates that the patterns may differ for various groups. A study in Hawaii found non-Caucasian girls outperforming boys in math and outnumbering boys in the highest-achieving groups. Other studies have reported fewer gender differences in mathematics for minority students than for white students.

Gender differences in tests of spatial skills are also declining. For example, a large study found that girls and boys gained equally from instruction in spatial-visualization skills, despite initial differences.

The research results reported here must be examined in light of the achievement of all American students, female and male, in mathematics. An international assessment of the mathematics skills of thirteen-year-olds found United States students scoring below students in the other four countries and four Canadian provinces participating. Korean students had the highest average score (567.8), while the U.S. students scored 473.9. In addition, the most recent National Assessment of Educational Progress reports that more than a quarter of fourth-graders failed to demonstrate the ability to do arithmetical reasoning, and only 5 percent of high school seniors demonstrated the skills needed for high technology or college-level work.

Achievement in Science. Gender differences in science achievement are not decreasing and may be increasing. While no meta-analyses of studies linking gender and science achievement have been done, the National Assessment of Educational Progress does track science performance. Its results indicate that for nine- and thirteen-year-olds, gender differences in achievement increased between 1978 and 1986, due to the combination of a lag in performance for females and significant increases in the performance of males. According to the NAEP, gender differences in science achievement are largest for seventeen-year-olds, and these differences have not changed since 1978. The areas of largest male advantage are physics, chemistry, earth science, and space sciences.

In addition, gender differences exist at various levels of achievement. NAEP found only 5 percent of seventeen-year-old girls as compared to 10 percent of seventeen-year-old boys scoring at or above NAEP's "highest cognitive level," defined as students' ability to integrate specialized knowledge. Advanced placement (AP) test scores show a similar pattern. The Educational Testing Service reports that in 1988, males scored on average 29 points higher than females on AP biology tests. This, incidentally, was the only science area tested by ETS where gender differences declined; the spread between male and female test scores shrunk eleven points from the forty-point gap measured in 1981. Males also scored about fifty-six points higher than females on the 1988 AP physics tests. However, once again girls receive grades in science that are as high or higher than those of boys.

As with gender differences in mathematics achievement, gender differences in science should be looked at in a larger context. American students, both female and male, are not doing well in science. Their low levels of scientific knowledge, even at the factual level, have been documented in both national and international studies. One international assessment of the science skills of thirteen-year-olds found United States students placing ninth among the twelve nations and provinces participating.

Mathematics Participation. Gender differences in math-course participation are small, occur only in higher-level courses, and appear to be stable. In 1989 the National Science Board of the National Science Foundation reported that from 1982 to 1987, the average number of math credits that a male high school student received increased from 2.61 to 3.04. During the same time period, the average number of math credits that a female student received increased from 2.46 to 2.93. In 1982 males received .15 more math credits than females; in 1987, .11 more. The National Science Board found that approximately the same percentages of females and males took the same math courses up to calculus, which was taken by 7.6 percent of the boys but only 4.7 percent of the girls. The 1991 NAEP reports that for the District of Columbia and the thirty-seven states participating in the study "Up to Algebra III/Pre-Calculus and Calculus" there were no gender differences in either course-taking or average proficiency." These results are similar to the findings of a 1990 survey by the Council of Chief State School Officers.

Science Participation. Gender differences in the number of science courses students take are small. However, the pattern of course-taking differs, with girls being more apt to take advanced biology and boys being more apt to take physics and advanced chemistry. In 1989 the National Science Board of the National Science Foundation reported that from 1982 to 1987, the average number of science and computer-science credits a male high school student received increased from 2.25 to 2.69. During the same time period the average number of science credits a female student received increased from 2.13 to 2.57. In both 1982 and 1987, males received .12 more science credits than did females. Another study based on 1987 data reports young women taking .2 fewer science courses than young men (2.93 versus 3.13). Using 1988 data, the National Science Foundation reported girls taking an average of 3.1 science courses compared to boys' 3.3.

All three studies found approximately the same numbers of females and males taking Biology I and Chemistry I but more males taking physics. In 1987 the National Science Board reported 25.3 percent of the males but only 15 percent of the females took physics. This is, however, an improvement. In 1982, 18.2 percent of the males but only 10 percent of the females enrolled in physics.

These results are mirrored by a 1991 survey by the Council of Chief State School Officers. The survey reports that 60 percent of the students enrolled in first-year high school physics are male and that 70 percent of second-year physics students are male.

Career Plans. Gender differences show up in career plans as well....

High school girls, even those with exceptional academic preparation in math and science, are choosing math/science careers in disproportionately low numbers. A study of Rhode Island seniors found that 64 percent of the male students who had taken physics and calculus were planning to major in science or engineering in college compared to only 18.6 percent of the female students who had taken these courses.

Girls who do go on in scientific fields after high school report that the encouragement provided by their teachers is very important. One study reports that girls who went on to study engineer-

ing felt that teachers encouraged them; unfortunately they also felt that counselors discouraged them. Clearly, differential treatment on the basis of sex contributes to the student choices reported here, but there are other factors as well.

Math and Science Influences. As they grow, girls and boys have different science experiences. Girls are more apt to be exposed to biology-related activities and less apt to engage in mechanical and electrical activities. One study found that by third grade, 51 percent of boys and 37 percent of girls had used microscopes, while by eleventh grade 49 percent of males and 17 percent of females had used an electricity meter. Gender differences in science-related activities may be reinforced in schools if children are allowed always to select science topics based on familiarity or interest.

Eighth-grade boys have been found to use more science instruments in class, particularly physical-science tools, such as power supplies. Although nine-year-old girls express interest in many science activities, they do not *do* as many as boys. This gender difference continues through ages thirteen and seventeen and is paralleled by an increasingly negative view of science, science classes, and science careers on the part of girls.

Gender differences in confidence are strongly correlated with continuation in math and science classes. Math confidence is the surety a student has of her or his ability to learn and perform well in mathematics. Math confidence has been found to be more highly correlated with math performance than any other affective variable.

Females, more than males, have been found to doubt their confidence in math. The Educational Testing Service reports that gender differences in perceptions of being good at math increase with age. Third-grade girls and boys think they are good in math in about the same percentages (64 percent versus 66 percent); by seventh grade, 57 percent of the girls agree, compared to 64 percent of the boys; by eleventh grade the gap widens to 48 percent of girls versus 60 percent of boys. In a classic study, researchers Elizabeth Fennema and Julia Sherman found a strong correlation between math achievement and confidence. Their research revealed a drop in both girls' math confidence and their achievement in the middle-school years. The drop in confidence *preceded* a decline in achievement.

One result of this diminished confidence is a lowering of the role that competence plays in girls' decisions about continuing in math and science. Researchers have found that competence is a more important prerequisite for the attainment of male career ambitions than it is for females. That is, females and males abandon math and science for different reasons. Males who drop out of math and science tend to do so because of a lack of competence—they cannot do the work; many females who drop out do so even though they can do the work.

Other researchers have also found that males are more apt than females to attribute their success to ability, while females are more apt to attribute failure to lack of ability. As boys get older, those who do not like math are more likely to attribute this feeling to the subject itself: they don't like math, they say, because it is "not useful." Girls, instead, interpret their problems with math as personal failures.

Concern about the difficulty or competitiveness of the field can also be an issue.

One study found that the perceived competitiveness of engineering was seen by girls as a major barrier to women entering the field. This finding is supported by research that shows girls who see themselves as highly competitive to be more interested in taking math and science courses than other girls. For boys, the degree of competitiveness is not related to interest in taking math and science.

While most students who dislike math do so because they consider it too hard, most students who dislike science say science is "not interesting." Adolescent girls are more likely than adolescent boys to find science uninteresting. Adolescent boys are more likely than girls to discount the importance of science itself.

In general, students' interest in and enthusiasm for math and science decline the longer they are in school. The poll commissioned by the American Association of University Women in 1990 found that all students' enthusiasm for math and science was greatest in the elementary years and dropped as they got older. However, losses for girls were larger than were those for boys.

In addition, males are more apt than females to envision themselves using math as adults. In assessing what factors they used to decide whether or not to continue math study, students listed the usefulness of math, followed by their confidence in their ability and their enjoyment of the subject.

Gender stereotyping also appears to influence whether girls persist in mathematics. Data from the National Assessment of Educational Progress indicate that girls who reject traditional gender roles have higher math achievement than girls who hold more stereotyped expectations. Moreover, girls in advanced math classes tend not to see math as a "male" subject.

Meta-analysis of affective variables associated with taking math courses indicate that gender differences are all small with the exception of the view of math as "something men do." Boys see math as very "male." A longitudinal study that tested students at sixth, eighth, tenth, and twelfth grades found that for girls a view of math as "male" was negatively correlated with math achievement at each grade level. This was the only affective variable for which consistent gender differences were found.

IMPLICATIONS

It is important that equal attention be given to both girls and boys in teaching reading and writing skills. The assumption that boys are in greater need of instruction in these areas should not be made. Furthermore, girls need particular encouragement to read more broadly in nonfiction areas and boys should be encouraged to read more fiction.

The gender gap is closing in math achievement but not in science achievement. Issues of gender and math have received more attention than issues of gender and science. Much of the work that has been done in science—beyond counting who is taking what courses—has been done in biology, a field in which there are many women, as opposed to physics, a field with very few women.

Since the growing gender gap in science is clearly related to males' climbing test scores, we need to ask why reforms in science education are apparently working for males and not for females. Just as the SAT-Math has been studied and found to underpredict women's achievement, science tests need to be checked for bias as well.

Building on the work done in math, we need to study more fully the possible causes of the gender gap in the sciences. Particular emphasis should be placed on issues of confidence.

Once students satisfy math and science requirements for graduation and college admission, gender differences in science and math course-taking emerge. More students are taking more science and math, but at the advanced levels the gender gap remains constant. It appears that messages about math and science as critical assets for later employment have been somewhat successful, at least for middle-school students. However, while we have more girls taking more math and science, the numbers and percentages of girls interested in careers in math and science is increasing minimally, if at all. During senior high school and college, female students drop out of the math/science pipeline because they choose not to pursue scientific careers.

Changing the public images of physics and chemistry to reflect the diversity of these fields and the way they tie in to our everyday lives can provide more girls with the "inside information" that daughters of scientists appear to get. Meeting, getting to know, and working with scientists also reduces negative and intimidating stereotypes about the field. Providing students, especially girls, with more real-life experiences with science and scientists may make a big difference.

Teaching methods to decrease to eliminate the gender gaps in math and science already exist. Having students read and try out math and science problems before they are covered in class appears to narrow the "experience" gap between girls and boys, thus helping to reduce gender differences in class performance. Providing a structure in which all students answer questions, pose questions, and receive answers, rather than one that emphasizes target students or those who call out answers loudest, increases girls' opportunities and interest. Girls also respond well to special programs where they work cooperatively in a relaxed atmosphere where math is fun. Such programs significantly increase the number of math and science courses girls take. However, while hands-on experience is more successful than the lecture approach, such experiences must allow sufficient time and opportunities for girls to reach the same level of performance that teachers expect from boys.

Schools can learn much from out-of-school programs that encourage girls in math and science. Girls are not required to take special out-of-school programs. Designers of successful out-of-school math and science programs have learned how to get girls to attend and, more important, how to keep them interested so that they will keep on attending. We need to continue and expand programs like those developed by Girls, Incorporated; the Girl Scouts; and several AAUW [American Association of University Women] branches. These offer unique opportunities for girls to learn together to overcome stereotypes. What's more, such programs also act as laboratories for developing effective techniques to keep girls involved in math and science. We can't rely on these programs alone, however. Compared to the school system, they can reach only small numbers of girls for relatively short periods of time. Since all girls go to school and go for many years, we must focus most of our effort there, incorporating techniques that work for girls throughout our schools, and doing so in ways that continue to work for girls systemwide.

POSTSCRIPT

Are Boys Better in Math Than Girls?

Mills, Ablard, and Stumpf tested mathematical reasoning ability in children in grades two through six. They found that boys performed better than girls at all five grade levels. This particular study differed from previous studies in that gender differences were found as early as second grade. This had not been previously reported. The researchers also found that math ability differences were more evident in academically talented students.

The AAUW report concluded that an analysis of studies done since 1975 shows that gender differences in math achievement have narrowed. Gender differences that do exist depend on the ages of the students tested, how academically selective the sample is, and what cognitive level the test is tapping. Math achievement and ability are correlated with confidence. Girls report having less confidence in their math ability and thus do not perform as well on math tests. In addition, because there are fewer girls in advanced math classes, they are not exposed to the same type of math education as boys.

When girls have trouble in math, is it considered normal? Why is there controversy over girls being discriminated against in math when boys are more likely to make lower grades in most other subjects, more likely to be in special education classes, and more likely to drop out of school?

What difference does it make if girls and boys differ in math skills? Math ability paves the way for a variety of lucrative careers; could there be a feeling of superiority in being able to master the skills of mathematics? Could this feeling be generalized to other aspects of a person's life? Whether a difference in math achievement is real or perceived, children are being done a disservice if their potential for learning in any subject is not maximized.

SUGGESTED READINGS

Arbetter, S. (1991, December). Boys and girls: Equal but not the same. *Current Health, 18,* 16–17.

Bracey, G. (1994, January). Sex and math revisited. *Phi Delta Kappan, 75,* 417–418.

Byrnes, J., & Takahira, S. (1993). Explaining gender differences on SAT-math items. *Developmental Psychology, 29,* 805–810.

Felson, R., & Trudeau, L. (1991). Gender differences in mathematics performance. *Social Psychology Quarterly, 54,* 113–126.

Goulding, M. (1992, February 21). Let's hear it for the girls (assessment of girls' performance in mathematics). *Times Educational Supplement,* pp. 38–39.

Nichols, R., & Kurtz, V. R. (1994, January). Gender and mathematics contests. *Arithmetic Teacher, 41,* 238–239.

Viadero, D. (1991, April 17). Math "gender gap" may be narrowing, researchers report. *Education Week, 10, 1,* 12.

ISSUE 11

Are Latchkey Children at a Disadvantage?

YES: Sherryll Kraizer et al., from "Children in Self-Care: A New Perspective," *Child Welfare* (November/December 1990)

NO: John L. Woodard and Mark A. Fine, from "Long-Term Effects of Self-Supervised and Adult-Supervised Child Care Arrangements on Personality Traits, Emotional Adjustment, and Cognitive Development," *Journal of Applied Developmental Psychology* (January–March 1991)

ISSUE SUMMARY

YES: Child advocate Sherryll Kraizer and her colleagues found that children in self-care, so-called latchkey children, did not respond to dangerous situations safely.

NO: Professors John Woodard and Mark Fine conclude that, under appropriate circumstances, self-care can be a positive learning experience for children.

How old should a child be before being left at home alone? Twelve? Fifteen? Is seven or eight years of age too young to be left without supervision? Of course the answer to this question depends upon many considerations: How long will the parent be gone? How safe is the environment? What are the capabilities of the child? There is a big difference between leaving a capable eight-year-old at home alone while a parent runs to the corner grocery store and leaving a nine-year-old alone overnight while parents work.

Child development specialists agree that by age eleven, most children have the intellectual and emotional maturity to stay home without adult supervision for short periods of time—two or three hours. Yet, in some states, it is illegal for parents to leave children under thirteen at home alone, and parents who do are at risk of being reported for child abuse and neglect. Conversely, it is not uncommon for parents to leave children as young as six at home alone from the time they get out of school until the parents get home from work. There seems to be a disparity between social and legal policies and parental practices on this issue.

Our society expects parents to be responsible for their children. At the same time, current economics frequently necessitates a two-worker family income to live even modestly. This makes it especially difficult for single-parent families. The educational system operates as if there is always one parent at home. Schools are usually open from 8:00 or 8:30 A.M. until 2:30 or 3:00 P.M.

Most jobs are scheduled from 8:00 A.M. to 5:00 P.M., which means that it is possible for children to be alone for approximately one hour in the morning to two or three hours in the afternoon. The U.S. Census Bureau reports that 2.1 million children five to thirteen years of age care for themselves after school. Estimates vary as to what percentage of the school-age population this number represents. Some studies report that 7 percent of school children care for themselves, while other studies show that 25 percent of school-age children are in self-care.

While being left at home without adult care has been useful to some children, studies also show that self-care can mean that children are left in risky and neglectful situations. In the following two selections, the benefits and disadvantages of children caring for themselves after school are debated.

YES

Sherryll Kraizer et al.

CHILDREN IN SELF-CARE: A NEW PERSPECTIVE

The inability of families to provide continuous care to children is not a new phenomenon in the United States. Since the 1950s, the need for nonparental child care has accelerated at an intimidating pace. Continuing changes in social structure, including a large increase in the proportion of women in the nation's labor force, increasing numbers of children living in single-parent households, the rise in family mobility and the decline of the availability of the extended family, have led professionals and policy makers to consider what these changes mean to the welfare of our nation's children [Galambos and Garbarino 1983; Long and Long 1982; Grollman and Sweder 1986; Robinson et al. 1986].

Although we know that many families leave their children unsupervised, it is not known precisely how many children are left in self-care, how and/or why the choice is made, and what the effects of self-care on the development and safety of the children may be.

Current estimates of the number of children in self-care range from 7% to 25% of the nation's 29 million school-age children [Long and Long 1982; Hofferth and Cain 1987; U.S. Bureau of the Census 1987; Vandell and Corasaniti 1985]. These large discrepancies in incidence exist partly because of inconsistent definitions and because parents are reluctant to give out information about their child care methods.

Researchers have had difficulty in acquiring sample populations to study due to the informal and undefined nature of the self-care arrangement and the low profile of children left without supervision [Long and Long 1982; Rodman et al. 1985; Jones 1980]. Guilt, social stigma, and awareness on the part of parents that leaving their children unattended may appear irresponsible and is considered a form of neglect in most states, have prevented parents from reporting their child care methods accurately.

More important than incidence, and more difficult to determine, are the effects self-care arrangements have on children. Few empirical studies exist, but recent studies of the attributes of children in self-care in rural and suburban settings suggest that unsupervised children do not differ significantly

From Sherryll Kraizer, Susan Witte, George E. Fryer, Jr., and Thomas Miyoshi, "Children in Self-Care: A New Perspective," *Child Welfare*, vol. 69, no. 6 (November/December 1990). Copyright © 1990 by Transaction Publishers. Reprinted by permission.

from supervised children in terms of academic achievement and school adjustment [Galambos and Garbarino 1983; 1985; Vandell and Corasaniti 1985], locus of control and self-esteem [Rodman et al. 1985; Steinberg 1986], or peer relations [Vandell and Corasaniti 1985; Steinberg 1986]. In striking contrast, studies of urban children in self-care suggest that children at home alone often feel bored, lonely, isolated, and terrified [Long and Long 1982], and that they have lower academic achievement and social adjustment than supervised children [Woods 1972].

Although these studies are important first steps in defining and exploring this important social problem, they do not resolve most issues associated with children in self-care. The studies vary widely in methodology and findings, and are characterized by small sample sizes, nonprobability sampling, short-term rather than long-term timelines, and the use solely of pencil and paper measures of such dependent variables as academic achievement, social adjustment, and personality characteristics [Robinson et al. 1986].

In response to this lack of scientific data, more definitive study to determine causes, patterns, and consequences of self-care has been called for by child development and child welfare researchers [Galambos and Garbarino 1983; Robinson et al. 1986; Rodman et al. 1985]. Experts cite the need for progressive research "in context," comparing groups of children in self-care in terms of family demographics, family histories, frequency and duration of unsupervised time, presence of siblings, and home structure imposed by absent parents [Galambos and Garbarino 1983; Robinson et al. 1986; Rodman et al. 1985].

Bronfenbrenner [1979] has put forth a model that encourages exploration of variables that can distinguish subgroups and causal factors in child care decisions, including the systems and settings of the child in self-care, the interaction between the child and various environments, family composition, social demographic characteristics, family power dynamics, communication styles, and sex roles.

Recognition of the need for more definitive research builds on the principal contribution of latchkey research to date, which is the conclusion that a great many variables seem to affect the experience and vulnerability of the child in a self-care setting [Garbarino 1981; Galambos and Garbarino 1983, 1985; Robinson et al. 1986]. Garbarino [1981] notes:

It is the premature granting of responsibility, particularly when it occurs in a negative emotional climate, that seems to be damaging. No social event affects all children or youth equally. Nearly all experiences are mediated by the quality and character of the family. Thus, we know that some kids will thrive on the opportunity of being a latchkey child. Others will just manage to cope. Still others will be at risk, and still others will be harmed. It is often difficult to separate the specific effects of the latchkey situation from the more general condition of the family.

Studies to date have not provided precise definitions of supervised and unsupervised environments, including clarification of the terms latchkey and self-care. Steinberg [1986] notes:

The most important conclusion from [his] study is that variations within the latchkey population—variations in the setting in which self-care takes place, variations in the extent to which absent parents maintain distal supervision of children, and variations in patterns of child rearing—are more important than are variations between adult care and self-care.

Finally, the most glaring omission in studies to date is the determination of vulnerability to child abuse and neglect when children are left in unsupervised settings. This article reports on a needs assessment and pilot study of risk to children, in kindergarten through grade 3, which dramatically highlights the need to study carefully the existing patterns of self-care and to develop resources responsive to need.

METHODOLOGY

To assess the need for programming to teach prevention skills to children in self-care, the authors conducted a needs assessment survey and piloted a behavioral simulation as a measure of risk. The combination of the survey and the behavioral simulation enabled a clearer and more valid assessment of self-care patterns with children ages five to nine years old than had previously been obtained.

The pivotal element of this study was the use of two self-care simulations that sought to extend the application of "measurable behavior" to evaluation of actual risk in a self-care situation [Fryer et al. 1987a, 1987b; Kraizer et al. 1988, 1989]. The simulations gave children a real-life opportunity to demonstrate behavioral skills on two tests associated with risk in self-care: answering the telephone and answering the door to a stranger trying to deliver a package.

Rural, urban, and suburban parents of 447 children were surveyed by telephone to determine patterns of self-care, if any. Virtually all the parents reported at first that they did not leave their children alone, but after describing to them the simulation that would be used to measure risk for children in self-care, the parents began to discuss their actual patterns of leaving children alone.

RESULTS OF SELF-CARE SURVEY

The authors found that 42% of the sample of 447 children (grades k–3) in rural, urban and suburban settings were left in self-care at least "occasionally," if not "regularly." It was apparent that as children got older, parents were more and more willing to leave them without supervision. Thus, the percentage of children left alone either occasionally or regularly in kindergarten was 28%, in first grade 37%, in second grade 45% and in third grade 77%. These figures far exceed any previously published estimates. The finding that 42% of the total sample of children were left alone occasionally or regularly was significant new information, and analysis by rural, urban and suburban groupings provided further insights.

Urban children were far more frequently left unattended occasionally at the kindergarten (k = 42%) and first grade level (1st = 45%) than were rural children (k = 21%, 1st = 25%) and suburban children (k = 25%, 1st = 22%). Urban children were also far more likely to be left along regularly, particularly in first (1st = 18%) and second grade (2nd = 19%) than rural children (1st = 8%, 2nd = 8%) and suburban children (1st = 5%, 2nd = 3%).

The finding that so many young urban children were left without supervision brings to mind many questions about the relationship of circumstance to risk.

In the interviews, these parents were matter-of-fact and pragmatic about their care decisions. They said they had no alternatives and were "doing the best they could." They consistently noted the resources they had tried to make available for their children, usually a neighbor or relative in an adjoining apartment or house.

Suburban parents were less likely to leave children in regular self-care situations but were considerably more likely to leave them unattended for the "occasional" trip to the grocery store (3% regularly vs. 35% occasionally). This is an interesting finding because these parents do not perceive themselves as leaving their children alone and were therefore less likely to have discussed safety issues with them. More traditional alternatives to self-care, such as day care, were not considered relevant by those parents who left their children alone spontaneously. This leaving young children without supervision provides its own special challenge to policymakers precisely because it appears to be spontaneous.

Although rural parents cited the relative isolation of the rural setting and the inability of younger children to get to a neighbor quickly as the reason for not leaving children alone regularly, the percentage of rural children left alone as young as kindergarten age (k = 21%) for the occasional errand was comparable to that of the suburban children (k = 25%). This once again brings into play the parental perception that a "quick trip" somehow puts children at less risk than does regular self-care.

ASSESSMENT OF RISK: BEHAVIORAL SIMULATION PILOT

Following the needs assessment portion of the study, and with parental permission and cooperation, the behavioral simulations were piloted with 16 children (human subjects' approval was obtained). Parents were contacted by telephone to establish a prearranged 15-minute block of them when their child would normally be home alone. During this 15-minute period, a member of the research team conducted the following simulations:

Telephone call: Call the children and ask to speak with their mother or father. Ask the children their name. Ask to leave a message and do so.

The optimal response in this situation is for the children to say that their mother or father cannot come to the phone, and that they would like to take a message. At no point should the children give their name.

The actual response of each child was recorded in detail. For example, the children may reveal that they are home alone, refuse to give their name but take a message, or simply not answer the telephone.

Package delivery: Go to each child's home, knock on the door. If the child opens the door, deliver the package for the parent and leave. If the child asks, through the door, "Who is it?" say, "I have a package for your mother (or father)." If the child opens the door, deliver the package and leave. If the child does not open the door, say "I'll drop by another time," or put the package where instructed by the child and leave.

The optimal response in this situation is that the child would go to the door, say, "Who is it?" without opening the door, and then handle the request. For example, "My mother can't come to the door right now, please leave the package on the porch."

Once again, the actual response of each child was recorded in detail. For example, the child may open the door and take the package, not respond to the knock, or respond to the individual without opening the door and handle the request without revealing that she or he is home alone.

RESULTS OF SIMULATIONS

Although these simulations were extremely time and labor intensive, they were invaluable for assessing actual risk. Only two of the 16 children performed well on the telephone portion of the simulation, handling the call properly. All other children readily engaged in conversation with the evaluator, offering information including their name and that they were at home alone.

None of the children handled the package delivery portion of the simulation effectively. Thirteen of the 16 children opened the door and took the package, leaving themselves at risk to whoever the adult at the door happened to be. Two pretended they were not home (this increases the risk to the child in the event of illegal entry once a perpetrator believes no one is home), and one, who was playing in the street, walked up to announce that his parents weren't home and he'd be happy to take the package. In this particular case, the child had been instructed not to leave the house and his mother was unaware that he played outside. Other parents, in the debriefing interview, constantly expressed surprise at their child's performance on the simulation. Not one of them had expected the child would open the door and take the package.

Although the sample in this pilot is small, the findings are compellingly clear. At the very least, these children are at risk, vulnerable to individuals from the outside. And it must be anticipated that they are also at risk in other ways. If parents have not prepared their children to handle telephone calls and people at the door, we must question their preparation for other problems, including emergencies.

In addition, the striking difference between the parents' expectation of their child's performance on the simulations and the actual performance of the child tells us that parents are not realistically assessing their children's ability to handle even the most common occurrences.

The number of children participating in the pilot of the simulations was substantially smaller than expected. Completion of the simulation protocol took over two hours per participant. The survey calls with parents became quite lengthy because they discussed not only their care arrangements but also their reasons for these arrangements, as well as other concerns about self-care. Arranging the simulation at a time when the child would be alone and the parents could expect that the simulation would take place often required several scheduling attempts. The simulation involved going to the vicinity of the child's home, making the telephone call, then making the delivery effort. Follow-up calls were also lengthy; parents wanted to talk about their surprise that their child had failed to handle the simulation properly, and to learn what steps they could take to prepare their child more adequately for future self-care. Researchers wishing to replicate or follow up on these findings should not underestimate the considerable time and resources that must be committed to each participant.

DISCUSSION

The results of this initial effort demand that we take a closer look at the thinking of parents and their children, the resources available to them, and the process by which so many families come to leave very young children without supervision and without adequate training to minimize risk.

Further research is needed to identify causal factors and patterns clearly, to formulate interventions, and to assess more fully the actual risks to children left without supervision. A preliminary assessment of need, as reported here, has been accomplished. The findings lay the groundwork for a more comprehensive and detailed analysis of need that would yield quantifiable data and establish operational definitions from which to shape future policy and initiatives.

The following are questions the authors recommend for further study:

1. What are the identifiers for families who leave young children without supervision?
2. What is the actual level of risk to these children in terms of outside elements, such as perpetrators and emergency situations, and to their personal well-being, considering effects such as fear, anxiety, and self-esteem?
3. What alternatives exist or could be provided within the framework of the realities these parents face, including

economics, transportation, quality of care, and so on?
4. What role can the school system play in providing preventive education and alternatives to "regular" before- and after-school self-care?

With a thorough analysis of the causes of self-care, including characteristics of the child, family, and community, policymakers will have the information they need to make policy decisions, formulate community objectives, implement educational programs, and enhance family resources.

Communities will have a solid basis for reviewing existing resources, establishing new options and increasing accessibility of services to those families with the highest-risk profiles. By identifying patterns of self-care, community planners will be able to target populations. For example, parents who say "My kids are never left alone," when, in fact, they *are* left alone while parents make the occasional run to the grocery store, will not be moved by public service campaigns that urge parents to choose supervised day care over self-care. These parents must be addressed in such a way that they are able to see that occasional risk is still risk. Different approaches must be made to parents who leave their children in self-care because they are uninformed, or have no transportation, or because children say the after-school care program is boring. Schools will have both a real picture of the need in their community and a blueprint for action. The findings would enable them to make their own recommendations for educational intervention and for public and private support to create alternatives to self-care, such as establishing after-school programs within the school.

The assessment of need and risk reported here offers new insights, but the short- and long-term consequences of unsupervised care are still not clear. Prevention programs and initiatives responsive to actual need can evolve once an accurate picture of what is actually happening in American homes is available. Only when we full understand how care patterns evolve can there be an effective national policy that enables families to reduce risk to children.

REFERENCES

Bronfenbrenner, Urie. The Ecology of Human Development: Experiences by Nature and Design. Cambridge, MA: Harvard University Press, 1979.

Fryer, George E.; Kraizer, Sherryll; and Miyoshi, Thomas. "Measuring Actual Reduction of Risk to Child Abuse: A New Approach." Child Abuse and Neglect 11, 2 (1987a): 173–180.

____ "Measuring Children's Retention of Skills to Resist Stranger Abduction: Use of the Simulation Technique." Child Abuse and Neglect 11, 2 (1987b): 181–186.

Galambos, Nancy, and Garbarino, James. "Identifying the Missing Links in the Study of Latchkey Children." Children Today 12, 4 (July–August 1983): 2–4.

____ "Adjustment of Unsupervised Children in a Rural Ecology." Journal of Genetic Psychology 146, 2 (June 1985): 227–231.

Garbarino, James. "Latchkey Children: How Much a Problem?" Education Digest 46, 6 (February 1981): 14–16.

Grollman, Earl, and Sweder, G. The Working Parent Dilemma: How to Balance the Responsibilities of Children and Careers. Boston, MA: Beacon Press, 1986.

Hofferth, Sandra, and Cain, Virginia. Study Findings Presented at the Population Association of America Meeting, National Institute of Child Health and Human Development, Bethesda, MD, 1987.

Jones, L. R. "Child Care: Who Knows? Who Cares?" Journal of the Institute for Socioeconomic Studies 5 (January 1980): 55–62.

Kraizer, Sherryll; Witte, Susan; and Fryer, George E. "Preventing Child Sexual Abuse: Measuring Actual Behavioral Change Attributable to a School-Based Program." Children Today 18, 5 (September–October 1989): 23–27.

Kraizer, Sherryll; Fryer, George E.; and Miller, Marilyn. "Programming for Preventing Sexual Abuse and Abduction: What Does It Mean When It Works?" CHILD WELFARE LXVII, 1 (January–February 1988): 69–78.

Long, Lynette, and Long, Thomas. "Latchkey Children: The Child's View of Self-Care." Washington, DC: Catholic University of America (ERIC Document Reproduction Service No. ED 211 229), 1982.

Robinson, Bryan E.; Rowland, Bobbie H.; and Coleman, Mick. Latchkey Kids/Unlocking Doors for Children and their Families. Lexington, MA: D. C. Heath and Co., 1986.

Rodman, Hyman; Pratto, David J.; and Nelson, Rosemary S. "Child Care Arrangements and Children's Functioning: A Comparison of Self-Care and Adult-Care Children." Developmental Psychology 21, 3 (May 1985): 413–418.

Steinberg, Laurence. "Latchkey Children and Susceptibility to Peer Pressure: An Ecological Analysis." Developmental Psychology 22, 4 (July 1986): 433–439.

U.S. Bureau of the Census. "After-School Care of the School-Age Child." Current Population Reports, Series p-23, No. 149 (January 1987).

Vandell, Deborah L., and Corasaniti, Mary Anne. After-School Care: Choices and Outcomes for Third Graders. Paper presented at the meeting of the American Association for Advancement of Science, Los Angeles, May 27, 1985.

Woods, M. B. "The Unsupervised Child of the Working Mother." Developmental Psychology 6, 1 (January 1972): 14–25.

NO John L. Woodard and Mark A. Fine

LONG-TERM EFFECTS OF SELF-SUPERVISED AND ADULT-SUPERVISED CHILD CARE ARRANGEMENTS ON PERSONALITY TRAITS, EMOTIONAL ADJUSTMENT, AND COGNITIVE DEVELOPMENT

This study investigated long-term effects of being in a "latchkey" or self-supervised child care situation compared with being in an adult-supervised arrangement. Data on former child care arrangements and several measures of cognitive development, emotional adjustment, and the personality traits of dominance, responsibility, and achievement via independence were collected from 248 college students. Students who reported having been in adult care did not differ from students who regularly cared for themselves during out-of-school hours on any of the dependent measures, which concurs with previous findings on short-term effects of the self-care arrangement. Age at which the self-care situation was initiated, and gender, individually and collectively, failed to predict outcome on any dependent measure. These results suggest that children are resilient to short-term separation from their parents and may be able to structure their time constructively during out-of-school hours.

Among the various forms of child care available to American families, perhaps none is more controversial than the "latchkey" or self-supervised situation (Rodman & Pratto, 1980), that is, allowing a child to care for himself/herself during out-of-school hours. The potential effects of the latchkey situation may have considerable impact on a large number of children. According to the U.S. Bureau of the Census (1987), there were 28.9 million children aged 5 to 13 who were enrolled in school in December of 1984. Although all of these children may potentially enter into a latchkey situation

From John L. Woodard and Mark A. Fine, "Long-Term Effects of Self-Supervised and Adult-Supervised Child Care Arrangements on Personality Traits, Emotional Adjustment, and Cognitive Development," *Journal of Applied Developmental Psychology*, vol. 12, no. 1 (January–March 1991), pp. 73–85. Copyright © 1991 by Ablex Publishing Corporation. Reprinted by permission.

at some point, approximately 2.1 million children 13 years of age and under *regularly* care for themselves after school (U.S. Bureau of the Census, 1987).

Vandell and Corasaniti (1988) speculated about potential effects that a latchkey situation may have on a child's academic, emotional, social, and behavioral development. Within the academic domain, a latchkey child may have poorer grades and standardized test scores because of the absence of direct adult supervision relative to nonlatchkey children. With respect to the emotional sphere, a latchkey child may spend more time alone, resulting in augmented feelings of loneliness, sadness, fearfulness, and isolation. Diminished opportunities for social interaction, which may be present in a latchkey arrangement, may inhibit the ability of these children to develop adequate social skills. Finally, the lack of direct adult supervision may result in an increase in conduct difficulties and a decrease in the effectiveness of discipline. In contrast to this grim scenario, Vandell and Corasaniti pointed out that the latchkey situation may alternatively provide the child with a chance to engage in and rehearse mature, responsible behavior that may be subsequently reinforced by parents.

Despite the potential impact that self-care arrangements may have on psychological function, surprisingly little research has addressed this issue. The few studies which have investigated possible outcomes of the latchkey situation have yielded inconsistent findings. One possible reason for these problems may be difficulty in operationalizing the concept of the latchkey child. Not all self-care arrangements are alike, and there are a number of variables that should be taken into account when examining the social and psychological development of the latchkey child. The age of the child at the time the self-care arrangement is initiated, the duration of the arrangement (both in terms of number of months or years and number of hours per week), the presence or absence of older siblings, the quality of parent–child relationships, parental attitude toward the arrangement, and whether the self-care arrangement was selected voluntarily (because of confidence in the child's competence) or involuntarily (due to financial constraints), have been proposed as important factors to consider in evaluating the overall effects of self-care on the child (Cole & Rodman, 1987; Etaugh, 1980; Rodman, Pratto, & Nelson, 1985). Because of the numerous variables which appear to be relevant in conceptualizing what is meant by a self-care arrangement, the exact nature of the impact of such an arrangement on children has been very difficult to evaluate.

Past research, which focused on immediate effects of the latchkey situation, occasionally suggested that adverse results are associated with allowing children to care for themselves. However, some of these studies have various methodological flaws. For instance, Woods (1972) assessed 108 fifth-grade black children from a low-income socioeconomic group on measures of personality and social adjustment, academic achievement, IQ, and rates for accidents, illnesses, and delinquency. Twelve out of 106 comparisons between self-care and adult-care children were significant beyond the $p < .05$ level, 11 of which were in the hypothesized direction. Woods concluded that children from a self-care arrangement (especially girls) had lower IQ scores, lower achievement scores, and were less socially adjusted than their adult-care counterparts.

However, Woods's conclusions must be questioned in light of the large number of comparisons that were made without adjustment for experimentwise Type 1 error rate and the potential for capitalization on chance.

Long and Long (1982) interviewed 85 first- through sixth-grade black children from an urban setting using a semistructured interview schedule. A number of areas were examined, including the degree of fear expressed by the children, the frequency of nightmares, and the adequacy of parental instructions for self-care for the children. Although their results were not based on the children's responses to standardized questions, and may have been subject to interviewer bias and/or inadequate precision in measuring the constructs of interest, the investigators concluded that latchkey children reported a greater degree of fear and a higher frequency of nightmares than children under continuous adult supervision.

In a more recent study, Diamond, Kataria, and Messer (1989) reported a pilot study that evaluated prevalence of the latchkey arrangement, as well as academic performance and behavior characteristics of latchkey children. Forty-four fifth and sixth graders from a rural setting served as subjects. The authors did not report socioeconomic status (SES) or race. Three groups were formed: (1) latchkey children who remained alone or with younger siblings for at least 2 hours per day after school for at least 1 year; (2) semilatchkey children who returned home to the presence of an older sibling under 17 years of age and/or were unsupervised fewer than 2 hours per day and/or were unsupervised fewer than 5 days per week; (3) nonlatchkey children who returned home from school each day to an adult figure who was at least 17 years of age. Using the California Achievement Test, Youth Self-Report (Achenbach & Edelbrock, 1987), and Teacher's Report Form of the Child Behavior Checklist (Achenbach & Edelbrock, 1986), the authors generally found few differences between the groups. The most salient finding was that latchkey boys had the most parent-acknowledged and self-acknowledged behavior problems and a nonsignificant trend toward lower academic achievement. However, the authors interpreted these findings cautiously in light of the small sample size employed.

In contrast to the studies citing negative effects of self-care, the majority of studies in this area reveal no significant differences between children from self-care situations and those from adult-care arrangements. Gold and Andres (1978a) sampled low and middle SES, 10-year-old white children from suburbs of a large Canadian city and measured personality and social adjustment, academic achievement, and sex role concept. No significant differences between latchkey and nonlatchkey children were obtained. Similar findings were obtained in a separate study that sampled low and middle SES, 14- to 16-year-old white children from the same area, using the same dependent measures (Gold & Andres, 1978b).

Galambos and Garbarino (1983) examined 77 low and middle SES, fifth- and seventh-grade white children from a rural area of New York State. Again, no significant differences emerged between self-care and adult-care children on: (1) the AML Behavior Rating Scale (Cowen et al., 1973), a measure of school adjustment; (2) Stanford Achievement Test score, a measure of academic achievement; and (3) the Scale of Intrinsic versus Extrinsic Orientation in the Classroom (Harter, 1981). Rodman et al. (1985) studied 48 pairs of children, matched on the basis of age, sex, race, family composition (one parent vs. two parents), and SES. No significant differences between the self-care group and the adult-care group were detected on the Coopersmith Self-Esteem Inventory (Coopersmith, 1967), the Personal Reaction Survey (Nowicki & Strickland, 1973), or social adjustment and interpersonal relations as measured by the Behavior Rating Form (Coopersmith, 1967).

Finally, Vandell and Corasaniti (1988) sampled 150 white, middle-class, suburban third graders and examined the relation between types of after-school care and social, academic, and emotional functioning. When comparing latchkey and adult-care children, no differences were found with respect to peer evaluations, academic grades, standardized test score, teacher's evaluation of conduct, parent and teacher ratings of social, emotional, and academic functioning, or self-ratings. However, children who attended day-care centers had significantly lower peer evaluations, lower academic grades, and lower standardized test scores than either latchkey or nonlatchkey children. It should also be noted that a number of studies compared cognitive development and emotional adjustment of children of working and nonworking mothers (cf. Etaugh, 1980; Hoffman, 1979), and generally found numerous *positive* benefits of maternal employment for lower SES families, and mixed results for children from middle- and upper-income families. However, it is important to note that there is no indication of whether children in these stud-

ies are under self-supervision or adult supervision.

Steinberg (1986) proposed that the type of *behavior* in which the self-care child engages after school (e.g., going directly home, going to a friend's house in the absence of adult supervision, or "hanging out" with friends) is an important variable for identifying potentially adverse effects of a self-care situation. Steinberg tested this hypothesis on a sample of fifth, sixth, eighth, and ninth graders using susceptibility to peer pressure as the outcome construct of interest. No differences emerged between children from adult-care and self-care situation. However, within the self-care group, Steinberg found that the more removed the children were from adult supervision, the more susceptible they were to peer pressure to engage in antisocial activity. Steinberg concluded that the proximity of adult supervision is a particularly relevant variable.

In summary, most studies suggested that there are no differences between latchkey and nonlatchkey children on a variety of measures. However, it is important to note that each of these studies did not operationalize the latchkey situation in exactly the same way. This raises the question of whether these previous studies are directly comparable. The lack of consensually adopted criteria to define the latchkey situation, and conflicting findings regarding the effects of the self-care arrangement, have been particularly vexing at this early stage of research. In addition, few studies examined a sample from the middle to upper SES range; much of the past research in this area focused on subjects from the lower SOS range. Related to this point is the fact that studies involving white children have found few significant differences between latchkey and nonlatchkey children, whereas studies of black latchkey children have found more negative effects. This trend suggests that racial/cultural differences may play an important role in the latchkey experience. Finally, to date, no studies have investigated potential long-term consequences of self-care arrangements.

The purpose of this study is to address some of the shortcomings in the literature from the perspective of potential long-term (adverse or positive) effects of being in a latchkey situation. First, individuals who formerly experienced a self-care situation were compared with individuals from adult-care arrangements to determine if differences would emerge on measures of cognitive development, academic achievement, emotional adjustment, self-esteem, and personality traits (responsibility, dominance, and achievement via independence). These three personality constructs were chosen because they are often cited in the literature as characteristics which may be influenced by the self-care situation.

A second focus of this study was to determine the extent to which gender, and age at which self-supervision was initiated, could predict outcome among individuals who experienced the latchkey arrangement. A significant relationship between the predictors and the outcome variables could further understanding of the impact of the latchkey child care arrangement. Given the lack of research in this area and conflicting research findings, it is premature to generate hypotheses regarding the nature of the expected relationships.

METHOD

Subjects

Subjects were 260 introductory psychology students at a large, private, midwestern university. In order to establish whether subjects had experienced a latchkey arrangement, the following question was asked on a demographic questionnaire, "During elementary school, junior high school, or high school, did you ever *regularly* come home from school to the absence of direct adult supervision?" If the subject answered "yes" to this question, he/she indicated the age at which this arrangement began. Following the recommendation of Rodman et al. (1985), subjects who indicated that they returned home from school to an empty house, or to younger siblings between the ages of 6 and 13, were classified as having experienced a latchkey arrangement. Next, for each of three periods (elementary school, Grades K–6; junior high school, Grades 7–9; high school, Grades 10–12), subjects were asked to indicate: (1) who was *usually* home when they got home from school; (2) the number of days per week not under direct adult supervision; (3) the number of hours per day not under direct adult supervision; and (4) whether one or both parents were employed during this period. There was a disproportionate number of white participants in the sample; therefore, all nonwhite participants were dropped from the study to render the sample more racially homogeneous. This manipulation yielded a sample size of 248.

Subjects were grouped according to whether their child care situation was self-care (21 males, 38 females) or adult-care (85 males, 104 females). The mean age of onset of the latchkey arrangement was 12.8 years of age ($SD = 2.6$). The mean age of all participants was 18.9 years ($SD = 0.8$ years). All groups were comparable in SES according to Hollingshead's (1977) four-factor index.

The majority of individuals came from intact families. Of the 27 subjects coming from nonintact families, 17 had experienced their parents' separation due to divorce, and 10 reported the death of one parent. There was a significant association between child care arrangement and parents' marital status (X^2 (2, $N = 248$) = 13.19, $p < .002$. Cramer's $V = 0.231$): Approximately half of the subjects from nonintact families reported having participated in self-care, compared to only 20% of the subjects from intact families. Subjects from intact families came predominantly from single-provider families during the elementary school years, although there was a substantial shift toward dual-provider families in the junior high and high school years. In addition, there was also a statistically significant association between being in a self-care situation and coming from a dual-provider family.

Instrumentation

All subjects completed the following five self-report instruments:

1. A short demographic questionnaire was used to identify gender, age, race, grade-point average (GPA), number and gender of siblings, community size, socioeconomic and occupational status of the subject's parents, and the latchkey status of the subject.

2. *The Quick Test* (Ammons & Ammons, 1962). The Quick Test is a brief test designed to provide an estimate of general intelligence. Traub & Spruill (1982) reported a Pearson correlation of .64 between Quick Test scores and Wechsler Adult Intelligence Scale-Revised (WAIS–R) full-scale IQ scores. A number of other studies (Joesting & Joesting, 1972; Ogilvie, 1965; Pless, Snider, Eaton, & Kearsley, 1965; Violato, White, & Travis, 1984) supported its use as a valid measure of global intelligence.

3. *Coopersmith Self Esteem Inventory–Adult Form (SEI)*; (Coopersmith, 1967). The 25-item adult form of the Coopersmith SEI was employed as a measure of self-esteem. Correlations of .59–.60 between the SEI short form and the Rosenberg (1965) scale for college students have been reported (*Manual for the Coopersmith Self-Esteem Inventory*, 1981). Bedeian, Geagud, & Zmud (1977) reported test–retest reliability coefficients of .80 for men and .82 for women.

4. *California Psychological Inventory (CPI)–Dominance (Do), Responsibility (Re) and Achievement via independence scales (Ai)* (Gough, 1975). These three scales were used to provide measures of the constructs of dominance, independence, and responsibility. Hase and Goldberg (1967) reported that short-term test–retest reliabilities of the CPI scales range between .71–.90 ($M = .83$). The individual scales of the CPI have also been subjected to extensive validation as measures of various personality traits (Groth-Marnat, 1984).

5. *Symptom Checklist 90–Revised (SCL–90–R*; Derogatis, 1983). This 90-item multidimensional self-report inventory measures an individual's perceived degree of psychological distress. Only the Global Severity Index (GSI) was used as a measure of emotional maladjustment in this study, as

Derogatis claimed that the GSI provides the most sensitive single measure of psychological distress on the SCL–90–R. Extensive evidence supporting the reliability and validity of the GSI and SCL–90–R is provided in Derogatis (1983).

Procedure

Testing was performed in groups of approximately 25. Subjects were initially asked to fill out the demographic questionnaire. Next, the Quick Test, SEI, and CPI scales were administered in a counterbalanced fashion for each group of subjects. The SCL–90–R was administered last, due to the emotional and symptomatic content of the items. When the material was collected, subjects received a description of the study and an invitation to ask further questions. Testing sessions ranged in length from 75 to 90 minutes.

RESULTS

Preliminary analyses of variance (ANOVAs) for each of the seven dependent measures revealed no significant interaction effects between the variables of interest (gender and group membership), and (a) marital status of the parents (intact, marital separation due to divorce, or marital separation due to death of one parent); (b) working status of the parents (single provider or dual-provider family); and (c) population of the community in which the subjects lived prior to college (large city, 1 million or more; suburb of large city; medium city, 100,000–999,999; suburb of medium city; small city, 25,000–99,999; suburb of small city; other urban area, 10,000–24,999; rural town, 5,000–10,000; rural village or farming community, 4,999 and below; or other rural area).

Therefore, the data were collapsed over these control variables.

Multivariate analyses of variance (MANOVAs) were performed in order to compare individuals from self-care arrangements with those from adult-care situations. The constructs of: (a) cognitive development (Quick Test score and college GPA); (b) emotional adjustment (SEI score and overall GSI); and (c) personality development (scores on the Re, Do, and Ai subscales from the CPI) were examined separately. Each analysis tested for the main effects of gender, group, and for their interaction. The regression approach to partitioning the sums of squares was selected. In this approach, each effect is adjusted for all other effects in the model and is appropriate when cell frequencies are unequal (Norusis, 1985). Table 1 depicts the means and standard deviations for each of the four groups. There were no significant ($p < .05$) effects for group, or for the group by gender interaction on any of the three sets of comparisons.

Relationship Between Mediating Variables and Outcome in Self-Care Children

It was also of interest to determine whether gender, age at which the latchkey situation was initiated, or an interaction between these variables could predict outcome on any of the seven dependent measures. To address this issue, a hierarchical multiple-linear regression analysis was then performed for each of the seven outcome measures.

Two sets of variables were entered sequentially into each of the regression equations. The first set contained two variables: gender, and age at which the latchkey situation was initiated. The second set of variables contained the

Table 1

Scores of Self-Care Individuals Versus Adult-Care Individuals on Dependent Measures Broken Down by Gender

	Self-Care				Adult-Care			
	Males N = 21		Females N = 38		Males N = 85		Females N = 104	
Test	*M*	*SD*	*M*	*SD*	*M*	*SD*	*M*	*SD*
CPI-*Do*	27.38	3.72	26.76	4.19	26.87	3.94	26.73	4.66
CPI-*Re*	24.76	4.55	24.41	5.44	25.05	4.64	27.08	4.82
CPI-*Ai*	18.14	3.35	18.03	4.21	18.37	3.71	18.64	3.99
Quick Test	130.01	16.59	123.16	16.97	119.72	17.73	123.01	16.82
GPA	2.82	0.43	2.89	0.49	2.72	0.57	2.76	0.57
GSI	0.89	0.47	1.12	0.60	1.08	0.52	0.96	0.50
SEI	76.57	16.16	68.63	21.42	74.45	16.16	75.65	19.32

interaction of the two variables described above. No significant interaction effects or main effects were obtained for any of the seven outcome measures. Therefore, none of the predictors was effective in predicting any of the outcome variables.

DISCUSSION

In summary, long-term differences in cognitive development, emotional adjustment, and personality development did not emerge between the self-care and adult-care individuals in this study. This finding concurs with previous studies which found no short-term differences between self-care and adult-care children on similar dependent measures (Galambos & Garbarino, 1983; Gold & Andres, 1978a, 1978b; Rodman et at., 1985; Steinberg, 1986). The absence of detectable long-term differences between self-care and adult-care individuals on global cognitive, affective, and personality indices suggests that self-care, in general, may not be as detrimental as previously imagined, at least for those individuals who later go on to college. There are several possible explanations for this finding. First, it may be that children are generally resilient to short-term separations from their parent(s). As long as children are aware that parents will return home shortly and are available in the case of emergency, they may not experience the potential fear and sense of isolation that Vandell and Corasaniti (1988) discussed. The absence of group differences on the dependent measures based on the age at which the latchkey arrangement was initiated suggests that children between the ages of 6 to 13 years may be developmentally capable of structuring their own time for short periods. This possibility may partially explain racial and SES differences reported in the literature, as middle to upper SES and white children may have more "enriched" home environments than their lower SES counterparts (Bouchard & Segal, 1985). The enriched home environments, possibly including educational videotapes and/or computers, for example, may provide more opportunity for children to structure time for themselves.

A second explanation for the lack of clear group differences is that differences among various self-care arrangements may actually exist and could potentially be a worthwhile focus for future study. According to Steinberg (1986), such differences may include degree of parent-child telephone contact, proximity of adult neighbors, or formality and rehearsal of rules and procedures with which the child must be familiar in the absence of adult supervision. In addition, the operational definition used in this study was relatively broad. Future studies with more specific criteria for differentiating self-supervision from adult supervision may find differences between these two groups by reducing the heterogeneity of the sample. Although no differences were observed on general measures of emotional adjustment and cognitive and personality development, differences within the self-care group may emerge on more specific or behaviorally oriented measures.

An attempt was made to examine the effects of potential sources of variation within the self-care arrangement by looking for a relationship between outcome measures, and age at which the arrangement commenced, and gender. The absence of any significant relationships between predictor and outcome variables suggests that the effect of the self-care experience on the outcome measures is likely to be relatively heterogeneous in nature. Such a finding points toward the need to focus on other variables that could potentially account for this heterogeneity, enabling practitioners and parents to identify children for whom this form of child care may be particularly detrimental. Previous research, and this study, have not yet been successful in identifying such relevant variables. Future research might fruitfully examine the potency of those (previously described) effects identified by Steinberg (1986).

One limitation to this study is that it relies on retrospective reports to determine latchkey status and duration of the latchkey arrangement. Halvorsen (1988) criticized the use of such information because it is difficult to trust peoples' memories without corroborating objective evidence. Ross and Conway (1986) also noted that adults tend to recall memories of complex events inaccurately. Thus, retrospective data tends to be biased and distorted, particularly with complex events. However, McCrae and Costa (1988) argued that memory for broad patterns of behavior is less susceptible to such distortions. Although this study is not immune to the potential flaws inherent in the use of retrospective data, it is directed toward recollection of general facts (i.e., who was usually home when the subject returned from school), which are likely to be recalled more accurately than more complex information (i.e., what did the subject usually do after school). Indeed, more detailed information requested in this study, such as number of hours per day and number of days per week of self-care, is more likely to be susceptible to retrospective bias: subjects were generally less able to provide this information consistently compared with the more general facts requested by the demographic questionnaire. In addition, it has been argued that an individual's perceptions of events may be as important as the objective accuracy of the actual incidents (McCrae & Costa, 1988) as reactions to situations are necessarily based upon subjective appraisals of their meaning.

Rodman, Pratto, and Nelson (1988) discussed the difficulties inherent in the operationalization of what is meant by "a latchkey child." A consensually adopted definition is necessary both to avoid confusion and to evaluate more reliably the effects of such arrangements. Moreover, a reliable definition will likely be used by parents, practitioners, and policymakers to make decisions regarding the best form of after-school care for a particular child. Although previous studies, and this study, have employed rather broad definitions of the latchkey situation (e.g., a child between the ages of 6 and 13 who comes home regularly to the absence of direct adult supervision), there is a trend in the literature toward using more narrow definitions (cf. Diamond et at., 1989; Rodman et at., 1985, 1988). There are advantages and disadvantages to each approach. Although it is usually easily and quickly applied, a broad definition may result in considerable heterogeneity within the sample, potentially resulting in erroneous conclusions that there are no negative effects of such arrangements. However, compared to a more narrow definition, a broad definition would be more likely to identify children who are potentially at risk of experiencing detrimental effects of self-care (should these effects exist). A more narrow definition of the latchkey construct would decrease heterogeneity, thereby enhancing the reliability of research findings. However, one may be more likely to miss identifying children who are potentially at risk, but who do not explicitly fit the narrow criteria when applied to the population as a whole. We suggest that the broad definition be used as a screening technique to identify children who may be at risk for

experiencing negative effects from self-care. Once these at-risk children have been identified, more specific definitions could pinpoint more sensitively those individuals for whom self-care might be particularly detrimental.

Clearly, the results of this study do not lay to rest the issue of whether or not the latchkey situation is detrimental to children and adolescents. Because the subjects in this study were all middle to upper SES college students, the results should not be generalized to all individuals who have experienced a self-care arrangement. College students are likely to be brighter than average, and perhaps more resourceful in adjusting to a self-care situation. Indeed, replication of this study using a sample who never attended college and/or a sample which possessed greater variability in SES would be an important contribution to this area of research. Moreover, the dependent measures used in this study do not exhaust the number of available constructs on which self-care and adult-care individuals may be expected to differ. In addition to the concepts of latchkey and nonlatchkey arrangements, the concept of the "semilatchkey" arrangement (Diamond et at., 1985) reserved for children who do not clearly fit the two former categories may be a useful category to examine in future research.

Finally, it would be worthwhile to refine further our understanding of the effects of a number of variables contributing to the heterogeneous latchkey experience. For example, detailed information on parental attitude toward the latchkey situation, whether the arrangement was chosen due to perceived necessity or because of confidence in the child, the quality of parent-child relationships, and related variables have not yet been examined in the context of the self-care arrangement.

REFERENCES

Achenbach, T. M., & Edelbrock, C. (1986). *Manual for the teacher's report form and teacher version of the child behavior profile.* Burlington: University of Vermont, Department of Psychiatry.

Achenbach, T. M., & Edelbrock, C. (1987). *Manual for the youth self-report.* Burlington: University of Vermont, Department of Psychiatry.

Ammons, R. B., & Ammons, C. H. (1962). *The Quick Test.* Missoula, MT: Psychological Test Specialists.

Bedeian, A. G., Geagud, R. J., & Zmud, R. W. (1977). Test–retest reliability and internal consistency of the short form of Coopersmith's self-esteem inventory. *Psychological Reports, 41,* 1041–1042.

Bouchard, T. J., Jr., & Segal, N. L. (1985). Environment and IQ. In B. B. Wolman (Ed.), *Handbook of intelligence: Theories, measurements, and applications* (pp. 391–464). New York: Wiley.

Cole, C., & Rodman, H. (1987). When school-age children care for themselves: Issues for family life educators and parents. *Family Relations, 36,* 92–96.

Coopersmith, S. (1976). *The antecedents of self-esteem.* Palo Alto, CA: Consulting Psychologists Press.

Cowen, E. L., Dorr, D., Clarfield, S., Kreling, B., McWilliams, S. A., Pokracki, F., Pratt, M., Terrell, D., & Wilson, A. (1973). The AML: A quick screening device for early identification of school maladaptation. *American Journal of Community Psychology, 1,* 12–35.

Derogatis, L. (1983). *SCL–90–R: Administration, scoring, and procedures manual for the revised version.* Baltimore, MD: Johns Hopkins University School of Medicine.

Diamond, J. M., Kataria, S., & Messer, S. C. (1989). Latchkey children: A pilot study investigating behavior and academic achievement. *Child & Youth Care Quarterly, 18,* 131–140.

Etaugh, C. (1980). Effects of nonmaternal care on children: Research evidence and popular views. *American Psychologist, 35,* 309–319.

Galambos, N. L., & Garbarino, J. (1983, July–August), Identifying the missing links in the study of latchkey children. *Children Today,* pp. 2–4, 40–41.

Gold, D., & Andres, D. (1978a). Developmental comparisons between 10-year-old children with employed and nonemployed mothers. *Child Development, 49,* 75–84.

Gold, D., & Andres, D. (1978b). Developmental Comparisons of adolescent children with employed and nonemployed mothers. *Merrill–Palmer Quarterly, 24,* 243–254.

Gough, H. G. (1975). *Manual for the California Psychological Inventory.* Palo Alto, CA: Consulting Psychologists Press.

Groth-Marnat, G. (1984). *Handbook of Psychological Assessment.* New York: Van Nostrand Reinhold.

Halverson, C. F. (1988). Remembering your parents: Reflections on the retrospective method. *Journal of Personality, 56,* 435–443.

Harter, S. (1981). A new self-report scale of intrinsic versus extrinsic orientation in the classroom: Motivational and informational components. *Developmental Psychology, 17,* 300–312.

Hase, H. D., & Goldberg, L. R. (1967). Comparative validity of different strategies of constructing personality inventory scales. *Psychological Bulletin, 67,* 231–248.

Hoffman, L. W. (1979). Maternal employment: 1979. *American Psychologist, 34,* 859–865.

Hollingshead, A. B. (1977). *Four-factor index of social status.* Unpublished manuscript, Yale University, New Haven, CT.

Joesting, J., & Joesting, R. (1972). Quick Test validation: Scores of adults in a welfare setting. *Psychological Reports, 30,* 537–538.

Long, T. J., & Long, L. (1982). *Latchkey children: The child's view of self-care.* Washington, DC: Catholic University of America. (ERIC Document Reproduction Service No. ED 211 229)

Manual for the Coopersmith Self-Esteem Inventory. (1981). Palo Alto, CA: Consulting Psychologists Press.

McCrae, R. R., & Costa, P. T. (1988). Do parental influences matter? A reply to Halverson. *Journal of Personality, 56,* 445–449.

Norusis, M. J. (1985). *SPSSX advanced statistics guide.* New York: McGraw-Hill.

Nowicki, S., Jr., & Strickland, B. R. (1973). A locus of control scale for children. *Journal of Consulting and Clinical Psychology, 40,* 148–154.

Ogilvie, R. D. (1965). Correlations between the Quick Test (QT) and the Wechsler Adult Intelligence Scale (WAIS) as used in a clinical setting. *Psychological Reports, 16,* 497–498.

Pless, I. B., Snider, M., Eaton, A. E., & Kearsley, R. B. (1965). A rapid screening test for intelligence in children. *American Journal of Diseases of Children, 109,* 533–537.

Rodman, H., & Pratto, D. J. (1980). *How children take care of themselves: Preliminary statement on magazine survey* (Report submitted to the Ford Foundation). Unpublished manuscript.

Rodman, H., Pratto, D. J., & Nelson, R. S. (1985). Child care arrangements and children's functioning: A comparison of self-care and adult-care children. *Developmental Psychology, 21,* 413–418.

Rodman, H., Pratto, D. J., & Nelson, R. S. (1988). Toward a definition of self-care children: A commentary on Steinberg (1986). *Developmental Psychology, 24,* 292–294.

Rosenberg, M. (1965). *Society and the adolescent self-image.* Princeton, NJ: Princeton University Press.

Ross, M., & Conway, M. (1986). Remembering one's own past: The construction of personal histories. In R. Sorrentino & E. T. Higgins (Eds.), *Handbook of motivation and cognition* (pp. 122–144). New York: Guilford.

Steinberg, L. (1986). Latchkey children and susceptibility to peer pressure: An ecological analysis. *Developmental Psychology, 22,* 433–439.

Traub, G. S., & Spruill, J. (1982). Correlations between the Quick Test and Wechsler Adult Intelligence Scale–Revised. *Psychological Reports, 51,* 309–310.

U.S. Bureau of the Census. (1987). *Current population reports, Series P-23, No. 149. After-school care of school-age children: December 1984.* Washington, DC: U.S. Government Printing Office.

Vandell, D. L., & Corasaniti, M. A. (1988). The relation between third graders' after-school care and social, academic, and emotional functioning. *Child Development, 59,* 858–875.

Violato, C., White, W. B., & Travis, L. D. (1984). Some concurrent, criterion-related data on validity for the Quick Test based on three Canadian samples. *Psychological Reports, 54,* 775–782.

Woods, M. B. (1972). The unsupervised child of the working mother. *Developmental Psychology, 6,* 14–25.

POSTSCRIPT

Are Latchkey Children at a Disadvantage?

Kraizer et al. found that urban children were left alone more often than rural children and that, as children got older, they were more likely to be left without supervised care after school. These researchers also found that the responses of unsupervised children who were faced with threatening situations put those children at significant risk of being exploited or abused.

Woodard and Fine compared self-care children to children who had adult supervision. Students who had been in adult care showed no differences in cognitive development, emotional adjustment, achievement, or responsibility when compared to children who had cared for themselves after school. At least for children who later attended college, self-care did not have any lasting detrimental effects.

Experts agree that successful self-care requires some maturity on the part of the child; good parental monitoring, such as phone calls; a secure home environment with clear rules and procedures; and an understanding, by the child, of basic safety skills. Other factors that affect the consequences of self-care are: the total amount of interaction the child has with adults, the amount of time the child is left alone, the number of siblings left in the self-care situation, food or entertainment left in the home, and how the child feels about the self-care option compared to other care options.

As long as there is a disparity between the number of hours that a parent works and the number of hours that a child is in school, after-school care will be an issue. This issue has not been satisfactorily answered by society since there are very few options open to parents.

SUGGESTED READINGS

Coleman, M., Robinson, B., & Rowland, B. (1993). A typology of families with children in self-care: Implications for school-age child care programming. *Child and Youth Care Forum, 22,* 43–53.

Galambos, N., & Maggs, J. (1991). Out-of-school care of young adolescents and self-reported behavior. *Developmental Psychology, 27,* 644–655.

Posner, J., & Vandell, F. (1994). Low-income children's after-school care: Are there beneficial effects of after-school programs? *Child Development, 65,* 440–456.

Seligson, M. (1993). Continuity of supervised child care for school-aged children. *Pediatrics, 91,* 206–208.

ISSUE 12

Is Home Schooling an Effective Method of Education?

YES: David Guterson, from "When Schools Fail Children: An English Teacher Educates His Kids at Home," *Harper's Magazine* (November 1990)

NO: Jennie F. Rakestraw and Donald A. Rakestraw, from "Home Schooling: A Question of Quality, an Issue of Rights," *The Educational Forum* (Fall 1990)

ISSUE SUMMARY

YES: David Guterson, an English teacher in the public schools, argues that home schooling is more effective than public schooling. Home schooling teaches children that learning is life, not separate from life. Guterson maintains that in public schools, children are not focused; they are simply free to retain any incidental learning that they may be exposed to throughout the day.

NO: Jennie F. Rakestraw and Donald A. Rakestraw, both professors at Georgia Southern College, state that by schooling their children at home, parents are undermining a fundamental social institution, the public school. They argue that interaction with a school peer group, which is usually missing in home schools, is imperative for the healthy social development of children.

Although home schooling was the accepted method of education in the United States until the 1850s, its comeback, beginning in the 1970s, has raised quite a bit of controversy. According to Michael Farris, president of the Home School Legal Defense Association, responsible home schooling is now legal in every state of the union.

In a 1991 article in *Essence* magazine, Constance Garcia-Barrio discusses reasons for home schooling. Factors related to why a parent would choose home school over public school include a parent's disagreement with the values presented in both public and private schools, as well as a dislike for certain curricula and particular teaching approaches. In addition, some parents who favor home schooling believe that public schools do not promote self-discipline and self-motivation or provide an environment in which each child's particular talents may flourish.

However, some experts fear that home schooling may be harmful to a child's overall development. Children schooled at home may not have the opportunity to develop and interact with a same-age peer group, through which children learn social skills. Another common concern is that home-school teachers may not have the appropriate skills, training, education, and knowledge to teach children effectively.

In the following selections, David Guterson provides an array of examples and reasons as to why he, a public school teacher, chose to educate his children at home. Jennie F. Rakestraw and Donald A. Rakestraw then offer their reasons as to why such a course of action may not be optimal for children.

YES

David Guterson

WHEN SCHOOLS FAIL CHILDREN

Although it remains unarticulated among us, we Americans share an allegiance to schools, an assumption that schools are the foundation of our meritocracy and the prime prerequisite to a satisfying existence. In fact, to the oft-cited triumvirate of what is ineluctable in life—birth, death, and taxes—we are prone to add an unspoken fourth: education in classrooms.

In my classroom at a public high school in an upper-middle-class milieu where education is taken relatively seriously, we read with great purpose precisely those stories that tacitly reaffirm this loyalty to schools: In *Lord of the Flies* a pack of schoolboys degenerate into killers because no teachers are around to preserve the constraints of civilization. In *To Kill a Mockingbird* the venerable Atticus Finch insists that, for all of its shortcomings—and despite the fact that his daughter, Scout, is best educated by his own good example and by life in the larger web of Maycomb County—Maycomb Elementary is *mandatory*. *The Catcher in the Rye* is in large part the story of its protagonist's maladjustment to schools, and J. D. Salinger is highly critical of the hypocrisy behind a good education; still he ultimately offers up Mr. Antolini—an English teacher—as Holden Caulfield's last best hope.

The doctrine that school is necessary, which we early imbibe while within the very belly of the beast, is inevitably reinforced after we are disgorged. The daily implacability with which the media report the decline of schools, the constant knell of ominous statistics on the sorry state of American education, the curious popularity of such books as E. D. Hirsch's *Cultural Literacy* and Allan Bloom's *Closing of the American Mind,* are signs and portents, yes—but they also serve to bolster our shared assumption that school is required not merely because we attended it but also because our common life is in such a precarious state. Our national discussion about education is a desperate one, taking place, as it does, in an atmosphere of crisis, but it does not include in any serious way a challenge to the notion that *every child should attend school.* Why? Because, quite simply, there is no context for such a challenge: We live in a country where a challenge to the universal necessity of schools is not merely eccentric, not merely radical, but fundamentally un-American.

From David Guterson, "When Schools Fail Children: An English Teacher Educates His Kids at Home," *Harper's Magazine* (November 1990). Copyright © 1990 by David Guterson. Reprinted by permission of Georges Borchardt, Inc., for the author.

Yet there *are* those who have challenged not exactly the schools' raison d'être but the reason for their children's being *in* them. The children of such people have come to be called by a powerful misnomer, by a Newspeak conjoining: "homeschoolers." These children are not really *home*schoolers at all but rather young persons who do not go to school and are educated outside of institutions, persons best defined by what they don't do as opposed to what they do. There are currently about 300,000 homeschoolers in the United States —truants from one perspective, but, from another, following in the footsteps of Thomas Jefferson, Thomas Edison, Woodrow Wilson, Margaret Mead, and Andrew Wyeth.

A substantial majority of homeschooling parents in America are fervently religious and view schools as at odds with Christian doctrine. Overall, however, they are a diverse lot—the orthodox and the progressive, the Fundamentalist Christian and the libertarian, the urban, the rural, the social skeptic, the idealist, the self-sufficient, and the paranoid. And studies show little or no correlation between the degree of religious content in a homeschooling program or the level of its formal structure—ranging from orthodox "structuralists," with homes set up as miniature schools, to informal programs guided only by a child's ability to learn—or the education or affluence of homeschooling parents (or lack of affluence; the median annual income of homeschooling families is somewhere between $20,000 and $30,000) and the surprising academic success of homeschooled children, who tend to score well above average on standardized achievement tests.

But despite this—and despite the fact that teaching one's own was the norm in the United States until the 1850s— homeschooling today is little more than a fringe movement, an uprising perceived by many as a sort of insult and by others as a severe admonishment: *Take more interest in your children, like us!* (A Gallup poll revealed that 70 percent of the American population disapproved of homeschooling.) The movement inspires guilt in the hearts of too many parents— a lot of them baby boomers energetically seeking money and success yet worried that their children are growing up estranged from them—guilt and the sort of rage normally reserved for heretics and cultists.

Few people realize that the homeschooling movement is populated by a large number of educators or ex-educators—parents who teach or who have taught in the schools but keep their children out of them. Their paradoxical behavior makes them at first a curiosity and finally an affront to the schools that hired them; their students are confounded by their apparent hypocrisy; their colleagues are apt to tread delicately around the subject. So saying, I'll add my own confession: I am one of these walking contradictions. I teach my neighbors' children in my high school classroom, but my wife and I teach ours at home.

* * *

We came to this decision, I should admit from the outset, viscerally, with our understanding incomplete, pondering no more than a year's trial run. We were like most parents in the turmoil we felt far in advance of our oldest son's first step onto the school bus but unlike most in our response to it: We became existentially worried.

At first it seemed this anxiety signified that something was fundamentally wrong with us. Were we overzealous, overprotective, paranoid? It was our duty, we tried to tell ourselves, to override our parental instincts; school, after all, was ineluctable. And so my wife attempted to visit the local kindergarten (to no avail—its principal's policy forbade such visits) in order to assure herself that nothing dreadful might occur within its walls. Meanwhile I sought to convince myself that my own experience of student life as nightmarishly dreary and an incomparable waste of time was my own experience, only that, and that nothing legitimate could be deduced from it. And this was true: I could deduce nothing.

I wish I could write that my wife and I had excellent reasons for deciding to homeschool. We didn't. It was in the gut, and the gut, we knew, could be wrong either way. In May of 1986 we read books, in June we talked, July we wrung hands, August felt deep and hot and still, September came, and then one morning the big yellow bus arrived, waited a minute with its doors open, and our child did not get on it.

That fall we took to answering our inquisitors—friends, acquaintances, siblings, grandparents—with the all-purpose and ultimately evasive assertion that to hold a child out of kindergarten was not really so unusual, that many people do it.

Not schoolteachers, they replied.

But since then, each of our three sons has missed the bus, so to speak, and we find ourselves flung headlong into a life neither of us would have predicted.

* * *

As it turns out, it is a life our family likes, and this is our chief reason for continuing to homeschool. Our days and our children's days are various.

They pass with no sense that learning is separate from life, an activity that begins at a specific point in the morning and arbitrarily ends at another in the afternoon. Instead, learning proceeds *from* our children, spurred by their interests and questions. A winter day on which snow falls is the natural starting point for discussion and reading about meteorology, weather fronts, road salts, sloped roofs, Alaska, polar bears, the invention of touring skis. A spring evening spent on a blanket in the yard as the stars begin to show themselves is a proper time for talk of constellations, for bringing out a star chart, for setting up a telescope, for questions about satellites, eclipses, comets, meteors, navigation, Columbus, the Apollo space program. When the weather is poor for roaming out of doors, our boys—five, seven, and nine —might spend hours playing Scrabble or chess, or read to one another, or draw pictures, or comb through atlases and encyclopedias because the maps and pictures interest them. At dinner, if it is impending war in the Middle East that is in the news, the atlases and encyclopedias might end up on the table, and we might be there for two hours or more, eating, asking questions, looking up precise answers, discovering how oil is formed in the ground, why people fight over it, how Islam differs from other religions, why a person has to drink more water when it's hot, and why camels have humps.

There are hours in the morning—two at most—when my wife sits down with our nine-year-old and is systematic about writing and mathematics; later, they will practice violin together. Evenings are my time for nurturing our children's interest in geography, for discussing the day's news, and for reading poems to them before they go to bed. We try to be consistent about these matters, and yet no two days are ever much alike, and the curriculum is devised by us according to our children's needs and implemented by us according to our strengths and weaknesses as parents and teachers. Thus:

AUGUST 30: Reading: *The Wooden Horse;* violin: *Witches' Dance;* writing: letter to Adam, final draft; science: gas cannon, carbon dioxide.

SEPTEMBER 26: Visit to the chicken-butchering plant and Point Defiance Zoo; violin practice; journal and writing.

OCTOBER 16: Neighborhood recycling; banking; violin practice; Chess Club; finished letter to Aunt Mary.

NOVEMBER 7: *Mouse and the Motorcycle,* Chapters 3 and 4; math drill, multiplying by 4 and 5; violin practice; cursive writing; swimming with Nathan.

What else? An ant farm, a bug jar, a pair of field glasses, a rabbit cage, old appliances to take apart. An aquarium, a terrarium, a metronome, a collection of petrified wood, another of shells, a globe, a magnifying glass, a calculator, a microscope. Felt pens, watercolors, dry cell batteries, paper-airplane kits. Swimming teachers, lithographers, bakers, canoe builders, attorneys, inventors, flutists, fishermen. And time to ponder all of them. To read the information on the backs of baseball cards, dig butter clams, dye rice paper, weave on a homemade frame loom. To plant potatoes, tell tall tales, watch birds feed. To fashion a self in silence.

And people too, many of them, a large and shifting variety. Friends from Little League and music lessons, acquaintances made on the basketball court and in art classes. The group of homeschoolers with whom our boys put on plays, beachcomb at low tide, play chess.

And salmon. Perhaps it began, one night, with merely eating one. Or with reading *Red Tag Comes Back.* Or with the man at the side of the road with the purse seine laid out in his yard. At any rate, the salmon life-cycle exhibit at the Seattle Aquarium and walking among the gill-netters at Fisherman's Terminal. And cleaning debris from a salmon stream, standing in it, one Saturday. Visiting the hatchery on the Elwha River, the fish ladders at the Rocky Reach Dam, the Pacific Science Center display on the Nootka people. Then seeing their grandfather's catch from the Hakai Peninsula, the bones and organs, the digestive tracts of fish—the blood and murder—and mulling over eating what was once living and the relative ethics of sportfishing. And then one day, abruptly —perhaps a plane has flown overhead or they have seen from the yard a crow fly—it is *flight* that interests them, the Wright Brothers, Charles Lindbergh, Amelia Earhart, draft and lift and thrust and wingspan, the Museum of Flight, the Boeing plant, pitch, yaw, and roll....

Their education is various, alive, participatory, whole—and, most of all, *theirs.* Quite frankly, no school can hope to match it. It is an education tuned to their harmonies, local and intimate as opposed to generic and imposed. They have not learned to be fearful of learning, to associate it with pain and dreariness, with competition, anxiety, dread. My wife and I hope that they will continue in this, that adolescence will find them earnestly seeking, that they will see enough of schools—by visiting them —to know what they are missing. We hope that colleges, if college is what they want, will recognize their strengths without school transcripts. (Admissions boards, incidentally, increasingly recognize homeschooled children as legitimate candidates.) And that their social lives will continue to be vigorous and sane, will continue to include people of all sorts and all ages. And finally that the life we have developed as a family will sustain itself on through *their* children, that our intimacy will not end when *they* are parents.

It is not always, of course, so idyllic, so wonderful, so easy to wax romantic over. Much of the time, though, it is satisfying and full, a fruitful existence for us all. We recognize that in the long run it may have drawbacks, but in the long run no life is perfect. We can't know, finally, if this is what is best for our children and, like all parents, we are playing it by ear to some extent, hoping to guess correctly what it is we should *do*. We do know that homeschooling has given us a life we wouldn't otherwise have, and we are thankful for that.

* * *

At the same time, I go on teaching English in a public high school. There my students might bemoan the dreary meaninglessness of classroom life and rail against its absurdities but also profess skepticism at the very mention of homeschooling. How are your kids going to make friends? they ask. Who's going to teach them algebra? How do you expect them to get into college? When do you find time to teach them anyway? What if you weren't a teacher—could you do it? Why are you *here*, Mr. Guterson?

Excellent questions, I say, sooner or later, in the approving voice of a high school English teacher. But answering them I feel the orbit of my reasoning widen—what high school students call "digression"—because in the end you can't discuss homeschooling as if it were divorced from other raging social issues. In fact, bring it up with your students' parents and you're soon fending off a touchy debate about such sacred matters as work, children, money, leisure time, and, above all, the self. Before long you are listening to hysterical pronouncements about democracy, capitalism, enculturation, the Japanese, and nearly everything else.

Let's take, for example, the assertion that children who don't go to school won't be "socialized." Most people believe school is the primary training ground for the social life we experience when we emerge from school: In its halls and classrooms, these skeptics recollect with mixed emotions, one sorts out the broad panoply of human types and then adjusts oneself to them, finds ways to modulate one's persona in the face of the great shifting tide of humanity. In this vision of things, the homeschooled child figures as an eternal outsider who, because he or she never attended school, will remain forever uninitiated in the tricky nuances of adult society. He will miss his cues at cocktail parties, he will not understand the subtleties of behaviors that come his way at the office or on the bus.

Furthermore, say homeschooling's detractors, homeschooling is *undemocratic*. They take at face value the portrait of schools as the irreplaceable agents of enculturation and, as E. D. Hirsch would have it, of cultural literacy. Jefferson's vision, after all, was that school would be democracy's proving ground, a place where all comers would take their best shot at the American Dream and where that dream would ultimately find its most basic and most enduring sustenance. Not to show up at all—at all!—is thus to give in to the forces of cultural decline, to withdraw at the moment of national crisis, and to suggest openly that if Rome is really burning, the best response is not to douse the flames or even to fiddle away beside the baths but to go home and lock the door.

Critics of homeschooling are likely to add that for America to work we must act in concert to repair our schools; that few parents are, in fact, well qualified to teach children the broad range of things they need to know; that homeschooling allows the bigoted and narrow-minded to perpetuate their types; that despite all the drawbacks to a peer-dominated world, such a world is required if children are to grapple with relationships more egalitarian than family ones. And more: Send your child to the school of hard knocks, they say, where some bigger boy will shove him from his place in line or steal his blocks or vandalize his fingerpaintings, where he will learn forbearance and self-reliance and meet in the form of his teacher an adult who is less than perfect and less than fully attentive to his every need—where, in short, life in all of its troubling glory will present itself daily to him. A dark inversion, perversely true, of Robert Fulghum's *All I Really Need to Know I Learned in Kindergarten*.

* * *

Let me address these criticisms in order. Evidence in support of homeschooling's academic virtues is both overwhelming and precisely what we would expect if we gave the matter some reflection. Public educators have complained, into a steady, implacable wind, that with much smaller classes and more one-to-one contact they might make better academic headway. Small wonder, then, that homeschoolers score consistently well above the norm on standardized achievement tests: They're learning under the ideal conditions—alone or in groups small enough to make real learning possible—that schoolteachers persistently cry out for.

Recently, a strong case has been made that achievement tests don't tell us anything that matters, because they are culturally biased and because they are *tests* —and tests are attended by various levels of anxiety and a wide range of test-taking habits. Here some facts about homeschoolers are in order: They come predominantly from the very middle-class backgrounds that standardized achievement tests reportedly favor, and their parents are, for the most part, deeply interested in their education as well as themselves better educated than the average American adult. Thus, homeschoolers' test scores might best be compared with those of schoolchildren who come from similar test-favoring backgrounds and whose parents also are well educated and involved. Furthermore, it's true that some homeschooling parents teach "to" standardized tests—some classroom teachers do also—because states require that their children take them or because college entry is largely contingent on test scores in the absence of a school grade-point average. (Harvard, for example, admits homeschooled children and takes their SAT scores very seriously.)

Researchers have probed as well the more slippery question of whether homeschooled children are properly socialized. John Wesley Taylor V, using the Piers-Harris Self-Concept Scale—a measure of the "central core of personality"—concluded that "few homeschooling children are socially deprived." Mona Maarse Delahooke placed them in the "well-adjusted" range on a personality measure known as the Roberts Apperception Test for Children; Jon Wartes, in surveys of 219 Washington State homeschoolers, found that at least half spent more than twenty hours a month in organized community activities and that more than two thirds spent twenty to thirty plus hours a month with other children of varying ages. Linda Montgomery, after studying the leadership skills of homeschooled children, concluded that "homeschooling is not generally repressive of a student's potential leadership, and may in fact nurture leadership at least as well as does the conventional system." In my experience, homeschoolers are less peer-dependent than schoolchildren and less susceptible to peer pressure. In this regard, the research merely corroborates what seems to most observers obvious.

But although homeschooling may work, it is by no means easy. Most American adults are fully competent, of course, to learn whatever they have to learn—facts, skills, methods, strategies—in order to teach their children. But should they want to do it, they should strive to be good at it, and they should face the endeavor seriously. It should bring them satisfaction; it should feel like important work. *No one* should undertake to homeschool without coming to terms with this fundamental truth: It is the fabric of your own life you are deciding about, not just your child's education.

* * *

This matter—the fabric of a homeschooling life—is the concern of some critics who assert that in practice homeschooling is patently sexist, that its most obvious result is the isolation of women in the home, away from the fulfillments of the workplace. (That there may be ful-fillments in the home, for both sexes, as educators of children, is another issue entirely.) Yet the question of who does what in a relationship is no more or less important with regard to homeschooling than with regard to anything else: who works outside the home, who works inside, who does the dishes, changes oil in the car, shops for food, flies to Miami on a business trip. The question of *who does what* remains: who takes responsibility for the child's introduction to long division, drives her to swimming lessons, teaches him to throw a baseball, shows her how to use a calculator. Homeschooling is, in fact, no more inherently sexist than anything else in a marriage (and is less so than schools), and if in many homeschooling families the mother is the prime mover and first cause of education and the father an addendum and auxiliary, this is a reflection on the culture at large and not on the phenomenon of homeschooling.

There are others who assert that although homeschooling might serve well for the American middle class, other groups—the poor, the disenfranchised, the immigrant—need schools to flourish. After all, the public schools have historically been a crucial conduit of upward mobility, they say, and point out the Vietnamese immigrants of the last twenty years, whose kids get full scholarships from places like the University of Texas and Columbia. Yet the mobility they describe is next to nonexistent; a permanent underclass is the reality in this country, and schools do as much as any other institution to reinforce this state of affairs. By systematizing unfairness, inequality, and privilege, schools prepare the children of the underclass to accept as inevitable the coming drudgery of their adult lives. At my school, for example, "basic" students are more likely to serve meals in Foods I while "honors" students join an organization called Future Business Leaders of America and enroll in courses like Leadership and Humanities. In both its social and academic structure, my school best instructs the disenfranchised in the cruel truth that disenfranchisement is permanent.

To say that homeschoolers, for the sake of American democracy, *must* be institutionalized is an undemocratic proposition. Both the courts and state governments recognize this, for homeschooling is legal in one form or another everywhere in the United States. The Supreme Court thus far has not ruled in any explicit way on homeschooling. The closest it came, in 1972, was to declare that Wisconsin's compulsory-education law could not, in fact, compel three Amish families to send their children to high school. Yet legal tension about homeschooling persists—mostly as First, Ninth, and Fourteenth Amendment issues: freedom of religion and the right to privacy—for the states have an interest in seeing children educated and are, rightly, concerned that in at least some cases "homeschool" ends up meaning no school. (When home-schooling parents in question are deemed incompetent, the courts have consistently—and properly—ruled against them.) Moreover, and more importantly, does anyone really believe that schools make students better democrats? Do they serve the individual and democratic society? I give them an A only for prompting peer-group relations of a sort conducive to the workings of our *economy:* Schools are in their social fabric nasty, competitive, mean-spirited, and status-conscious in the manner of the adult institutions they mimic.

Could there be something in the very nature of the school as an institution that prevents it from fully realizing its mandate to inform, educate, and develop both the individual and his or her society? Or, to put it another way, could there be something in its *manner* of being that prevents it from realizing its *reason* for being? At the high school where I teach, as at most, students come and go in sets of thirty or so at approximately one-hour intervals, an arrangement convenient to the daunting task of administering a crowd of more than 800 young people but not necessarily conducive to their education or in the best interests of society. The arrangement is instead both relatively expedient and indicative of the schools' custodial function—in essence, their primary one, since we have structured schools in such a manner as to allow this function to precede all others. Schools *keep* students first, and any education that happens along the way is incidental and achieved against the odds. It may be, finally, that schools temporarily *prevent* us from getting the education we persist in getting outside and beyond schools, where the conditions of life provide more natural motivations and learning is less abstract. *Never let your schooling get in the way of your education,* advised Mark Twain, who never attended school.

* * *

The school I teach in is fortunate to employ some excellent teachers, honorable and earnest men and women who are quietly heroic for the sake of their students and whose presence does much to salvage some good from an otherwise untenable institution. They bring humanity to an inhumane setting and pit it against the *design* of schools, which were envisioned as factories dedicated to the efficient production of predictable, formulaic human beings.

But I find myself, like many teachers, beating my head against the classroom wall on a daily, even hourly, basis. My students are compelled to herd themselves from room to room, to sit in daily confinement with other people of precisely their age and approximately their social class, to hear me out on "Sailing to Byzantium" whether or not they are ready. They are scrutinized, sorted, graded, disciplined, and their waking hours are consumed by this prison life: thirty hours a week, thirty-six weeks a year, seven to ten hours a week of "homework" twelve years running—the heart of their young lives consumed by it. What can we expect of them as adults, other than that they become, as New York City Teacher of the Year John Taylor Gatto says, "dependent human beings, unable to initiate lines of meaning to give substance and pleasure to their existence"? Penned up and locked away, shaped by television and school instead of by their community, they must struggle as adults for a satisfying life they can neither grasp nor envision.

* * *

Confining children to school is emblematic of the industrialized twentieth century, but it is also convenient for our current generation of young parents, which might best be characterized in general terms as terrifyingly selfish, persistently immature, and unable to efface its collective ego for the sake of the generation that will follow it and is *already* following it. While these people go about the business of saving the world—or of extracting everything they can from it— their children (they can hardly believe

they have children, can hardly grasp the privilege of nurturing them when they are so thoroughly occupied by their attentions to themselves) need *someplace* to go. The truth is that for too many contemporary parents the school system is little more than convenient day care—day care they can feel good about as long as they don't reflect on it too deeply.

Many parents I know put more hours into their golf games or their wardrobes or into accumulating enough capital for the purchase of unnecessary luxuries than into their child's education. Because they are still children themselves, it simply doesn't occur to them to take an active role in their child's learning—in part because they expect the schools to do it all, in part because there isn't room in their souls for anybody to loom as large as themselves. For many the solution is simply to buy an education as one buys a BMW—your child's school as yet another commodity to show off. So when I talk about homeschooling I am talking about choosing less affluence in the name of more education. I am talking about giving matters intense and vital thought before one ships one's child off to school.

And while it's easy—and understandable—for parents to protest that one hasn't the time or energy for homeschooling, there is much, short of pulling children out of school, that parents can undertake today. Homeschooling is only the extreme form of a life in which all of us can and should take part. The notion of parents as educators of their children is, in the broad sense, neither extreme nor outlandish, and we should consider how instinctively parents engage in the instruction of their children—at the dinner table, for example—and how vital a role an expanded homeschooling movement might play in repairing families. We should think clearly about the problems of schools, ask ourselves why every attempt to correct them seems doomed to fail, replace in our hearts the bankrupt notion of "quality time" with a reassessment of our role as parents. We should recognize that schools will never solve the bedrock problems of education because the problems are problems of *families*, of cultural pressures that the schools reflect and thus cannot really remedy.

Today it is considered natural for parents to leave their children's education entirely in the hands of institutions. In a better world we would see *ourselves* as responsible and our schools primarily as resources. Schools would cease to be *places* in the sense that prisons and hospitals are places; instead, education would be embedded in the life of the community, part of the mechanics of our democracy, and all would feel a devotion to its processes. Parents would measure their inclinations and abilities and immerse themselves, to varying degrees and in varying ways, in a larger educational system designed to *assist* them. Schools—educational resource centers—would provide materials, technology, and expertise instead of classrooms, babysitters, and bureaucrats.

Admittedly, I am a professional educator, part of this vast bureaucracy. Yet I see no contradiction in what I am doing: coming each day to where young people are, attempting within the constraints of the institution to see to their education. Each year I come to admire many of my students, to like them so well that I am sad to see them go; each year there are moments in which I am gratified, even moved, by a sentence a student has written in an essay, by a question somebody asks. Yet for all this, for all the quiet joys of the classroom, I am forever aware of some amorphous dissatisfaction, some inkling that things might be better. It seems to me that many of my students should simply be elsewhere, that they would be better served by a different sort of education, that their society would be better served by it, too. I believe this education is one their parents can best provide and that they should expect schools to assist them. These parents love their children with a depth that, finally, I can't match—and finally, teaching is an act of love before it is anything else.

NO

Jennie F. Rakestraw and Donald A. Rakestraw

HOME SCHOOLING: A QUESTION OF QUALITY, AN ISSUE OF RIGHTS

Home schooling is an educational practice that is spreading throughout grass-roots America. Fifteen years ago it was rare to find parents teaching their children at home rather than sending them to traditional schools. But in recent years, there has been a surprising increase of interest in, and commitment to, home schooling. In 1986, Lines, a policy analyst for the U.S. Department of Education, estimated that there were between 120,000 and 260,000 home-schooled children in the United States. Public school officials, state legislators, and professional educators have had to take notice of the presence of these home-schooling families and, at times, take action about them. When parents educate their children at home, they depart from the mass-schooling ethic that has been perceived as a cornerstone of the 20th-century American way of life. This departure has raised questions concerning who holds responsibility for providing education and who is accountable for insuring quality education. Not surprisingly, such questions have been fundamental issues of home schooling and keynotes of continuing debate.

Although states have had reasonable and obvious interest in education, advocates of home schooling have regarded their parental freedom to educate as a Constitutional right, a moral duty and, for some, a Biblical command. With their opinions concerning educational philosophy, curriculum, socialization, institutionalization of children, and teacher qualifications usually at variance with public school practices, home educators have felt their decisions to home-school a matter of conscience. Home schooling, meanwhile, has a foundation in American history and has developed a legal foundation in most states. Even so, home schools face skepticism. They have reappeared

From Jennie F. Rakestraw and Donald A. Rakestraw, "Home Schooling: A Question of Quality, an Issue of Rights," *The Educational Forum*, vol. 55, no. 1 (Fall 1990). Copyright © 1990 by Kappa Delta Pi, an international honor society in education. Reprinted by permission. References omitted.

out of the past with a new face, one that looks unfamiliar and maybe even unsafe. Are parents able to meet *all* the needs of their children in the home setting? Can we concede that parents are ultimately responsible and accountable for the education of their children?

THE HISTORICAL BACKGROUND

We believe that the historical perspective must be taken when deciding on the advisability of home schooling. And we would be wise to examine how the contemporary movement toward home schooling evolved, as well as how effective these schools are in meeting children's academic and social needs.

During America's colonial and early national periods, home schooling was commonplace and, as a matter of fact, a predominant form of education. The primary responsibility for education clearly rested with parents. Although the Constitution of the United States addressed a wide range of powers, limitations, and duties, it did not expressly mention education. It was only after the passing in 1791 of the Tenth Amendment in the Bill of Rights that education became a function of the states. At that point, the states were empowered to provide education, but schooling still was not universal, compulsory, or tax supported. Although state-sponsored "charity schools" were established to provide formal schooling locally to those in need, American education remained a private and religious effort until the late 1800s. Private schools, many of which were church supported, assumed a large role in providing academic as well as religious instruction. There was no division between religious and secular authority and the Bible was considered the moral guide for the nation

and, consequently, for the developing educational system.

During the 19th century, the state's interest in education grew. Universal public education was the means by which individual liberty and a democratic state would be guaranteed. The interests and goals of the state, in contrast with those of the church, were considered to be representative of the people. The purposes of the state, namely, to promote cultural, economic, and social equality, gradually superseded the purposes of the church in American education. After the Civil War, the majority of states passed legislation providing for free public education. Even though the concept of public education had been slow to gain acceptance, every state established public schools by the early 1900s. Nevertheless, the presumption of family responsibility and control remained, and parents could use the "right of excusal" to have their children excused from any objectionable course or programs of study. Parents believed schools should conform to their values and reinforce their authority, while preparing their children for success in American society. Public education was regarded as a service to families, "an opportunity to which children were entitled, not as a requirement to be imposed."

The free educational opportunities offered by public schools were not always accepted. Indifferent parents, inadequate school facilities, rejection of a regimented school setting by children, opportunities for child labor, and the generally low standard of living—all worked against the efforts of public education. In due time, the problems of child neglect and exploitation prompted the passage of compulsory school attendance laws and child labor laws. By 1918 every state had a compulsory attendance law in effect, and the relationship between families and schools changed. The locus of responsibility had shifted from the family to the institutionalized school operated by the state. Since schools were responsive to group, rather than individual, demands, various social groups began to battle over whose values, pedagogy, and world view should be adopted by public schools. This created a problem for parents who, while accepting the idea of public education itself, perhaps did not realize that public education, when mandated by compulsory attendance laws, would usurp their rights over their children's education. By yielding to state compulsory attendance laws, parents found themselves increasingly removed from the responsibility for their children's education.

The goals of public education, generally condoned, reflected a national concern over (a) advancing the ideals of, and preserving, a democracy, (b) economically strengthening the country, and (c) equalizing opportunity among races and classes of people. In addition, the socialization of children in the school was a major emphasis of compulsory education, as it provided a powerful means of political control. Indeed, some have claimed that the essence of the common school movement was "its rhetorical commitment to the deliberate use of education as a tool for social manipulation and social progress."

Naturally, many Americans questioned the appropriateness and effectiveness of school socialization and, from the beginning, public education has been challenged and pressured to reform. In the more recent past, when Sputnik was launched by the Soviet Union in 1957, the event shocked the American public and its educational system. The satellite undermined the American people's confidence in their educational and technological superiority, as well as their sense of national security. Fear and survival became the motive for change. The attitudes and emotions thus provoked during the late 1950s greatly affected American educational policies and created an era of self-inspection, criticism, and disequilibrium. Many of the educational innovations and practices of the present can be traced to this period. Not only were alternative public schools established to counteract the growth of private schools, but some parents withdrew their children from traditional schools and initiated the contemporary home education movement. Since the 1960s, skepticism has continued to increase over how acceptable and even necessary public education is to the education and socialization of children and to the maintenance of American democracy. The renewed interest in home schooling has been an outgrowth of this sentiment.

Present-day home schools have thus evolved from a dissatisfaction with organized public schooling, a dissatisfaction based on philosophical differences in educational thought. For instance, during the 1960s and early 1970s, educators and noneducators alike called for reforms. Many recognized the need for changes but felt they should be implemented within the framework of the existing educational system. For example, Silberman described the schools as "grim, joyless places" but argued that they need not be: "Public schools *can* be organized to facilitate joy in learning and esthetic expression and to develop character.... This is no utopian hope." Yet, for some, this unrealized hope is indeed utopian and has not been fulfilled.

Others believed in a radicalization of the school, while still others contended that reform was impossible and that schools should simply be abolished. Holt, as an example, once felt that school reform was possible, but has since reconsidered his position. He now believes that the conditions for true education "do not exist and cannot be made to exist within compulsory, coercive, competitive schools." According to him:

> While the question "Can the schools be reformed?" kept turning up "No" for an answer, I found myself asking a much deeper question. Were schools, however organized, however run, necessary at all? Were they the best place for learning? Were they even a good place? Except for people learning a few specialized skills, I began to doubt that they were.

Holt has therefore encouraged concerned parents to withdraw their children from institutionalized schools and to teach them at home. Moore has also advocated home schooling on the basis of his research, through the Hewitt Research Foundation, on the effects of institutionalizing young children. He suggested that children should not be enrolled in formal school programs before ages 8 to 10 unless they are severely disadvantaged or handicapped. Instead, parents should be assured their rights by the state to teach their children "systematically" at home.

While the home schooling movement, under the leadership of Holt and Moore, has expanded and stabilized in every state, the fundamental issue still remains: Who holds responsibility for the education of American children? With this question unanswered, many local school officials faced difficult, multi-faceted decisions involving home-schooling families. These decisions sometimes led to the charging, prosecution, and imprisonment of parents for child neglect and/or violation of state compulsory school attendance laws. Nevertheless, every state has been allowing home schooling in some form or another, even while imposing some regulations to protect the right of the state to an educated citizenry.

The legal foundation of home schooling has involved numerous court rulings and individual state's compulsory education statutes. The acceptance of home schooling implies that, although states have assumed a prominent role in providing education over the years, ultimate responsibility stays with parents. Many public educators cringe at the notion, but President Reagan was voicing a widely-held opinion when he in 1984 stated that, "The primary right, duty and responsibility of educating children belongs to parents. Their wishes should be heeded."

THE QUESTION OF QUALITY

In heeding the parental wishes, however, we must be careful that the quality of education is preserved. Public educators have often contended that some parents do not have the ability or the patience to teach their children well. Observations have been made that home-schooled children tend to be students with better-than-average potential but that their achievement is uneven due to a "spottiness" in the parents' preparation. Some school officials have been concerned about the lack of documentation and objective evaluation of home-schooled children. Some state legislators and school officials have addressed these concerns, and, since 1980, 28 states have adopted home school statutes or regulations. Compulsory attendance laws in 31 states now explicitly recognize an exception for home schooling. In legally providing for home schooling, most of these statutes established varying sets of requirements for home schools, including such criteria as teacher qualifications, achievement testing, and record keeping. . . .

In addition to academic concerns, the socialization of home-schooled children has been a primary consideration. Many educators insist that peer interaction in the school environment is necessary for normal development and speculate that home schooling will produce social isolates. Home schooling has also been criticized as elitist, appealing mainly to educated, middle-class families. Critics also fear that the domination of parents over their children would deny the protection of society to the neglected or indoctrinated child. Some have even questioned the motives of parents who home-school their children, suspecting that some mothers use home schooling as a rationalization to stay home while others home-school for status or ego reasons. These criticisms and concerns have mounted in parallel with the growth of home schooling. . . .

THE EFFECTIVENESS OF HOME SCHOOLING

In spite of concerns over academic progress, several studies have found that home-schooled children achieve higher than national averages on standardized measures. For example, the Tennessee Education Department reported that home-schooled students in Grades 2, 3, 6, and 8 in that state scored higher in every major area of the Stanford Achievement Test than the statewide public school averages for the 1985–1986 school year. Similar results were reported in studies

by the New York and Washington State Departments of Education. In Alabama, home-schooled children in Grades 2, 3, 5, and 6 scored in 1986 at or above the national norms in all areas of the Stanford Achievement Test. In Illinois, a study concluded that home-schooled children are not disadvantaged academically by their home-school setting.

A few studies have examined the achievement of home-schooled children working with differing home-school curricula. Two such studies were conducted by home-school curriculum publishers: the Hewitt Research Foundation found that the average standardized test score of children, who use the Hewitt-Moore Child Development Center home-school curriculum, was approximately at the 80th percentile, while researchers at the Christian Liberty Academy found that home-schooled children who use their curriculum performed two to three grade levels above the national norms. In addition, studies done since 1981 by the Alaska Department of Education have found that the home-schooled children in the first through eighth grades outperformed their classroom counterparts on the California Achievement Test and the Alaska Statewide Assessment Tests.

Now, the effects of home schooling on the socialization of children have been more difficult to examine, since there is apparently no convenient instrument available to measure the equivocal elements of socialization. However, Taylor, himself a proponent of home schooling, used a self-concept inventory with a sampling of home-schooled children and found that these children scored higher than conventionally-schooled children in all areas on the scale. His conclusion was that few home-schooled children are socially deprived. Other studies that have surveyed parents' reasons for home-schooling commonly report that parents see socialization as a negative aspect of school. They wish to help their children develop social skills without negative peer influences, learning socialization skills from parent models in the home rather than from peer models in the school. While those wary of home schooling worry about the children's socialization, the parents worry about the quality of socialization that takes place in traditional schools.

THE "THREAT" OF THE HOME SCHOOLING MOVEMENT

Home schooling has been regarded as a major educational movement in America even though the actual number of home-schooled children is still negligible, being less than 1 percent of the school-age children. Nevertheless, there is apprehension over possible negative effects that this movement could have on public schooling. Even as the function and effectiveness of public education in today's society have been questioned, schools seem to have maintained a certain level of general support. Thus, Jackson, for one, advanced an argument that previous challenges to public education simply reaffirmed how deep-rooted our society's allegiance to public education had become.

On their part, advocates of home schooling have maintained that granting the right to educate their children would not significantly deplete public school attendance or damage the system. For any family not to opt for the convenience of public schooling would be not only impractical but also inconsistent with the typical American lifestyle. Rather than rocking the foundations of American

schooling, the definition and concept of education would merely be revised and broadened. Toffler, for instance, visualized an increased role of families in the education of children and maintained that home schoolers should be aided by the schools and not regarded as "freaks or lawbreakers."

Of course, the prevalence of home schooling in the future of American education cannot be clearly foreseen now. Nevertheless, [it] is ironic to note that several current trends have encouraged the growth of home schooling. The increased emphasis on parent education, parental choice and participation in the educational process, and alternative educational options worked indirectly to promote the home-schooling movement. Widely-publicized issues concerning secular humanism in public education and the reassessment of teacher certification requirements have provided added incentives for home schoolers. In addition, recent national reports such as A Nation at Risk, offering many sweeping indictments and reform recommendations, have been seen as evidence that public education is moving farther away from the educational ideals of home-schooling parents. Any future dissatisfactions with public education will increase the possibility of more families turning to home schooling.

* * *

Compulsory public schooling in the United States originated from genuine societal needs and has grown strong as an American institution. However, future needs might create a more distinctive place for home schooling. Parental freedom to home school has been promoted as a right which a democratic society should allow. Before it can become a viable educational alternative, nevertheless, underlying issues regarding the balance of power between parents and society over the education of children must be settled. Only mutual interest in the welfare of the child, a cooperative spirit, and a genuine objectivity in discussing the sensitive issues surrounding home schooling will provide satisfactory solutions.

POSTSCRIPT

Is Home Schooling an Effective Method of Education?

Parents who do not want their children to be shaped by hours of rigid institutional learning may opt for the more flexible home-school setting. However, it should be noted that home schooling is challenging and difficult at best. Parents must be willing to take the time to learn so as to be able to teach their children effectively. Home schooling can be a full-time job and may therefore necessitate a separate income source for the parent-educator.

Another issue that must be considered is college recognition of high school credits earned through home schooling. Although increasing numbers of colleges and universities are accepting home-schooled students with adequate ACT or SAT scores, parent-teachers must be mindful of meeting state and local requirements for certification. Class meeting times and course content must be sanctioned by authorities so that home-school credits will be recognized by local boards of education.

There is also a possibility that home schooling will promote parental enmeshment with children in some families. Abuse and neglect could go unnoticed if children remain within the family for schooling, whereas abusive situations are more likely to be detected by school officials in public and private schools. Furthermore, home educators must provide their children with social outlets and activities. If not, children could become overly dependent upon their parents and unable to function effectively in social situations, especially among peers. On the other hand, in the public and private schools, children may model themselves after their peers and adopt behaviors and values that are unacceptable.

Parents can choose to educate their children at home or send them to a public or private school. While one type of setting may look more attractive than the other, it would seem prudent for parents to remember to look at their children individually and offer each the type of educational environment that considers the child's unique needs.

SUGGESTED READINGS

Gahr, E. (1991). Home and not alone. *Insight, 7,* 10–13.

Garcia-Barrio, C. (1991). Home is where the school is. *Essence, 22,* 104–106.

Pike, B. (1992). Why I teach my children at home. *Phi Delta Kappan, 73,* 564–565.

Smith, D.S. (1993). Home schooling. *Mother Earth News, 139,* 53–54.

PART 4

Adolescence

Many people use the term teenage years *to describe adolescence. This is the period of time from age 13 through 19. During this period of development the child experiences puberty, and there are dramatic physical changes that occur as the child becomes a young adult. Much less obvious than the physical changes are the cognitive changes in children at this stage of development. In early adolescence the child is increasingly able to think on an abstract level. Adolescents also undertake the process of identity development, defining who they are. This final section considers some of the key issues related to developmental tasks in adolescence.*

- Should Bilingual Education Programs Be Abandoned?

- Should Parents Be Doing More to Impart Values to Children?

- Is an Adolescent's Sexual Orientation Important in Understanding Causes for Youth Suicide?

- Is Abstinence Education the Best Sex Education?

- Are Gangs Created by a Need for Family?

ISSUE 13

Should Bilingual Education Programs Be Abandoned?

YES: Diane Ravitch, from "Politicization and the Schools: The Case of Bilingual Education," *Proceedings of the American Philosophical Society* (June 1985)

NO: Donaldo Macedo, from "English Only: The Tongue-Tying of America," *Journal of Education* (Spring 1991)

ISSUE SUMMARY

YES: Professor Diane Ravitch, who has written widely on educational issues, questions the effectiveness of bilingual programs. She suggests that they have become simply a means to attain certain political ends. Do these programs operate in the best interests of the children who are placed in them? she asks.

NO: Linguistics professor Donaldo Macedo believes that English should *not* be the only language used for educating children. He maintains that bilingual education programs are effective for educating children who cannot speak or read English and that they improve the academic performance of non-English-speaking children. In addition, these programs also contribute to furthering the cause of racial equality in our society.

There are several types of bilingual education programs in the United States, each with its own strengths and shortcomings. For example, in one type of billingual curriculum, a child who does not speak English is placed in a class taught by a teacher who speaks both English and the child's original language. The intent is to teach the child in English and in his or her native tongue, as well as to maintain the child's appreciation of the native culture of his or her parents. Problems can arise in such a program, however, when a language is common to many cultures. Consider the teacher who is from one Spanish-speaking country, Guatemala for example, and who teaches a class composed of Spanish-speaking students from diverse countries, such as Spain, Mexico, San Salvador, Bolivia, and so on. These children may enter high school with a thorough understanding of the Spanish language and Guatemalan culture, but they will likely have little idea of their own culture. To further exacerbate the problem, these children often lack sufficient immersion in the dominant, American culture. As a consequence, these children, who may be just as intelligent as their English-speaking counterparts, could do poorly on culturally relevant standardized tests and thus become discouraged.

Some bilingual education programs give the parents of non-English-speaking children the choice of enrolling their children in a completely native-speaking classroom or a completely English-speaking classroom, where they will receive no extra help or assistance. The problem here is that neither option may benefit the children. If children go to native-speaking classrooms, it can impede their acquisition of English. If they are put into English-only classrooms, they may become frustrated and discouraged.

Some bilingual programs, however, seem to be enjoying great success in recognizing a child's native culture and language and teaching them about American culture. In so-called English immersion programs, children are enrolled in classrooms where they are "immersed" in the English language, but only after they have been oriented to the language and the happenings of an American classroom. However, these immersion programs seem to work best in preschool curricula, since children acquire language more readily in early childhood.

In the following selections, the authors offer different arguments regarding bilingual education. As you read each selection, take note of the ways in which non-English-speaking children can be integrated most effectively into the educational system, according to Diane Ravitch and Donaldo Macedo. Which arguments seem to be most closely aligned with the best interests of the children?

YES

Diane Ravitch

POLITICIZATION AND THE SCHOOLS: THE CASE OF BILINGUAL EDUCATION

There has always been a politics of schools, and no doubt there always will be. Like any other organization populated by human beings, schools have their internal politics; for as long as there have been public schools, there have been political battles over their budget, their personnel policies, their curricula, and their purposes. Anyone who believes that there was once a time in which schools were untouched by political controversy is uninformed about the history of education. The decision-making processes that determine who will be chosen as principal or how the school board will be selected or whether to pass a school bond issue are simply political facts of life that are part and parcel of the administration, financing, and governance of schools. There is also a politics of the curriculum and of the profession, in which contending forces argue about programs and policies. It is hard to imagine a school, a school system, a university, a state board of education, or a national department of education in which these kinds of political conflicts do not exist. They are an intrinsic aspect of complex organizations in which people disagree about how to achieve their goals and about which goals to pursue; to the extent that we operate in a democratic manner, conflict over important and even unimportant issues is inevitable.

There is another kind of politics, however, in which educational institutions become entangled in crusades marked by passionate advocacy, intolerance of criticism, and unyielding dogmatism, and in which the education of children is a secondary rather than a primary consideration. Such crusades go beyond politics-as-usual; they represent the politicization of education. Schools and universities become targets for politicization for several reasons: First, they offer a large captive audience of presumably impressionable minds; second, they are expected to shape the opinions, knowledge, and values of the rising generation, which makes them attractive to those who want to influence the future; and third, since Americans have no strong educational philosophy or educational tradition, almost any claim—properly clothed in rhetorical appeals about the needs of children or of American society—can make its way into the course catalogue or the educational agenda.

From Diane Ravitch, "Politicization and the Schools: The Case of Bilingual Education," *Proceedings of the American Philosophical Society*, vol. 129, no. 2 (June 1985). Copyright © 1985 by The American Philosophical Society. Reprinted by permission.

Ever since Americans created public schools, financed by tax dollars and controlled by boards of laymen, the schools have been at the center of intermittent struggles over the values that they represent. The founders of the common school, and in particular Horace Mann, believed that the schools could be kept aloof from the religious and political controversies beyond their door, but it has not been easy to keep the crusaders outside the schoolhouse. In the nineteenth century, heated battles were fought over such issues as which Bible would be read in the classroom and whether public dollars might be used to subsidize religious schools. After the onset of World War I, anti-German hostility caused the German language to be routed from American schools, even though nearly a quarter of the high school population studied the language in 1915. Some of this same fervor, strengthened by zeal to hasten the process of assimilation, caused several states to outlaw parochial and private schools and to prohibit the teaching of foreign language in the first eight years of school. Such laws, obviously products of nationalism and xenophobia, were struck down as unconstitutional by the United States Supreme Court in the 1920s. The legislative efforts to abolish nonpublic schools and to bar the teaching of foreign languages were examples of politicization; their purpose was not to improve the education of any child, but to achieve certain social and political goals that the sponsors of these laws believed were of overwhelming importance.

Another example of politicization in education was the crusade to cleanse the schools of teachers and other employees who were suspected of being disloyal, subversive, or controversial. This crusade

began in the years after World War I, gathered momentum during the 1930s, and came to full fruition during the loyalty investigations by state and national legislative committees in the 1950s. Fears for national security led to intrusive surveillance of the beliefs, friends, past associations, and political activities of teachers and professors. These inquiries did not improve anyone's education; they used the educational institutions as vehicles toward political goals that were extraneous to education.

A more recent example of politicization occurred on the campuses during the war in Vietnam. Those who had fought political intrusions into educational institutions during the McCarthy era did so on the ground of academic freedom. Academic freedom, they argued, protected the right of students and teachers to express their views, regardless of their content; because of academic freedom, the university served as a sanctuary for dissidents, heretics, and skeptics of all persuasions. During the war in Vietnam, those who tried to maintain the university as a privileged haven for conflicting views, an open marketplace of ideas, found themselves the object of attack by student radicals. Student (and sometimes faculty) radicals believed that opposition to the war was so important that those who did not agree with them should be harassed and even silenced.

Faced with a moral issue, the activist argued, the university could not stand above the battle, nor could it tolerate the expression of "immoral" views. In this spirit, young radicals tried to prevent those with whom they disagreed from speaking and teaching; towards this end, they heckled speakers, disrupted classes, and even planted bombs on campus. These actions were intended to politicize schools and campuses and, in some instances, they succeeded. They were advocated by sincere and zealous individuals who earnestly believed that education could not take place within a context of political neutrality. Their efforts at politicization stemmed not from any desire to improve education as such, but from the pursuit of political goals.

As significant as the student movement and the McCarthy era were as examples of the dangers of politicization, they were short-lived in comparison to the policy of racial segregation. Segregation of public school children by their race and ancestry was established by law in seventeen states and by custom in many communities beyond those states. The practice of assigning public school children and teachers on the basis of their race had no educational justification; it was not intended to improve anyone's education. It was premised on the belief in the innate inferiority of people whose skin was of dark color. Racial segregation as policy and practice politicized the schools; it used them to buttress a racist social and political order. It limited the educational opportunities available to blacks. Racial segregation was socially and politically so effective in isolating blacks from opportunity or economic advancement and educationally so devastating in retarding their learning that our society continues to pay a heavy price to redress the cumulative deficits of generations of poor education.

The United States Supreme Court's 1954 decision, *Brown v. Board of Education*, started the process of ending state-imposed racial segregation. In those southern states where segregation was the cornerstone of a way of life, white resistance to desegregation was prolonged and intense. The drive to disestablish racial segregation and to uproot every last vestige of its effects was unquestionably necessary. The practice of assigning children to school by their race and of segregating other public facilities by race was a national disgrace. However, the process through which desegregation came about dramatically altered the politics of schools; courts and regulatory agencies at the federal and state level became accustomed to intervening in the internal affairs of educational institutions, and the potential for politicization of the schools was significantly enlarged.

The slow pace of desegregation in the decade after the *Brown* decision, concurrent with a period of rising expectations, contributed to a dramatic buildup of frustration and rage among blacks, culminating in the protests, civil disorders, and riots of the mid-1960s. In response, Congress enacted major civil rights laws in 1964 and 1965, and the federal courts became aggressive in telling school boards what to do to remedy their constitutional violations. Initially, these orders consisted of commands to produce racially mixed schools. However, some courts went beyond questions of racial mix. In Washington, D.C., a federal district judge in 1967 directed the school administration to abandon ability grouping, which he believed discriminated against black children. This was the first time that a federal court found a common pedagogical practice to be unconstitutional.[1]

In the nearly two decades since that decision, the active intervention of the federal judiciary into school affairs has ceased to be unusual. In Ann Arbor, Michigan, a federal judge ordered the school board to train teachers in "black English," a program subsequently found to be ineffectual in improving the education of black students. In California, a federal judge barred the use of intelligence tests for placement of students in special education classes, even though reputable psychologists defend their validity. In Boston, where the school board was found guilty of intentionally segregating children by race, the federal judge assumed full control over the school system for more than a decade; even reform superintendents who were committed to carrying out the judge's program for desegregation complained of the hundreds of court orders regulating every aspect of schooling, hiring, promotion, curriculum, and financing. In 1982, in a case unrelated to desegregation, a state judge in West Virginia ordered the state education department to do "no less than completely reconstruct the entire system of education in West Virginia," and the judge started the process of reconstruction by setting down his own standards for facilities, administration, and curriculum, including what was to be taught and for how many minutes each week.[2]

Perhaps this is as good a way of bringing about school reform as any other. No doubt school officials are delighted when a judge orders the state legislature to raise taxes on behalf of the schools. But it does seem to be a repudiation of our democratic political structure when judges go beyond issues of constitutional rights, don the mantle of school superintendent, and use their authority to change promotional standards, to reconstruct the curriculum, or to impose their own pedagogical prescriptions.

Now, by the definition of politicization that I earlier offered—that is, when educational institutions become the focus of dogmatic crusaders whose purposes are primarily political and only incidentally related to children's education—these examples may not qualify as politicization, although they do suggest how thin is the line between politics and politicization. After all, the judges were doing what they thought would produce better education. The court decisions in places like Ann Arbor, Boston, California, and West Virginia may be thought of as a shift in the politics of schools, a shift that has brought the judiciary into the decision-making process as a full-fledged partner in shaping educational disputes, even those involving questions of pedagogy and curriculum.

The long struggle to desegregate American schools put them at the center of political battles for more than a generation and virtually destroyed the belief that schools could remain above politics. Having lost their apolitical shield, the schools also lost their capacity to resist efforts to politicize them. In the absence of resistance, demands by interest groups of varying ideologies escalated, each trying to impose its own agenda on the curriculum, the textbooks, the school library, or the teachers. Based on the activities of single-issue groups, any number of contemporary educational policies would serve equally well as examples of politicization. The example that I have chosen as illustrative of politicization is bilingual education. The history of this program exemplifies a campaign on behalf of social and political goals that are only tangentially related to education. I would like to sketch briefly the bilingual controversy, which provides an overview of the new politics of education and demonstrates the tendency within this new politics to use educational programs for noneducational ends.

Demands for bilingual education arose as an outgrowth of the civil rights movement. As it evolved, that movement contained complex, and occasionally contradictory, elements. One facet of the movement appealed for racial integration and assimilation, which led to court orders for busing and racial balance; but the dynamics of the movement also inspired appeals to racial solidarity, which led to demands for black studies, black control of black schools, and other race-conscious policies. Whether the plea was for integration or for separatism, advocates could always point to a body of social science as evidence for their goals.

Race consciousness became a necessary part of the remedies that courts fashioned, but its presence legitimized ethnocentrism as a force in American politics. In the late 1960s, the courts, Congress, and policymakers—having been told for years by spokesmen for the civil rights movement that all children should be treated equally without regard to their race or ancestry—frequently heard compelling testimony by political activists and social scientists about the value of ethnic particularism in the curriculum.

Congress first endorsed funding for bilingual education in 1968, at a time when ethnocentrism had become a powerful political current. In hearings on this legislation, proponents of bilingual education argued that non-English-speaking children did poorly in school because they had low self-esteem, and that this low self-esteem was caused by the absence of their native language from the classroom. They claimed that if the children were taught in their native tongue and about their native culture, they would have higher self-esteem, better attitudes toward school, and higher educational achievement. Bilingual educators also insisted that children would learn English more readily if they already knew another language.

In the congressional hearings, both advocates and congressmen seemed to agree that the purpose of bilingual education was to help non-English speakers succeed in school and in society. But the differences between them were not then obvious. The congressmen believed that bilingual education would serve as a temporary transition into the regular English language program. But the bilingual educators saw the program as an opportunity to maintain the language and culture of the non-English-speaking student, while he was learning English.[3]

What was extraordinary about the Bilingual Education Act of 1968, which has since been renewed several times, is that it was the first time that the Congress had ever legislated a given pedagogical method. In practice, bilingual education means a program in which children study the major school subjects in a language other than English. Funding of the program, although small within the context of the federal education budget, created strong constituencies for its continuation, both within the federal government and among recipient agencies. No different from other interest groups, these constituencies pressed for expansion and strengthening of their program. Just as lifelong vocational educators are unlikely to ask whether their program works, so career bilingual educators are committed to their method as a philosophy, not as a technique for language instruction. The difference is this: techniques are subject to evaluation, which may cause them to be revised or discarded; philosophies are not.

In 1974, the Supreme Court's *Lau v. Nichols* decision reinforced demands for bilingual education. The Court ruled against the San Francisco public schools for their failure to provide English language instruction for 1,800 non-English-speaking Chinese students. The Court's decision was reasonable and appropriate. The Court said, "There is no equality of treatment merely by providing students with the same facilities, textbooks, teachers, and curriculum; for students who do not understand English are effectively foreclosed from any meaningful education." The decision did not endorse any particular remedy. It said "Teaching English to the students of Chinese ancestry who do not speak the language is one choice. Giving instruction to the group in Chinese is another. There may be others."[4]

Despite the Court's prudent refusal to endorse any particular method of instruction, the bilingual educators interpreted the *Lau* decision as a mandate for bilingual programs. In the year after the decision, the United States Office of Education established a task force to fashion guidelines for the implementation of the *Lau* decision; the task force was composed of bilingual educators and representatives of language minority groups. The task force fashioned regulations that prescribed in exhaustive detail how school districts should prepare and carry out bilingual programs for non-English-speaking students. The districts were directed to identify the student's primary language, not by his proficiency in English, but by determining which language was most often spoken in the student's home, which language he had learned first, and which language he used most often. Thus a student would be eligible for a bilingual program even if he was entirely fluent in English.[5]

Furthermore, while the Supreme Court refused to endorse any given method, the task force directed that non-English-speaking students should receive bilingual education that emphasized instruction in their native language and culture. Districts were discouraged from using the "English as a Second Language" approach, which consists of intensive, supplemental English-only instruction, or immersion techniques, in which students are instructed in English within an English-only context.

Since the establishment of the bilingual education program, many millions of dollars have been spent to support bilingual programs in more than sixty different languages. Among those receiving funding to administer and staff such programs, bilingual education is obviously popular, but there are critics who think that it is educationally unsound. Proponents of desegregation have complained that bilingual education needlessly segregates non-English speakers from others of their age. At a congressional hearing in 1977, one desegregation specialist complained that bilingual programs had been funded "without any significant proof that they would work.... There is nothing in the research to suggest that children can effectively learn English without continuous interaction with other children who are native English speakers."[6]

The research on bilingual education has been contradictory, and studies that favor or criticize the bilingual approach have been attacked as biased. Researchers connected to bilingual institutes claim that their programs resulted in significant gains for non-English-speaking children. But a four-year study commissioned by the United States Office of Education concluded that students who learned bilingually did not achieve at a higher level than those in regular classes, nor were their attitudes toward school significantly different. What they seemed to learn best, the study found, was the language in which they were instructed.[7]

One of the few evidently unbiased, nonpolitical assessments of bilingual research was published in 1982 in the *Harvard Educational Review*. A survey of international findings, it concluded that "bilingual programs are neither better nor worse than other instructional methods." The author found that in the absence of compelling experimental support for this method, there was "no legal necessity or research basis for the federal government to advocate or require a specific educational approach."[8]

If the research is in fact inconclusive, then there is no justification for mandating the use of bilingual education or any other single pedagogy. The bilingual method may or may not be the best way to learn English. Language instruction programs that are generally regarded as outstanding, such as those provided for Foreign Service officers or by the nationally acclaimed center at Middlebury College, are immersion programs, in which students embark on a systematic program of intensive language learning without depending on their native tongue. Immersion programs may not be appropriate for all children, but then neither is any single pedagogical method. The method to be used should be determined by the school authorities and the professional staff, based on their resources and competence.

Despite the fact that the Supreme Court did not endorse bilingual education, the lower federal courts have tended to treat this pedagogy as a civil right, and more than a dozen states have mandated its use in their public schools. The path by which bilingual education came to be viewed as a civil right, rather than as one method of teaching language, demonstrates the politicization of the language issue in American education. The United States Commission on Civil Rights endorsed bilingual education as a civil right nearly a decade ago. Public interest lawyers and civil rights lawyers have also regarded bilingual education as a basic civil right. An article in 1983 in the *Columbia Journal of Law and Social Problems* contended that bilingual education "may be the most effective method of compensatory language instruction currently used to educate language-minority students."[9] It based this conclusion not on a review of educational research but on statements made by various political agencies.

The article states, for example, as a matter of fact rather than opinion: " ... by offering subject matter instruction in a language understood by language-minority students, the bilingual-bicultural method maximizes achievement, and thus minimizes feelings of inferiority that might accompany a poor academic performance. By ridding the school environment of those features which may damage a language-minority child's self-image and thereby interfere with the educative process, bilingual-bicultural education creates the atmosphere most conducive to successful learning."[10]

If there were indeed conclusive evidence for these statements, then bilingual-bicultural education *should* be imposed on school districts throughout the country. However, the picture is complicated; there are good bilingual programs, and there are ineffective bilingual programs. In and of itself, bilingualism is one pedagogical method, as subject to variation and misuse as any other single method. To date, no school district has claimed that the bilingual method succeeded in sharply decreasing the dropout rate of Hispanic children or markedly raising their achievement scores in English and other subjects. The bilingual method is not necessarily inferior to other methods; its use should not be barred. There simply is no conclusive evidence that bilingualism should be preferred to all other ways of instructing non-English-speaking students. This being the case, there are no valid reasons for courts or federal agencies to impose this method on school districts for all non-English speakers, to the exclusion of other methods of language instruction.

Bilingual education exemplifies politicization because its advocates press its adoption regardless of its educational effectiveness, and they insist that it must be made mandatory regardless of the wishes of the parents and children who are its presumed beneficiaries. It is a political program whose goals are implicit in the term "biculturalism." The aim is to use the public schools to promote the maintenance of distinct ethnic communities, each with its own cultural heritage and language. This in itself is a valid goal for a democratic nation as diverse and pluralistic as ours, but it is questionable whether this goal is appropriately pursued by the public schools, rather than by the freely chosen activities of individuals and groups.

Then there is the larger question of whether bilingual education actually promotes equality of educational opportunity. Unless it enables non-English-speaking children to learn English and to enter into the mainstream of American society, it may hinder equality of educational opportunity. The child who spends most of his instructional time learning in Croatian or Greek or Spanish is likely to learn Croatian, Greek, or Spanish. Fluency in these languages will be of little help to those who want to apply to American colleges, universities, graduate schools, or employers, unless they are also fluent in English.

Of course, our nation needs much more foreign language instruction. But we should not confuse our desire to promote foreign languages in general with the special educational needs of children who do not know how to speak and read English in an English-language society.

Will our educational institutions ever be insulated from the extremes of politicization? It seems highly unlikely, in view of the fact that our schools and colleges are deeply embedded in the social and political mainstream. What is notably different today is the vastly increased power of the federal government and the courts to intervene in educational institutions, because of the expansion of the laws and the dependence of almost all educational institutions on public funding. To avoid unwise and dangerous politicization, government agencies should strive to distinguish between their proper role as protectors of fundamental constitutional rights and inappropriate intrusion into complex issues of curriculum and pedagogy.

This kind of institutional restraint would be strongly abetted if judges and policymakers exercised caution and skepticism in their use of social science testimony. Before making social research the basis for constitutional edicts, judges and policymakers should understand that social science findings are usually divergent, limited, tentative, and partial.

We need the courts as vigilant guardians of our rights; we need federal agencies that respond promptly to any violations of those rights. But we also need educational institutions that are free to exercise their responsibilities without fear of pressure groups and political lobbies. Decisions about which textbooks to use, which theories to teach, which books to place in the school library, how to teach, and what to teach are educational issues. They should be made by appropriate lay and professional authorities on educational grounds. In a democratic society, all of us share the responsibility to protect schools, colleges, and universities against unwarranted political intrusion into educational affairs.

REFERENCES

1. *Hobson v. Hansen*, 269 F. Supp. 401 (D.D.C., 1967); Alexander Bickel, "Skelly Wright's Sweeping Decision," *New Republic*, July 8, 1967, pp. 11–12.
2. Nathan Glazer, "Black English and Reluctant Judges," *Public Interest*, vol. 62, Winter 1980, pp. 40–54; *Larry P. v. Wilson Riles*, 495 F. Supp. 1926 (N.D. Calif., 1979); Nathan Glazer, "IQ on Trial," *Commentary*, June 1981, pp. 51–59; *Morgan v. Hennigan*, 379 F. Supp. 410 (D. Mass., 1974); Robert Wood, "The Disassembling of American Education," *Daedalus*, vol. 109, no. 3, Summer 1980, pp. 99–113; *Education Week*, May 12, 1982, p. 5.
3. U.S. Congress, Senate, Committee on Labor and Public Welfare, Special Subcommittee on Bilingual Education, 90th Cong., 1st sess., 1967.
4. *Lau v. Nichols*, 414 U.S. 563 (1974).
5. U.S. Department of Health, Education, and Welfare, "Task Force Findings Specifying Remedies Available for Eliminating Past Educational Practices Ruled Unlawful under *Lau v. Nichols*" (Washington, D.C., Summer 1975).
6. U.S. Congress, House, Subcommittee on Elementary, Secondary, and Vocational Education of the Committee on Education and Labor, Bilingual Education, 95th Cong., 1st sess., 1977, pp. 335–336. The speaker was Gary Orfield.
7. Malcolm N. Danoff, "Evaluation of the Impact of ESEA Title VII Spanish/English Bilingual Education Programs" (Palo Alto, Calif.: American Institutes for Research, 1978).
8. Iris Rotberg, "Some Legal and Research Considerations in Establishing Federal Policy in Bilingual Education," *Harvard Educational Review*, vol. 52, May 1982, pp. 148–168.
9. Jonathan D. Haft, "Assuring Equal Educational Opportunity for Language-Minority Students: Bilingual Education and the Equal Educational Opportunity Act of 1974." *Columbia Journal of Law and Social Problems*, vol. 18, no. 2, 1983, pp. 209–293.
10. Ibid., p. 253.

NO

Donaldo Macedo

ENGLISH ONLY: THE TONGUE-TYING OF AMERICA

During the past decade conservative educators such as ex-secretary of education William Bennett and Diane Ravitch have mounted an unrelenting attack on bilingual and multicultural education. These conservative educators tend to recycle old assumptions about the "melting pot theory" and our "common culture," assumptions designed primarily to maintain the status quo. Maintained is a status quo that functions as a cultural reproduction mechanism which systematically does not allow other cultural subjects, who are considered outside of the mainstream, to be present in history. These cultural subjects who are profiled as the "other" are but palely represented in history within our purportedly democratic society in the form of Black History Month, Puerto Rican Day, and so forth. This historical constriction was elegantly captured by an 11th-grade Vietnamese student in California:

> I was so excited when my history teacher talked about the Vietnam War. Now at last, I thought, now we will study about my country. We didn't really study it. Just for one day, though, my country was real again. (Olsen, 1988, p. 68)

The incessant attack on bilingual education which claims that it serves to tongue-tie students in their native language not only negates the multilingual and multicultural nature of U.S. society, but blindly ignores the empirical evidence that has been amply documented in support of bilingual education.... [T]he present overdose of monolingualism and Anglocentrism that dominates the current educational debate not only contributes to a type of mind-tied America, but also is incapable of producing educators and leaders who can rethink what it means to prepare students to enter the ever-changing, multilingual, and multicultural world of the 21st century.

It is both academically dishonest and misleading to simply point to some failures of bilingual education without examining the lack of success of linguistic minority students within a larger context of a general failure of public education in major urban centers. Furthermore, the English Only position points to a pedagogy of exclusion that views the learning of English as education itself. English Only advocates fail to question under what conditions

From Donaldo Macedo, "English Only: The Tongue-Tying of America," *Journal of Education*, vol. 173, no. 2 (Spring 1991). Copyright © 1991 by the Trustees of Boston University. Reprinted by permission.

English will be taught and by whom. For example, immersing non-English-speaking students in English as a Second Language [ESL] programs taught by untrained music, art and social science teachers (as is the case in Massachusetts with the grandfather clause in ESL Certification) will hardly accomplish the avowed goals of the English Only Movement. The proponents of English Only also fail to raise two other fundamental questions. First, if English is the most effective educational language, how can we explain that over 60 million Americans are illiterate or functionally illiterate (Kozol, 1985, p. 4)? Second, if education solely in English can guarantee linguistic minorities a better future, as educators like William Bennett promise, why do the majority of Black Americans, whose ancestors have been speaking English for over 200 years, find themselves still relegated to ghettos?

I want to argue in this paper that the answer lies not in technical questions of whether English is a more viable language of instruction or the repetitive promise that it offers non-English-speaking students "full participation first in their school and later in American society" (Silber, 1991, p. 7). This position assumes that English is in fact a superior language and that we live in a classless, race-blind society. I want to propose that decisions about how to educate non-English-speaking students cannot be reduced to issues of language, but rest in a full understanding of the ideological elements that generate and sustain linguistic, racial, and sex discrimination. That is, educators need to develop, as Henry Giroux has suggested, "a politics and pedagogy around a new language capable of acknowledging the multiple, contradictory, and complex subject posi-

tions people occupy within different social, cultural, and economic locations" (1992, p. 27). By shifting the linguistic issue to an ideological terrain we will challenge conservative educators to confront the Berlin Wall of racism, classism, and economic deprivation which characterizes the lived experiences of minorities in U.S. public schools. For example, J. Anthony Lukas succinctly captures the ideological elements that promote racism and segregation in schools in his analysis of desegregation in the Boston Public Schools. Lukas cites a trip to Charlestown High School, where a group of Black parents experienced firsthand the stark reality their children were destined to endure. Although the headmaster assured them that "violence, intimidation, or racial slurs would not be tolerated," they could not avoid the racial epithets on the walls: "Welcome Niggers," "Niggers Suck," "White Power," "KKK," "Bus is for Zulu," and "Be illiterate, fight busing." As those parents were boarding the bus, "they were met with jeers and catcalls 'go home niggers. Keep going all the way to Africa!'" This racial intolerance led one parent to reflect, "My god, what kind of hell am I sending my children into?" (Lukas, 1985, p. 282). What could her children learn at a school like that except to hate? Even though forced integration of schools in Boston exacerbated the racial tensions in the Boston Public Schools, one should not overlook the deep-seated racism that permeates all levels of the school structure....

Against this landscape of violent racism perpetrated against racial minorities, and also against linguistic minorities, one can understand the reasons for the high dropout rate in the Boston public schools (approximately 50%). Perhaps racism and other ideological elements are part of a school reality which forces a high percentage of students to leave school, only later to be profiled by the very system as dropouts or "poor and unmotivated students." One could argue that the above incidents occurred during a tumultuous time of racial division in Boston's history, but I do not believe that we have learned a great deal from historically dangerous memories to the degree that our leaders continue to invite racial tensions as evidenced in the Willie Horton presidential campaign issue and the present quota for jobs as an invitation once again to racial divisiveness.

It is very curious that this new-found concern of English Only advocates for limited English proficiency students does not interrogate those very ideological elements that psychologically and emotionally harm these students far more than the mere fact that English may present itself as a temporary barrier to an effective education. It would be more socially constructive and beneficial if the zeal that propels the English Only movement were diverted toward social struggles designed to end violent racism and structures of poverty, homelessness, and family breakdown, among other social ills that characterize the lived experiences of minorities in the United States. If these social issues are not dealt with appropriately, it is naive to think that the acquisition of the English language alone will, somehow, magically eclipse the raw and cruel injustices and oppression perpetrated against the dispossessed class of minorities in the United States. According to Peter McLaren, these dispossessed minority students who

populate urban settings in places such as Howard Beach, Ozone Park, El Barrio, are more likely to be forced to learn

about Eastern Europe in ways set forth by neo-conservative multiculturists than they are to learn about the Harlem Renaissance, Mexico, Africa, the Caribbean, or Aztec or Zulu culture. (McLaren, 1991, p. 7)

While arguing for the use of the students' native language in their educational development, I would like to make it very clear that the bilingual education goal should never be to restrict students to their own vernacular. This linguistic constriction inevitably leads to a linguistic ghetto. Educators must understand fully the broader meaning of the use of students' language as a requisite for their empowerment. That is, empowerment should never be limited to what Stanley Aronowitz describes as "the process of appreciating and loving oneself" (1985). In addition to this process, empowerment should also be a means that enables students "to interrogate and selectively appropriate those aspects of the dominant culture that will provide them with the basis for defining and transforming, rather than merely serving, the wider social order" (Giroux & McLaren, 1986, p. 17). This means that educators should understand the value of mastering the standard English language of the wider society. It is through the full appropriation of the standard English language that linguistic minority students find themselves linguistically empowered to engage in dialogue with various sectors of the wider society. What I must reiterate is that educators should never allow the limited proficient students' native language to be silenced by a distorted legitimation of the standard English language. Linguistic minority students' language should never be sacrificed, since it is the only means through which they make sense of their own experience in the world.

Given the importance of the standard English language in the education of linguistic minority students, I must agree with the members of the Institute for Research in English Acquisition and Development when they quote Antonio Gramsci in their brochure:

> Without the mastery of the common standard version of the national language, one is inevitably destined to function only at the periphery of national life and, especially, outside the national and political mainstream. (READ, 1990)

But these English Only advocates fail to tell the other side of Antonio Gramsci's argument, which warns us:

> Each time that in one way or another, the question of language comes to the fore, that signifies that a series of other problems is about to emerge, the formation and enlarging of the ruling class, the necessity to establish more "intimate" and sure relations between the ruling groups and the popular masses, that is, the reorganization of cultural hegemony. (Gramsci, 1971, p. 16)

This selective selection of Gramsci's position on language points to the hidden curriculum with which the English Only movement seeks to promote a monolithic ideology. It is also part and parcel of an ongoing attempt at "reorganization of cultural hegemony" as evidenced by the unrelenting attack by conservative educators on multicultural education and curriculum diversity....

In contrast to the zeal for a common culture and English only, these conservative educators have remained ominously silent about forms of racism, inequality, subjugation, and exploitation that daily serve to wage symbolic and real violence against those children who by virtue of their language, race, ethnicity, class, or gender are not treated in schools with the dignity and respect all children warrant in a democracy. Instead of reconstituting education around an urban and cultural studies approach which takes the social, cultural, political, and economic divisions of education and everyday life as the primary categories for understanding contemporary schooling, conservative educators have recoiled in an attempt to salvage the status quo. That is, they try to keep the present unchanged even though, as Renato Constantino points out:

> Within the living present there are imperceptible changes which make the status quo a moving reality.... Thus a new policy based on the present as past and not on the present as future is backward for it is premised not on evolving conditions but on conditions that are already dying away. (1978, p. 201)

One such not so imperceptible change is the rapid growth of minority representation in the labor force. As such, the conservative leaders and educators are digging this country's economic grave by their continued failure to educate minorities. As Lew Ferlerger and Jay Mandle convincingly argue, "Unless the educational attainment of minority populations in the United States improves, the country's hopes for resuming high rates of growth and an increasing standard of living look increasingly dubious" (1991, p. 12).

In addition to the real threat to the economic fabric of the United States, the persistent call for English language only in education smacks of backwardness in the present conjuncture of our ever-changing multicultural and multi-lingual society. Furthermore, these conservative educators base their language policy argument on the premise that English education in this country is highly effective. On the contrary. As Patrick Courts clearly argues in his book *Literacy for Empowerment* (1991), English education is failing even middle-class and upper-class students. He argues that English reading and writing classes are mostly based on workbooks and grammar lessons, lessons which force students to "bark at print" or fill in the blanks. Students engage in grudgingly banal exercises such as practicing correct punctuation and writing sample business letters. Books used in their classes are, Courts points out, too often in the service of commercially prepared ditto sheets and workbooks. Courts's account suggests that most school programs do not take advantage of the language experiences that the majority of students have had before they reach school. These teachers become the victims of their own professional ideology when they delegitimize the language experiences that students bring with them into the classroom.

Courts's study is basically concerned with middle-class and upper-middle-class students unburdened by racial discrimination and poverty, students who have done well in elementary and high school settings and are now populating the university lecture halls and seminar rooms. If schools are failing these students, the situation does not bode well for those students less economically, socially, and politically advantaged. It is toward the linguistic minority students that I would like to turn my discussion now.

THE ROLE OF LANGUAGE IN THE EDUCATION OF LINGUISTIC MINORITY STUDENTS

Within the last two decades, the issue of bilingual education has taken on a heated importance among educators. Unfortunately, the debate that has emerged tends to recycle old assumptions and values regarding the meaning and usefulness of the students' native language in education. The notion that education of linguistic minority students is a matter of learning the standard English language still informs the vast majority of bilingual programs and manifests its logic in the renewed emphasis on technical reading and writing skills.

I want to reiterate in this paper that the education of linguistic minority students cannot be viewed as simply the development of skills aimed at acquiring the standard English language. English Only proponents seldom discuss the pedagogical structures that will enable these students to access other bodies of knowledge. Nor do they interrogate the quality of ESL instruction provided to the linguistic minority students and the adverse material conditions under which these students learn English. The view that teaching English constitutes education sustains a notion of ideology that systematically negates rather than makes meaningful the cultural experiences of the subordinate linguistic groups who are, by and large, the objects of its policies. For the education of linguistic minority students to become meaningful it has to be situated within a theory of cultural production and viewed as an integral part of the way in which people produce, transform, and reproduce meaning. Bilingual education, in this sense, must be seen as a medium that consti-

tutes and affirms the historical and existential moments of lived culture. Hence,
it is an eminently political phenomenon,
and it must be analyzed within the context of a theory of power relations and an
understanding of social and cultural reproduction and production. By "cultural
reproduction" I refer to collective experiences that function in the interest of the
dominant groups rather than in the interest of the oppressed groups that are
objects of its policies. Bilingual education
programs in the United States have been
developed and implemented under the
cultural reproduction model leading to a
de facto neocolonial educational model.
I use "cultural production" to refer to
specific groups of people producing, mediating, and confirming the mutual ideological elements that merge from and
reaffirm their daily lived experiences. In
this case, such experiences are rooted in
the interest of individual and collective
self-determination. It is only through a
cultural production model that we can
achieve a truly democratic and liberatory
educational experience. I will return to
this issue later.

While the various debates in the
past two decades may differ in their
basic assumptions about the education
of linguistic minority students, they all
share one common feature: they all ignore
the role of language as a major force in
the construction of human subjectivities.
That is, they ignore the way language
may either confirm or deny the life
histories and experiences of the people
who use it.

The pedagogical and political implications in education programs for linguistic minority students are far-reaching and
yet largely ignored. These programs, for
example, often contradict a fundamental principle of reading, namely that students learn to read faster and with better
comprehension when taught in their native tongue. The immediate recognition
of familiar words and experiences en-
hances the development of a positive self-
concept in children who are somewhat insecure about the status of their language
and culture. For this reason, and to be
consistent with the plan to construct a
democratic society free from vestiges of
oppression, a minority literacy program
must be rooted in the cultural capital of
subordinate groups and have as its point
of departure their own language.

Educators must develop radical pedagogical structures which provide students with the opportunity to use their
own reality as a basis of literacy. This
includes, obviously, the language they
bring to the classroom. To do otherwise
is to deny minority students the rights
that lie at the core of a democratic education. The failure to base a literacy program on the minority students' language
means that oppositional forces can neutralize the efforts of educators and political leaders to achieve decolonization
of schooling. It is of tantamount importance that the incorporation of the minority language as the primary language of
instruction in education of linguistic minority students be given top priority. It is
through their own language that linguistic minority students will be able to reconstruct their history and their culture.

I want to argue that the minority
language has to be understood within the
theoretical framework that generates it.
Put another way, the ultimate meaning
and value of the minority language is
not to be found by determining how
systematic and rule-governed it is. We
know that already. Its real meaning has to
be understood through the assumptions
that govern it, and it has to be understood

via the social, political, and ideological relations to which it points. Generally speaking, this issue of effectiveness and validity often hides the true role of language in the maintenance of the values and interests of the dominant class. In other words, the issue of effectiveness and validity becomes a mask that obfuscates questions about the social, political, and ideological order within which the minority language exists.

If an emancipatory and critical education program is to be developed in the United States for linguistic minority students in which they become "subjects" rather than "objects," educators must understand the productive quality of language. James Donald puts it this way:

> I take language to be productive rather than reflective of social reality. This means calling into question the assumption that we, as speaking subjects, simply use language to organize and express our ideas and experiences. On the contrary, language is one of the most important social practices through which we come to experience ourselves as subjects.... My point here is that once we get beyond the idea of language as no more than a medium of communication, as a tool equally and neutrally available to all parties in cultural exchanges, then we can begin to examine language both as a practice of signification and also as a site for culture struggle and as a mechanism which produces antagonistic relations between different social groups. (Donald, 1982, p. 44)

It is to the antagonistic relationship between the minority and dominant speakers that I want to turn now. The antagonistic nature of the minority language has never been fully explored. In order to more clearly discuss this issue of antago-nism, I will use Donald's distinction between oppressed language and repressed language. Using Donald's categories, the "negative" way of posing the minority language question is to view it in terms of oppression—that is, seeing the minority language as "lacking" the dominant standard features which usually serve as a point of reference for the minority language. By far the most common questions concerning the minority language in the United States are posed from the oppression perspective. The alternative view of the minority language is that it is repressed in the standard dominant language. In this view, minority language as a repressed language could, if spoken, challenge the privileged standard linguistic dominance. Educators have failed to recognize the "positive" promise and antagonistic nature of the minority language. It is precisely on these dimensions that educators must demystify the standard dominant language and the old assumptions about its inherent superiority. Educators must develop liberatory and critical bilingual programs informed by a radical pedagogy so that the minority language will cease to provide its speakers the experience of subordination and, moreover, may be brandished as a weapon of resistance to the dominance of the dominant standard language of the curriculum.

In this sense, the students' language is the only means by which they can develop their own voice, a prerequisite to the development of a positive sense of self-worth. As Giroux elegantly states, the students' voice "is the discursive means to make themselves 'heard' and to define themselves as active authors of their worlds" (Giroux & McLaren, 1986, p. 235). The authorship of one's own world also implies the use of one's own language, and relates to what Mikhail Bakhtin describes as "retelling a story in one's own words" (Giroux & McLaren, 1986, p. 235).

A DEMOCRATIC AND LIBERATORY EDUCATION FOR LINGUISTIC MINORITY STUDENTS

In maintaining a certain coherence with the educational plan to reconstruct new and more democratic educational programs for linguistic minority students, educators and political leaders need to create a new school grounded in a new educational praxis, expressing different concepts of education consonant with the principles of a democratic, multicultural, and multilingual society. In order for this to happen, the first step is to identify the objectives of the inherent colonial education that informs the majority of bilingual programs in the United States. Next, it is necessary to analyze how colonialist methods used by the dominant schools function, legitimize the Anglocentric values and meaning, and at the same time negate the history, culture, and language practices of the majority of linguistic minority students. The new school, so it is argued, must also be informed by a radical bilingual pedagogy, which would make concrete such values as solidarity, social responsibility, and creativity. In the democratic development of bilingual programs rooted in a liberatory ideology, linguistic minority students become "subjects" rather than mere "objects" to be assimilated blindly into an often hostile dominant "common" culture. A democratic and liberatory education needs to move away from traditional approaches, which emphasize the acquisition of mechanical basic skills while divorcing education from its ideological

and historical contexts. In attempting to meet this goal, it purposely must reject the conservative principles embedded in the English Only movement I have discussed earlier. Unfortunately, many bilingual programs sometimes unknowingly reproduce one common feature of the traditional approaches to education by ignoring the important relationship between language and the cultural capital of the students at whom bilingual education is aimed. The result is the development of bilingual programs whose basic assumptions are at odds with the democratic spirit that launched them.

Bilingual program development must be largely based on the notion of a democratic and liberatory education, in which education is viewed "as one of the major vehicles by which 'oppressed' people are able to participate in the sociohistorical transformation of their society" (Walmsley, 1981, p. 74). Bilingual education, in this sense, is grounded in a critical reflection of the cultural capital of the oppressed. It becomes a vehicle by which linguistic minority students are equipped with the necessary tools to reappropriate their history, culture, and language practices. It is, thus, a way to enable the linguistic minority students to reclaim "those historical and existential experiences that are devalued in everyday life by the dominant culture in order to be both validated and critically understood" (Giroux, 1983, p. 226). To do otherwise is to deny these students their very democratic rights. In fact, the criticism that bilingual and multicultural education unwisely question the traditions and values of our so-called "common culture" as suggested by Kenneth T. Jackson (1991) is both antidemocratic and academically dishonest. Multicultural education and curriculum diversity did not create the

S & L scandal, the Iran-Contra deba-cle, or the extortion of minority proper-ties by banks, the stewards of the "com-mon culture," who charged minorities exorbitant loan-sharking interest rates. Multicultural education and curriculum diversity did not force Joachim Maitre, dean of the College of Communication at Boston University, to choose the hypocrit-ical moral high ground to excoriate the popular culture's "bleak moral content," all the while plagiarizing 15 paragraphs of a conservative comrade's text.

The learning of English language skills alone will not enable linguistic minor-ity students to acquire the critical tools "to awaken and liberate them from their mystified and distorted views of them-selves and their world" (Giroux, 1983, p. 226). For example, speaking English has not enabled African-Americans to change this society's practice of jailing more Blacks than even South Africa, and this society spending over 7 billion dol-lars to keep African-American men in jail while spending only 1 billion dollars ed-ucating Black males (Black, 1991).

Educators must understand the all-encompassing role the dominant ide-ology has played in this mystification and distortion of our so-called "common culture" and our "common language." They must also recognize the antagonis-tic relationship between the "common culture" and those who, by virtue of their race, language, ethnicity, and gen-der, have been relegated to the margins. Finally, educators must develop bilin-gual programs based on the theory of cultural production. In other words, lin-guistic minority students must be pro-vided the opportunity to become actors in the reconstruction of a more democratic and just society. In short, education con-ducted in English only is alienating to lin-guistic minority students, since it denies them the fundamental tools for reflection, critical thinking, and social interaction. Without the cultivation of their native language, and robbed of the opportunity for reflection and critical thinking, lin-guistic minority students find themselves unable to re-create their culture and his-tory. Without the reappropriation of their culture, the valorization of their lived ex-periences, English Only supporters' vac-uous promise that the English language will guarantee students "full participa-tion first in their school and later in Amer-ican society" (Silber, 1991, p. 7) can hardly be a reality.

REFERENCES

Aronowitz, S. (1985, May). "Why should Johnny read." *Village Voice Literary Supplement*, p. 13.

Black, C. (1991, January 13). Paying the high price for being the world's no. 1 jailor. *Boston Sunday Globe*, p. 67.

Constantino, R. (1928). *Neocolonial identity and counter consciousness*. London: Merlin Press.

Courts, P. (1991). *Literacy for empowerment*. South Hadley, MA: Bergin & Garvey.

Donald, J. (1982). Language, literacy, and schooling. In *The state and popular culture*. Milton Keynes: Open University Culture Unit.

Ferlerger, L., & Mandle, J. (1991). *African-Americans and the future of the U.S. economy*. Unpublished manuscript.

Giroux, H. A. (1983). *Theory and resistance: A pedagogy for the opposition*. South Hadley, MA: Bergin & Garvey.

Giroux, H. (1991). *Border crossings: Cultural workers and the politics of education*. New York: Routledge.

Giroux, H. A., & McLaren, P. (1986). Teacher education and the politics of engagement: The case for democratic schooling. *Harvard Educational Review*, 56(3), 213–238.

Gramsci, A. (1971). *Selections from Prison Notebooks*, (Ed. and Trans. Quinten Hoare & Geoffrey Smith). New York: International Publishers.

Jackson, D. (1991, December 8). The end of the second Reconstruction. *Boston Globe*, p. 27.

Jackson, K. T. (1991, July 7). Cited in a *Boston Sunday Globe* editorial.

Kozol, J. (1985). *Illiterate America.* New York: Doubleday Anchor.

Lukas, J. A. (1985). *Common ground.* New York: Alfred A. Knopf.

McLaren, P. (1991). Critical pedagogy: Constructing an arch of social dreaming and a doorway to hope. *Journal of Education, 173*(1), 9–34.

Olsen, L. (1988). *Crossing the schoolhouse border: Immigrant students and the California public schools.* San Francisco: California Tomorrow.

Silber, J. (1991, May). *Boston University Commencement Catalogue.*

Walmsley, S. (1981). On the purpose and content of secondary reading programs: Educational and ideological perspectives. *Curriculum Inquiry, 11,* 73–79.

POSTSCRIPT

Should Bilingual Education Programs Be Abandoned?

Macedo blames an ineffective bilingual education program for the fact that the vast majority of the country's high school dropouts are minorities. He maintains that learning English alone will not assist minority students in becoming equal members of society. Bilingual programs must do more to acculturate students.

Is bilingual education effective? Although Macedo thinks it can be, some studies suggest that bilingual programs may be ineffective. What can society do? Can we, in good conscience, take a "sink or swim" attitude and do nothing while some children become so frustrated and discouraged that they no longer want to go to school? Is society willing to continue to support those people who cannot earn a living because they cannot read and write in English? Is it possible that current bilingual programs are not very effective because they are designed in such a way that children are actually taught little English and instead spend their time in special "transitional" classes?

A. M. Thernstrom, in his article "Bilingual Miseducation," *Commentary* (vol. 88, 1990), encourages bilingual educators to teach the English language while emphasizing the culture of the students' new country. This could prevent the children from feeling like strangers in a foreign land.

The debate on the utility of bilingual education rages on in courtrooms, school boards, and families. However, as we engage in these arguments, we must not lose sight of the true focus of our discussion—the children. What approach will provide the most expedient way to give non-English-speaking children the best possible education?

SUGGESTED READINGS

Citrin, J. (1990). Language, politics, and American identity. *Public Interest, 99,* 96–109.

Hokuta, K. (1992). At issue: Do bilingual education programs help Hispanic children learn English and assimilate into American culture? *CG Researcher,* 2, 945.

Imhoff, G. (1990). The position of the U.S. English on bilingual education. *Annals of the American Academy of Political and Social Science, 508,* 48–51.

Miller, J. A. (1990). Native-language instruction found to aid L.E.P.'s. *Education Week, 10,* 1, 23.

Porter, R. P. (1991). Language choice for Latino students. *The Public Interest, 105,* 48–60.

ISSUE 14

Should Parents Be Doing More to Impart Values to Children?

YES: William J. O'Malley, from "Don't Upset the Kids," *America* (September 28, 1991)

NO: Kathleen Kennedy Townsend, from "Why Johnny Can't Tell Right from Wrong," *The Washington Monthly* (December 1992)

ISSUE SUMMARY

YES: William J. O'Malley, a professor of theology and English, posits that as children move into adolescence, they lack the ability to understand the implications of adulthood and its responsibilities. He contends that parents are largely to blame for this because they do not want their children to encounter any discomfort. As a result, parents unknowingly undermine the purpose of adolescence, which is the development of a personally validated adult self, arrived at through decision making and encounters with adversity.

NO: Kathleen Kennedy Townsend, who was a key administrator for the Maryland Department of Education at the time she wrote this selection, agrees that many children lack socially constructive values. However, she contends that expecting parents to instill values is not realistic. She states that in many homes parents simply are not around or motivated to teach children. In others, family role models can include close relatives who are criminals, making it less likely that children will develop positive values. She concludes that teaching values in the schools can yield excellent results for children and for society.

Few would argue that a solid moral foundation can empower children as they move into adolescence, providing them with the ability to resist cheating, abusing drugs and alcohol, sexual exploitation, and the multitude of other temptations that will confront them. It would be impossible for parents or educators to provide children with prescriptions for what to do and what not to do in every questionable situation that will confront them in life. However, in addition to the issues and suggestions stated in the selections that you will read in this debate, you need to realize one important fact: morality and appropriate values are not easily verbalized. This is one reason why it may be difficult to teach good values.

Children and adolescents learn most readily from observing how people around them conduct their lives. Children model behavior, and the role models in children's lives can include parents, other family members, teachers, peers, politicians, and television, sports, and movie stars. The fact is, the more a child identifies with a role model, the more apt the child is to imitate the behavior of that person. What message does the high school basketball player get when a professional basketball superstar inexcusably cuts practice or flagrantly fouls an opponent? Or what message does pop singer Madonna send when she intimates that she enjoys numerous, casual, sexual liaisons? The message becomes even more significant when it is a family member who acts in questionable ways.

It is incumbent upon society for children and adults to embrace the responsibility of acting morally, and role models should discuss moral decisions with the children in their lives. Certainly, these discussions should be offered at a developmentally appropriate level for the intended child, and they should be to the point (children tend to tune out long sermons). People sometimes fail to be clear when talking with children. While adolescents can certainly think and understand abstract concepts and analogies, younger children need more concrete examples of the values one is trying to impart.

In the selections that follow, William O'Malley and Kathleen Townsend both maintain that the level of value impartation today is cause for concern, but they disagree as to who is at fault and who could best improve the situation.

YES

William J. O'Malley

DON'T UPSET THE KIDS

A few years ago, a father came to me and said, "I'd like to talk to you about marketing my sons to colleges." Gasp! In the first place, he didn't even realize he was trying to solve his sons' first genuine adult challenge *for* them. In the second place, he didn't realize that his question tacitly admitted that his sons were inferior academic goods that needed a little belated parental razzmatazz to mesmerize—and dupe—college admission officers into accepting them.

I had taught both boys, and they hadn't bestirred their (quite modest) talents in any way, but they were "nice kids": well-mannered, sharp-looking, savvy, "popular," which apparently had been enough—up to the crunch point —for their parents. Actually, they should have been working twice as hard as their classmates, and I shouldn't have been the only one who consistently failed them. Of course, they graduated and were accepted into colleges. But they got high school diplomas without getting the education the diplomas fraudulently testified to. Their number is legion.

In *Iron John: About Men*, Robert Bly makes a strong case for the deleterious effect, on any society, neutering adolescent initiation rituals to meaningless "gestures." In "less enlightened" societies, after the onset of puberty, young people are stranded in the wilderness away from their families, starved for days, subjected to ritual scarring and terrifying midnight tableaux that, almost literally, scare them into "growing up." After such an ordeal, the youngster willingly—and most often placidly—takes his or her place in the adult-world, accepting both its privileges and its responsibilities.

Not so with us, either as a church or as a nation. In Christian churches, caring adults prepare the candidate *cognitively* for Confirmation, but amid symbols more meaningful to experts than to ordinary children. As with Christmas, most weddings and even many liturgies, the surface trappings have all but smothered any genuine conviction that something truly important is going on beneath them. There is little *affective* content to the confirmation/initiation ritual other than a bit of dress-up and fuss and presents, and very little internalized sense of a personal shift in the recipient's relationship to the community.

From William J. O'Malley, "Don't Upset the Kids," *America*, vol. 165, no. 8 (September 28, 1991). Copyright © 1991 by William J. O'Malley. Reprinted by permission.

What's more, it occurs usually before the child has any genuine understanding of what the church and he or she are mutually "confirming." (Most often, as with all religious rituals, it is not a mutual acceptance; rather, the church takes over any assertions of the will, other than submission.) Metaphors like "Now you are soldiers of Christ" might have appealed to children in a simpler age, when we felt beleaguered by all those predatory Masons, Protestants and Jews. Now, however, the metaphor seems more than slightly corny to youngsters, especially since most of the people in the parish don't appear very aggressively apostolic. Worst of all, Confirmation frequently occurs *before* puberty and certainly with no overt connection whatever with that life-shaking sexual event and (judging from the results) with no felt realization of a new, more demanding role in the community.

* * *

Outside the churches, other than the few fortunates who remain in the Scouts or young people who enter military service, there aren't even any mediocre rituals to body forth a realization, not only of a new physical status in society, but also (and in large part *because* of that physical change) of a new *moral* relationship to the self, to the family, to lovers, to those under whom they work, to the community at large. In the prosperous First World, puberty is merely an opportunity to remain a child while enjoying the advantages of an adult body.

* * *

Not that a new Confirmation ritual, rigorously revamped by poets and dramatists rather than academics, would automatically usher in the brave new world. But the near total lack of such means to internalize a new-found adulthood and its responsibilities, coupled with a more laid-back—or even absent—style of parenting and with an even more indulgent school system, have left us with a world that is to a great extent spiritless and spineless. It is a world of children in adult bodies, wherein men and women in their forties—and even later—dump spouses and families to go off to "finally find myself," a task most psychologists believe should have been at least tentatively wrapped up at the end of chronological adolescence.

The radical cause, I believe, is overly pliant parents and an embarrassingly untaxing school system, public and private.

In an article called "A Bedtime Story That's Different" (The New York Times, 4/8/91), Carol Lawson details interviews she conducted with parents who, however reluctantly, had learned to live with their teen-age children and their dates having sex upstairs while the parents watched television downstairs. (Understandably, they were even more reluctant to be identified.) The justification the parents offered were painfully mealy-mouthed: at least the young people don't have to have sex in unsafe places and with people the parents don't know; better to have sex and be honest than to lie about it; "You can't tell people not to do things they are going to do anyway." Teen-agers, the parents say, feel uncomfortable if they are fooling their parents. The bottom line seems to be that we don't want young people to be uncomfortable about anything—despite the fact that that is precisely the purpose of adolescence: to surmount the uncomfortable, to achieve a personally validated adult self by conquering unnerving challenges.

The evidence that teen-agers are avoiding those challenges—with the connivance of parents and the educational system—is both overwhelming and disheartening.

According to an Alan Guttmacher Institute survey in 1988, 53 percent of girls 15–19 had had intercourse, contrasted to 36 percent in 1973. That's a quantum leap in a mere 15 years. In that age group in 1988, 60 percent of boys had had intercourse. (All of which makes the chaste minority feel left out and nerdy, but no one seems concerned about *their* discomfort.) Proposals to distribute condoms in senior high schools not only throw in the sponge on any attempt to encourage abstinence or to treat human sexual intercourse as anything but merely a *practical* problem, but they also fortify youngsters' convictions that more efficient birth control devices have severed any link whatever between sex and commitment.

According to the National Center for Health Statistics, at least 19 million unmarried young women between 15 and 24 use birth control—which says nothing of how many young men do, and makes one wonder if (and why) the only reason is that a woman needs a doctor's prescription for birth control devices and a man doesn't. Despite that fact, however, there were in one year 828,124 unwanted births and 1,368,987 abortions, and most of them to very young women—which, in the long run, is a great deal more upsetting than being told that sex is not just another indoor sport, that it has *inescapable* human consequences.

Morality cannot be taught explicitly in public schools because of the mind-withering belief—among otherwise educated people—that to teach morality is somehow to teach religion. On the contrary, one must be moral to be a good human being; immorality is a rending of the objective web of human relationships we have with everybody and everything on this planet, whether there is a God or not. Religion adds a completely different, trans-terrestrial dimension to those relationships. But because norms for human behavior can't be taught in public schools and because parents are incapable or unwilling to do it themselves or even to discomfit their young, we are faced with a generation who are to a terrifying extent what John McLaughlin, S.J., used to call "moral morons."

But even in the religious schools and colleges where I have taught, the vast majority of students routinely say sex with one's steady or with a willing stranger is at worst a venial sin. Class after class estimate that 60–70 percent of their classmates routinely cheat on homework and exams. The majority consistently (and unblushingly) say they do not give their parents an honest day's work for an honest day's pay. There seems to be no guilt about that. Guilt, in fact, is something too upsetting to be allowed. Ditto, responsibility. Ditto, gratitude. One begins to long for an aboriginal Australian subincision ritual.

Moral behavior is not the only area in which one can discern that we dare not upset the kids. According to a 1990 survey conducted by the Institute for Social Research at the University of Michigan, U.S. senior high school students spend 30 hours weekly on school work (26.2 hours in class, 3.8 hours a week at homework) whereas Japanese senior high school students spend 60.4 hours (41.5 hours in class, 19 hours a week at homework). U.S. students spend 1.6 hours a week reading, while Japanese students spend 3.3 hours a week, and yet Japanese students watch three hours more television a week. One major difference is that Japanese students spend less than one hour a week at sports, contrasted to the U.S. seven hours, and the Japanese sleep seven hours less a week than American senior high students. The cult of the body may be more subtly in control of our values than we suspected.

* * *

Out of 13 countries, U.S. students rank 13th in biology, 11th in chemistry, ninth in physics; in all three subjects, only Italy is lower in scientific performance than the United States and Canada. One would have a far greater chance of a strong scientific education in Hungary. There seems to be a difference in national priorities, not to mention a difference in attitudes about who calls the shots in the requirements for a young person's *gradual* growth as an adult.

According to the National Assessment of Educational Progress, only 44 percent of high school *graduates* could read at the 11th-grade level. They had difficulty in finding solutions for everyday problems: Four out of five had difficulty deciphering a bus schedule; two out of three could not follow map directions; three out of four could not understand a long newspaper feature. Nearly one-third of our citizens are functionally illiterate. They can decipher street signs, but they cannot read a recipe or the helpful guidelines the government publishes for making the most out of a meager food budget. They cannot even make and adhere to a budget because they cannot add numbers.

In 1987, 26.9 percent of America's high school students dropped out. In the District of Columbia, the figure was 40.5 percent; in New York, 33.3; in California, 31.5. The effects on the job market, welfare and street crime are both obvious and incalculable. Average SAT scores across the nation out of a possible 800/800 in 1967 were: Verbal—466, Math—492; 20 years later in 1988, they were: Verbal—428; Math—476. One must remember that a candidate gets 200 simply for signing his or her name. Our schools are not improving. The *average* high school senior in the U.S., with a combined score of 904, is not likely to run for public office or win a Nobel Peace Prize or even vote, and roughly half of our students are *below* average. The only way to raise at least verbal scores is by reading books, beginning in kindergarten if not before, not by memorizing lists of words or taking a crash course, which is the academic equivalent of steroids. But kids don't *want* to read books; they'd rather watch a film. So give them a film.

Our purpose as parents and teachers *is* to upset the kids. As Dr. Lawrence Aber, an associate professor of psychology at Barnard College, says: "Parents need to set limits, and it is the children's job to push them. But when parents don't set limits, it can be scary and disruptive for children." Every parent and teacher knows what an abrasive hassle it is to face down kids with their chins set, snarling over not getting their own way. But if we don't want that job, we should have remained childless or become hermits. To allow students to graduate without facing the inescapable *fact* of failure—or at least less than satisfying success—is to send them out into a minefield with no other skills than the ability to play volleyball. Too many young people have a false sense of security that leads them to believe that, at least until age 22, life is going to be pretty much spring break. Or it ought to be, and anybody who tries to disrupt that is a mean-spirited Puritan.

Most parents I know believe their job is to *reassure* their young: to shield them from harm and to provide "the best" they can for them. But to shield them from harm is to shield them from risk, from loss, from the galvanizing and soul-searing experience of surmounting suffering. If the only major setback a boy has is failure to move an inflated pig bladder through eleven other boys on a field with white stripes, if the only major challenge a girl faces is being cut from the musical, our socializing mechanisms —parents and school—not only do no long-range service to our young, but we hamstring them with a perniciously false sense of security.

If a game is worth playing, it is worth losing—and that is true both of the interpersonal family game and of the academic game as well. As Francis T. (Fay) Vincent Jr. said recently in these pages, "We learn that failure often teaches us more than success. We never forget that test or paper we failed and why. A perfect grade or paper gets forgotten much more quickly. Failure is searing... it burns. Success is a liquid... it evaporates." The operative two words in that wise statement are: "and *why*" ("Education and Baseball," 4/6/91).

But children *can't* fail if their overly protective parents continue to make their decisions for them, type out the envelopes for their college applications, yield to their whims (sexual and otherwise) lest the kids be upset—or worse, dislike the parents. Our children *can't* fail —and learn by failing—if kindly (and overworked) teachers let the 10-minute swamp-gas essay slide by, if a child has gotten to senior year without the verbal and mathematical skills that Hun-garian children take for granted, if they *know* they can get a diploma while finessing an education. How can we hold the self-deceptive hope that our children will have spine when we refuse to display it ourselves?

* * *

Any truly caring parent should find out, with as close to conviction as possible, just what the child's capabilities are. If the counseling department offers a picture more bleak than the parent is willing to accept, there are agencies more than willing to test the child out for a fee. But after two or three reliable opinions, the parent—and the child—have to accept serenely that this is not the child of one's dreams but the child of one's love, then work with what they have. Settle for what the child is capable of *now*—but absolutely no *less* than that. And demand performance on that level, not only of the child, but of the *teachers* as well—to say nothing of the administration, which is, especially in schools depending on financial support, loath to upset parents and, *ipso facto*, to upset kids.

A youngster needs time to unwind, but many of the young I've taught in the last 30 years find it essential to keep taking breaks—to play handball, to shoot the breeze, to play the guitar, to watch television, to talk on the phone, to go to the movies—and many of their breaks are breaks from their breaks. And when I say that, they almost inevitably grin, with a "knowing" though tolerable guilt. Get a job.

If our knowledge of young people over the past 3,000 years has not become somehow obsolete overnight, there is no youngster who is lazy—just unmotivated. There has to be a *reason*— apprehended as valid *by* the adolescent

—to do this "stuff." And yet many parents and teachers are incapable of demonstrating why any sane person would submit to ingesting this "stuff." The data one may not remember, but the difference is what working on ever more complex data does to the thinking machine.

For a high school senior, five or six years down the road is a nearly limitless (and subsidized) length of time. As a result, many of the college students I deal with evenings in the dorm still can't believe, in March of their senior year, that Oz time is over; even at that late date, they do not know what they want to do with their lives. Unless students begin to internalize, at least as early as junior high, that welfare is going to come to an end in a few years, we will continue to have a nation of children in grown-up bodies. Let them begin to pay their own tuition, to put money in the bank —not for college spending money, but for tuition. Let them begin to contribute to family vacations—not just for their own pleasures, or the family's. "If we go to Florida, you'll have to contribute 200 bucks." After puberty, they are— objective fact—no longer babies.

Most high school students are subsidized to the tune of at least $15,000: tuition, food, heat, insurance, clothes, car. At that cost, taking an honest day's pay without giving an honest day's work is *grand* larceny. Yet many parents blithely collude in their own children's larcenous habits.

* * *

Psychiatrist Erik Erikson shows that life is a natural series of upsets, stages of disequilibrium that have a *purpose:* to crack open the individual's comfortable security and lead him or her out into a wider, richer humanity. Birth itself is an upset: forced from the warm serenity of the womb out into the cold and noise, and the first present is a whack on the rear end. But without that pain, the child would die. A child resents the upset of weaning and potty training, but without them the child remains a mewlying baby for a lifetime. A child resents being hauled from the television and shoved outside to play with the other children, but without that the child is impoverished. There is no bigger upset in a small child's life than being stranded at the kindergarten door by a woman who has suddenly changed from Fairy Godmother into Wicked Stepmother, but without that upset the child would lack the skills he or she needs to survive as a breadwinner working with other people. And none of us would want to face the upset of adolescence again. But its natural purpose is to force a child to cope with life as an adult, to achieve and understand a personally validated identity, which—as anyone blessed with the upset of therapy knows—is a painful process many choose to avoid.

It is much more comfy in the womb, being pampered by Mommy and Daddy, sprawled in front of the television, dumping school, living off the family. But comfy is the Freudian death wish, like giving candy to a diabetic or booze to an alcoholic because they whine and pout for them. With painful irony, our very attempts to shield our young and give them the best is depriving them of precisely what their puberty invites them to.

NO   Kathleen Kennedy Townsend

WHY JOHNNY CAN'T TELL RIGHT FROM WRONG

"What would you like to be when you graduate?" asked a grade school teacher of her students in a Baltimore County classroom I visited recently. A young man raised his hand: "A pimp. You can make good money." The teacher then turned to a female student and asked, "Would you work for him?" "I guess so," the young woman replied lethargically.

In my five years in the Maryland Department of Education, I've heard hundreds of similar stories—rueful teachers' lounge chronicles of abject moral collapse by children barely old enough to make grilled cheese sandwiches by themselves. But these days you don't need to work in education to hear such mind-numbing tales. Turn on the TV news and there you have it: Our schools are hotbeds of violence, vandalism, and unethical behavior. Recently we've heard of a student-run LSD ring in one Virginia school and the bartering of stolen college entrance exams in one of New York City's most selective high schools. Sixty-one percent of high school students say they cheated on an exam during the past year. Nationwide, assaults on teachers are up 700 percent since 1978. Each month 282,000 students are attacked. And for the first time ever, the risk of violence to teenagers is greater in school than on the streets.

Obviously, we've got a problem here—a problem not just of violence, but of values. Plain and simple, many of our kids don't seem to have any, or at least any of a socially constructive kind. But what to do about 12-year-old aspiring pimps and cheaters? You might think the solution lies with that "family values" constituency, the Republicans. Yet a year of podium-thumping in favor of "values" by the Bush administration was not backed by a single concrete plan of action. In his four years as president, George Bush offered nothing more substantial than a PR stunt—his Thousand Points of Light Foundation. Still, at least the Republicans have been willing to *talk* about values. For all of Bill Clinton's 12-point plans, he has yet to come up with a specific agenda for restoring values.

To explain away that omission, Democrats argue that the ultimate responsibility for inspiring values lies not with the government, but with the family.

From Kathleen Kennedy Townsend, "Why Johnny Can't Tell Right from Wrong," *The Washington Monthly*, vol. 24, no. 12 (December 1992). Copyright © 1992 by The Washington Monthly Company, 1611 Connecticut Avenue, NW, Washington, DC, 20009, (202) 462-0128. Reprinted by permission of *The Washington Monthly*.

A day in one of the nation's public schools might well convince the average citizen that those Democrats need a reality check. Face it: In some homes, parents simply aren't paragons of civic or ethical virtue. If we rely on the family alone to instill values, we will fail. As one 21-year-old ex-con said, "Kids grow up with a father or an uncle who is robbing stores. They figure, 'If my father can do it, so can I.'" In other homes, parents simply aren't around. In a series of recent workshops sponsored by the Maryland state government, high school students suggested a number of solutions they thought would help them better withstand the antisocial pressures that buffet them. While much of what they said was expected—more information about drugs, greater student participation in school and county decisions—one was a real eye-opener: They asked that their parents have dinner with them more often.

Ultimately, the goal should be to help parents raise kind and law-abiding children. But how do we get there? Why not turn to the one institution that sees the problem more closely than any, and that touches children on a regular and sustained basis: the public school. Why not teach values in school?

Before you dismiss this suggestion as a William Bennettesque ploy to end calls for more school resources, additional jobs programs, or parental-leave legislation—all worthy goals—hear me out. Teaching values does *not* mean using the classroom to push a particular point of view on any political issue—say, abortion or the death penalty—that has worked its way to the core of the values debate. We're not even talking about school prayer or requiring the Pledge of Allegiance. It's much simpler than that: Teaching values means quietly helping

kids to learn honesty, responsibility, respect for others, the importance of serving one's community and nation—ideals which have sufficiently universal appeal to serve as the founding and guiding principles of this country. In the schools, values education means lessons about friendship and anger, stealing and responsibility, simply being polite, respecting others, serving the needs of those who may be less fortunate—all lessons sadly absent from today's curriculum.

Teaching these sorts of values does more than yield heart-warming anecdotes of students helping old ladies across the street. It brings results—tangible improvement to the lives of children and their families. A survey of 176 schools that have adopted a values curriculum found that 77 percent reported a decrease in discipline problems, 68 percent boasted an increase in attendance, and 64 percent showed a decrease in vandalism. Three years after the Jackie Robinson Middle School in New Haven, Connecticut, initiated a values curriculum, the number of student pregnancies went from 16 to zero. After the Merwin Elementary School in Irwindale, California, instituted a character education program, damage due to vandalism was reduced from $25,000 to $500; disciplinary action decreased by 80 percent; and—could it be?—academic test scores went up.

Teaching values is clearly worth the trouble. So why is "values education" still one of education's neglected stepchildren? Why is it that schools that now teach values are rare—most often independent efforts by one or two inspired educators? Because, despite the family values chitchat, there's been no political or popular consensus that values should be as much a part of the curriculum as reading and writing. We need a more organized approach. If we are ready to instill a sense of values in America's youth, it will take a concerted effort by both political leaders and educators to make it happen.

SELECTIVE SERVICE

So where to begin? How about with a notion relegated to the back burner in the get-it-while-you-can eighties: community service. Serving others is held in such low regard among our youth that 60 percent of high school students said in a recent survey they simply would not be willing to "volunteer to serve their community for a year." That's a remarkable figure not only because so many aren't willing to serve, but because so many of those who responded negatively have never served to begin with. The students' distaste for service could largely be a distaste for the unknown. But when students are exposed to this unknown—through activities such as tutoring, visiting the elderly, rehabilitating homeless shelters, lobbying for new laws—their reaction is appreciably different.

Alethea Kalandros, as a ninth-grade student in Baltimore County, missed more than 70 days of school and was tempted to drop out. The next year she missed two days of school. What happened? She enrolled in a program that allows her to volunteer at the Maryland School for the Blind. "It gives me a reason to come to school," she says. Alethea is part of Maryland's pioneering effort in promoting community service. While the program is now voluntarily offered by only a couple of schools, Maryland, after years of heated debate, recently became the first state to require all high school students to perform community service in order to graduate. Starting next year, all students entering the ninth grade must complete 75 hours of service or classes which incorporate service into the lesson, such as stream testing in an environmental course or writing about visits to the elderly in an English class. As part of the program, students are required to "prepare and reflect." This means, for instance, complementing working in a soup kitchen with learning about the most common cause of homelessness.

Any of a wide variety of activities fulfill the requirement, from repairing a local playground to tutoring fellow students. The impact, however, goes beyond helping the needy. Community service, as the limited experience in schools has shown, teaches students values and citizenship. For instance, while fourth, fifth, and sixth graders at Jackson Elementary School in Salt Lake City, Utah, were studying ground water pollution, they discovered that barrels of toxic waste were buried just four blocks from their school. They waged a vigorous public relations and fundraising campaign to clean up the site, eventually winning the support of the city's mayor. When this effort was stymied—Utah state law does not allow for private donations to clean up such sites—they lobbied the legislature and changed the statute. And while service programs can help students make a difference outside the school, they also have an impact inside the classroom: They make learning more interesting by simply helping students to understand how to apply textbook lessons in the real world.

Despite successes in experimental programs, stubborn resistance to community service from educators is still the norm, even in Maryland where the Superintendents Association, the PTA, and the local boards of education all fought against the new service requirement. One of the most common knee-jerk reactions is cost. But ask educators in Atlanta, Georgia, who have been operating a regional service program for eight years, and they'll tell you it doesn't cost a dime. Of course, that doesn't mean all service programs can be run as efficiently, but it does show that costs can be kept low.

Beyond that, the arguments against service become more strained. The president of the Maryland Teachers Association, for example, called the proposal "enforced servitude" and claimed that it violated the Thirteenth Amendment. What's really bothering the educators? Probably the fact that they would be required to change their teaching methods. As Pat McCarthy, vice-president of the Thomas Jefferson Center, a non-profit foundation specializing in values education, says, "The biggest impediment to values education is teacher education." You can't teach community service out of a textbook; it takes time and thought, which, of course, takes effort. And that, for some educators, is a tough concept to accept.

While community service teaches values through hands-on experience, that's but one piece of the puzzle. If we want to instill values, why not take an even more straightforward approach: Teach them directly. It may sound radical, especially when we are talking about methods like memorizing passages from the Bible, "bribing" kids with discounts at the school store to behave decently, permitting students in class discussions to describe problems they face at home, and allowing teachers to make it clear that they might not approve of some parents' values. But while students are

sometimes taught that what happens at home is not always a good thing, teaching values does not mean separating the parents from the lessons. Quite the contrary, a smart values program includes parents, too. Before a values program at Gauger's Junior High in Newmark, Delaware, was implemented, 100 people —parents, teachers, students and community representatives—attended a two-day conference in which they learned about the purpose and goals of the program and the ways they could help implement it. Parents provided input and teachers knew they had community support. And in the end, nobody had to worry that little Petey would bounce home from values class clutching the collected works of Lyndon LaRouche.

Is it really possible to teach values that we all agree upon? Of course. In fact, schools in an indirect way already present students with a set of values that is universally respected: What are our efforts to integrate our schools and prohibitions against stealing or drinking in school if not an education in values? It's not difficult to take this type of thinking one step further, creating a curriculum that teaches other values that are universally accepted but are almost never actually taught directly to our youth. In districts such as Sweet Home, New York, and in Howard and Baltimore counties, Maryland, superintendents formed representative groups of community leaders that included people as ideologically diverse as fundamentalist ministers and ACLU attorneys. They held public forums and listened to community opinion and after months of extensive discussion, the groups produced a list of values with which everyone was comfortable. Now, when people in these communities ask,

"Whose values?" they can proudly say "Ours."

At places like Hebbville Elementary in a low-income section of Baltimore County, the results are impressive. There, teachers hold out the promise of tutoring the mentally retarded as a reward for children who have finished their assignments, done well on a test, shown improvement, or been helpful in class. The students actually vie for the privilege. Tiesha was picked to help out in a class of 15 seven- and eight-year-olds whose IQs are in the 30–45 range. "I like being a helper," she says. "I tried to teach my cousin that 100 percent and 100 percent equal 200 percent. When I saw her write two, I was so happy."

At the Waverly Elementary school in Baltimore City, values lessons are taught through discussions about peer pressure. The teacher chooses 15 students, divides them into four groups, and asks them to perform skits about peer pressure. One skit involves Daniel, whose three hip classmates mock him because he wears non-brand-name tennis shoes. Daniel persuades his parents to buy Nikes and when he returns to school, the gang accepts him. In reflecting upon the skit, Daniel says, "All the friends were making the decision rather than me making my own decision." Another student said, "Daniel could have decided to be different." It is significant that the students made up this fact pattern. In the kids-and-sneakers stories you usually hear, children are assaulting each other for Air Jordans. Here, they are girding themselves to accept an alternative.

That's well and good, but we're still missing one crucial element: accountability. For values education to succeed and prosper, schools need to show that it's paying off in tangible ways. That means, for instance, keeping track of indicators such as rates of crime and vandalism in schools or the number of students involved in community service where values are being taught.

CLASS WAR

Many may resent this call for values as a way for parents to shirk their own responsibility onto someone else, or may see it as another passing fad. As for parents, they may cling to concerns about which values their children should learn. But our collective trepidations pale next to the alternative: another generation of children growing up without a moral compass.

Changing will take courage, but we can take heart from one fifth-grade class I watched where the topic was "the right to be an individual." The purpose was to help the children decide when their own actions are inappropriate and to develop strategies for improving their classmates' behavior. The discussion began with a very simple story about a boy named Bobby who never washed himself and had no friends. Eventually he realized that he'd have to take a bath if he wanted his classmates to ask him to play. The immediate lesson was about cleanliness —about as innocuous a value as you can find. But the moral had pertinence even for frequent bathers: Sometimes change is not only good, but necessary. That's a lesson that should resonate, not just with fifth-graders, but with the next administration. Clearly, the old ways of inculcating values in our kids are no longer working. We grownups have got to change our thinking, too.

POSTSCRIPT

Should Parents Be Doing More to Impart Values to Children?

According to a 1992 article in *Education Week*, there seems to be a movement to include values education in school curricula across the country. Educators are promoting efforts to develop good character in young people. A network called the Character Education Partnership has been formed by leaders from education, business, religion, and youth groups across the country.

The issue of values or character education was a central mission of most school districts through the 1960s. It had little attention in the ensuing 30 years. Now, in the 1990s, it is enjoying a renewed prominence among school policymakers.

Educational institutions in our society have distanced themselves from teaching values in their curricula for fear of being controversial and because they are vulnerable to litigation from any of a number of oppositional groups. Also, many teachers educated in the 1960s and 1970s were taught not to impose their values on students. This renewed interest in teaching values in the schools is a direct result of some of the youth-related problems that currently plague society at large. Consider, for example, that among leading industrial nations, the United States has the highest murder rate for 15–24-year-olds; in excess of 1 million adolescent girls become pregnant each year; 76 percent of college freshmen admit to having cheated in high school; and 25 percent of college women have been victims of rape or attempted rape by dates or acquaintances (Viadero, 1992). These types of statistics lend a sense of urgency to the feeling many people have that things must change, and perhaps the time is ripe for a frank, constructive discussion of values and morality and the role parents play in developing these in their children.

SUGGESTED READINGS

Buchholz, T. G. (1992, April 15). Teaching virtue. *Vital Speeches of the Day, 58,* 396–397.

Edelman, M. W. (1992, April). The challenges of the 90s: Saving our children, *Social Education, 56,* 240–243.

Roberts, Y. (1993, December 3). Teaching children to be bad. *New Statesman & Society, 6,* 14–15.

Ryan, K. (1993, November). Mining the values in the curriculum. *Educational Leadership, 51,* 16–18.

Sommers, C. H. (1993, December 13). How to teach right and wrong. *Christianity Today, 37,* 33–37

ISSUE 15

Is an Adolescent's Sexual Orientation Important in Understanding Causes for Youth Suicide?

YES: Scott A. Hunt, from "An Unspoken Tragedy: Suicide Among Gay and Lesbian Youth," *Christopher Street* (January 6, 1992)

NO: Douglas Foster, from "The Disease Is Adolescence," *Rolling Stone* (December 9, 1993)

ISSUE SUMMARY

YES: Scott A. Hunt, a writer with a special interest in social problems and transpersonal psychology, suggests that gay and lesbian youths suicide rates have reached epidemic proportions. He reports that current research has failed to adequately examine the issue of suicide among homosexual youths and offers reasons as to why it is important to undertake more research in this area.

NO: Douglas Foster, a former editor of *Mother Jones* magazine, reports that the combination of alcohol and firearms accounts for the vast majority of adolescent deaths. He contends that sexual orientation is but one variable in the risk factor equation that contributes to the youth suicide rate.

Adolescence is a time when a child is confronted with many developmental tasks. Perhaps the two most important are establishing an individual identity that is similar to one's family of origin, yet unique, and developing the ability to engage in meaningful intimate relationships outside of one's family of origin. For most adolescents, embracing these tasks is difficult and challenging. However, the vast majority successfully meet the challenge and effectively move through this stage of development. There are some adolescents who, for various reasons, find this time in their lives especially turbulent, stressful, and depressing. It is within this group that suicide is usually found.

As one reads literature on suicide, there are several typical predictors of adolescent suicide. Most experts in the field would agree that depression, poor relations with one's primary support group (typically one's family), substance abuse (drugs and alcohol), failure in school, and even the loss of something very important to the person—one's health, a close friend, a dating partner or parent, one's home, or even money—are factors predisposing an adolescent toward suicide. Absent from this list of predictors is an adolescent's sexual preference, specifically being gay or lesbian.

In 1974 the American Psychiatric Association concluded that if individuals are not dissatisfied with their homosexuality and if this sexual preference does not typically impair social functioning, then it should not be considered a disorder. Despite this conclusion, many in our society continue to believe that the homosexual lifestyle is immoral, perverted, and unnatural. There is a particularly hostile attitude among heterosexual adolescent males toward gays. There seems to be a convoluted notion among many adolescent males that contemptuous behavior toward gay men affirms their masculinity. Some people believe that the effects of these social attitudes on children who may be predisposed to homosexuality (particularly males) as they move into adolescence and encounter issues related to sexual identity can be deadly.

In the following two selections, both authors agree that adolescent suicide is an increasing problem in our society in general and among adolescents in particular. Scott Hunt states that being gay or lesbian puts teens at an additional and significantly greater risk of suicide than heterosexual teens. This is because in addition to the typical developmental tasks that are encountered by all teens, gay and lesbian teens must also endure the burden of both accepting and disguising their sexual orientation from a hostile society. However, as compared to the research and discussion on adolescent suicide in general, suicide in the gay and lesbian adolescent population is an area about which very little is known. Hunt concludes that these issues are serious and worthy of empirical investigation.

Douglas Foster believes that suicide is largely precipitated by the lack of positive role modeling by caring and consistent adults. This, he suggests, can enhance the feelings of alienation that many adolescents experience and consequently decrease the sense of hope that is so vital to successfully moving through this stage of development. Moreover, young people today are the least likely age group to get the medical services needed to maintain a healthy lifestyle. The adolescent population does not always get the guidance they need to help them make responsible choices in their intimate relationships with peers. The resultant problems can become so insurmountable that the only solution for some seems to be escape through suicide.

As you read the following selections, consider for yourself the issues facing today's youth. Do you think that gay and lesbian youths are at greater risk of committing suicide than heterosexual youths? Or do you believe that the increase of teen suicide involves so many factors that sexual orientation is of minor concern as compared to all the other variables?

YES

Scott A. Hunt

AN UNSPOKEN TRAGEDY: SUICIDE AMONG GAY AND LESBIAN YOUTH

Government officials, scientists, writers, commentators, and activists have been criminally silent on the issue of suicide among gay and lesbian youth. Despite the fact that the problem has reached epidemic proportions, a comprehensive review of hundreds of the most well-known national magazines in the United States reveals not a single article on adolescent homosexual suicide. Additionally, some of the best researched and best written books and studies on adolescent suicide fail even to mention the issue of sexuality.

The lack of scientific information on this issue is particularly troublesome in a country that tends to ignore social problems until they are researched and quantified. Unfortunately, in a society of varied interests and limited resources, statistics have become a way of determining which problems will be addressed. This is precisely why it is so important to facilitate further research on suicide among gay and lesbian youth. Only by presenting statistically meaningful evidence is there a chance of attracting attention to this unspoken tragedy.

EXTENT OF THE PROBLEM

Recently, the Centers for Disease Control (CDC), which is part of the Department of Health and Human Services (DHHS), released a report in its journal *Morbidity and Mortality Weekly Report*, identifying the overall problem of suicide among adolescents. The report, entitled "Attempted Suicide Among High School Students," noted that suicide rates for adolescents 15 to 19 years of age have quadrupled from 2.7 per 100,000 in 1950 to 11.3 in 1988. As part of the CDC's Youth Risk Behavior Surveillance System and its associated Youth Risk Behavior Survey, the CDC surveyed 11,631 students in grades 9 through 12 in all 50 states, the District of Columbia, Puerto Rico, and the Virgin Islands. Students were asked whether they had seriously thought about attempting suicide in the year preceding the survey, whether they had made a specific plan about how they would attempt suicide, how many times

From Scott A. Hunt, "An Unspoken Tragedy: Suicide Among Gay and Lesbian Youth," *Christopher Street*, vol. 14, no. 3 (January 6, 1992). Copyright © 1992 by Scott A. Hunt. Reprinted by permission.

they had actually made a suicide attempt, and whether their suicide attempts resulted in an injury or poisoning that necessitated medical treatment.

The survey found that 27.3 percent of all students in grades 9–12 reported that they had thought seriously about attempting suicide. Over 16 percent of the students stated that they had made a specific plan to attempt suicide, and about half(8.3 percent) of those who did make a plan actually attempted suicide. Medical treatment was necessary in two percent of those who reported that they had made a suicide attempt. Translating these percentages into real numbers, the data indicate that about 276,000 high school students in the United States made at least one suicide attempt requiring medical attention during the 12 months preceding the survey. Although these numbers on self-reported suicide attempts are shocking, it is even more shocking that the report is absolutely silent on the issue of sexuality. Despite the fact that the CDC researched issues of gender and race, the CDC did not utilize its Youth Risk Behavior Survey to try to identify and quantify attempted suicides by youths who had difficulties with their sexual orientation. In so doing, the CDC sent a tacit message that sexuality is unimportant in understanding the causes of suicide among youth.

The omission of sexuality from the recent CDC report was a conscious decision designed to avert criticism from conservatives who espouse so-called traditional family values. Prior to this report, the federal government had addressed the issue of suicide among gay and lesbian youth. In the "Report of the Secretary's Task Force on Youth Suicide" released by the DHHS in 1989, the government reported that gay and lesbian youth are two to three times more likely to commit suicide than heterosexual youth. Consequently, the members of the task force called for an "end [to] discrimination against youths on the basis of such characteristics as disability, sexual orientation, and financial status." The task force further declared that "religions need to reassess homosexuality in a positive context within their belief system." The members of the task force were trying to initiate positive steps to reduce suicide attempts among gay and lesbian youth. But HHS Secretary Louis Sullivan, under pressure from conservative religious and family groups (in the persons of Reverend Lou Sheldon and California State Representative William Dannemeyer), repudiated the report, precluding further government research on the issue of sexuality and youth suicide.

Fear of criticism as well as a large dose of institutional homophobia within the federal government has prevented the nation's top health organization from addressing this epidemic. Fortunately, a few sources outside of the government have picked up where the DHHS has left off. In a study last June reported in *Pediatrics*, researchers from the University of Minnesota and the University of Washington found that 30 percent of homosexual and bisexual male youths aged 14 to 21 attempted suicide. Half of these youths attempted suicide more than once. Over 20 percent of those who attempted suicide were treated medically or with psychiatric care. This study, although using a relatively small sample size, demonstrated that the attempted suicide rate among homosexual males is two or three times higher than the rate among heterosexual males in the same age group.

It is important to note that the statistics on suicides, and particularly on adolescent homosexual suicides, almost certainly understate the problem. As in other cases of unnatural death, suicides are subject to police investigation and a host of various forms of subsequent action ordered by investigators. A determination at any time during an investigation that a death was accidental alters the process of gathering evidence, making it increasingly unlikely that a finding of suicide will be made.

The discretion of the coroner is of paramount importance in the investigation. Yet there is no single list of criteria for a coroner to make a finding of suicide. Some coroners are reluctant to declare that a death is the result of suicide unless the victim leaves a note clearly stating his or her intent. In one case, a coroner declared that a person who shot himself through the head must have been cleaning the barrel of the gun with his tongue. Although this case is an extreme example, it does illustrate the enormous amount of discretion afforded to the coroner in determining whether a death is the result of accident or suicide. But even if a death is ruled a suicide, coroners' reports hardly ever provide data on sexuality, ensuring that the data we do have is erroneously low.

Suicide statistics also understate the problem because evidence of suicide is often suppressed by family and friends of the victim who fear the dual stigmas of suicide and homosexuality. As a result, no one will ever know how many so-called accidental deaths caused by poisoning, falling from high places, drowning, car crashes and the like are actually suicides carried out by gays and lesbians. Because of these difficulties in quantification, several studies have estimated that the overall number of suicides may be understated by one-fourth to one-third.

BREAKING THE SILENCE

The reluctance to talk about the topic of suicide in our society has one sure effect: It perpetuates the problem, and tens of thousands of people die each year as a result. Suicide has touched the lives of literally millions of people in the United States, yet for various personal, moral, and legal reasons, the subject remains taboo.

Before the early 1960s, the United States did not have a single community-based suicide prevention program. Through the courage, vision, and hard work of a gay Episcopal priest from Great Britain, San Francisco opened the first community suicide prevention agency in the United States in 1962. Since that time, suicide prevention centers have opened throughout the country. The veil of silence around the topic of suicide, however, has lifted very little. "We recoil from the word," says Eve Meyer, Executive Director of San Francisco Suicide Prevention. "We recoil from the thought. And we recoil from the responsibility."

One of the reasons that people recoil from responsibility is that they attempt to avoid unpleasant situations. According to Meyer, "People who are suicidal are often depressed, and depression has a magic quality that makes people invisible to their friends." People are often unsure of what to say to someone who is depressed. They find it uncomfortable to talk about issues involving pain, grief, and death. And many people fear that talking about suicide introduces the idea into an already volatile situation, making them responsible should someone actually commit suicide.

There is another less apparent reason that society fails to deal with the issue of sexuality and suicide. The problem touches on a collective guilt that society seems unwilling to bear. If the words and actions of our leaders and institutions contribute to the deaths of tens of thousands of people each year, then there must be something wrong with the message being sent to gay and lesbian youth. But society as a whole is not willing to accept the blame for the deaths of our young people. And so the message to gay and lesbian youth continues to be that they are sinful, shameful, and inferior.

Many people believe that suicide is a hopeless problem. If that were true, then there would be no reason to address this issue at all. But experts point out that suicide is often preventable. Paul Gibson, a clinical social worker who was involved in the 1989 DHHS report, notes, "While the problems faced by lesbian, gay, and bisexual youth may seem overwhelming, they are also one of the easiest groups of young people to help. Once they gain a positive understanding of their sexual orientation, acceptance from others, and support in dealing with the conflicts they face from others, many of their problems are greatly diminished. Most importantly, this includes suicidal feelings and behavior once they recognize they have a life that is worth living." Eve Meyer agrees. "I believe we can prevent most, but not all suicides," she says. The important thing according to Meyer, is to break the silence on the issue of suicide: "We should all become very comfortable with the word so that we can turn to our friend and say, 'Are you thinking about suicide?' And our friend can say, 'Yes.' And we can say, 'Let's talk about it.'" It is clear that unless we do become comfortable talking about it, gay and lesbian youths will continue to die by their own hands.

TOWARD A SOLUTION

Although there are no clear cut solutions to the problem of adolescent homosexual suicide, gay and lesbian youth could benefit immediately from youth suicide hotlines, shelters, crisis centers, and anti-slur policies in the schools. But perhaps the most effective solution is to initiate programs in the public schools designed to provide gay and lesbian youth with comfort and guidance. One such program has proven very effective in high schools within the Los Angeles School District. In 1984, Virginia Uribe, a teacher at Fairfax High School in Los Angeles, responded to the total lack of services for gay and lesbian youth by establishing an informal lunchtime discussion group for gay and lesbian teens. To Uribe's surprise, the number of students coming to the group grew to 25 in a short period of time. The response of the students confirmed Uribe's suspicion that there was a serious need that had not been addressed. "They represented all of the things that I had read were the result of being stigmatized in the school system," Uribe says. "Many of them were very, very intelligent kids. They had been individually tested for one reason or another, but most were not performing at a level that you would expect. They had a history of family difficulties in connection with their sexual orientation. A lot of them had run away. They had a history of harassment, many of them."

Uribe decided to increase the size of the group to address the needs of other students in the district. She eventually formalized a program called Project 10, using the group at Fairfax as a pilot. School District officials admitted that a need for specialized gay and lesbian services existed. Uribe was granted three class periods a day to devote to the project, making Project 10 the first of its kind in the nation to receive school district approval.

Project 10 was designed to meet the needs of students dealing with issues of sexual orientation and to educate counselors and other students about gay and lesbian issues. Project 10 not only coordinates training and education sessions, but also produces educational material which it sends around the country. Funding for the program comes exclusively from a private organization called Friends of Project 10. Currently, Project 10 has discussion groups in 20 of L.A.'s 50 high schools and maintains a contact person in each of the high schools.

Uribe concedes that it is difficult to measure the success of the program, but adds, "We know that there's such a desperate need for affirmation [and] if we're giving that affirmation, we know we have to be doing some good." Over the years, many of Project 10's participants have declared that the program was instrumental in helping them through difficult times. Uribe is justifiably angry that there are so few school districts that have followed the lead of Los Angeles. She would ultimately like to see the implementation of the 1988 National Educators Association resolution calling for every school district to provide counseling for students who are struggling with their sexual orientation. "I think that a program of affirmation for gay and lesbian people would certainly do something toward helping our youth," Uribe says. "I mean, I know that means a change of attitudes, but I think we have to begin to base our policies on good science and social justice instead of some old, Bible concept of homosexuality. I suppose that if enough is said and enough people are educated

that maybe a general change in attitudes about homosexuality could happen. And that could only help young people. You know, if they didn't think they were horrible, sick perverts, maybe they wouldn't try to kill themselves."

Despite the low number of school districts that provide services specifically designed to meet the needs of gay and lesbian youth, and the rejection of such programs in places like Long Beach, Virginia Uribe has been the catalyst for the creation of other programs outside of Los Angeles. For example, just over a year ago the San Francisco School District began what Uribe calls a "real program" to help gay and lesbian youth. The program is "real" because the School Board has allocated funds received from Drug Free America and the Center for Disease Control to the program, and employs a full-time coordinator in the district. The program is called Support Services for Gay and Lesbian Youth (SSGLY). The current Director of SSGLY, Kevin Gogin, points out that gay and lesbian youth often experience confusion, isolation, and fear. "Discovery of their feelings," Gogin states, "might cause them to be the victims of verbal or physical violence; they may be shunned by former friends. Worse still, these young people may also be ostracized from their families—told they are unwanted and unloved." SSGLY, like Project 10, is designed to respond to the needs of gay and lesbian youth in a number of ways. First, the program offers confidential sessions with students and families concerning issues of sexuality. Second, it attempts to foster a safe and nurturing atmosphere within the schools by providing training to faculty and counseling departments, and by making presentations to students on the topic of homosexuality. The point is to eliminate the isolation and pain felt by gay and lesbian youth that may lead to self-destructive behavior, and ultimately to suicide.

CONCLUSION

Programs in the public schools offer a key element in eliminating suicide among gay and lesbian youth: hope. Hope is essential if we are to prevent suicides. Individuals need hope that their current condition is temporary and will change for the better. They need hope that they will be accepted and loved as individuals, or at the very least that they won't be attacked, denounced, and devalued.

In other words, they need hope that society will stop punishing them with the full force of its opinions, customs, and laws that condemn them for being who they are.

As a society, we should be ashamed at our lack of attention to this epidemic. We will not make the problem disappear by ignoring it. The truth is that some of our children are gay and lesbian. That is a plain fact. It is also a plain fact that at this very moment thousands of gay and lesbian youth all over the United States are calling out for help in the face of bigotry, ignorance, and hatred. How we decide to answer them will literally make the difference between life and death.

NO

Douglas Foster

THE DISEASE IS ADOLESCENCE

"This ankle is most assuredly broken," Dr. Barbara Staggers says, sounding almost gleeful.

Staggers is tall, 39 years old, African American, a physician. She smiles broadly and turns. Her 16-year-old Latino patient, laid out on a few chairs, narrows his eyes, perhaps startled by the pleasure he can hear in her voice. Staggers pats the boy's hand, surveys his pale face. Her eyes follow his long, muscled leg, stopping to study the spot where his foot draws down to the south. There, the bone takes a sharp detour east, its trajectory sketched by a plum-colored bruise, the fruit of basketball played too hard.

Staggers raises her arms in a *V* of triumph and grins. "Yep. Broken. Yes!"

After following Staggers on rounds—here in a clinic at Fremont High School and at the Teen Clinic of Children's Hospital in north Oakland, Calif.—even a casual observer might understand her glee. This is the first clean break of the day. The patient, suffering from the kind of injury doctors are trained to handle, will be treated and sent on his way. Within a few months, he will be playing ball too aggressively again.

Many of Staggers' other patients suffer far murkier ailments. So far today she has seen teenagers who are suicidal and homicidal; victims of sexual abuse; sufferers of serious diseases, from asthma to AIDS; and kids who are addicts to everything from alcohol to crack and junk. She has also seen teenagers who are pregnant or love starved and too many who have given up all hope.

The crisis among patients like Staggers' has been widely reported as a tale of inner-city poverty and youth crime, but her weekly schedule is a rebuke to that simple notion. Many of her patients are poor, minority teenagers, but she also draws patients from more privileged neighborhoods. One kind of patient comes to her after taking a bullet in the belly during a downtown shootout. Another kind arrives bruised and broken, having drunk himself sick before wrecking his parents' luxury car in a high-speed crash.

"As a physician, I'm dealing with people who are incredibly resilient physically," Staggers says in her cramped office at the school clinic, just before the injured athlete arrives. "Yet they still see their most positive option as

From Douglas Foster, "The Disease Is Adolescence," *Rolling Stone*, no. 671 (December 9, 1993). Copyright © 1993 by Straight Arrow Publishing Company, L.P. All rights reserved. Reprinted by permission.

being dead." In conversation, Staggers rolls her shoulders forward for emphasis and explains things in well-crafted bursts. "Guns and cars are different kinds of weapons. But they can be weapons all the same. Different presenting symptoms. The same disease."

What are the different presenting symptoms Staggers confronts? While black teen-agers are far more likely to be shot to death, white teens are more likely to be injured or killed in an automobile crash —or to kill themselves. But both groups share this underlying condition: Three-quarters of the deaths of young people from ages 10 to 24—a total of 30,000 each year—occur not from disease but from preventable causes.

For most other age groups in the country, the risk of a violent death or injury from these causes has leveled off or declined. Not so for adolescents—or for young people in their 20s, whose escalating risk of violent injury and death begins in their teens. Among youths from 15 to 19 years of age, the risk of being shot to death more than doubled in the last decade.

Consider this toll: 5,749 teens were killed—and tens of thousands injured— in automobile crashes in 1991. Among youths 10 to 19, 3,398 were murdered, and 2,237 killed themselves in 1990. During the 1980s, 68,997 teen-agers died in car crashes, 19,346 were murdered, and 18,365 killed themselves. That added up to 106,718 for the decade. Today's teenager runs roughly twice the risk of being murdered or becoming a victim of suicide compared with teens during most years of the turbulent 1960s. (The risk of death from car crashes has declined, perhaps as a result of safety laws, public education and lower speed limits.) As if the old dangers were not threatening enough,

HIV infection has begun to cut a wider swath.

Across lines of race and class among teen-agers, the number of preventable deaths is rising at an alarming rate. Adolescence has become a high-risk activity.

* * *

As the athlete with the broken ankle hobbles off to have his bone set, Staggers tugs at the MD credentials hanging from a chain around her neck and surveys a waiting room full of difficult cases. Few of Staggers' patients readily reveal the underlying reasons for their visits. The receptionist's sign-in sheet contains a litany of mundane complaints —aching ears, persistent coughs, upset stomachs. Inside the examining room, the more serious business will tumble out if Staggers can find a way to dredge it up. On this morning, it turns out that the earache was caused by a beating, the cough by parental neglect and the stomachache by a suicide attempt.

Staggers sees several patients, including one young man, who are exploring their sexuality. "This school has a fair number of kids who openly identify [themselves] as gay or bisexual," she says. Staggers has doubled-barreled concerns about the boy: Does he know everything he needs to know about safer sex? Are the older men he has been staying with overnight—perhaps trading sex for shelter—taking advantage of his youth and naiveté?

The boy is handsome, soft-spoken, painfully shy. He has had several near-fatal bouts of asthma, but his family is scattered, and nobody seems to be in charge of his care. Treating teens like this boy seems to require a kind of double vision: Staggers is treating the asthma but also trying to anticipate an underlying danger, counseling him to avoid exploitation, drug abuse, AIDS.

Next door, three young women have arrived—a few days after their junior prom—for pregnancy tests. As she reads their names, Staggers raises her eyebrows in disappointment. There's a faint, nearly inaudible growl in her throat. These three girls know better. They've been taught how to protect themselves from sexually transmitted diseases and pregnancy.

Like these young women, teen-agers all over the country, most of whom are sexually active, increasingly risk serious illness and death through sex. A recent report by the Centers for Disease Control found that among teens, new infections with HIV are occurring at a startlingly high rate.

Preparing to meet with the girls individually, Staggers suppresses an exasperated scowl and replaces it with a stoic, neutral expression. This part of her practice—inspiring teens to make use of what they already know—is by far her biggest challenge. It demands the ability to hector and persuade without seeming to nag or lecture.

"It's hard when you're angry, but you have to take time with these kids if you expect to make a difference," Staggers says outside the examining room. "To make an impact, you have to push past the facts. You have to press the girls for more information and look for the underlying causes. I ask them, 'Is an orgasm worth dying for?' and 'Why do you want to be pregnant?' They'll tell you they want to get an education first. But then they'll go and have unprotected sex. Many of them don't think they have any control. The boys tell them they don't like the feel of a condom. The boys say, 'Trust me.' And the girls desperately want to trust somebody."

Staggers is a vicious mimic, and she pauses to take on the role of a teen-age boy, wheedling: "I just don't like how it feels. Please, baby. Trust me." She rolls her eyes and whirls. "Please, girls. Let's trust ourselves."

Staggers believes there's an "influential connection" between the 1 million teen-agers who get pregnant each year and the violence that pervades their lives. "Even though, in many ways, they don't want to get pregnant, they do it to replace some of the people they've lost," she says. At first blush, this sweeping statement seems hyperbolic, a shade New Age. To blame teen-age pregnancies on violence in the streets seems a bit of a stretch. But during her examination, one of the three prom revelers, a striking and articulate high-school senior, proves a spot-on example. This young woman can rattle off safe-sex guidelines so expertly that she could work for the CDC. Still, here she is waiting for the results of her pregnancy test, having picked up a bad case of herpes after the big dance.

I ask if there's anything else bothering her. At that, the forthright teenager becomes querulous. She hems and dodges. Finally, her hands flapping back and forth, she admits to having a hard time keeping a clear head ever since the recent murder of her 25-year-old cousin. The killing has left her feeling betrayed. Her cousin was called out of his home by his friends—among them people she knows from the neighborhood. Clearly, the young man was set up. She puffs big clouds of air through her cheeks. You learn not to trust anybody, she says.

* * *

Perhaps Staggers can chart the perils of adolescence so well because she grew up in an upwardly mobile home that was thoroughly guarded against teen dangers. Her greatest influence was her father, one of the first African American doctors in a surgical subspecialty (urology) in the Navy. When Dr. Frank Staggers Sr. left military service, he moved the family to Castro Valley, an archetypal California suburb. The Staggers family settled above a sleepy commercial strip in one of the Eichler homes dotting the hills. Eichler's design, distinguished by expansive panes of glass and open redwood beams, was the architectural corollary to the family's upward arc.

Barbara Staggers' great-grandmother was born to a slave woman and an Irish slaveholder. On her father's side, there was a railroad switchman and his wife, who never went to high school. Among her parents' generation, there were great social strides; all of her father's siblings and many of his 35 cousins have advanced degrees.

Under the watchful eye of two attentive parents, Staggers' younger brother became an ordained minister and teacher and her elder brother a doctor specializing in the treatment of addiction. Staggers wobbled between her desire to dance, her wish to pursue veterinary medicine and her ambition to become a doctor like her dad. At 18, she worked in a summer camp for inner-city Oakland teen-agers. There, she got hooked on the idea of doctoring teens. "Black physicians are social engineers," her father says. "I told her it was pretty hard to pursue a doctor's career as a dancer. But it would be possible to keep dancing if she trained to be a doctor."

For Barbara Staggers, being an upwardly mobile black in the 'burbs was a sometimes mixed experience. Her junior-high-school counselor told her she would "never be able to achieve anything higher than a job washing dishes," she remembers, and she was tracked out of the class of high achievers she'd studied with until then. Her father intervened forcefully with school officials.

"What if my parents hadn't been watching out for me? I think about that a lot," she muses. "Lots of kids just fall through the cracks because nobody is paying attention when they need it the most. It's in that moment when the crack is opening up for a kid that it's most important to intervene."

* * *

"Boy! Oh, my! Don't tell me!" Staggers hunches over the telephone, as if the sheer weight of her concern can be brought to bear on her umpteenth case of life or death.

At the Teen Clinic of Children's Hospital in Oakland, she's packed into her chair, surrounded by papers and correspondence and piles of telephone messages. Boxes of research files, speech materials and papers spill out of pink milk crates.

This is the first time I've heard Staggers stopped cold. She scuffs her Reeboks beneath her chair and nestles the receiver against her cheek. A patient is nearing physical collapse from starving herself.

"Uh, oh! Anorexia and psychosis, too. She's hearing voices. Ah, man," Staggers says, frowning. "Do we know how much she weighs?

"Excuse me. She weighs how much? Boy, oh, boy. Is she pale and blue-looking? When anorectics need hospital care, we're talking cardiovascular trouble.

And so we're talking risk of instant death."

Staggers quickly refers the doctor to Lucile Salter Packard Children's Hospital at Stanford, across the bay. Packard has a specialized eating-disorders clinic and in-patient psychiatric care. It's the appropriate place for this particular teenager. Swiveling in her chair, Staggers looks glum. "That was a tough one. You know, among anorectics, the odds aren't terrific. One-third of those who get treated get better, one-third or more stay the same—and up to a fifth die."

She's up and out before finishing the sentence, clearly discomfited by the notion that there are cases even she can't get traction on. We've been talking about some of the others troubling her sleep. There's a 14-year-old female patient who lives with a 28-year-old pimp and drug dealer. So far, he's not sexually involved with the girl, and he doesn't show any signs of trying to pressure her into prostitution. "I've been watching to see if he would try to pimp her out," Staggers says. "He seems to genuinely care for and protect her."

Staggers could turn the girl over to Child Protective Services. But that public agency is overwhelmed with urgent cases, and the best they could offer is foster care. Staggers still remembers, with a shiver of disgust, an 11-year-old girl with chronic illness turned over to the agency a few years ago. The girl's parents were homeless, and CPS officials believed she could not be adequately cared for on the street. So they separated the girl from her parents.

"She ended up getting hospitalized as a psychiatric case," Staggers remembers. "Her parents were good to her, and she missed them. What we did initially, by referring the case, was take a tragedy and make it worse. In the end, we got the parents jobs and a house. The kid is doing wonderfully now." With that experience as a backdrop, Staggers calculates that her current 14-year-old patient may be better off staying with the one person who has cared for her, even if he's a pimp.

Staggers hurries off to meet with a middle-class teen-age girl, a runaway from her suburban home. "I can't tell you how many middle-class girls I have who get involved with the gangs at this age," she says. "This girl was an A student. Now she's failing." Staggers sends two peer counselors, young women who have graduated from gang-involvement and drug-treatment programs themselves, in for some straight talk with the teen. Then the doctor follows up, both with the girl and with her parents—getting her to agree to go to family therapy and advising them to lighten up once they get their daughter home.

As the parents and daughter file out, reunited, Staggers allows herself a moment of relief. Her eyebrows bobble, and she grins. About her advice to the parents, she explains, "We don't get very far by just telling teen-agers not to take risks because it scares us. When we demand to know why they've screwed up, the kid says, 'I had to. Everybody else was doing it.' The adult replies, 'If everybody else jumped off the cliff, would you, too?'

"The honest answer to that question," continues Staggers, "is *yes*. It's really important that we understand this. For the teen at that moment, being down at the bottom together feels better than being on the edge of a cliff alone. What we need to engage our teens in discussing is this question: What else can you do to be part of a group and still survive, while taking reasonable risks? If you've got to jump off the cliff, can't you choose one that's not 50-feet high? Can you jump off the cliff that's 2-feet high instead?"

Staggers' approach to treating teen-agers involves more engaged listening than most doctors or parents ever muster. Her method uncovers underlying symptoms. She mentions a 16-year-old white boy who came into the clinic for treatment of his swollen knees. By probing further, she learned that he'd jumped from the second story of a building while high on PCP and needed help with his drug habit. Another boy was in the hospital recovering from injuries suffered in an automobile accident. Since his breath smelled as if he'd been drinking at the time of the accident, alcohol treatment was recommended. But nobody asked him why he'd crashed into the wall in the first place. Staggers did ask. "He told me, 'I've done this before. Several times,'" Staggers recalls. "And so we knew he needed suicide-prevention couseling, too. The experience left me wondering: How many suicides are really homicides? And how many homicides are really suicides?"

From experiences like these, Staggers first developed her theory about the common problems of teen-agers. She believes a festering generational grievance cuts across differences of income, ethnic background or particular trauma.

But if adolescence itself has become a high-risk activity—a disease to be treated with preventive therapy, as Staggers believes—what is the most effective treatment? Collecting her belongings at the end of a day, Staggers considers this question carefully and answers a bit haltingly. "With all the kids I know who make it, there's one thing in common: an individual contact with an adult who cared and who kept hanging in with the teen through his hardest moments," Staggers says. "People talk programs, and that's important. But when it comes down to it, individual, person-to-person connections make the difference.... Every kid I know who made it through the teen-age years had at least one adult in his life who made that effort."

* * *

When Staggers leaves work in downtown Oakland, she beats a retreat to the suburbs where she was brought up—and where she presently lives with her second husband, 8-year-old son and 9-year-old stepson. Zipping along in her new Acura Integra at 75 mph, it's a short drive but a world away. The freeway slices around inner-city Oakland like a melon spoon, cutting southeast past a string of suburban villages, to Castro Valley.

"Notice anything?" Staggers laughs as we emerge from the car outside Castro Valley High School. At Fremont High, most of the school gates were chained shut, and security guards roamed the hallways, two-way radios at the ready. The average grade-point average is 1.7, and only a small fraction of the students will go on to college. At Castro Valley High, students wander freely. Most students come from two-parent families, and incomes are high. Almost all of them will go on to college.

"You're about to find out the problems for teens are similar even in very different settings," Staggers insists, bustling down the hallway to the school's counseling office. "Sure, it looks better out here. It is better. But there are plenty of scary things happening here, too."

Just last spring, one Castro Valley teen-ager was killed with a baseball bat in a brawl after a Little League game. Although not reported at the time, tensions at the school had been fierce in the weeks before the brawl. The school's wrestling coach had been charged with making sexual advances to a boy on his team. That had led to gay-baiting teasing aimed at the wrestlers, some of whom were also baseball players. Then, ongoing racial skirmishes between Anglo and Latino students resulted in a series of confrontations.

Natalie Van Tassel, an ebullient white woman who has worked in Castro Valley schools for 25 years, was Staggers' counselor during high school. She still treats Castro Valley's troubled teens. Within a minute of hitting the door of Van Tassel's office, the two are deep into cases.

The women compare notes about sexual activity among their patients. "I don't think I'm misrepresenting the past," Van Tassel says. "I mean, I came from a small Midwestern town where most of the girls got married the day after graduation because they were all pregnant. But what has happened is that the explosion of sexual activity moved down in the age groups—12, 13, 14..."

Staggers interrupts. "Among mine: 10, 11, 12—"

"And the big difference," Van Tassel continues, "is, if you wanted to be sexually active in your high-school years, you could do it without running the risk of dying because of it."

The risk of HIV infection is an increasing danger for all teen-agers. Among the thorniest issues in prevention work is the ambiguous sexuality of many teenagers —and the disdainful disapproval or loaded silence from adults concerning same-sex exploration. In this more privileged setting, oddly enough, there seems to be even less acceptance of gay teen-

agers than at Fremont High. Only one young man is open about his homosexuality here.

Van Tassel finds it toughest of all to deal with teen-agers who have no meaningful relationship with any adult. Suburban teen-agers are set loose to fend for themselves far too early, Van Tassel tells Staggers. "The parents here have a great capacity to give their kids things. Giving them so many material things masks what they're failing to give—time. What I see are kids without real parents."

Staggers is pounding the table. "See, it's the same disease, different symptoms. Here the kids have economic opportunity, but no real family life." She's worked up now. "I'm tired of hearing people say, 'I'm too busy.' If you have kids— or you're related to kids—and they don't have adults in their lives, it's your job to either take care of them yourself or find some other grown-up who can do it for you. Either do it or find someone who can. But just throwing up your hands and saying, 'Time, time, there's no time'—that just doesn't cut it with me. How can we get that message through to the adults?"

*　*　*

Staggers doesn't wear a watch. Sometimes her schedule seems chaotic, full of what appears—to some of her superiors, at any rate—to be overly generous amounts of time for her patients. She has a way of locking on to whoever is in her presence and letting all the others wait. There have been rumblings about her supposed failings as an administrator and turf fights with the hospital administration. Staggers' department has been hit with a series of cutbacks in staff and resources in a hospital–wide restructuring.

In the midst of the cutbacks, even Staggers' clinic at Fremont High may be in jeopardy. "That's where services should be—in the schools, in the community," Staggers says firmly. "Can you imagine those kids turning up at a hospital clinic? With no insurance, no parent support, no information? Yet they're the kids who need treatment most."

But Staggers knows that her real beef is not with the budget-cutting administrators at her hospital. She's at odds, fundamentally, with the way medicine is currently organized. Staggers is trying to practice public-health medicine in a fee-for-service world. No matter which proposal is eventually adopted to reform the nation's health-care system, the underlying problem for doctors like Staggers will remain. Her focus on prevention, no matter how socially important, simply does not generate the fees that would fund such a practice.

Preventive medicine is not rewarded under the current system. Consider one example: While researching this story, I watched in the emergency room of Oakland's Children's Hospital one Friday afternoon as a 13-year-old gang member was treated for a gunshot wound suffered in a drive-by shooting. A 9mm slug was lodged in his thigh, and like dozens of other teen-age shooting victims treated over the summer, his case generated a hefty bill. These kinds of bills are paid off either by a private insurance company or by the state.

By contrast, if Staggers succeeds as Doctor to the Teens—talking an angry young man out of a gang, in one instance—her efforts often don't generate a bill. Since her time isn't billable, she and her institution are left holding the bag. Her model of health care makes sense, particularly in treating teen-agers, but Staggers' efforts at prevention are never rewarded as well as the standard program of stitch-then-release.

When she gets agitated on this subject, Staggers sets her jaw and waves her arms. Teen-agers are less likely to receive medical care than any other age group in the country, she insists, and rarely do they get the kind of care they need, even when they are treated. For all the hazy rhetoric floating around in Washington about the domestic agenda, Staggers can't understand how anyone expects to make headway without taking into account the special problems of teens.

Staggers often gives speeches around the country. She's a doctor of publicity, too, turning out between appointments on one day, for example, to support the efforts of community groups in Oakland trying to shut down alcohol outlets. ("You put alcohol and firearms together, and you account for 50 to 75 percent of all adolescent deaths," she says.) She's also a regular fixture in testimony before state legislative committees.

The uphill nature of her cause was evident at an afternoon hearing last May in Sacramento, the state capital. With teens and their advocates from all over the state waiting and ready to testify about their problems, a special hearing about teen-age health was abruptly canceled because legislators were busy downstairs grappling with a state budget that was $9 billion from balancing. In times of such stark shortage, it's harder than ever to get teen-agers the attention they desperately need.

When Staggers was honored with the Lewis Hine Award in New York this year for her service to young people, Hillary Rodham Clinton, a fellow honoree, asked for her advice. The first lady got an impassioned briefing about adolescent medicine.

"She listened carefully, and I hope it made a difference in her thinking," Staggers says. "If only the federal government could restructure health care so there's community-based operations and more school-based clinics, we might get a grip on some of these problems."

*　*　*

On my last day with Staggers at the school clinic, a tall, lively African American teen-ager stops by to share the good news: She has been accepted at San Jose State University, and she'll be starting college in the fall. Dressed in a red blouse and stretch pants, Ebony Hawthorne acknowledges that her prospects seemed rather bleak not so long ago. She had gotten pregnant at 15, and she nearly decided to carry the baby to term. It was a dicey conflict. On the one hand, she would not have been likely to have gone on to college if she had had the baby. But her family was dead set against an abortion, and she felt a powerful need to "have somebody to call my own."

At home, it was difficult to find support. Ebony's father, estranged from her mother, is a drug dealer who has been in and out of prison. Her mother is an addict. At the school clinic, she had opened up about her problems at home, her hopes and fears, and she ultimately decided to have an abortion.

As it turned out, her unwanted pregnancy was the prelude to a period of raw travail, which hit during last year's holiday season. First, her stepfather died of a heart attack. Then, last November, Ebony and her mother were evicted from their home on Thanksgiving Day. Ebony was distracted, to say the least, from her schoolwork. She worried that notices from the colleges she'd applied to would never catch up with her.

On their way to a homeless shelter, mother and daughter stopped for fuel. There, at the gas station, they bumped into Ebony's father, out of prison and back into business. He allowed them to stay for a week in an apartment he had rented nearby. Then he tossed them out, because he needed the apartment back "for work."

Ebony sets her chin, speaking crisply, as if she's desperately trying to distance herself from the bitterness she feels. "Does this make any sense to you? He told me he was throwing us out for my own good. For my own good! Why? Because he needed the apartment to sell his drugs from. And if he didn't make any money, he wouldn't be able to give me any Christmas money. Tell me, would you rather have a roof over your head —or Christmas money? That's when I decided: As far as I'm concerned, I have no father."

Luckily, Ebony salvaged a relationship with her mother, who is now in a drug treatment program in San Francisco. She has been clean for eight months. "She's trying to get my respect back," Ebony says, frowning. "I don't feel I lost my respect for her. Not at all. But she feels I have. She went through a hard task to get sober. And I'm proud of her."

Hawthorne betrays a hint of pride in herself as well. She has managed to finish high school in an environment of homelessness, drug addiction, violence and neglect. Most of her classmates are headed for the streets, while she is going off to college. From a deep reservoir of will and hope, Ebony Hawthorne has mustered a quality in scant supply among today's teen-agers. She has ambition.

"The difference between me and some of the others is that I push myself, because I've seen how my mother ended up,"

Hawthorne says. "And I have people here at the clinic who push me, too.

"I want to be a psychiatrist," she adds tentatively, as if ready to be challenged. "Because I want to really understand it all better. I want to understand myself— what happened to me and all the anger I have—much better. And then I want to be in a position to help people. I want to help the kind of people... who have problems like mine."

Outside the door, another set of patients is waiting. In one room, peer counselors are giving a lecture about safer sex, practicing rolling condoms onto rubber phalluses with their mouths. A couple of students need prescriptions. Another doctor is on the line. But Staggers has already moved on to the next examining room, her face upturned and open, anxious to dig out the essence of her next case.

POSTSCRIPT

Is an Adolescent's Sexual Orientation Important in Understanding Causes for Youth Suicide?

In contemporary society, there is a tremendous amount of human misery caused by people's lack of understanding. The issues of suicide and homosexuality are ones to which considerable social and religious stigma are attached. Taking one's own life is thought to be immoral, as is being sexually intimate with someone of the same sex. It is attitudes like these that cause anxiety and inhibit greater understanding of suicide and homosexuality. As a result, families are quick to try to cover up suicide and sidestep any queries as to the sexual preferences of family members.

Our society appears to pride itself on the idea that we enjoy many freedoms, including the freedom of expression. But where issues of sexuality are concerned, there is considerable debate over freedom of expression and tolerance. When it comes to understanding sexual preferences, society generally has had tremendous reservations about any deviation from strictly heterosexual norms. The implications for adolescent gays and lesbians are considerable. Should they come out? If so, for what reason and to whom? To everyone? To friends? To parents? How do these adolescents understand and cope with their first love affairs? Who can they trust and turn to for guidance? If these questions cannot be satisfactorily addressed by the adolescent, perhaps it is not surprising that frustration, dissatisfaction, depression, and even suicide result. On the other side of the issue, some would argue that closeness to one's family, dealing with a first love, and having someone to talk to are equally significant issues for all adolescents, regardless of sexual orientation. Predisposition toward suicide is a complex issue, and gay and lesbian youths may not necessarily be at greater risk.

For those in society who may have difficulty with the concept that each individual should have the right to decide his or her own lifestyle, including sexual preference, the key may lie in the realization that people who choose lives that are different are not necessarily asking others to condone their lifestyles. They only ask that society understand and allow them the privacy and freedom to live with dignity. If this were the case, the major adolescent developmental tasks of forging an adult identity and developing intimate relationships outside of the family could be embraced much more effectively by children. Furthermore, adolescents who found themselves to be gay or lesbian would not have to endure the hostility that currently faces them. Regardless of whether or not one believed that sexual orientation is a significant factor in adolescent suicide rates, social tolerance would enhance a child's ability to embrace the developmental tasks of adolescence much more readily.

SUGGESTED READINGS

Bromfiled, R. (1993, February). On skulls, coffins and bloodied wrists. *School Arts, 92*, 46–47.

Goode, E. E. (1993, August 9). The mind in its despair. *U.S. News & World Report, 115*, 58–59.

Hoagland, E. (1988, March). The urge for an end. *Harper's, 276*, 45–52.

Kamberg, M.-L. (1990, September). America's 10 least wanted. *Current Health, 17*, 4–10.

_____. (1990, November). Suicide brains: Naturally prone to pain? *Science News, 138*, 301.

Weiss, R. (1989, November). Teen suicide clusters: More than mimicry. *Science News, 136*, 342.

ISSUE 16

Is Abstinence Education the Best Sex Education?

YES: Thomas Lickona, from "Where Sex Education Went Wrong," *Educational Leadership* (November 1993)

NO: Jessica Gress-Wright, from "The Contraception Paradox," *The Public Interest* (Fall 1993)

ISSUE SUMMARY

YES: Thomas Lickona, a developmental psychologist, states that Americans need to promote a higher standard of sexual morality in our society through "directive" sex education, which promotes abstinence before marriage. He argues that traditional sex education programs, such as "comprehensive" sex education and "abstinence but" sex education, have not only failed to reduce teen pregnancy but may also, inadvertently, be promoting it.

NO: Jessica Gress-Wright, a researcher and writer, analyzes teen pregnancy rates and sex education in the United States, Sweden, and Great Britain. She comes to very different conclusions than does Lickona as to why teen pregnancy and abortion rates are so high in the United States. She argues that the problems of teen childbearing and abortion cannot be solved by sex education programs alone.

The number of adolescent females in our society who bear out-of-wedlock children continues to rise. Most people understand that teenage pregnancy is a serious and epidemic problem. Unwed adolescent mothers lack sufficient skills and education to support themselves and their children. They are unlikely to receive emotional or financial support from the fathers of their children, for the fathers are too young and unprepared for the financial and emotional responsibilities of parenthood as well. The adolescent mother's needs are often met by her parents or, more often, through publicly supported programs. It is no surprise that the cost of providing such services, not only during pregnancy and at the time of birth but often throughout the life of the mother and child, is very high. Teen mothers and their children are at a distinct disadvantage in their ability to function successfully in society. As a consequence, they often turn to welfare programs, such as Aid to Families with Dependent Children, and other social programs for help.

The obvious solution is to lessen the number of out-of-wedlock births that are occurring. Sexuality education is the current method through which

U.S. society has confronted the problem. However, what constitutes effective sexuality education? Professionals continue to debate which sex education approach to this emotionally and financially costly societal problem will yield the intended results. The sexuality programs considered acceptable by some researchers, teachers, clinicians, clergy, and parents are seen by others as contributing to the problem. As a result, the arguments about what is appropriate sex education continue, even as the century comes to a close. These arguments might be conceptualized into two extremes: (1) We have been much too liberal in our approach to teaching our children about sexuality. In our zeal to be nonjudgmental and open-minded, we have forgotten our responsibility to teach our children the morality and safety of abstinence in this world of unwanted infants and sexually transmitted diseases. (2) Comprehensive sex education in the schools, which begins in kindergarten and continues through grade 12, has not been given a chance in America. Virtually no school district has integrated teaching about the social and psychological aspects of human sexuality, along with its physical dimensions, into their curricula from the beginning of a child's school years until they end. If this were to occur, we could make significant progress in solving the problem of adolescent pregnancy.

Thomas Lickona's selection elaborates a typical rationale for the morality and safety argument. He cites research studies to make his case. The selection by Jessica Gress-Wright contradicts Lickona and extols the virtues of a comprehensive, locally appropriate sex education program.

As you read the following debate, consider not only your own personal views, and how they compare with the ones presented, but also the current social climate toward sex education. What societal attitudes impede or contribute to possible solutions to this problem?

YES

Thomas Lickona

WHERE SEX EDUCATION WENT WRONG

Most of us are familiar with the alarming statistics about teen sexual activity in the United States. Among high school students, 54 percent (including 61 percent of boys and 48 percent of girls) say they have had sexual intercourse, according to a 1992 Centers for Disease Control study. The number of 9th graders who say they have already had sex is 40 percent.[1]

In the past two decades, there has been an explosion in the number of sexually transmitted diseases. Twelve million people are infected each year; 63 percent of them are under 25.

Each year, 1 of every 10 teenage girls becomes pregnant, and more than 400,000 teenagers have abortions. One in 4 children is born out of wedlock, compared to 1 in 20 in 1960.

But statistics like these do not tell the whole story. The other side—one that should concern us deeply as moral educators—is the debasement of sexuality and the corruption of young people's character.

A LEGACY OF THE SEXUAL REVOLUTION

A 1993 study by the American Association of University Women found that four out of five high school students say they have experienced sexual harassment ("unwanted sexual behavior that interferes with your life") in school. Commented one 14-year-old girl: "All guys want is sex. They just come up to you and grab you."

In suburban Minneapolis, a mother filed state and federal complaints because 3rd and 4th grade boys on the school bus had tormented her 1st grade daughter daily with obscene comments and repeated demands for sexual acts. A 6th grade teacher taking my graduate course in moral education said, "The boys bring in *Playboy*, the girls wear make-up and jewelry, and the kids write heavy sexual notes to each other."

At an Indiana high school, a teacher said, "Kids in the halls will call out—boy to girl, girl to boy—'I want to f— you.'" At Lakewood High School in an affluent Los Angeles suburb, a group of boys formed the "Spur Posse," a

From Thomas Lickona, "Where Sex Education Went Wrong," *Educational Leadership*, vol. 51, no. 3 (November 1993), pp. 84–89. Copyright © 1993 by The Association for Supervision and Curriculum Development. All rights reserved. Reprinted by permission.

club in which participants competed to see how many girls they could sleep with.

Growing up in a highly eroticized sexual environment—a legacy of the sexual revolution—American children are preoccupied with sex in developmentally distorted ways and increasingly likely to act out their sexual impulses. The widespread sexual harassment in schools and the rising rates of teen sexual activity are not isolated phenomena but an outgrowth of the abnormal preoccupation with sex that children are manifesting from the earliest grades.

The sexual corruption of children reflects an adult sexual culture in which the evidence continues to mount that sex is out of control. In 1990, 29 states set records for the sex-and-violence crime of rape. By age 18, more than a quarter of girls and one-sixth of boys suffer sexual abuse. One in four female students who say they have been sexually harassed at school were victimized by a teacher, coach, bus driver, teacher's aide, security guard, principal, or counselor.[2] By various estimates, sexual infidelity now occurs in a third to one-half of U.S. marriages.

Sex is powerful. It was Freud who said that sexual self-control is essential for civilization. And, we should add, for character.

Any character education worthy of the name must help students develop sexual self-control and the ability to apply core ethical values such as respect and responsibility to the sexual domain. Against that standard, how do various contemporary models of sex education measure up?

The history of modern sex education offers three models. The first two are variations of the nondirective approach:

the third, by contrast, is a directive approach.

COMPREHENSIVE SEX EDUCATION

"Comprehensive sex education," which originated in Sweden in the 1950s and quickly became the prototype for the Western world,[3] was based on four premises:

1. Teenage sexual activity is inevitable.
2. Educators should be value-neutral regarding sex.
3. Schools should openly discuss sexual matters.
4. Sex education should teach students about contraception.

The value-neutral approach to sex soon showed up in American sex education philosophy, as in this statement by the author of the *Curriculum Guide for Sex Education in California*: " 'Right' or 'wrong' in so intimate a matter as sexual behavior is as personal as one's own name and address. No textbook or classroom teacher can teach it."[4]

What was the impact of nondirective, value-neutral, comprehensive sex education on teenage sexual behavior?

• From 1971 to 1981, government funding at all levels for contraceptive education increased by 4,000 percent. During that time teen pregnancies increased by 20 percent and teen abortions nearly doubled.[5]
• A 1986 Johns Hopkins University study concluded that comprehensive sex education did not reduce teen pregnancies,[6] a finding replicated by other studies.
• A 1986 Lou Harris Poll, commissioned by Planned Parenthood (a leading sponsor of comprehensive sex educa-

tion), found that teens who took a comprehensive sex education course (including contraceptive education) were significantly *more likely* to initiate sexual intercourse than teens whose sex education courses did not discuss contraceptives.[7]

THE "ABSTINENCE, BUT" MODEL

Negative results like those cited did not lead comprehensive sex educators to alter their approach—but AIDS did. AIDS led to two modifications: (1) teaching students to practice "safe [or "safer"] sex" through the use of barrier contraception (condoms); and (2) grafting an abstinence message onto the old comprehensive model. These changes resulted in what can be called the "Abstinence, But" approach, which says two things to students:

- Abstinence is the only 100 percent effective way to avoid pregnancy, AIDS, and other sexually transmitted diseases.
- But if you are sexually active, you can reduce these risks through the consistent, correct use of condoms.

This hybrid model, still found in many public and private schools, seems to many like a "realistic" compromise. But closer examination revels fundamental problems in the "Abstinence, But" model.

1. It sends a mixed message.
"Don't have sex, but here's a way to do it fairly safely" amounts to a green light for sexual activity. The problem is that "Abstinence, But" is still nondirective sex education. Abstinence is presented as the safest contraceptive option,[8] but "protected sex" is offered as a "responsible" second option. The emphasis is on "mak-

ing your own decision" rather than on making the right decision.

As a rule, if educators believe that a given activity is ethically wrong—harmful to self and others (as teen sexual activity clearly is)—we help students understand why that is so and guide them toward the right decision. We don't say, for example, "Drug abuse is wrong, but make your own decision, and here's how to reduce the risks if you decide to become drug active."

2. An abstinence message is further weakened when schools provide how-to condom instructions and/or distribute condoms.
Teachers providing condom instruction will commonly demonstrate how to fit a condom to a model (or students may be asked to put a condom on a banana). In the same nonjudgmental atmosphere, discussion often includes the pros and cons of different lubricants, special precautions for oral and anal sex, and so on. Some schools also take what seems like the next logical step of actually distributing condoms to students. Both actions signal approval of "protected sex" and further undermine an abstinence message.

3. Condoms do not make sex physically safe. For all age groups, condoms have a 10 percent annual failure rate in preventing pregnancy; for teens (notoriously poor users), the figure can go as high as 36 percent.[9] By one estimate, a 14-year-old girl who relies on condoms has more than a 50 percent chance of becoming pregnant before she graduates from high school.[10]

Contraceptive sex educators often cite AIDS as the main justification for "safe sex" education, but research shows that condoms do *not* provide adequate protection against AIDS (and, especially among teens, may generate a false sense of security). In a 1993 University of Texas study, the average condom failure rate for preventing AIDS was 31 percent.[11]

While AIDS is still relatively infrequent among teens, other sexually transmitted diseases are epidemic. Many of these diseases—and 80 percent of the time there are no visible symptoms—can be transmitted by areas of the body that are not covered by contraceptive barriers. Human Papilloma Virus, once very rare, is perhaps the most common STD among teens, infecting 38 percent of sexually active females ages 13 to 21. Victims may suffer from venereal warts, painful intercourse, or genital cancer. The virus can also cause cancer of the penis. Condoms provide no protection against this virus.[12]

Chlamydia infects 20 to 40 percent of sexually active singles; teenage girls are most susceptible. In men, chlamydia can cause infertile sperm; in women, pelvic inflammatory disease and infection of the fallopian tubes. A single infection in a woman produces a 25 percent chance of infertility; a second infection, a 50 percent chance. Medical research has found that condoms do not significantly reduce the frequency of tubal infection and infertility stemming from this disease.[13]

Given teenagers' vulnerability to pregnancy despite the use of condoms and the fact that condoms provide inadequate protection against AIDS and no protection against many STDs, it is irresponsible to promote the myth that condoms make sex physically safe.

4. Condoms do not make sex emotionally safe.

The emotional and spiritual dimensions of sex are what make it distinctively human. If we care about young people, we will help them understand the destructive emotional and spiritual effects that can come from temporary, uncommitted sexual relationships.

These psychological consequences vary among individuals but include: lowered self-esteem (sometimes linked to sexually transmitted diseases), a sense of having been "used," self-contempt for being a "user," the pain of loss of reputation, compulsive sexual behavior to try to shore up one's damaged self-image, regret and self-recrimination, rage over rejection or betrayal, difficulty trusting in future relationships, and spiritual guilt if one has a faith tradition that prohibits sex outside marriage (as world religions typically do).[14] Condoms provide zero protection against these emotional consequences.

5. Nondirective sex education undermines character.

From the standpoint of character education, the nondirective "Abstinence, But" model fails on several counts:

- It doesn't give unmarried young people compelling ethical reasons to abstain from sexual intercourse until they are ready to commit themselves to another person. Instead, students learn that they are being "responsible" if they use contraception.

- It doesn't help students develop the crucial character quality of self-control —the capacity to curb one's desires and delay gratification. To the extent that sex education is in any way permissive toward teenage sexual activity, it fosters poor character and feeds into the societal problem of sex-out-of-control.

- It doesn't develop an ethical understanding of the relationship between sex and love.
- It doesn't cultivate what young people desperately need if they are to postpone sex: a vision of the solemn, binding commitment between two people in which sex is potentially most meaningful, responsible, and safe (physically and emotionally)—namely, marriage.

DIRECTIVE SEX EDUCATION

By any ethical, educational, or public health measure, nondirective sex education has been a failure. As a result, schools are turning increasingly toward directive sex education—just as the national character education movement is embracing a more directive approach to promoting core ethical values as the basis of good character.

A directive approach means helping young persons—for the sake of their safety, happiness, and character—to see the logic of an "Abstinence, No Buts" standard, often called "chastity education." This standard says three things:

1. Sexual abstinence is the *only* medically safe and morally responsible choice for unmarried teenagers.
2. Condoms do not make premarital sex responsible because they don't make it physically safe, emotionally safe, or ethically loving.
3. The only truly safe sex is having sex *only* with a marriage partner who is having sex *only* with you. If you avoid intercourse until marriage, you will have a much greater chance of remaining healthy and being able to have children.

There are now many carefully crafted curriculums, books, and videos that foster the attitudes that lead teens to choose chastity—a moral choice and a lifestyle that is truly respectful of self and others. Here are some examples:

1. Decision-Making: Keys to Total Success. Facing a serious teen pregnancy problem (147 high school girls known to be pregnant in 1984–85), the San Marcos, California, school system implemented a multifaceted program, which included six-week courses for junior high students on developing study skills, self-esteem, and positive moral values;[15] daily 10-minute lessons on "how to be successful"; a six-week course for 8th graders using Teen Aid's curriculum on the advantages of premarital abstinence and how to regain them (for example, self-respect and protection against pregnancy and disease) after having been sexually active; *Window to the Womb*, a video providing ultrasound footage of early fetal development to show students the power of their sexuality to create human life; and summaries of all lessons for parents plus a parent workshop on teaching sexual morality to teens.[16]

After San Marcos implemented this program, known pregnancies at the high school dropped from 20 percent in 1984 to 2.5 percent in 1986 to 1.5 percent in 1988. Meanwhile, scores on tests of basic skills went up, and in 1988 San Marcos won an award for the lowest drop-out rate in California.

2. Teen S.T.A.R. (Sexuality Teaching in the context of Adult Responsibility) is currently used with more than 5,000 teens in various regions of the United States and in other countries. The program teaches that fertility is a gift and a power to be respected. Its premise is that "decisions about sexual responsibility will arise from inner conviction and knowledge of the self." More than half of the teens who enter the program sexually active stop sexual activity; very few initiate it.[17]

3. *The Loving Well Curriculum*, a literature-based program, uses selections from the classics, folktales, and contemporary adolescent literature to examine relationships from family love to infatuation and early romance to marriage. An evaluation finds that of those students who were not sexually active when they started the curriculum, 92 percent are still abstinent two years later, compared to 72 percent abstinent in a control group not exposed to the curriculum.[18]

4. *Postponing Sexual Involvement* was developed by Emory University's Marion Howard specifically for low-income, inner-city 8th graders at risk for early sexual activity. Of students in the program, 70 percent said it taught them that they "can postpone sexual activity without losing their friends' respect." Participants were *five times less likely* to initiate sexual activity than students who did not take the program.[19] ...

ANSWERS TO COMMON QUESTIONS

Educators committing to directive sex education must be prepared to answer some common questions. Among them:

What about all the teens who will remain sexually active despite abstinence education? Shouldn't they be counseled to use condoms? Obviously, if a person is going to have sex, using a condom will reduce the chance of pregnancy and AIDS, but not to an acceptable level. Condoms offer no protection against many other STDs and their long-term consequences, such as infertility. Schools have the mission of teaching the truth and developing right values—which means helping students understand why the various forms of contraception do not make premarital sex physically or emotionally safe and how premature sexual activity will hurt them now and in the future.

Isn't premarital sexual abstinence a religious or cultural value, as opposed to universal ethical values like love, respect, and honesty? Although religion supports premarital abstinence, it can be demonstrated, through ethical reasoning alone, that reserving sex for marriage is a logical application of ethical values. If we love and respect another, we want what is in that person's best interest. Does sex without commitment meet that criterion? Can we say that we really love someone if we gamble with that person's physical health, emotional happiness, and future life? Given the current epidemic of sexually transmitted diseases, it's possible to argue on medical grounds alone that premarital sexual abstinence is the only ethical choice that truly respects self and other.

Isn't the recommendation to save sex for marriage prejudicial against homosexual persons, since the law does not permit them to marry? All students can be encouraged to follow the recommendation of the U.S. Department of Education's guidebook, *AIDS and the Education of Our Children:*

Regardless of sexual orientation, the best way for young people to avoid AIDS and other STDs is to refrain from sexual activity until as adults they are ready to establish a mutually faithful monogamous relationship.[20]

Is abstinence education feasible in places, such as the inner city, where poverty and family breakdown are harsh realities? Programs like Atlanta's Postponing Sexual Involvement have a track record of making abstinence education work amid urban poverty. Virginia Governor Douglas Wilder has argued that "the black family is teetering near the abyss of self-destruction" and that "our young, male and female alike, must embrace the self-discipline of abstinence."[21] Sylvia Peters, who won national acclaim for her work as principal of the Alexander Dumas School (K-8) in inner-city Chicago, made the decision to tell her students (6th graders were getting pregnant before she arrived), "Do not have sex until you are married—you will wreck your life."[22] These two black leaders know that the problem of black illegitimate births—up from 35 to 65 percent in little more than two decades— won't be solved until there is a new ethic of sexual responsibility.

Sexual behavior is determined by value, not mere knowledge. Studies show that students who have value orientations (for example, get good grades in school, have high self-regard, consider their religious faith important, have strong moral codes), are significantly less likely to be sexually active than peers who lack these values. These internally held values are more powerful than peer pressure.[23]

Our challenge as educators is this: Will we help to develop these values and educate for character in sex, as in all other areas? If we do not move decisively—in our schools, families, churches, government, and media—to promote a higher standard of sexual morality in our society, we will surely see a continued worsening of the plague of sex-related problems —promiscuity, sexual exploitation and rape, unwed pregnancy, abortions, sexually transmitted diseases, the emotional consequences of uncommitted sex, sexual harassment in schools, children of all ages focused on sex in unwholesome ways, sexual infidelity in marriages, pornography, the sexual abuse of children, and the damage to families caused by many of these problems.

Non directive sex education obviously didn't cause all of these problems, and directive sex education won't solve all of them. But at the very least, sex education in our schools must be part of the solution, not part of the problem.

NOTES

1. Centers for Disease Control and Prevention, (1992), "Sexual Behavior Among High School Student, U. S.," in *Morbidity and Mortality Weekly Report 40*, 51–52.

2. American Association of University Women "Report on Sexual Harassment," (June 1993).

3. D. Richard, (1990), *Has Sex Education Failed Our Teenagers?*, (Colorado Springs: Focus on the Family Publishing).

4. S. Cronenwett, (1982), "Response to Symposium on Sex and Children," in *Character Policy*, edited by E. A. Wynne, (Lanham, Md.: University Press of America), p. 101.

5. R. Glasow, (1988), *School-Based Clinics* (Washington, D.C.: NRL Educational Trust Fund).

6. D. A. Dawson, (1986), "The Effects of Sex Education on Adolescent Behavior," *Family Planning Perspectives* 18, 4: 162–170.

7. L. Harris, (1986), "American Teens Speak: Sex, Myth, TV, and Birth Control," poll commissioned by the Planned Parenthood Federation of America.

8. Thanks to Onalee McGraw for this point.

9. E. Jones and J. Forrest, (May/June 1989), "Contraceptive Failure in the United States." *Family Planning Perspectives*.

10. W. Kilpatrick, (1992), *Why Johnny Can't Tell Right From Wrong*, (New York: Simon & Schuster).

11. Reported by CBS Evening News, 1993.

12. Source: Dr. Joe McIlhaney, Medical Institute for Sexual Health, Austin, Texas. For an in-depth treatment of sexually transmitted diseases, see McIlhaney's 1991 book *Safe Sex: A Doctor Explains the Realities of AIDS and Other STDs* (Grand Rapids: Baker Book House).

13. *Safe Sex: Slide Program Lecture Notes*, (1993), (Austin: Medical Institute for Sexual Health).

14. Thanks to Carson Daly for her contribution to this list.

15. These lessons are available from the Jefferson Center for Character Education, Suite 240, 202 S. Lake Ave., Pasadena, CA 91101.

16. Teen Aid, N. 1330 Calispel, Spokane, WA 99201-2320. For information on a similar program with comparable positive outcomes, contact: SEX RESPECT, P.O. Box 349, Bradley, IL 60915-0349

17. C. Balsam, (October 1992), "Letter to the Editor," *New Oxford Review*. For information about Teen S.T.A.R., contact Hanna Klaus, P.O. Box 30239, Bethesda, MD 20824-0239.

18. Based on an article by S. Ellenwood in *Character* (April, 1993), the newsletter of Boston University's Center for the Advancement of Ethics and Character. For information about the Loving Well Curriculum, contact Nancy McLaren, Project Coordinator, College of Communication, Boston University, 460 Commonwealth Ave., Boston, MA 02215

19. M. Howard and J. McCabe, (1990), "Helping Teenagers Postpone Sexual Involvement," *Family Planning Perspectives* 22: 1.

20. *AIDS and the Education of Our Children*, (1988), (Washington, D.C.: U.S. Department of Education).

21. L. D. Wilder, (March 28, 1991), "To Save the Black Family, the Young Must Abstain," *The Wall Street Journal*.

22. S. Peters, (February 1993), comments as a panel member at the annual conference of the Character Education Partnership, Washington, D.C.

23. I am indebted to William Bennett for this point.

NO

Jessica Gress-Wright

THE CONTRACEPTION PARADOX

The debate over contraception is an old one. In 1916, Margaret Sanger, the founder of Planned Parenthood, was thrown in jail for offering advice and contraceptives to married women in Brooklyn. But the present controversy over giving contraceptives to teenagers dates, like so much else in the American culture wars, from the early 1970s, when contraceptives first became available to teens through publicly funded family planning programs.

As births to unwed teens rose throughout the 1970s, conservatives increasingly resented the thought that they were paying taxes to support programs that encouraged the sexual misbehavior of their own children. This resentment found formal expression in January 1981, when Richard Schweiker, President Reagan's newly appointed Secretary of Health and Human Services, declared that doctors treating unmarried teenagers under Medicaid should not be permitted to prescribe contraceptives. This statement aroused such sharp criticism that Schweiker was silenced. His Assistant Secretary of Health, Dr. Edward Brant, Jr., was soon at pains to reassure the public (and the interest groups responsible for much of the outcry) that the government considered support of family planning services a "necessity."

Such support is not cheap. Since 1970, the federal Office for Family Planning has spent more than $4 billion to provide women with physical exams, counseling, and contraceptives. Federally funded programs serve 4.5 million women today, of whom a million and a half are teens. Services are provided through 5,100 family planning agencies, of which the oldest and largest is Planned Parenthood. Through its network of 691 affiliated clinics, Planned Parenthood offers contraceptive counseling and prescriptions to over a million clients, while its education programs serve another million. To conservatives, Planned Parenthood's influence, public funding, and stand on teenage sex have made it the very symbol of deliberate decadence. Catholics United for Life once wrote that "Planned Parenthood is anti-life and anti-family and opposes all our Christian values."

While there are obvious differences of opinion here, liberals and conservatives do share some common ground. Both sides agree that raising children

From Jessica Gress-Wright, "The Contraception Paradox," *The Public Interest*, no. 113 (Fall 1993), pp. 15–25. Copyright © 1993 by National Affairs, Inc. Reprinted by permission.

is not something to be undertaken lightly. Both sides also agree that it is best if teenagers delay reproduction. The disagreement is over how.

PREVENTING PREGNANCY, CONTROLLING SEX

Sex education programs, such as those sponsored by Planned Parenthood, seek to delay reproduction by preventing pregnancy rather than preventing sex. Advocates of such programs assume that sex among teenagers is commonplace and neither can nor should be stopped. In this view, the better the sex education and the easier the access to contraceptives, the lower the rate of teenage pregnancy.

Conservatives, particularly among the religious right, seek to delay reproduction by controlling sex. They argue that the federal policy of making counseling and contraceptives easily available has done nothing to stabilize, much less reduce, teenage pregnancy. Indeed, they argue, the policy has had the perverse effect of increasing teen pregnancy. Distributing contraceptives encourages early and inappropriate sex, they say, by adding tacit adult approval to already existing social pressures. Moreover, since teens are such poor users of contraceptives, more sexual intercourse results in more pregnancies, while the moral assumptions implicit in the contraceptive approach guarantee that many of these pregnancies will end in abortion.

SEX IN SWEDEN

As the contraception debate rages on, the pregnancy rate continues to rise. Around one million teens—10 percent of American teenage girls—become pregnant each year. Conservatives point to this and ar-

gue that the policies of the past two decades have been a miserable failure, while liberals argue that what is needed is more—not less—of the same.

Evidence from other countries, however, suggests that both sides are mistaken. Consider the case of Sweden. Unlike the U.S., Sweden has low and even falling rates of teen pregnancy and abortion. Yet Sweden does not have abstinence programs like those advocated in America—quite the opposite.

In 1974, the Swedish sex-education curriculum was officially revised. Under the new curriculum, commitment was still stressed, but "panegyrics to marriage" were dropped. The curriculum also eliminated "the general recommendation of restraint when young." The curricular reform commission, accommodating and encouraging changes already taking place in popular opinion, directed that teachers emphasize to students that sex is natural; that a person without a developed sexuality is deficient; that premarital sex is to be expected; that cohabitation and childbearing outside of marriage are acceptable; and that even adultery is tolerable. The new curriculum constituted a decisive repudiation of all Judeo-Christian teaching on sex.

Unsurprisingly, perhaps, surveys have found Swedish teens to be quite sexually active. A 1976 study in Stockholm found that 80 percent of boys and 89 percent of girls were sexually experienced by age nineteen. Other studies have come up with figures of around 80 percent for both sexes.

When the first reliable American survey was taken in 1971, it found that just 30 percent of unmarried girls between fifteen and nineteen were sexually active. By 1979, 50 percent of girls were sexually active by nineteen, yet American nineteen-year olds were still four times as likely as Swedish nineteen-year olds to be virgins.

SEX EDUCATION

The sharp difference in U.S. and Swedish teen pregnancy rates must have some explanation other than the level of sexual activity—and that explanation is contraception. Nearly two-thirds of the tenth-grade girls in an Uppsala survey used a contraceptive at first intercourse, as opposed to 20 percent of Americans in a similar study. Later, the Uppsala teenagers were even more careful. Eighty-two percent used contraception, and they were more likely than American teens to use highly effective methods such as the pill and IUD. A 1979 survey of sexually active teens in America found that only 34 percent always used contraceptives; another 39 percent used them inconsistently. Twenty-seven percent never used contraceptives at all.

Why are Swedish teens more conscientious than Americans? Better sex education would seem to be one answer. Sex education has been compulsory in Sweden since 1956, and today Sweden has the most comprehensive sex education program in the world. Those who measure the sexual knowledge of American teens, on the other hand, routinely deplore the ignorance they discover.

Yet lack of sex education cannot explain everything. Even very young, very poor American teens know the basics of how babies are made, and that it is possible to prevent pregnancy. Sex education is available, moreover, in 80 percent of urban school districts and to an estimated 70 percent of girls aged fifteen to nineteen. Yet teen pregnancy rates are highest in precisely those areas where sex education is most available and most sophisticated.

Sex education may not even be necessary. A study that compared the contraceptive knowledge of Italian and Swedish adolescents found that 98 percent of the teens from a small town in a very traditional area of southern Italy, where the schools were forbidden to teach sex education, strongly believed that the schools ought to provide such education. The Italian teens assumed that, without formal instruction, they must be ignorant. Yet they scored as well or better than the Swedes on tests of reproductive and contraceptive knowledge. (Nonetheless, the Swedish teens seem able to use contraceptives successfully even on the basis of shaky knowledge.)

If sex education is not the whole answer, then perhaps easy access to contraceptives is. If only contraceptives were available at low cost, without guilt or shame, it is frequently argued, then American teens, who are having sex anyway, would at least not have babies, too.

It is true that Swedes have easy access to low-cost, effective contraceptives, and that, in general, Americans must search somewhat harder and pay more. But even if easy access to contraceptives and good sex education could somehow explain the different teen pregnancy rates in Sweden and America, they cannot explain the differences *within* America. And those differences are big.

RACE MATTERS

Adolescent motherhood is a problem for both black and white Americans. The incidence of unwed motherhood is actually rising faster for whites than blacks; unwed mothers now account for 23 percent of all white births. But the problem is far greater among blacks. Sixty-four percent of black births are out-of-wedlock. Of births to black teens in 1983, nine out of ten were out-of-wedlock (compared to four out of ten for whites). Forty-one percent of black women have a child by the time they are twenty. The black adolescent pregnancy rate is the highest in the developed world.

Of course, many black adolescents do not have babies. A black teen is more, not less, likely than a white to abort a given pregnancy; 65 percent of black teen pregnancies end in abortion. Moreover, black teens who use contraception are more likely than whites to use modern, effective methods such as the pill, rather than old-fashioned methods such as withdrawal, perhaps because they are more likely to have access to a clinic and to free prescriptions. But the sheer number of black teen pregnancies overwhelms these moderating effects.

How can we explain the difference in black and white teen pregnancy rates? Differences in income and educational level might seem obvious answers, but once these are controlled for, the black rate is still higher. (Poverty and poor education, moreover, cannot explain why teen motherhood is so much more prevalent among blacks today than forty years ago, when overt discrimination was rampant, poverty worse, and schools formally segregated.)

As for access to family planning services, it seems to be somewhat easier for black teens. They are more likely than whites to be eligible for free or low-cost contraceptives and counseling at government-funded clinics. White teens tend to see private doctors—often their family doctors—and frequently must pay full price for counseling and contraceptives. And while white teens tend to fear discovery by their parents, black teens are more confident that parents and neighbors will approve.

One reason for the high black pregnancy rate could be that black teens are sexually active at an early age, on average a full year earlier than white American teens. But adolescents in other countries also start sex early, and the sexual pattern of American black teens is, in fact, remarkably similar to that of Swedes. For both groups, intercourse typically begins in the mid-teens, and about 85 percent are sexually experienced by the time they are nineteen. Yet the Swedish teens do not get pregnant.

A QUESTION OF MOTIVATION

The evidence from Sweden undermines the conservative hypothesis that sex is the root of the teen pregnancy problem. And the comparative evidence from America undermines the liberal hypothesis that contraceptives and sex education are the answer. Out-of-wedlock births are most likely in the very urban neighborhoods where family planning services are cheapest, where school clinics are available, and where elaborate programs to encourage teens to use contraceptives are most prevalent.

Precisely because the familiar explanations no longer suffice those who study teenage pregnancy, including those most sympathetic to the plight of teenage mothers, are beginning to ask themselves whether a lack of motivation to prevent pregnancy, rather than a lack of opportunity, may explain why American teens —especially black teens—have such high rates of pregnancy and are so likely to bear children young.

We know that there are sharp cultural differences between American blacks and whites in the expectations and attitudes that surround sex and childbirth. Both groups value marriage and both groups have high educational and job aspirations. But unlike white teens, black teens perceive little stigma in premarital sex or out-of-wedlock childbirth, and many expect approval from their peers and support from their families.

Early childbirth is also something of a tradition among blacks. In 1950, for example, many more black than white teens were mothers, and these black teens later went on to have much larger families. Black communities tend to tolerate and even expect early motherhood. And blacks have traditionally relied upon relatives and extended family for aid, which makes adolescent childbearing easier.

But appeals to a distinctive black culture cannot explain changes over time within the black community. In the early 1950s, 74 percent of black mothers had their first child within marriage. Of those mothers who did have a child out-of-wedlock, three-quarters eventually married. Even as late as 1970, 30 percent of black teen births were to married girls.

Today teen marriage has nearly disappeared, but black Americans, unlike whites, have not delayed childbearing, even though the prospects of supporting a family on one youthful income are dim. A substantial minority of black teens, in fact, *wants* to have a child before marriage. For more than a third of black women, the connection between family formation and childbearing has not just shifted but reversed. Reproduction is preceding its prerequisites, independence and adulthood. The consequences are severe. By refusing to delay childbearing, many black teens are condemning themselves to lives of dependency.

WORK AND FAMILY

There is one other developed country that has suffered a sudden increase in unwed teen motherhood: Great Britain. Britain, like Sweden, is a welfare state with a national health care system. Contraceptives and abortion are easily available, as in Sweden. But Britain's rate of unwed teenage motherhood, like America's, is rising fast and has become a major public issue. In 1957, less than one in twenty British babies were illegitimate; in 1985, one in five were. British teens are much more likely than Swedish teens to be indifferent users of contraceptives, to become pregnant, to oppose abortion, and to carry the child to term. Even more than American teens, they are likely to keep the child and raise it on the dole. Clearly, availability of contraceptives, even paired with a national health system, is not enough to prevent teen motherhood.

But if neither poverty, lack of contraceptives, lack of sex education, nor even sex itself can explain the rise in unwed teen motherhood, what can? How is it that adults in Sweden have succeeded in persuading teenage girls to delay childbearing, while equally well-meaning adults in Great Britain and America have not?

One possible explanation is the very different life cycles in the three countries. While Swedish women begin sex at an early age, they are serious about their education. As they grow older, they become strongly attached to the labor market. Eighty-six percent of mothers with children under six are in the labor force (although at any one time, many are temporarily unemployed or on paid maternity leave).

This strong labor market attachment results in childbearing that is precise and uniform. Ninety percent of Swedish women, near the biological maximum, become mothers. Very large families are rare, however; women have an average of two children. It can be difficult and expensive to accommodate more, as cars, houses, and even the packages of frozen food at the supermarket are designed with the four-person family in mind. The government subsidies that make raising two children so affordable, moreover, are paid for by high taxes that make raising four children almost impossible.

This uniformity of childbearing extends not just to the number of children, but to the timing of their births. The strong emphasis on school and work means that childbearing is delayed very long, until an average age of twenty-six. Swedish mothers then space their children, on average, about twenty-two months apart, which enables mothers to take maximum advantage of a special maternity leave provision and, incidentally, allows them to finish their childbearing quickly and return to the labor market.

In Great Britain, by contrast, women have entered the labor market more slowly. The image of a young mother at home with her children, obsolete in Scandanavia for two decades or more, is still plausible to many British teens. American women, too, have much more ambivalent attitudes toward combining work and family than do Swedish women. Despite the rise of the two-income family, a majority of American women would prefer to be home with their young children if they could afford it. In both the U.S. and Great Britain, many still see the role of housewife and mother as an honorable alternative to a lifelong career outside the home, and the family as the most important institution in society.

We know that work outside the home both delays and depresses childbearing. This is one of the best established facts of demographics. It should not surprise us, then, that girls who expect to work outside the home are much more likely than girls who do not to use contraceptives carefully and delay childbearing. One way to find out whether teens expect to work is to ask them about their educational and employment aspirations. American girls, it turns out, have high aspirations, yet still become pregnant. They seem not to act in a way that would allow them to fulfill their ambitions. This is even more true for black teens. Their educational and employment aspirations are higher than those of whites, once family background is controlled for. It seems that while virtually all Swedish teens concretely prepare for a job, many American teens —especially black teens—aspire vaguely to a career.

MOTHERHOOD AND MONEY

This leaves us with a conundrum. What is it about living in America and Britain that makes the disastrous decision to become an unwed teen mother so attractive? There are no firm answers, but there are some hints. In America, opportunity cost appears to be a very important influence on the decision to abort. Women who expect relatively high wages are far more likely to abort an unplanned pregnancy than are women who expect lower wages. In Sweden, wages even for unskilled women are frequently two to three times the American minimum wage.

Another, more significant, difference between the countries lies in welfare payments to single mothers. In Sweden, only a quarter of single mothers receive means-tested benefits. Swedish mothers expect state support, but in the form of unemployment and maternity-leave benefits, which are available only to women attached to the labor market. In the U.S. and Great Britain, unwed mothers can rely on a dole that permits them (pace nominal workfare requirements) to stay home. When free time and health benefits are added to the secure, if low, income of welfare, teen motherhood may seem a reasonable alternative to a lonely independence eked out on the minimum wage.

This is an old and controversial argument. Many have disputed the suggestion that teenage mothers are much influenced by economic incentives. It is frequently pointed out that the number of unwed mothers has continued to rise despite declines in the real value of welfare grants. But while it is true that the value of cash grants has declined from a high in the mid-1970s, new calculations suggest that once the value of additional benefits, such as food stamps, Medicaid, and free school lunches, is calculated in, the total economic value of the welfare package has risen in tandem with the growth of welfare caseloads. Life on welfare may indeed be economically rational in countries such as the U.S., where the wages of unskilled women are relatively low.

This is not to say that the problem of teen motherhood can be solved overnight by a tripling of the minimum wage. The high minimum wage is a blunt tool, and, as the Swedes are discovering, a tool that even committed welfare state governments can hardly afford. Nor is this to suggest that mandatory workfare is the solution. In the Netherlands, mothers with young children are less likely to work than in America, yet the teen pregnancy and abortion rates there are even lower than in Sweden.

AMERICAN AMBIVALENCE

Comparisons with Sweden and Great Britain suggest that America's difficulties with teen childbearing and abortion can be traced partly to continued cultural ambivalence about chastity, childbearing, and working. White American teens— the vast majority of American teens— are in some ways like Swedish teens. They are very likely to combine work and motherhood, and, on average, will delay childbearing well into their twenties. Unlike Swedish teens, however, most American teens must contend with their parents' and society's continued disapproval of premarital sex. The ironic result is that American teens are more likely than Swedish teens to get pregnant and abort for the same reason that they are less likely to have sex—ambivalent attitudes toward sex and contraception.

Black American teens also are like Swedish teens in some ways. Both groups come from milieux that tolerate early sexual activity and out-of-wedlock childrearing. Both groups are ensured access to sex education and contraception through government programs. But, unlike black teens, Swedish teens use the contraception they have so as to delay childbearing for as long as a decade after they begin having sex.

Black or white, it seems that American teens are both too liberated—they have sex, and not liberated enough— they don't use contraceptives. Those who make policy must decide whether the conservative approach—abstinence—or the liberal approach—providing contraceptives—is more desirable in the local context. Programs of birth control will probably be highly effective for those teens, white and black, who want to delay reproduction and who come from families and neighborhoods where teen sex is largely accepted. Teaching abstinence may work where ambivalence about sex is still strong.

But the decision to use contraceptives consistently and the decision to abstain both depend on a prior conviction that it is worthwhile to delay childbearing. It is just this conviction that can no longer be assumed.

Teenage girls can be helped to become efficient users of contraceptives. This is easiest to do, however, when they expect to work throughout their lives and when work seems to them worthwhile. Only then do they put a high value on completing their education and delaying childbearing. Only then do they conceive of motherhood as the culmination of, rather than a substitute for, independent adulthood.

POSTSCRIPT

Is Abstinence Education the Best Sex Education?

Out-of-wedlock births to adolescent mothers has become problematic in our society for several reasons. The onset of the menarche (first ovulation and subsequent menstruation) is coming at increasingly earlier ages for young females. This combined with the tendency for delaying marriage means that the adolescent female faces longer periods of singlehood during her fertile years than did her great-grandmother. Consider, for example, that it was not uncommon for a women born at the turn of the century to be married at age 17 or 18. Consider, too, that this woman's menarche was a year or more later than that of a contemporary adolescent female. The result is fewer years of singlehood and fewer opportunities for premarital sexual endeavors.

Current notions regarding adolescent sexuality suggest that teens will inevitably express themselves sexually as part of the developmental process of adolescence. Therefore, unless they are taught to exercise restraint and sexual abstinence, they should be apprised of the risks of early sexual activity and empowered with information about how to express themselves sexually while avoiding pregnancy and sexually transmitted diseases. But on the basis of current rates of teen pregnancy, the information teens are now receiving is not encouraging more responsible behaviors, be those behaviors abstinence or the use of contraceptives.

SUGGESTED READINGS

Darling, C., Kallen, D., & VanDusen, J. (1992). Sex in transition, 1900–1980. In A. Skolnick and J. Skolnick (Eds.), *Family in Transition* (pp. 151–160). New York: HarperCollins.

Donovan, P. (1989). *Risk and responsibility: Teaching sex education in America's schools today*. New York: Alan Guttmacher Institute.

Kantor, L. M. (1993). Scared chaste? Fear-based educational curricula, *SIECUS Report, 21*, 1–15.

Miller, B. C., & Moore, K. A. (1990). Adolescent sexual behavior, pregnancy and parenting: Research through the 1980s. *Journal of Marriage and the Family, 52*, 1025–1044.

Robinson, I., Ziss, K., Ganza, B., & Katz, S. (1991). Twenty years of the sexual revolution, 1965–1985: An update. *Journal of Marriage and the Family, 53*, 216–220.

Whitehead, B. D. (1994, October). The failure of sex education. *Atlantic Monthly*, 55–80.

ISSUE 17

Are Gangs Created by a Need for Family?

YES: Jim Burke, from "Teenagers, Clothes, and Gang Violence," *Educational Leadership* (September 1991)

NO: John M. Hagedorn, from "Gangs, Neighborhoods, and Public Policy," *Social Problems* (November 1991)

ISSUE SUMMARY

YES: Jim Burke, a high school English teacher in California, describes how gang members wear certain clothes to communicate membership in a particular group. He contends that if children feel no security at home, they will seek it through the group affiliation that gangs provide.

NO: John M. Hagedorn, a researcher at the Urban Research Center, University of Wisconsin–Milwaukee, claims that economic problems, such as low wages and lack of jobs, are the reasons why young people join gangs. He suggests that gang membership would be short-lived if members had access to good jobs

Twenty-five or 30 years ago, when people heard the term *street gang* they conjured up an image of the Jets and the Sharks from the popular Broadway musical and movie *West Side Story*. Gangs today are vaguely similar to those in *West Side Story* in that they are comprised of minors and young adults, have a name, have identifiable leadership, and claim some geographic territory as their own. But contemporary gangs are dangerous, motivated by violence, and engaged in extortion, intimidation, and illegal trafficking in drugs and weapons. In order to be accepted by the group, gangs have some type of membership initiation, which usually involves violence. Members associate on a regular basis, often engaging in delinquent or criminal behaviors, such as assault, rape, robbery, vandalism, and even murder.

The gang culture has its own characteristic vocabulary. Common gang-related jargon includes words like *maddogging* (intimidating others by staring them down or other, more aggressive acts); *home-boy* or *homie* (one of the neighborhood boys); *tap* or *cap* (to shoot someone); *smacking* or *talking smack* (criticizing the reputation or character of someone); and *turf* (the gang's claimed territory). Other elements of gang culture include the use of graffiti to mark a gang's territorial boundary and the use of tattoos and various modes of dress to differentiate one gang from another.

Large metropolitan areas with inner cities are not the only places gangs can be found. They are now spreading throughout suburban and even rural communities. Membership in gangs includes young people from most racial and ethnic backgrounds. Perhaps most troubling is the fact that schools are the major recruiting grounds for gangs. While it is true that most gang members drop out of school, younger members still attend school and actively recruit other students.

There are several factors that have been strongly associated with putting adolescents at risk for gang recruitment. It is interesting to note that many of these factors are identical to ones that put them at risk for dropping out of school, abusing drugs and alcohol, and engaging in premature sexual activity:

1. Children who do not feel competent in either their ability to function effectively in their families or to learn in school are at risk.
2. Children who seldom receive any validation or affirmation from family members and school staff regarding positive aspects of their behavior are at risk.
3. The child who does not bond or feel a sense of connectedness with the family or school is at risk.

Many child and adolescent development specialists suspect that unmet needs predispose children to affiliate with gangs, but there is still much debate as to what needs are going unmet and how to remedy the situation. The following selections try to determine what needs drive individuals to join gangs. One basic need of all human beings is to feel a sense of belongingness. This fosters a sense of security for the person. If this does not occur in the family system, do children turn to gangs to fulfill this need?

A different need, that of validation and affirmation that one can make it in society, is fulfilled by learning to function economically. This is most typically achieved through employment and earning power. Do children turn to gangs because they can earn more respect among their gang peers and more money through illicit activities than they could with a legitimate job in mainstream society?

YES
Jim Burke

TEENAGERS, CLOTHES, AND GANG VIOLENCE

Students cannot learn if they do not feel safe. No matter how you define safety—emotional or physical—it is a necessity in both the school and the classroom. While this seems obvious, perhaps even unnecessary to point out, the fact is that the school is becoming an arena of increasingly serious and constant violence.

And this violence no longer limits itself to the inner city. Witness the fiasco at San Leandro High School in the fall of 1990, where 3 to 20 students (depending on whom you talk to) were injured in a riot stemming from racial tensions that had erupted on that particular day. At a Bay Area high school near San Francisco, a locker search following some trouble yielded 62 guns, more than 40 of which turned up in girls' lockers. Recently, two students from my own school, a suburban school in the East Bay, entered the parking lot of a nearby convenience store to buy their lunch; one of them left in an ambulance, unconscious. He had been savagely beaten by 10 to 15 students while reportedly out cold—all this over a girl one of the gangsters went out with. One of my own students currently hides from a gang from a neighboring town because he is dating a girl whose ex-boyfriend is in a gang. Last week a freshman in another of my classes told me her boyfriend had been robbed of his Raiders jacket while the thief held a gun to his head. She herself reports having been shot at several weeks ago for wearing black and red—colors associated with a gang not welcome where she was.

GANG MEMBERS AND CLOTHES

To become better informed as we attempt to manage these new and difficult problems, my school recently invited Joe Angeles to speak with our faculty on the topic of gangs. Angeles works with the Alameda County schools as a sort of gang guru, having a background in law enforcement, counseling, and education. At our meeting, he focused on the clothes these youths wear. At our school, and the surrounding area, Raiders jackets can mark one as a member of an exclusive club, which the kids may or may not define as a

From Jim Burke, "Teenagers, Clothes, and Gang Violence," *Educational Leadership*, vol. 49, no. 1 (September 1991), pp. 11–13. Copyright © 1991 by The Association for Supervision and Curriculum Development. Reprinted by permission.

gang. I find many of these students in my English classes. Curious, I asked Angeles what distinguished the actual gang member from the kid who liked to wear Raiders regalia. He said that the gang member wears the prescribed clothes intentionally, hoping by means of his dress to communicate publicly his membership with a group to those around him; the gang member will frequently alter or individualize his clothes—having his nickname embroidered on, or writing his gang's name under, the bill of his hat. Such a "uniform" will, if the individual shows up in the wrong place, put him in danger should he come into contact with a rival gang. Related to this, I would add, is the degree to which such students are willing to go to protect their comrades who wear similar "membership only" items of clothing.

The role of females in these groups is especially troubling. Why would such nice young women as fill two of my classes spend their time with boys who, as Angeles said, see them only as "objects, possessions, holders of illicit goods"? In an era when the role and esteem of women in our society should be on the rise, why do these girls seek such subservience, such emotional, if not physical, degradation? Perhaps it is because they, too, want protection. Or they are afraid to say, "No, I won't hold your drugs or keep your gun in my locker."

KIDS NEED SECURITY AT HOME

A recent report by the National Center for Health Statistics attempts to lay full blame for many of these children's troubles on their parents—specifically, single parents. An article from the *Chicago Tribune*, discussing the findings of this report, summed it up well: "Emotional and behavioral problems were two to three times higher among children in single-parent homes or in families with one step-parent."[1] This tells me these parents may be absent both physically and emotionally from their children's lives, that they may pay little or no attention to the kids their child hangs out with or what they wear.

When these parents go shopping for Christmas or birthday presents to compensate for their absence, will they buy the requested Raiders, or Kings, or other sports team jacket? Most of these kids do not purchase these items with their own money. Parents must be aware of what their children wear, especially if an item of clothing seems to indicate some connection to other kids they see around. What kids wear can put them in danger today.

Security is a feeling that should begin at home; it begins with children knowing their parent or parents are watching out for them. If they feel no security from home, they will seek it elsewhere.

KIDS CREATE THEIR OWN "FAMILIES"

Every other week, for 10 minutes at the end of the day, I supervise the area at our school where cars come to pick up students. It is here that the students who belong to The Great Disconnected—who signify their membership by wearing their large black Raiders jackets and black and red clothes—"hang" with each other. Week after week, I see these kids trying to create their own families. They do this because so many of them have no family at home that provides them with affection, with a sense of belonging. They feel that no one at home cares about them so much that they would smash someone who insulted them, as their Raiders-jacketed friends would do.

I think of the things I've read earlier in the day in the journals of some of these same students. What they spelled out for me was that they do not feel safe alone in our society. So they resort to the purchased security of a certain jacket and run with others who feel similarly ostracized from school, friends who lead friends far from the security that a good education might provide. They hope that if they wear a Raiders jacket, some lunatic who has a gun in his or her locker will leave them alone. What they fail to understand is that the Raiders jacket or the Ben Davis work shirt or the red bandanna—or whatever it is—is often a signal that sends fear or anger into the other kid, who runs for his gun, his bat, his friends, so that he, too, can feel safe in a school where they all feel too scared or distracted to learn or participate in the larger community of the school.

BRIDGES FROM THE SCHOOL TO THE COMMUNITY

We cannot create some national curriculum that will magically solve the need for safety, for membership in the community. Nor can we, in most cases, involve the family in such a way as would improve the "curriculum" of the home. We can, however, develop a curriculum that incorporates the school into the community and gets the community into the schools.

We can make positive rites of passage available to students through various programs at school that, we hope, will draw them away from the hazardous rites of passage they now seek out. These connections would provide students with a sense of belonging to the society; they would also, significantly, impress upon the community the realization that these kids are not villains, but their kids, *our* kids.

We must also look to the thousands of teachers who daily perform acts of personal kindness and work to bring such teens into the fold. It is teachers, more than anyone, who are in a position to erect these bridges to the community. And, if built, such bridges will bring students like Richard—one of my freshmen who recently returned from jail for a gang-related assault—into the community, where they can see, as he did recently, his picture in the newspaper, the community recognizing him, along with other students, for his work with a group of retired older adults. It is only by providing a positive, humane, and safe "gang" of youths who participate in the community and are recognized by the community that we will get them away from the other gangs that spread the fear we all feel.

NOTES

1. R. Korulak, (December 9, 1990), "Survey Links Youth Problems to One-Parent Families," *San Francisco Examiner*, p. A-5 (This article originally appeared in the Chicago Tribune).

NO

John M. Hagedorn

GANGS, NEIGHBORHOODS, AND PUBLIC POLICY

Are today's youth gangs part of an "underclass"? What policies should communities adopt to control their gang problem? Based on recent gang research and experience in reforming Milwaukee's human service bureaucracy, we can address these questions and suggest practical local policies that go beyond the usual nostrums of "more cops" and "more jobs."

In the last few years a number of researchers have suggested that today's gangs have changed in some fundamental ways and may be part of an urban minority "underclass" (Moore 1985, Short 1990b, Taylor 1990, Vigil 1988). The nature of the "underclass," however, has been the subject of controversy (Aponte 1988, Gans 1990, Jencks 1989, Ricketts, Mincy, and Sawhill 1988, Wilson 1991). This paper uses data gathered from three different Milwaukee studies over the past five years to examine the changing nature of Milwaukee's gangs, the characteristics of Milwaukee's poorest African-American neighborhoods, and the relationship between gangs and neighborhoods.

For the first study, completed in 1986, 47 of the founding members of Milwaukee's 19 major gangs, including 11 of the 19 recognized leaders, were interviewed (Hagedorn 1988). That study described the origins of Milwaukee gangs, their structure and activities, and documented how gangs came to be seen as a social problem. It also tracked the education, employment, drug use, incarceration experience, and the level of gang participation of the 260 young people who founded the 19 gangs, including the 175 founders of 12 African-American male gangs.

A brief follow-up study in spring of 1990 looked at the patterns of drug abuse and the structure of gang drug dealing in three African-American gangs. This pilot study tracked the employment, incarceration, and drug use status of the 37 founding members of the three gangs since the original study. It began a process of exploring the relationship between Milwaukee gangs and drug dealing businesses or "drug posses."

Finally, as part of a human services reform plan, Milwaukee County commissioned a needs assessment in two neighborhoods where several of Milwaukee's gangs persist (Moore and Edari 1990b). Residents were hired to

From John M. Hagedorn, "Gangs, Neighborhoods, and Public Policy," *Social Problems*, vol. 38, no. 4 (November 1991), pp. 529–542. Copyright © 1991 by The Society for the Study of Social Problems. Reprinted by permission. References omitted.

survey heads of households drawn from a probability sample of 300 households in ten census tracts in two neighborhoods. These neighborhoods had a high percentage of residents living in poverty and a clustering of social problems associated with the "underclass."

This article first looks at how Milwaukee gangs have changed due to deindustrialization. Second, the paper explores some volatile social dynamics occurring within poor but still heterogeneous African-American neighborhoods. Finally, based on the analysis of gangs and their neighborhoods, other underclass research, and on the author's own experience in reforming the delivery of social services, the article suggests several local policies to strengthen and assist community institutions with gang troubles.

MACRO-ECONOMIC TRENDS AND GANGS IN MILWAUKEE

The underclass has been conceptualized as a product of economic restructuring that has mismatched African-American and other minority workers with radically changed employment climates (Bluestone and Harrison 1982, Kasarda 1985, Sullivan 1989). Milwaukee epitomizes this mismatch: between 1979 and 1986 over 50,000 jobs were lost or 23 percent of Milwaukee's manufacturing employment (White et al. 1988:2–6). African-American workers were hit especially hard. In 1980, prior to the downturn, 40 percent of all African-American workers were concentrated in manufacturing (compared to 31 percent of all city workers). By 1989, research in five all-black Milwaukee census tracts found that only about one quarter of all black workers were still employed in manufactur-

ing (Moore and Edari 1990b). African-American unemployment rates in Milwaukee have reached as high as 27 percent over the past few years.

Another way to view economic changes in the African-American community is to look at social welfare over the last thirty years. Like European immigrants before them, African-Americans came to Milwaukee with the hopes of landing good factory jobs (Trotter 1985), and large numbers succeeded. But as industrial employment declined and good jobs were less available, reliance on welfare increased (Piven and Cloward 1987:83). In 1963, when black migration to Milwaukee was still rising, fewer than one in six of Milwaukee's African-Americans were supported by AFDC. However by 1987, nearly half of all Milwaukee African-Americans and two thirds of their children received AFDC benefits. Seven out of every ten Milwaukee African-Americans in 1987 were supported by transfer payments of some kind accounting for half of all 1987 black income in Milwaukee County (Hagedorn 1989a).

Coinciding with reduced economic prospects for African-Americans, Hispanics, and other working people, gangs reemerged in Milwaukee and other small and medium-sized cities across the Midwest. While the popular notion at the time was that these gangs had diffused from Chicago, gangs in Milwaukee and the Midwest developed from corner groups and break-dancing groups in processes nearly identical to those described by Thrasher fifty years before (Hagedorn 1988, Huff 1989). The economy may have been changing, but the way gangs formed had not.

In 1986 we interviewed 47 of the 260 Milwaukee gang founders or members of the initial groups of young people who started the 19 major gangs in the early 1980s. At the time of our interviews, the founders were in their early twenties and at an age when young people typically "mature out" of gang life. We asked the 47 founders to report on the current status of all the members who were part of the gang when it started. To our surprise, more than 80 percent of all male gang founders were reported as still involved with the gang as twenty to twenty-five year old adults.

We concluded at the time that the *economic basis* for "maturing out" of a gang—those good paying factory jobs that take little education, few skills, and only hard work—was just not there anymore. As Short wrote in a review recent of gang literature, "There is no reason to believe that boys hang together in friendship groups for reasons that are very different now than in the past.... What has changed are the structural economic conditions..." (Short 1990a).

Moore (1991) has also documented economic effects of deindustrialization on the "maturing out" process of Chicano gangs. She finds that members of recent gang cliques in East Los Angeles are less likely to have found good jobs than members of older gang cliques. She concludes, "It is not that the men from recent cliques were more likely to have dropped out of the labor market, nor were they more likely to be imprisoned. It may be that they could not get full-time, stable jobs."

The difficulty in finding a good job today is offset by the abundance of part-time jobs in the illegal drug economy. In preparation for a proposal to the National Institute on Drug Abuse to examine the impact of drug abuse and drug dealing on Milwaukee's gangs, we updated our rosters on the current status of the

37 founding members of three African-American gangs. By 1990, less than one in five (19 percent) of the founders, now in their mid to late twenties, were engaged in full-time work. However, three times as many of the founders (59 percent) graduated from the gang into drug "posses" or high-risk small businesses selling drugs. "High risk" is perhaps an understatement. Almost all of the 37 (86 percent) had spent significant time in prison since 1986, most for drug offenses. Three quarters (76 percent) had used cocaine regularly within the last three years, and three had been murdered. While five of the 37 were said to be working as entrepreneurs (called "hittin' 'em hard"), the others involved with drug distribution worked part time ("makin' it") or sporadically ("day one"), and continued to live on the margins.

As Don, a leader of the 1-9 Deacons told us in 1985: "I can make it for two or three more years. But then what's gonna happen?" The answer to Don's question is now clear. The lack of access to good jobs has had a direct effect of making illegal drug sales, no matter how risky, more attractive to Milwaukee's gang founders as an occupation for their young adult years.

Frederick Thrasher pointed out sixty years ago: "As gang boys grow up, a selective process takes place; many of them become reincorporated into family and community life, but there remains a certain criminal residue upon whom gang training has, for one reason or another, taken hold" (Thrasher 1963:287). The loss of entry level manufacturing jobs appears to have turned Thrasher's "selective process" on its head. Today most of the young adult gang founders rely on the illegal economy for guarantees of survival. It is only the "residue" who, at this time in Milwaukee, are being "reincorporated into family and community life."

There are also some indirect effects of economic changes. In Milwaukee, most of the founders still identify somewhat with their old gang and often hang out in the same neighborhoods where they grew up, coexisting with a new generation of gang youth. This mixing of older members of drug "posses" with younger siblings and other young gang members has produced disturbing intergenerational effects. Older gang members with a street reputation employed in the fast life of drug dealing are modeling dangerous career paths for neighborhood youth. These intergenerational effects also appear in Anderson's latest work (1990). He finds that "old heads," older residents who upheld and disseminated traditional values, are being replaced by *new* "old heads" who "may be the product of a street gang" and who promote values of "hustling," drugs, and sexual promiscuity (103). This "street socialization" may contribute to reproducing an underclass rather than socializing young people into conventional lifestyles (Short 1990b, Vigil 1988).[1]

In summary, contemporary gangs have changed from the "delinquent boys" of fifties literature: There is a growing relationship between the youth gang, illegal drug-based distribution, and survival of young adult gang members in a postindustrial, segmented economy. Clearly, powerful *economic* forces are affecting contemporary gangs as Wilson and other underclass theorists would predict. But when we take a closer look at the impact of economic, demographic, and institutional changes on processes within Milwaukee's poorest African-American neighborhoods, the situation becomes more complicated.

GANGS AND NEIGHBORHOOD SEGMENTATION

Gangs have always been associated with neighborhoods, and African-American gangs have been no exception. Thrasher found "Negroes" had "more than their share" of gangs (Thrasher 1963:132) as far back as the 1920s. In the neighborhood that Suttles studied, gangs were functional "markers" or signs by which neighborhood youth could know who may be harmful and who is not and thus were an important part of a neighborhood's search for order. Suttles' black gangs were not in any significant way distinct from white ethnic gangs (Suttles 1968:157). Similarly, the black Chicago gang members that Short and Strodtbeck (1965:108) studied were quite similar to non-gang black youth, though they were more lower class than white gang members. Until the 1960s, the sociological literature largely viewed black gangs as functional parts of black neighborhoods.

But things have been changing. Perkins, summarizing the history of black Chicago gangs, wrote that gangs first became disruptive to their communities in the 1960s due to the influence of drugs, corrupting prison experiences, and the failure of community-based programs (Perkins 1987:40–42). Cloward and Ohlin theorized that housing projects and other big city "slums" tended to be disorganized and "produce powerful pressures for violent behavior among the young in these areas" (Cloward and Ohlin 1960:172). They correctly predicted that "delinquency will become increasingly violent in the future as a result of the disintegration of slum organization" (203).

Increasing violence in central cities has prompted angry responses from residents. Cooperation by broad elements of the black community with police sweeps of gang members in Los Angeles and elsewhere and the founding of "mothers against gangs" and similar organizations throughout the country are examples of community hostility toward gangs. Gangs today are seen by both law enforcement and many community residents as basically *dysfunctional*. Today's gangs are a far cry from the "Negro" street gangs of Suttle's Addams area which contained the "best-known and most popular boys in the neighborhood" (Suttles 1968:172).

Based on our Milwaukee interviews, we concluded that gang members reciprocated the hostility of "respectables." While the gang founders were hostile toward police and schools as expected, they also severely criticized African-American community agencies which they felt were mainly "phoney." The black founders agreed their gangs were dysfunctional for their neighborhoods: two thirds of those we interviewed insisted that their gang was "not at all" about trying to help the black community. Some were shocked at even the suggestion that their gang would be concerned about anything but *"green* power" (i.e., money). The role model of choice for many of the founders we interviewed was not Dr. Martin Luther King, Jesse Jackson, or any African-American leader, but Al Capone.

One explanation for this intra-community alienation in Milwaukee is the peculiar way black gangs formed. Gang formation in Milwaukee coincided with desegregation of the schools: a one-way desegregation plan that mandato-

rially bused only black children. While gangs originally formed from neighborhood groups of youth in conflict with youth from other neighborhoods, busing complicated the situation. School buses picking up African-American students often stopped in many different neighborhoods, mixing youth from rival gangs and transforming the buses into battlegrounds. Gang recruitment took place on the buses and in the schools as well as from the neighborhood. The black founders told us in 1985/86 that a majority of the members of their gangs no longer came from the original neighborhood where the gang formed.

Consequently, when the gang hung out on neighborhood corners, they were not seen by residents as just the "neighbors' kids" messing up. "I'll tell your Mama" did not work when no one knew who "mama" was or where she lived. Informal social controls were ineffective, so calling the police became the basic method to handle rowdiness and misbehavior as well as more serious delinquency. Hostility between the gangs and the neighborhood increased with each squad car arriving on the block.

A second explanation for intra-community hostility is provided by 1989 research in five of Milwaukee's poorest and all-black census tracts (Moore and Edari 1990b) where several of the gangs I had studied were founded. These neighborhoods exhibit many of the criteria of an "underclass" area, but they also differ in many respects from very poor ghetto neighborhoods described by Wilson and others.

Household income of the tracts was very low—1980 census data (*before* the eighties downturn) show more than 30 percent of the families in the five tracts living below poverty. The five tracts experienced a 42 percent population loss between 1960 and 1985. In 1989, when the interviews were completed, most (53.8 percent) respondents received AFDC and nearly twenty percent (19 percent) did not have a phone. A majority of residents in the five tracts presently live below the poverty line. The tracts certainly qualify as "underclass" areas by standard definitions (Ricketts and Mincy 1988).

But these neighborhoods are not uniformly poor. One quarter of the residents (28.6 percent) owned their own home—fifteen percent less than the city-wide average, but still a stable base within a very poor neighborhood. Half of the household heads lived at their current residence for five or more years. While stable employment had drastically declined in these tracts since 1980, still nearly one third of working respondents had held their current job for 10 or more years. Unlike the "densely settled ghetto areas" Sampson describes (1987:357) where residents have "difficulty recognizing their neighbors," 80 percent of the Milwaukee respondents said the best thing about their neighborhood *was* their "neighbors." Nearly three in five (59.2 percent) visited with neighbors at least once a week.

More striking were strong kinship ties, supporting earlier work by Stack (1974) and others. Nearly half of all respondents visited their parents every day and over ninety percent visited parents monthly. An even higher percentage visited siblings at least once a month. Finally, more than three quarters belonged to families that held family reunions—and 77 percent of those respondents regularly attended those reunions. Even child protective clients, who are among the most transient residents, had extensive kinship networks (Moore and Edari 1990a).[2]

But the neighborhoods are not regarded positively by most residents. Less than one fifth (19.7 percent) said the neighborhood was a "good place to live," and 52 percent said they would move if they could. While respondents liked their neighbors as the best thing about their community, the top three worst things were said to be drugs (64 percent), violence (52 percent), and gangs (20 percent). About half said things had gotten worse the past two years, and a majority (54.5 percent) believed things will continue to get worse. And the problems were not "around the corner" or in an adjacent neighborhood, but right on the blocks where the interviews took place. The interviewers were often told by respondents to not go to a certain house or to avoid a certain side of the street because of dangerous drug or gang problems.

The area also has few basic social institutions. Zip code 53206 is a 20 by 20 square block area with 40,000 residents in the heart of Milwaukee, containing the census tracts where the interviews took place. This area has no large chain grocery stores. There are no banks or check-cashing stores in the entire zip code area. Bars and drug houses are in plentiful supply and the area has the highest number of Milwaukee drug arrests. Still, in 1989, this zip code area did not have a single alcohol/drug treatment facility. Even community agencies are located overwhelmingly on the periphery of 53206, circling the neighborhoods they serve, but not a part of them.[3] Community programs, churches, and social workers were seldom mentioned by survey respondents as a resource to call in times of neighborhood trouble.[4]

In summary, while these poor African-American neighborhoods have characteristics of Wilson's notion of the underclass, they also exhibit important differences. On the one hand, central city Milwaukee neighborhoods have been getting poorer due to deindustrialization and have experienced substantial population loss. They are home to the poorest and most troubled of all Milwaukee's residents. The area's lack of basic institutions is reminiscent of descriptions by Thrasher (1927) and Shaw and McKay (1969) and supports aspects of Wilson's underclass thesis.

On the other hand, large numbers of working class African-American families still reside in these neighborhoods. Some want to leave but cannot because of residential segregation (Massey and Eggers 1990) or lack of affordable housing. But many stay because they want to. Rather than neighborhoods populated overwhelmingly by a residue left behind by a fleeing middle and working class, as Wilson has described, Milwaukee's "underclass" neighborhoods are a checkerboard of struggling working class and poor families, coexisting, even on the same block, with drug houses, gangs, and routine violence.

This ecological coexistence explains much of the intra-community tension between poor and working families and underclass gangs. Clearly when drug deals gone bad turn into midnight shoot-outs, residents of a neighborhood will be scared and angry. Contrary to Wilson's claim, events in one part of the block or neighborhood are often of vital concern to those residing in other parts (Wilson 1987:38). With a lack of effective community institutions, residents can either ignore the gunshots in the night, arm themselves for self-protection, call "911"—or give in to the fear and despair by moving out.[5]

While Milwaukee neighborhoods are not the socially disorganized underclass areas reported by Wilson, neither are they the highly organized neighborhoods described by Whyte (1943) or Suttles (1968). Milwaukee's poor neighborhoods have segmented and an uneasy peace reigns between nervous factions. Suttles (1968) saw the 1960s Addams area as representing "ordered segmentation," where firm boundaries between ethnic neighborhoods helped make "a decent world within which people can live" (234). Instead, Milwaukee's neighborhood segments have become a prime source of instability.

This picture of neighborhood segmentation is consistent with Anderson's portrait of "Northton," a poor African-American community in a large eastern city (Anderson 1990). "Old heads" in Northton are not so much missing, as they have become demoralized and their advice shunned (78–80). Respectable residents are confronted by a growing street culture that increases community distrust of young people, victimizes neighborhood residents, and lures children into dangerous activities (92). Police simplistically divide the neighborhood between the "good people" and those linked to drug trafficking (202–3). Conflict between neighborhood segments inevitably increases, and "solidarity" is sacrificed to the imposed order of police patrols, vigilante justice, and prisons.

These heterogenous but segmented neighborhoods in "Northton" and Milwaukee may be characteristic of many "underclass" communities across the United States (Jencks 1990). How to stabilize such neighborhoods is one of the major policy debates of the nineties.

GANGS, NEIGHBORHOODS, AND PUBLIC POLICY

In light of these findings, what do we make of this contradictory picture of gangs and their neighborhoods? What policies ought to be followed? The data suggest the drug economy flourishes in large part because of the absence of good jobs. It is hard to argue with the response from a 1986 interview:

> Q: OK, we're at the end here. The Governor comes in. He says, Darryl, I'm gonna give you a million dollars to work with gangs. Do what you want with it.
> A: Give 'em all jobs.

But while jobs are certainly needed, there is no reason to believe hundreds of thousands of good paying, entry-level jobs will appear anytime soon from either the private or public sector. In the absence of sufficient jobs, pressure will continue to mount for more police and more prisons as the policy option of choice to curtail violence. This militarization of our neighborhoods is inevitable unless community residents and public officials can be persuaded that alternative policies are plausible and can be effective. But what alternative policies should be advocated?

One popular option is to work with city hall and call for more federal resources to come to cities. While we clearly need more resources, a more critical issue is how money is spent. As Spergel says in summarizing his recommendations in the National Youth Gang Survey "the implications of our findings is that more resources alone for police or even human service programs would not contribute much to dealing effectively with the youth gang problem" (Spergel and Curry 1990:309). In the absence of institutional reform and guarantees that resources will get to those that need it, more resources alone will not necessarily contribute to solving gang problems.[6]

The development of effective policy will require a struggle within cities over where new and existing programs are physically located, who will be served, and how the massive public bureaucracies (which gobble most resources intended for the poor) should be structured. Rather than proposing specific new model gang programs or narrowly calling for a federal office of gang control (Miller 1990), our data suggest a focus on strengthening neighborhood social institutions. Our experience in reforming Milwaukee's human service system suggests that we should adopt four policies to strengthen neighborhood-level social control.

(1) Public spending and private investment must be concentrated in the most impoverished areas. This does not mean spend more human service dollars "for" the underclass by funding well intentioned programs run by middle-class white providers located on the periphery of the poorest neighborhoods. Rather, I suggest we should insist that money be spent mainly on programs physically located *in* underclass neighborhoods, run by people with ties to the neighborhoods they intend to serve. This policy has the effect of targeting programs for the underclass while also strengthening minority agencies or creating new agencies within very poor neighborhoods. These agencies provide not only services but also can provide jobs for neighborhood residents. As employment opportunities increase and better funded local agencies become centers for social action, pressures for working- and middle-class residents to flee should decrease.

For example, in Milwaukee, close examination of where human service dollars were spent by zip code exposed that less than 1 percent of $100 million of Department of Health and Human Service contract dollars in 1988 was spent on programs located in two of Milwaukee's poorest zip code areas (53206 and 53204). These two areas contain only eight percent of Milwaukee County's population but are home to 25 percent of Milwaukee's human service clients. These figures were used by our reform administration to direct several million dollars in purchase contracts to agencies physically located in the two zip code areas, helping build an institutional infrastructure. Boarded up buildings are being rehabilitated to house the new agencies, employing neighborhood youth in the rehabbing effort.

Redirecting existing money is not an easy task. When we sent more than "crumbs" to neighborhood organizations, the mainly white traditional agencies—which are located downtown or in integrated, more stable neighborhoods—howled "reverse discrimination" and lobbied against us. Funding new programs is a zero sum game: if agencies located in poor neighborhoods are to get funded, agencies located elsewhere stand to lose. Those providers will almost certainly have more political power and connections than poor neighborhood organizations.

But as our research shows, while very poor neighborhoods have been devastated by economic and demographic changes, they also have important strengths to build on. The residents who live in poor neighborhoods need stable, well-funded agencies and institutions in which to participate. This recommendation is a call for sustained local political struggle over *where* money is spent to better stabilize impoverished neighborhoods.

(2) Programs should be fully evaluated to see if they are having a positive impact on gangs or those most in need. It is not only important where the money is spent, but it is also critical whether anyone besides the agency or bureaucracy benefits. The inability of traditional agencies to serve the "hard to reach" has a long history: the Chicago Area Project (Schlossman, Zellman, and Schavelson 1984) was initiated to fill just such a gap. Geis cites the 1960s New York City Youth Board as an example of the need for innovative programming to replace the traditional agencies which were unable "to respond readily to new ideas and approaches" (Geis 1965:43). And some programs do "work." Lizbeth Schorr lists numerous contemporary programs that have been effective and could be replicated (Schorr 1988).

Large public bureaucracies are seldom concerned with formal results of programs. Once programs are funded, their continuation is often all that is offered as proof of effectiveness. In Milwaukee, research on agencies which received more than $20 million dollars worth of contracts to work with delinquents discovered the Department of Social Services kept no records at all of client outcomes of these programs. Funding decisions were based almost solely on routine approval of the re-funding of those agencies funded the year before (Hagedorn 1989b).

Programs thus continue with no regard for their effectiveness for clients. Lindblom points out the apparent absurdity that "In an important sense, therefore, it is not irrational for an administrator to defend a policy as good without being able to specify what it is good for" (Lindblom 1959:84). James Q. Wilson, in a forum on "Can Government Agencies be Managed?" recommended the novel idea that managers be judged on program results, a prospect he doubted would happen because "It is in no one's interest in Washington, D.C.," to do it (Wilson 1990:33). Many organizational theorists have pointed out that program evaluation serves only ceremonial functions for public bureaucracies (Meyer and Rowan 1981, Weick 1976). If sociologists are not among those insisting that social programs be evaluated and show results for the clients they are intended to serve, who will?

(3) *Fund family preservation programs.* One of the most encouraging developments in the past decade in social work has been family preservation programs (Nelson, Landsman, and Duetelman 1990). These short-term, intensive, empowerment model programs, which focus not on an individual client, but rather the needs of the entire family, have been remarkably successful.[7] In dozens of states and cities, these programs, many of them modeled after the successful "homebuilders" projects funded by the Edna McConnell Clark Foundation, have reduced out of home placements and helped families learn how to stay together during a crisis.

Families where an older sibling is involved with gangs may be ideal candidates for these types of intensive, coordinated efforts. Our data show that many child protective clients have extensive family networks whose strengths could be utilized by intensive interventions. Milwaukee received a $1 million dollar grant from the Philip Morris Com-

panies to fund a "homebuilders" model program. An agency located in one of the poorest areas of the city was awarded the contract to implement the program and collaborate with the public school system. As noted above, there was considerable resistance to the program from elements within the social welfare bureaucracy, where family-based, results-oriented programming was viewed as a threat to business as usual (Nelson 1988). Yet, strategies were developed to confront the opposition, and the program was implemented.

(4) *Finally, large public bureaucracies should become more neighborhood based and more open to input from clients and the neighborhoods they serve.* Reminiscent of the 1960s community control movement (Altshuler 1970), current research suggests that social control is least effective when imposed by outside forces. Community controls are strengthened most when informal community level networks are voluntarily tied to external bureaucracies and other resources (Figueria-McDonough 1991).[8] Public dollars for social programs today are largely used to support "street level bureaucrats" whose structure of work often makes it difficult to deliver services that improve the quality of life of their clients (Lipsky 1980). Diverse reform trends in policing, education, and social services all stress more community involvement in public bureaucracies (Chubb and Moe 1990, Comer 1972, Goldstein 1977, Kamerman and Kahn 1989). These reforms, insofar as they increase client and neighborhood control and break down existing bureaucratic barriers, merit support.

While Lipsky and others comment that it will be difficult to reform public bureaucracies in the absence of a social movement (Lipsky 1980:210, Wineman 1984:240), unfavorable conditions should not be an excuse for inaction. The Milwaukee experience of creating multidisciplinary teams of human service workers, moving them into the neighborhoods, and creating neighborhood councils to increase accountability is one example of such a reform.

CONCLUSION

Deindustrialization has altered the nature of gangs, creating a new association between the youth gang, illegal drug-based distribution, and survival of young adult gang members in a post-industrial, segmented economy. While it would be a mistake to see all gangs as drug-dealing organizations, the lack of opportunity for unskilled delinquents creates powerful strains on gang members to become involved in the illegal economy. Without a major jobs program, illegal trade in drugs and related violence seem likely to continue at unacceptable levels (Goldstein 1985, Johnson et al. 1989).

Although neighborhood changes are clearly relevant to gang activities, Wilson's characterization of the underclass as living in neighborhoods from which middle and working class African-Americans have fled and abandoned social institutions (Wilson 1987:56) does not fully apply in cities like Milwaukee. Instead, there are deteriorating neighborhoods with declining resources and fractured internal cohesion. In cities like Milwaukee, it is not the absence of working people that define underclass neighborhoods but more the absence of effective social institutions. Without community controlled institutions, conventional values will have diminished appeal, neighborhoods will segment, sol-

idarity will weaken, and working residents will continue to flee. The research on Milwaukee is consistent with the basic tenet of social disorganization theory, that the lack of effective institutions is related to crime and delinquency. The data support Spergel and others who call for "community mobilization and more resources for and reform of the educational system and job market" (Spergel and Curry 1990:309) as the most effective approach to gang control.

This article does support Wilson and others who call for massive new federal jobs programs. While lobbying for new state and federal job programs, social scientists should also focus on ways to encourage private and public investment in poor neighborhoods and advocate for more community control of social institutions. This means a stepped up involvement by academics in the workings of the large public bureaucracies which control resources needed to rebuild these communities.[9]

In the words of C. Wright Mills, bureaucracies "often carry out series of apparently rational actions without any ideas of the ends they serve" (Mills 1959:168). All too often the ends public bureaucracies serve are not helpful for poor communities. This article can be read as a call for social scientists to step up the struggle to make public bureaucracies more rational for the truly disadvantaged.

NOTES

1. Moore (1991) also finds a mixing of gang cliques in Los Angeles gangs. Short's (1990) 1960 Nobles were mainly employed in the early 1970s when they were restudied, in contrast to Vicelords, virtually all of whom had more prison experience, many of whom still identified with the Vicelords

and were involved in illegal operations more than a decade after they were first studied.

2. Child protective clients, however, more than other residents, turned to police for help with problems than asking help from their relatives or neighbors.

3. In contrast, zip code 53204, a predominantly Hispanic area home to several Hispanic gangs, is dotted with community agencies, banks, merchants, and grocery stores. While this neighborhood is an area of first settlement for Mexican immigrants, it does not have the characteristics of social disorganization of the predominantly African-American 53206 neighborhoods. Those who use "percent Hispanic" as a proxy for social disorganization should take note of these findings (cf. Curry and Spergel 1988:387).

4. There are other institutions in the area with a high profile, particularly law enforcement. But the strong police presence plays to a mixed review. While most residents (38.3 percent) called the police for any serious problems in the neighborhood before they called relatives or friends, one in eight (12.1 percent) listed police as one of the three top "bad things" about the neighborhood. Police are still viewed with suspicion and fear in African-American communities.

5. It must be remembered, however, that the illegal drug economy, while disruptive, is also sustained by local demand. Workers in drug houses assert that most Milwaukee cocaine sales are to people within the neighborhood, not to outsiders (in contrast to Kornblum and Williams [1985:11]). But when illegal activities bring trouble to the neighborhood, particularly violence, police are often welcomed in ousting drug dealers and combatting gang problems (Sullivan 1989:128).

6. City hall may be as capable today of using academics against Washington for its own purposes as Washington in the sixties was adept in using academics to attack city hall (Gouldner 1968, Piven and Cloward 1971).

7. Recent control group evaluations have questioned these programs' effectiveness in reducing out of home placements. The main conclusion from the evaluations is the incapacity of social service bureaucracies to refer the appropriate clients to the programs. The evaluations found family preservation programs are so effective that social workers try to place families in the programs even though they do not fit project guidelines (cf. Feldman 1990, Schuerman et al. 1990, Yuan 1990). These evaluations also point out the important role social scientists can play in insisting programs be properly implemented.

8. This was also Suttles' conclusion: as community ties to external forces increased, so did its internal social control—it became more "provincial" (1968:223–224). Social disorganization and social control, Sullivan also points out, is not linear, but varies widely between poor neighborhoods (Sullivan 1989:237).

9. This recommendation is not a call for revisiting the Chicago Area Project which relied on private financing and performed a "mediating role" with local institutions (Schlossman and Sedlak 1983, Sorrentino 1959), nor is it a call for a new war on poverty with built in antagonism between city hall and short lived federally funded agencies (Marris and Rein 1967, Moynihan 1969). Rather, it is a call for academics to directly engage in local struggles over how and where large public bureaucracies distribute existing resources.

POSTSCRIPT

Are Gangs Created by a Need for Family?

The May 1992 issue of *Education Digest* lists several myths about gangs. Selected ones are summarized below to provide further insight into contemporary street gangs:

Myth: Most gang members are juveniles.
Fact: Approximately one in five gang members is under the age of 18. Nationally, the age range is 9 to over 40.
Myth: Gang crime is primarily gang versus gang.
Fact: More than 50 percent of the time, those who are assaulted or murdered by gang members have no gang affiliation.
Myth: Females are not allowed to be gang members.
Fact: About 5 percent of gang members are female, and the number increases yearly.
Myth: Graffiti is merely an adolescent art form.
Fact: Graffiti is a form of gang advertising and aggression. It stakes out a given gang's turf and challenges other gangs to keep their distance.

The proliferation of gangs is a serious social problem. Most of those who study gangs agree that preventing children from involving themselves with gangs is the only workable long-term solution. Intervention must come early in a child's development, as early as first or second grade, before the onset of delinquent behaviors, which can occur in the later elementary grades.

Perhaps the key element in prevention is the enhancement of self-esteem in children and the consequent elevation of self-confidence. In addition to supportive family and school systems, mentoring programs like Big Brothers and Big Sisters, accessibility to social and organized recreational programs, tutoring, and other special needs programs all could help children believe that they can lead meaningful lives and could offer children the skills that will help them make it in society.

SUGGESTED READINGS

Cantrell, R. P. (1993, November 1). Countering gang violence in American schools. *Principal, 73,* 6+.

Lasley, J. R. (1992, June). Age, social context and street gang membership: Are "youth" gangs becoming "adult" gangs? *Youth and Society, 23,* 434–451.

Williams, J. W., Jr. (1992, July). A structured subculture: Understanding how youth gangs operate. *Corrections Today, 54,* 86–88.

CONTRIBUTORS
TO THIS VOLUME

EDITORS

ROBERT L. DelCAMPO is a professor of family science at New Mexico State University in Las Cruces, New Mexico, and a licensed marriage and family therapist. He is a clinical member of the American Association for Marriage and Family Therapy, and he holds memberships in the International Family Therapy Association, the National Council on Family Relations, and the New Mexico Association for Marriage and Family Therapy. His major research interests include multicultural and cross-cultural issues related to children and families. He received a B.S. from the State University of New York, an M.S. from Virginia Polytechnic Institute and State University, and a Ph.D. in family relations and child development from Florida State University. His work has appeared in numerous journals, including *Family Relations.*

DIANA S. DelCAMPO is a family life specialist with the New Mexico Co-operative Extension Service and an associate professor of child development at New Mexico State University in Las Cruces, New Mexico. She is a member of the National Council on Family Relations, the National Association for the Education of Young Children, and the National Extension Family Life Specialists' Association. Her research interests focus on child development and parent education. She received a B.S. from Concord College, an M.S. from Virginia Polytechnic Institute and State University, and a Ph.D. in early childhood education from the University of Michigan. She is currently working on a project, supported by the Children's Trust Fund, that targets preventing child abuse and neglect in the state of New Mexico.

STAFF

Mimi Egan   Publisher
Brenda S. Filley   Production Manager
Libra Ann Cusack   Typesetting Supervisor
Juliana Arbo   Typesetter
Lara Johnson   Graphics
Diane Barker   Proofreader
David Brackley   Copy Editor
David Dean   Administrative Editor
Richard Tietjen   Systems Manager

AUTHORS

KAREN E. ABLARD is a professor in the Center for Talented Youth Research at Johns Hopkins University in Baltimore, Maryland.

AMERICAN ASSOCIATION OF UNIVERSITY WOMEN is an organization of college and university graduates that was founded in 1881 to work for the advancement of women.

CHRISTOPHER BAGLEY is a professor of social work at the University of Calgary in Calgary, Alberta, Canada, and the director of the Center for Applied Social Research at City Polytechnic of Hong Kong in Hong Kong, China.

MARGUERITE STEVENSON BARRATT is a developmental psychologist in the Department of Child and Family Studies at the University of Wisconsin–Madison. Her research interests focus on infant social interactions, particularly parent-child interactions, and she is currently investigating how reciprocal exchange is affected by characteristics of the mother.

NAZLI BAYDAR is a researcher with the Battelle Human Affairs Research Center in Seattle, Washington.

JEANNE BROOKS-GUNN is the Virginia and Leonard Marx Professor in Child Development and Education at Columbia University's Teachers College in New York City and the director of the university's Center for Young Children and Families. She is a member of the National Institute of Child Health and Human Development's Consortium on Child and Family Well-Being and of the National Institutes of Mental Health's Family Research Consortium. She is on the editorial boards of the *Journal of Research on Adolescence*, the *Journal of Youth and Adolescence*, and *Psychosomatic Medicine*.

JIM BURKE is an English teacher at Burlingame High School in San Francisco, California. He writes on educational issues for various publications, including *Educational Leadership*.

BARBARA BYRD is an associate of the Department of Professional Psychology at Seton Hall University in South Orange, New Jersey.

BRANDON S. CENTERWALL is an assistant professor of epidemiology in the School of Public Health and Community Medicine at the University of Washington in Seattle, Washington.

KAREN K. COLBERT is a lecturer at Iowa State University in Ames, Iowa, whose research interests focus on child development and parent-child relationships. She received an M.A. and a Ph.D. from the University of Wisconsin–Madison in 1980 and 1984, respectively, and she is currently involved in a national research project that is studying the transition of Head Start students as they enter the school system.

STEPHEN S. CRAIG is a professor in the Department of Professional Psychology at Seton Hall University in South Orange, New Jersey.

ARNOLD P. DeROSA is a professor in the Department of Counseling Psychology at Seton Hall University in South Orange, New Jersey.

MARK A. FINE is a professor in the Department of Psychology at the University of Dayton in Dayton, Ohio.

DOUGLAS FOSTER is a John S. Knight Fellow of Stanford University in Stanford, California, and a former editor of *Mother Jones* magazine.

DAVID GATELY was a graduate student of psychology at the Ohio State University in Columbus, Ohio, when he coauthored "Favorable Outcomes in Children After Divorce" for the *Journal of Divorce and Remarriage*.

CHARLOTTE GOODLUCK is a professor at Northern Arizona University in Flagstaff, Arizona.

JESSICA GRESS-WRIGHT is a senior fellow of the Manhattan Institute for Public Policy in New York City, an affiliated scholar at the Institute for American Values in New York City, and a visiting scholar at Cambridge University's Newnham College in Cambridge, England.

DAVID GUTERSON is an English teacher at Bainbridge High School in Bainbridge Island, Washington. His publications include *The Country Ahead of Us, the Country Behind* (Harper & Row, 1989).

JOHN M. HAGEDORN is a professor in the Urban Reseach Center at the University of Wisconsin–Milwaukee.

SCOTT A. HUNT is a writer based in San Franciso, California, whose research interests focus on social problems and transpersonal psychology. He graduated from Harvard University with a degree in government and political philosophy.

DOREEN KIMURA is a neuropsychologist and a professor in the Department of Psychology at the University of Western Ontario in London, Ontario, Canada. Her research interests focus on the brain and hormonal bases of human intellectual abilities.

SHERRYLL KRAIZER is the director of the Coalition for Children and Health Education Systems in Palisades, New York.

THOMAS LICKONA is a professor of education at the State University of New York College at Cortland, in Cortland, New York, the director of the State University of New York's Center for the Fourth and Fifth Rs (Respect and Responsibility), and a member of the board of directors of the Character Education Partnership, a national coalition working to promote character development in schools and communities. He is a frequent consultant to schools throughout the United States, and he has lectured in Canada, Japan, Switzerland, Ireland, and Latin America on teaching moral values in the school and home.

DONALDO MACEDO is an associate professor of linguistics at the University of Massachusetts–Boston. He is the author of *Literacies of Power: What Americans Are Not Allowed to Know* (Westview, 1994) and the coauthor, with Paulo Freire, of *Literacy: Reading the Word and the World* (Greenwood, 1987).

JOAN McCORD is a professor of criminal justice at Temple University in Philadelphia, Pennsylvania, where she has been teaching since 1987. She has received the Prix Emile Durkheim Award from the International Society of Criminology and the Edwin H. Sutherland Award from the American Society of Criminology for her research. A former president of the American Society of Criminology, she has authored or coauthored more than 100 articles, books, and essays on theory, treatment effects, crime, alcoholism, protective factors, and socialization.

STEVEN MELLOR is a professor in the Department of Psychology at the University of Connecticut in Storrs, Connecticut.

MICHAEL F. MEYERS is a professor at the University of Massachusetts–Boston in Boston, Massachusetts.

CAROL J. MILLS is the director of research in the Center for Talented Youth Research at Johns Hopkins University in Baltimore, Maryland.

WILLIAM J. O'MALLEY teaches theology and English at Fordham Preparatory School in Bronx, New York.

DONALD A. RAKESTRAW is an assistant professor in the Department of History at Georgia Southern College in Statesboro, Georgia.

JENNIE F. RAKESTRAW is an associate dean of the College of Education at Georgia Southern College in Statesboro, Georgia.

JANAKI RAMANAN is an instructor at the University of Texas in Dallas, Texas.

DIANE RAVITCH is the senior research scholar at New York University in New York City and a fellow of the Brookings Institution, a private nonprofit organization devoted to research, education, and publication in economics, government, foreign policy, and the social sciences. She also served as assistant secretary of education during the Bush administration. She is the author of *The Schools We Deserve* (Basic Books, 1985) and the coauthor, with Chester E. Finn, Jr., of *What Do Our Seventeen-Year-Olds Know?* (Harper-Collins, 1987).

MARY A. ROACH is an assistant scientist in the Waisman Center on Mental Retardation and Human Development at the University of Wisconsin–Madison. Her current research focuses on identifying the factors that promote the cognitive, linguistic, and social well-being of young children and their families, and she has a particular interest in how child characteristics, parenting styles, and environmental factors affect young children with developmental disabilities. She received her Ph.D.in 1985 from the University of Wisconsin–Madison.

ANDREW I. SCHWEBEL is a professor in the Department of Psychology at the Ohio State University in Columbus, Ohio.

LAWRENCE J. SCHWEINHART is the chair of the research division of the High/Scope Educational Research Foundation in Ypsilanti, Michigan.

BRIAN SIANO is a writer and researcher based in Philadelphia, Pennsylvania. His column "The Skeptical Eye" appears regularly in *The Humanist*.

MURRAY A. STRAUS is a professor of sociology and the codirector of the Family Research Laboratory at the University of New Hampshire in Durham, New Hampshire. He has held academic appointments at Cornell University, the University of Minnesota, the University of Wisconsin, and Washington State University, as well as at universities in England, India, and Sri Lanka. He is the author or coauthor of over 150 articles and 15 books on the family, research methods, and South Asia, including *Physical Violence in American Families: Risk, Factors, and Adaptations to Violence in 8,145 Families* (Transaction, 1989), coauthored with Richard J. Gelles.

HEINRICH STUMPF is a professor in the Center for Talented Youth Research at Johns Hopkins University in Baltimore, Maryland.

CAROL TAVRIS is a social psychologist and an author based in Los Angeles, California, and a member of the American Psychological Association. Her publications include *The Longest War: Sex Differences in Perspective*, 2d ed. (Harcourt Brace, 1984), coauthored with Carole Wade, and *Anger: The Misunderstood Emotion* (Simon & Schuster, 1989).

KATHLEEN KENNEDY TOWNSEND was the director of the Maryland Student Service Alliance of the Maryland Department of Education, and in 1994 she was elected lieutenant governor of Maryland.

DEBORAH LOWE VANDELL is a professor in the Department of Educational Psychology at the University of Wisconsin–Madison in Madison, Wisconsin. She is the author of numerous articles on the effects of child care and maternal employment on children's development.

DAVID P. WEIKART is the president of the High/Scope Educational Research Foundation in Ypsilanti, Michigan.

BARBARA DAFOE WHITEHEAD is a research associate at the Institute for American Values in New York City, a nonpartisan research organization devoted to issues of family and civic well-being. She received a degree in history from the University of Wisconsin–Madison.

JOHN L. WOODARD is a professor at Wayne State University in Detroit, Michigan.

ANDREW L. YARROW is a columnist for the *New York Times*.

INDEX

Aber, Lawrence, 311
Ablard, Karen E., on gender differences and math, 218–228
abuse, child, and spanking, 104–126
Adaptability Cohesion Evaluation Scale, 132
adoption, transracial, 58–76
African-American mothers, poverty of, in single-parent families, 154–155
age, of child, and formal schooling, 200–212
AIDS, sex education and, 342–357
Alaska Statewide Assessment Test, 278
Allen, Laura S., 83
American Association of University Women, on gender differences and math, 229–237
androgyny, in children of divorce, 169–170
Annett, Marion, 88
Ansbacher, Adler, 134
Armed Forces Qualifications Test, 9, 10, 18, 22
Aronowitz, Stanley, 297
Auletta, Ken, 154

Bagley, Christopher, on transracial adoption, 68–76
Bakhtin, Mikhail, 302
Barnett, W. Steven, 202
Barratt, Marguerite Stevenson, on older parents and children, 30–45
Basic Word Vocabulary Test, 139
Baydar, Nazli, on the effects of a mother's job on children, 4–14
Behan, Peter, 91–94
Behavioral Problems Index, for assessing the effects of a mother's job on children, 9, 10, 18
Belson, William, 183
Benbow, Camilla P., 85
Bennett, William, 295, 296
Berenbaum, Sheri A., 81
bilingual education, 286–304
Bilingual Education Act, 290
black mothers, poverty of, in single-parent families, 154–155
Bleier, Ruth, 94–96, 98
Bloch, Donald A., 51
brain, and gender differences, 80–98
Brant, Edward, Jr., 350

Brooks-Gunn, Jeanne, on the effects of a mother's job on children, 4–14
Brown, Laurene Krasny, 151–152
Brown, Marc, 151–152
Brown v. Board of Education, 288
Burke, Jim, on gangs, 362–364
Bush, George, 314
Byrd, Barbara, on only children and independence, 130–135

California Achievement Test, 220, 251, 278
Cambridge-Somerville Youth Study, 113, 118
cartoons, controversy over violence in, 188–189, 193, 194–195
Census, U.S. Bureau of the, 163, 242, 249, 250
Centerwall, Brandon S., on television and children, 180–187
Chambers, David, 159–160
Cherlin, Andrew, 149, 157, 160
child abuse, spanking and, 104–126
child development, and transracial adoption, 58–76
children: divorce and, 148–174; effect of mother's job on, 4–25; "latchkey," 249–260; television and, 180–195; values and, 308–318
civil rights, 289–291, 292
Civil War, 275
Clark Doll Test, 70, 71
class war, 318
Clinton, Bill, 204, 314
Clinton, Hillary Rodham, 335
clothing, and gangs, 362–363
Colbert, Karen K., on older parents and children, 30–45
College Ability Test, 219, 221
community service, as a method of imparting values to children, 316–317
Conflict Tactics Scales, for juvenile crime data collection, 110
Constantino, Renato, 298
Construct Theory, 116, 117, 121–124
contraception, 344–345, 347, 350, 351, 352, 357
corporal punishment, and child abuse, 104–126
Couchie, Catherine, 85